The Holocaust

by Bea Stadtler

~~~~~~

edited by
MORRISON DAVID BIAL

illustrated by
DAVID STONE MARTIN

New York, New York

The Holocaust

~~~~~~

A HISTORY OF COURAGE AND RESISTANCE

Behrman House, Inc.
Publishers

Library of Congress Cataloging in Publication Data

Stadtler, Bea.
    The holocaust.

    SUMMARY: Describes the experiences of Jews in Germany and other
European countries during the twelve years of the Third Reich when more
than six million of their number were systematically destroyed.
    Edition for 1973 published under title: The test. Bibliography: p.
    1. Holocaust, Jewish (1939–1945)—Juvenile literature. 2. World War,
1939–1945—Underground movements—Jews—Juvenile literature. 3. Religious
education, Jewish—Text-books for children. [1. Holocaust, Jewish (1939–
1945). 2. World War, 1939–1945—Underground movements—Jews] I.
Martin, David Stone, illus.

II. Title.
BM105.S69   1974   940.53'1503'924   74–11469
ISBN 0-87441-224-2

*In memory of the six million Jews who
were murdered during the Holocaust*

Contents

ACKNOWLEDGMENTS

*My thanks go, first of all, to Arthur Weyne, and Jerry Barach,
editors of the* Cleveland Jewish News, *where most of this material
originally appeared. Some of these chapters appeared as articles
in other papers as well, including the* Boston Jewish Advocate, *the*
Baltimore Jewish Times, *the* Pittsburgh Jewish Chronicle, *the*
Kansas City Jewish Chronicle, *the* Philadelphia Jewish Exponent,
the Jewish Journal *of New York City and the* American Jewish
World *of Minneapolis.*

*I would also like to thank Aaron Intrater, Executive Vice President
of the Cleveland Bureau of Jewish Education, and Henry Margolis,
Director of the Bureau, as well as Rabbi Marvin Spiegelman, for
encouraging me to prepare this work in its original experimental
form. To Frank Stern, Administrative Director of the Bureau of
Jewish Education in Cleveland, goes a special thanks for his help
with many little details that went into the production of this
volume. For their support, my gratitude to Dr. Martin Goldstein,
President of the Cleveland College of Jewish Studies and to Sidney
Vincent, Executive Director of the Jewish Community Federation.*

To my husband, Dr. Oscar Stadtler and my daughter, Miriam, a special thank you for assistance in undertaking this project and help in completing it.

And, most assuredly, to Seymour Rossel for lending his nice hand and fine judgment in the preparation of the manuscript for publication.

Finally, I would like to thank Rabbi Daniel Jeremy Silver of The Temple in Cleveland, Ohio, for his support and Henry Tyrangiel, former Educational Director of The Temple, who permitted me to devote time to the study of the Holocaust in my fifth-grade class—and to my fifth graders for responding so favorably to the experimental volume.

Bea Stadtler

x

Preface

~~~~~~

THE events described here should never have happened, and then there would have been no need for such a book. But we cannot run away from ourselves. We must tell the story, the true story. And yet, for our young audiences, present it in a way that they will understand, and thereby understand themselves. This has not been attempted before. Mrs. Bea Stadtler is the first author to do this tremendous service, and one hopes and prays with her that this wonderful little book will become a household item for Jewish youngsters all over the United States.

Why the Jews? Were not other people killed in that terrible upheaval called World War II—a war in which more people lost their lives than in any other war in human history until now? True, there were others. Hitler killed four million Soviet prisoners of war (and none of them resisted . . .). Millions of other European civilians died in this war too. But there was only one people who was destined to be destroyed completely, because in Nazi eyes they stood for the opposite of what Nazism represented. If Nazism stood for extreme nationalism, dictatorship, racism, inequality and brutality of man to man, denial of the moral values inherited from the great monotheistic religions—then the Jews, apparently, represented the opposite.

Other people in Europe were killed too. They were killed because they resisted the Nazis, or because they happened to be in a place where the Nazis needs were not satisfied, or because of some whim of Nazi brutality. But Jews were killed because they were Jews. They were dispossessed and singled out, humiliated and killed for no other reason but that they were Jews. Even when they did not consider themselves to be Jewish at all, they were defined as Jews by the Nazis. Their beliefs, opinions, attitudes, religion, social life made no difference at all. That is the uniqueness of the story, which is clearly brought out in this volume.

How did other people behave? Did they help the victims? The picture is complicated, and Bea Stadtler tells both sides of the story. And what of the reaction of the victims themselves? Did some of them collapse morally under the pressure? Did they stand the test? What did those do who stood up to the challenge? Finally— can it happen again? Bea Stadtler does not give an an-

Preface

swer to the youngster reading her book. He must find the answer himself, and perhaps searching for the answer is part of the answer too.

This is an important book. A book with a mission of truth to young people who want to know the truth. It is told with a great love for those who perished and for those who survived. Young Jews may find in it answers to questions about themselves—who they are and where they come from. Surely, they must realize that they, too, are Holocaust survivors. Is it not a mere accident that their immediate ancestors left Europe while other relatives remained behind? Surely it could have been the other way around. Young non-Jews may find in the book both problems and partial answers. Who are these people who suffered so much? Why?

All youngsters who read this book will find in it a story which they must understand and absorb if they wish to understand the world in which we must live. They will, I am sure, be deeply thankful to Bea Stadtler for having written it.

Yehuda Bauer
Professor of Holocaust Studies
Institute of Contemporary Jewry
Hebrew University
Jerusalem, Israel

one

Before the Beginning

~~~~~~

YOU have probably heard about a period of time, not so long ago, known as "The Holocaust." A holocaust, according to Webster's dictionary, is "a complete destruction by fire." In Europe, during this period, there *was* a complete destruction by fire—of Jewish homes, Jewish businesses, Jewish neighborhoods—and Jewish people. This destruction was carried out under the direction of Adolf Hitler, during the years 1939–1945. But it began even earlier—in 1933.

On January 30, 1933, the Third Reich * was established in Germany, with Adolf Hitler as chancellor and

* A Reich is a state. The First Reich lasted from 962–1220; the Second Reich from 1871–1918.

1

Before the Beginning

dictator. During the next twelve years Hitler, through deceit and force, almost conquered Europe. Twelve years is like a moment in recorded history, but so much evil was done during this time that it touched almost everyone in the world, and will continue to cause problems for hundreds of years to come. But how did one man, Adolf Hitler, come to have so much power?

Adolf Hitler was born in 1889, in a small town on the Austro-German frontier. He was short and dark, a mixture of many kinds of people. Originally his family name was Schicklgruber, but along the way it became Heidler, which finally became Hitler. As he grew up, he became convinced that tall, blonde, blue-eyed persons from Germany were the most pure-blooded, superior people. He called them Aryans.

Adolf was a very poor student—in fact, a high-school drop-out. He never blamed himself for his poor grades. Rather he blamed his teachers, calling them "mad," "abnormal," "tyrants," and other names.

After Hitler's father died, his mother found it difficult to make a living for the family. Although he was very close to her, Adolf refused to go to work, preferring instead to daydream about becoming a great artist. At the age of 18, he went to Vienna where he applied for admission to the Vienna Academy of Fine Arts. He was turned down. He applied a second time, but the school officials turned him down again, saying perhaps he should try architecture. Although he never followed through, nevertheless he was interested in architecture all his life.

After the death of his mother, Hitler lived in poorhouses and ate in charity soup kitchens. He seemed unable to concentrate on anything, had no friends, no home, no family, no profession, no sweetheart, and no country. He was so poor that a Jewish secondhand clothes dealer, taking pity, gave him a coat too large for him. With his unshaven face and long matted hair, and his outsized overcoat, he looked very strange. As a matter of fact, he later described the Jews, whom he hated so much, as looking the way he himself looked in those days. In Vienna there was a great deal of anti-Jewish literature circulated, and Hitler read it all. He moved to Munich in 1913.

In 1914, at the outbreak of World War I, he enlisted in the German army. He served four years. He became a corporal, was gassed, and received the Iron Cross for bravery. In 1918, when Germany was defeated, he felt cheated. He did not understand how the Aryans could be defeated. The German army slowly dissolved, but some soldiers did not want to leave military service. These were mostly the misfits who could not get along in a peaceful society. One of these soldiers gave a series of lectures and discussions which Hitler attended. During these lectures, Hitler spoke about his own opinions and ideas. These opinions and ideas were anti-everybody except the pure-blooded German, and against every

From *Mein Kampf,* Hitler's life and opinions, which he wrote
while in prison. *Mein Kampf* became the Nazi handbook.

*"Every animal mates only with a member of the
same species. The titmouse seeks the titmouse, the
finch, the finch, the stork, the stork . . . the wolf,
the she-wolf. . . . The fox is always a fox, the
goose a goose, the tiger a tiger . . . but you will
never find a fox who might show humanitarian
tendencies toward geese, as similarly, there is no cat
with a friendly feeling toward mice.*

country except Germany. They were full of hate and
violence and appealed to the lowest human instincts.
The other misfits who attended the lectures and discussions wholeheartedly praised Hitler and his ideas.

. In 1919 Hitler became a member of the German
Worker's Party, a tiny political group numbering seven
people including himself. Hitler soon took over the group
and sought new members. More people began attending
meetings. Hitler found he had a talent—he could
"hypnotize" people with his speeches.

· In 1920 he changed the name of his party to
Nationalist Socialist German Worker's Party, the "Nazi"
party. He drew up a program of things he wanted to
accomplish. Many of these things appealed to the lowest
element in the country. He promised that when he would

4

head the government, they could take from the Jews "wealth" and possessions. To those upset by their country's defeat in the war, he promised to restore Germany's pride and glory. He blamed the defeat of World War I on the Communists and Jews, a trick he would use over and over in the future.

During these years most people thought him to be a crackpot. He was the butt of many jokes. At his meetings he had ex-servicemen stationed around the hall to quiet hecklers or to throw them out. Then he organized a bunch of tough, unemployed war veterans. They were dissatisfied bullies who became his strong-arm squads. He clothed them in brown uniforms, and these roughnecks not only kept order at his meetings, but made it their business to break up meetings of other respectable groups. It was the beginning of might over right.

Hitler's first attempt to gain control of the government ended in disaster, with him in jail. He was sentenced to five years, but served only three months. During his time in jail he wrote a book—*Mein Kampf (My Struggle)*, which told anyone who cared to read it exactly what he thought about Jews and other minorities and what he would do to them if he had the chance. Those who did read this book said it was the work of an unimportant maniac. Most people paid no attention.

When he was released from jail, the Nazi party was in disgrace. Gradually he rebuilt the party, until in 1928, he had 108,000 dues-paying members. From 1925–1929 conditions in Germany were relatively good, and the masses of people no longer wanted an extreme change in the government. Hitler and his ideas made little headway. But in 1929 a worldwide depression occurred and Hitler seized this chance to appeal once more to the lower elements in the society.

In the 1930 elections, the Nazi party received four times as many votes as in the previous election, and obtained 107 seats in the *Reichstag* (Parliament). Hitler's emphasis on *Deutschland über alles* (Germany above all

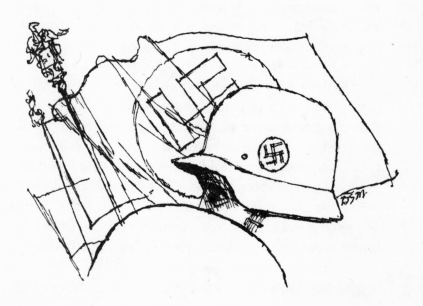

else) appealed to many Germans. Still Hitler himself was unable to take over the government. There were two more elections. Hitler with all his campaigning did not have enough votes to win a majority. But President Hindenburg appointed him chancellor in January of 1932. He decided that he wanted even more power and felt that the German constitution was in his way. So in February 1933, the Parliament building was set ablaze. Although the Nazis insisted the Communists had set the fire, later it was discovered that the Nazis themselves had set the fire. In the confusion following this fire, Hitler managed to convince the Reichstag that the Communists were an immediate threat. President Hindenburg signed a decree for the "protection of the people and the state." This decree took away all individual and civil liberties of the population. It gave the Nazis permission to do whatever they wanted to do in the Third Reich. They could enter homes without search warrants, listen in on telephone conversations (bugging), confiscate property, jewels, money, clothing, furniture, and bank accounts. They could open mail and read telegrams. They forced newspaper editors and radio broadcasters to say only what the Nazis wanted said, and refused to allow meetings of opposition parties. By March 23, 1933, Hitler was made dictator of the Reich. When General von Hindenburg died in 1934, 88 percent of the people voted to make Hitler chancellor and president of Germany, but he preferred being called *Fuehrer* (Leader)!

During the next few years, Hitler took over press

and radio, education and culture. It seemed that all of Germany became nazified. New textbooks were written and a new culture produced. He took over Austria in 1938 without firing a shot, and then became "protector" of Czechoslovakia and finally, on September 1, 1939 attacked Poland with full military force. This act marked the beginning of World War II. Poland fell in less than a month. Germany easily defeated France, Belgium, Denmark, Yugoslavia, Holland, and Norway. Italy joined the German side as did Romania and Hungary. By the middle of 1940, much of Europe was under the domination of Nazi Germany and Adolf Hitler.

Things to think about

1 When Hitler committed suicide on April 30, 1945, the only monument he left behind was a country tired of war, its cities bombed and blasted, its farms burned and deserted, its homes and families in ruins, and the name of Germany hated throughout the world. From what you have read in this chapter and from what you already knew about Adolf Hitler, how do you think the German people feel about Hitler now?

2 The Third Reich was an "absolute dictatorship." In a dictatorship, one person or a small group of people rule the entire country. In an absolute dictatorship, one person alone rules the entire country. Hitler had the power to change the law at will or to work outside the law, to

arrest whom he pleased, to put anyone to death, to declare war, and to command the armies of Germany. Could any one person ever have so many powers in our country? Could our country ever become an absolute dictatorship?

✦3 Much of the reason that the Nazi party and Adolf Hitler were successful lay in the fact that they often lied to the people of Germany. When a government lies and deceives us, who is responsible for seeking out the truth?

two

Night
of the
Broken Glass

FROM 1933–1939 Adolf Hitler, by bluffs and threats, gained control of Germany, Austria, and Czechoslovakia, and conquered Poland. This was the beginning of his attempt to conquer the world. At the same time that he was striving to conquer the world, he also wanted to get rid of those people whom he believed were "inferior," and of less value than other people. This included several minority groups, but Hitler expressed against the Jews most of his hate and anger. He ordered the Aryan Germans not to do business with Jews, and placed signs forbidding Jews in their shops and in their businesses. Aryans were not permitted to marry Jews, mingle with Jews, go to Jewish doctors, or live near Jews.

Night of the Broken Glass

At first Hitler tried to expel the Jews from Germany and any other country he conquered, but that was too difficult—other countries refused to accept them! Then he drew up his "Final Solution." "Final Solution" was a cover-up name for the murder of all the Jews of Europe. Some German people who were not Jewish opposed these acts. He murdered them too. Hitler did not kill a hundred Jews, or a thousand, or even a million. He put six million Jews to death. Many Germans had to work on the "solution" to this problem: How to kill all of Europe's Jews.

November 9, 1938, marked the real beginning of tragedy for the Jews. There are many Jews still alive who were in Germany at the time. When you mention November 9, 1938, to them they shudder. On that night all the synagogues in Germany were destroyed. Small, and large, elegant and plain, costly and inexpensive, small town shuls and huge city showplaces—all were destroyed. Glass was smashed, buildings burned. Torah scrolls, arks, curtains, prayer books were torn and burned. Homes, offices, stores, and any other property belonging to Jews were also destroyed. This night became known as *Kristallnacht* (Night of Glass), but it was really the Night of the Broken Glass. What excuse did the Nazis use to cause such destruction?

On November 7, 1938, a crazed seventeen-year-old German-Jewish refugee named Herschel Grynszpan shot and killed Ernst vom Rath, the third-secretary of the German embassy in Paris. Herschel was Polish, but had been raised in Germany, and had escaped to France

12

because of the Nazi persecutions of Jews. The boy's
father had been among thousands of Jews deported to
Poland in sealed boxcar trains. Herschel received letters
from his father describing the terrible journey and the
inhuman conditions in the camp. The boy felt he had to
do something to protest these happenings, so he went
to the German embassy, planning to kill the ambassador,
but instead shot and killed the third-secretary.

This murder by the young lad was followed by
what the German press called a "spontaneous" demonstration. "Spontaneous" means on the spot . . . un-
planned. Dr. Goebbels, the German propaganda minister,
claimed the demonstration was a reaction to the murder.
Later, however, documents were discovered showing

13

that this spontaneous demonstration on Kristallnacht had been planned to the tiniest detail, weeks in advance, by the Nazis. They were only waiting for some incident to set it off. The murder of Vom Rath became that incident.

It was a night of horror throughout Germany. It was as though a single enormous torch suddenly passed over the entire country. The Nazis used kerosene to start the fires and bombs to destroy the synagogues.

Newspapers in Germany described the fires, but they never mentioned how the fires came to be lit. The destruction in broken glass alone came to millions of dollars. The Nazis insisted that the destruction had to be paid for by the Jews. After all, the Nazis claimed, the Jews started the trouble.

In Nuremberg, one German city, Jewish homes were destroyed with hatchets. Why hatchets? Early on the evening of November ninth, there was a rally of about 30,000 Nazis in Nuremberg. A Nazi official made a speech which angered the crowd against the Jews. Then each Nazi was given a hatchet and permission to do whatever he wanted to the Jews. Twelve years later in Nuremberg Nazi war criminals were put on trial.

Many Germans "got even" with Jews of whom they were jealous or whom they hated or feared. They forced their way into Jewish homes. Then beat, killed, and humiliated the people. They stole or destroyed their property. One Jewish woman saw an architect smash the furniture in the home he had built for her twelve years earlier.

Following are remembrances of two people who lived in Germany during Kristallnacht:

> I lived in Cologne, a city of about 100,000, on a street opposite an Orthodox synagogue, in a two-story apartment house. Next door was our small restaurant. My room was upstairs under the roof and the window faced the synagogue. About four houses away was the 4711 factory—a place that manufactured perfume. I woke up in the middle of the night hearing noises—as though heavy barrels were being rolled about. I climbed out of bed onto the slanted roof and thought I saw people at the factory.
>
> Nazis were going in and out of apartments. Some Nazis rolled heavy kegs from the factory into the synagogue and put it on fire. I ran downstairs and woke my parents. We took a small amount of jewelry and ran back to my room, locked the door, and hid the jewelry on the roof. We heard lots of noise, both in the house and in the restaurant. Finally the Nazis left. We went downstairs. Everything in the apartment and restaurant was smashed to pieces, including my beautiful grand piano. It was overturned and every single string had been cut. Sofas and chairs were upside down and books and valuables had been stolen. My father was taken by two Nazis and put into jail. . . .

Another first-hand report comes from a small town called Kassel. This girl was only fourteen years old when Kristallnacht occurred:

> I was visiting my aunt nearby when my father came to get me. He was very upset for he had just seen freight trains

Night of the Broken Glass

packed with Jews. We went to our small home, and about two o'clock in the morning, my uncle from another village knocked on the door. He told us Nazis had come into his village and arrested all the Jewish men. He hid, and later walked 25 kilometres [about 14 miles] to our home. My cousin, who was seventeen years old, had been tied onto a horse and dragged about the village. The two large synagogues in my town were burned. At night I went back to stay with my aunt, because she was alone. She wept all night, and recited the *Shema* over and over. The next morning all the Jewish apartments in my town were ransacked. Feather-beds were torn and feathers scattered. When I returned home, nothing was left but the house. My mother and sister were in jail. Every piece of china had been smashed, every piece of clothing stolen. I thought of my two violins. One was new and the other an older, ¾ child-size. The new one was gone and the ¾ one smashed. I had a mama doll with a china head. The arms, legs, and head were torn off. The furniture had been hacked with saws and axes.

My father was sent to Buchenwald [a concentration camp] for five weeks. We had almost nothing to eat, and no one would sell us anything. My mother had a heart attack and the doctor refused to come. Jewish children were not allowed to go to public schools. At that time Jews could still be ransomed, and we finally were able to ransom my father. When he returned home, he had lost 60 pounds. Later, no one could be ransomed. We were fingerprinted and forced to wear a yellow star on the front and back of our clothing and on armbands. A large *J* was stamped on our passports. . . .

There are hundreds of true life accounts from the Night of the Broken Glass. This was bad enough—but it was only the beginning.

16

Night of the Broken Glass

Things to think about

1 On the night of November 9, 1938 almost all the synagogues in Germany were destroyed; the sacred books of Judaism were burned—Torah, Talmud, prayerbooks, and Codes. Why did Hitler and the Nazis who helped him to plan the "Final Solution" choose to strike at buildings and books first?

2 Many Jewish homes were robbed, looted, or destroyed; and many Jewish men were hauled to concentration camps during the night and morning of *Kristallnacht*. Do you think it was possible that the Nazis alone were responsible for such a terrible event?

3 We have heard of people in large apartment buildings watching a person being robbed and murdered in the courtyard and not even calling the police for help. Is this any different from the attitude of Germans who watched their Jewish neighbors being taken away, or beaten, or robbed, without saying a word? Would you be able to sleep through a *"Kristallnacht"*?

three

The Right
to Live

IN 1935 Hitler arranged for the passing of Nuremberg
Laws, which took away the citizenship of Jews born in
Germany and turned them into "subjects." A citizen of
a country has status, he belongs to the country. But a
subject has no rights and is not a particularly welcome
person. Certainly a subject has much less value than does
a citizen. That was exactly the feeling Hitler wanted the
Germans to have about the Jews—that Jews were
untermenschen (subhuman).

It was also the feeling he wanted the Jews to have
about themselves. The Nuremberg Laws forbade mar-
riages between Jews and Germans. Jews were not
allowed to employ German female servants under the

age of 35. Jews were not allowed to hold public office, nor were they allowed to hold civil service jobs. If they were journalists or worked at radio stations, they were fired. They were not permitted to teach or to be farmers or to act in the theater. They were thrown out of the stock exchange and were not allowed to practice medicine or law except for other Jews.

Jewish businesses were taken away from their owners by the Nazis and placed in the hands of German "trustees." These included huge department stores and little family shops. If people could not practice their professions or work in stores or own businesses, they could not earn a living.

In addition, signs saying "Jews Not Admitted" were placed on the doors of stores, theaters, parks, and hotels. Jews were not permitted to even walk or ride on certain streets. The name Israel was added to the identity

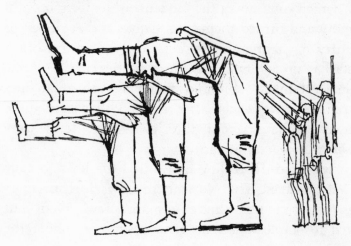

card of each Jewish male, and the name Sarah was added to that of each Jewish female. Jewish children were no longer permitted to go to public schools.

By 1939 other laws forbade Jews to leave their houses except for a few hours a day. Jews were forced to deposit all their money in banks. Then laws were enforced that forbade them to take the money out. The money was confiscated by the Nazis. Jews were forced to turn over their radios to Nazi authorities. Telephones were taken away from them. Gradually, everything but the clothes on their backs was taken from them.

Kristallnacht on November 9, 1938, was the turning point. Before this time Jews were often beaten or forced to clear the streets, but now brutality and public shaming became everyday affairs. Jews were stripped naked in public theaters. Grandfathers had their beards pulled out. Jewish children in school were forced to sit apart from the rest of the pupils and had to listen to their teachers calling them traitors to the Fatherland.

Meanwhile many Jewish leaders, liberals, Communists—and anyone else—who annoyed a Nazi were taken to the dread concentration camps. At first these were not death camps, but the unfortunate people within them were subjected to the utmost degradation, starvation, beatings, even torture and death.

In October 1941, the first transport of Jews left Berlin and was shipped to Lodz in Poland. This was a transport of human beings—Jews who had over the years come to Germany from Poland and were now being

A police order dated September 1, 1941. The careful description tells us that the Nazis had thought long and hard about what they were doing to the Jews.

Jews who have completed their sixth year of age are forbidden to appear in public without a Jewish star.

The Jewish star consists of a six-pointed star, the size of the palm of a hand, drawn in black on yellow material, with the inscription "Jew" in black. It is to be worn on the left breast of clothing, clearly visible and strongly sewn on.

sent back. They traveled under terrible conditions, crowded into sealed boxcars or cattle cars, with no food, water, or toilet facilities. But this was still the beginning.

In order to isolate Jews and keep them more easily under control, the Nazis decided to concentrate them in ghettos. During 1940 the Nazis established ghettos in several Polish towns and cities. These ghettos were governed within by a Jewish council, usually picked by the Germans. Hunger and disease killed off thousands of people, for when people live together in overcrowded, unsanitary circumstances, disease easily finds victims. In addition Jews in the ghettos were given only about 230 calories a day, compared to 1500–3000 that are usually eaten. Many Jews starved, and others were so weak from hunger they could scarcely drag themselves about. There was no fuel for heating and fur coats had to be turned over to the Nazi authorities. Many Jews in the ghettos froze to death.

Life in the ghetto was dismal except for one thing —the Jews all lived together and most of them tried to help each other to the best of their ability. They produced plays and cultural programs. They organized classes for the children and even had concerts. All these things had to be carried out in secret, because of the strict Nazi rules.

When Jews walked in the streets to try to find food or medicine, or to go to work, they were kidnapped by the Nazis for forced labor and never seen again by their families. Frequently drunken Nazis would come into the ghetto and beat elderly Jews, drag women by the hair, and shoot passersby just for their own amusement. It soon reached the point that people tried to stay in their apartments during the day.

In each country in Europe occupied by the Germans, the Jews were forced to submit to the same laws as those in Germany and Poland.

When the Nazis overran an area their first concern —after setting up their headquarters—was to kill many Jews; and organize the rest into workgangs or send them to the death camps. At Babi Yar in Russia 100,000 Jews were shot and dumped into a ravine. The number in other cities and towns may have been smaller, but the procedure was the same: kill, terrorize, use strong Jews

The Right to Live

to work at slave labor for the Nazi war machine, and send the rest to the death camps.

At first the death camps had signs on their gates *Arbeit macht frei* (work will liberate), but these were cover-ups for the true purpose of the camps. So too the doors to the gas chambers bore the sign "showers," and the Jews were forced to strip before they entered. The piles of clothing and shoes were, of course, confiscated by the Nazis.

The Nazis, with legendary German thoroughness, kept records of the millions who entered the death camps, and so it is not difficult to prove that at least six million Jews died at their hands.

Things to think about

1 Imagine that you were a Jew living during the rise of Nazi power in Germany. What signs could you have seen of the Holocaust coming? How do you think you would have reacted to the Nuremberg laws? What freedoms (that you treasure) would you have lost?

2 In what ways do you think the Jews of Germany were helpless to stop the persecution against them? In what ways did they react? Why did most of their German neighbors not help at all? How is fear a weapon?

3 All of us always hope for "better times" when things are bad. Yet we in the United States have been in a protected situation for many years because of our great

military strength. Not since the time of the Civil War have we felt the destructive force of war in the mainland of the United States.

How did this great fear of war and its destructive power help Hitler and the Nazis to overrun much of Europe with little resistance? How did it help them in their private war against the Jews? Why do you think Hitler chose the Jews as a special target for destruction? Was Hitler right to believe that none of the other countries in the world cared about what happened to the Jews? Would European countries today care if Israel is threatened with destruction?

four

The Yellow Badge

~~~~~~

THE Germans did many things to humiliate and shame the Jews and make them feel less than human. One of the things they thought would be very embarrassing was to make the Jews stand out from everyone else. Jews were forced to wear a symbol of their Judaism—a yellow six-pointed star, outlined in black, with the word *Jude* written in black. *Jude* is the German word for Jew. In some countries occupied by the Nazis, the Jews had to wear the star on an armband. In other countries the star had to be pinned to the front and back of the outer garment.

Nazi-occupied Poland was the first country to enforce the wearing of the star. It became a law in November 1939. Those wearing the "Jew Badge" could not travel on trains or public vehicles without a permit, nor could they walk on certain streets, or sit in parks. They could be arrested without cause, and sent to hard labor or death. Jews ten years of age and over had to wear the star on the right sleeve of their clothing or overcoats. It was placed on a white armband, not less than four inches wide. The armband had to be provided by the Jews themselves.

In addition to wearing this sign, the star also had to be placed in all Jewish shops, offices, and apartments.

When the German government announced the enforcement of the wearing of the badge in 1941, it said, "Jews who have completed their sixth year are forbidden

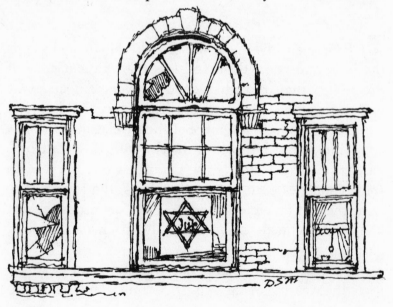

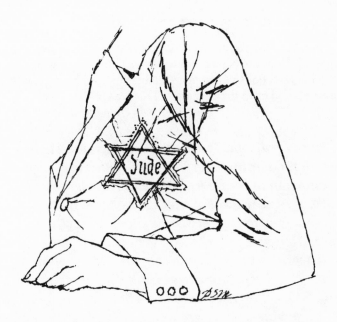

to show themselves in public without the Jew-Star. . . . It must be worn visibly and firmly sewed to the left breast of clothing. . . ."

The reaction to this order in Germany was what the Nazis expected. Most people looked away from their Jewish friends and neighbors and behaved as if they did not notice them. Some Germans spat on Jews wearing the stars. Only a few brave people tried to make the Jews feel accepted, and smiled or shook hands. One German general was very upset about the badge. He wrote his relatives, ". . . this star is unworthy of a supposedly cultured nation . . . someday we shall pay for it." One wonders what that general thought later when the deportations, murders, and burnings began.

From *The Nazi Primer*, a textbook which was written
completely from the Nazi point of view. The Nazis wrote
new textbooks which changed history and biology,
literature, and even mathematics. This was just one way
that the Nazis changed schools.

*. . . the Nordic man grows tall and slender. He has,
according to our discoveries, limbs which are large
in proportion to the body. That suits our sense of
beauty . . . the skull of the Nordic man, likewise,
grows narrow, long. The face is small . . . the
nose is high set . . . the skin is light, rosy-white
and delicate . . . the hair is smooth, wavy, thin
and fine . . . its color varies from light to golden
blond. As to eyes, the Nordic race has light-colored
eyes, blue, blue-grey to grey. . . . The Nordic race
is uncommonly gifted mentally. It is outstanding
for truthfulness and energy. . . .*

Unfortunately only a few people in each country
were upset and dared defy the Nazis. For the most part,
people did not care.

Jews who were always observant or Orthodox were
forced to wear the badge; and Jews who did not consider
themselves to be Jews were sought out by the Nazis and
forced to wear the badge. Some startled Christians found
they had Jewish blood from some grandfather or grand-
mother. They also had to wear the star.

30

The Yellow Badge

In March 1942 the Germans tried to bring the badge to France. The French officials refused to cooperate. They were replaced. But the new officials still hesitated. Finally the decree was enforced in June. The badge had to be worn by all French Jews from the age of six. Jews had to pay a clothing coupon to purchase it. In France, clothing coupons were used during the war for purchasing badly needed clothing. Jews had to purchase the badge instead.

Some Frenchmen were in sympathy with wearers of the badge, and Nazis complained that Jews proudly wore their badges in cafés and restaurants where German soldiers ate. Some Frenchmen appeared in public wearing yellow handkerchiefs in their breast pockets, and holding yellow stars in their hands. The angry Nazis arrested many of these sympathizers and sent them to concentration camps, forcing them to wear a white armband that said "Jew Friend."

The Germans hired several textile firms to prepare 400,000 badges. With the usual systematic German thoroughness, it was decided that each French Jew owned at least three garments as well as an overcoat. However, much to their disappointment, only 83,000 stars were claimed. The rest rotted in warehouses.

A legend grew up that when King Christian of Denmark was approached by the Nazis to force the Jews in Denmark to wear the badge, he said, "The Jews are a part of the Danish nation. We have no Jewish problem in our country. If the Jews are forced to wear the Yellow

The Yellow Badge

Star, I and my whole family shall wear it as a Badge of Honor." The legend arose because of the brave resistance of the Danish people against the Nazi deportations of Danish Jews.

Very small groups of people in other countries, too, showed their sympathies at the beginning when the Jews were forced to wear the badge. The Jews wore the badge without shame. In Hungary, Jews put their badges on a week before they were supposed to. When asked why, one girl answered, "We are Jews—why should we be ashamed?"

In 1945, when the Palestinian Jews came across the Alps to try to help the remnant of Jewry in Europe, they wore the Jewish star on their clothing and said: "This was to be a sign of shame—we consider it a Badge of Honor."

Things to think about

1 The story of the Yellow Badge teaches us that one of the greatest dangers of life in modern times is the danger of "not caring," the danger of *apathy*. Apathy is a lack of emotion or interest, it is not being concerned about others. Do you think the German people were more afraid of Hitler or more afraid of "getting involved," or just did not care altogether?

2 In those countries where the people or the govern-

The Yellow Badge

ment was not apathetic, were the Germans able to force the Jews to wear badges? Having seen what happened in France—knowing that although many Gentiles became "Jew Friends," the Jews were forced to wear the badge anyway—do you think it was of any use to be a "Jew Friend?" Is it better not to demonstrate and protest when demonstrating and protesting do no good?

3 When the Palestinian Jews said, "This was to be a sign of shame; we consider it a Badge of Honor," they were speaking of the same Yellow Star which Jews in Europe had been forced to wear. Can we really change things by changing the way we think about them? Can a sign of shame really become a "Badge of Honor"?

five

The Judenrat Government

~~~~~~

WE all know the saying "Do not judge your neighbor until you have been in his shoes." Probably as you watch a film, or view TV, you think about how you would feel and act if you were the hero or the victim. Would you be brave? Or would you really be a coward? Immediately, of course, you answer—you would be brave. But in the secret hiding place of your heart you are not so sure.

It is not often easy to be brave. Sometimes we are surprised by the criminal, and we don't think of being brave—just give him money and get it over with. Sometimes the crime begins as something very small, and every few days additional elements are added, until it becomes a very large and horrible crime.

35

The Judenrat Government

In the ghettos, the Nazis appointed Jews to be heads of the community (called the *Judenrat*). These Jews were placed in the position of choosing who would go to their death and who would remain alive—at least for the moment. It is not easy to be appointed to a position of power and leadership when that power is only for the death of your own people.

In Warsaw, Poland, Adam Czerniakow was appointed head of the Jewish Council. He had been born in Poland in 1880, into an educated, middle-class family. Although he received a degree in chemical engineering, he did not become successful as an engineer. He did become a successful teacher in a vocational school. In addition to his work, he devoted a great deal of energy to public activities, pioneering in the organization of other vocational schools in leading Jewish centers in Poland.

In 1916 he became chairman of the Central Federation of Jewish Artisans (skilled craftsmen) and fought for the acceptance of Jews into the guilds. In 1928 he won an election to the Polish senate, but never got to sit in the senate because he was Jewish and the Polish authorities declared the election invalid.

When the Germans appointed him to head the *Kehilla* or community, they ordered him to set up a council of 24 elders—the *Judenrat*. Most of the people he appointed tried to get out of serving, but Czerniakow

pleaded with them, and finally they accepted positions on the council.

Most people in the ghetto disliked Czerniakow, but when his diary was found, people began to realize what a great man he really was. He was caught between the Germans' impossible demands and the struggle to ease the terrible restrictions on his people. He was blamed for everything that went wrong in the Ghetto.

One day, for no apparent reason, Nazi soldiers broke into his office, beat him, kicked him, and threw him down the stairs, and then took him to jail. As he discovered more about the evil intentions of the Nazis, he began carrying poison with him.

Just before he died, he wrote: "Because employees of the Judenrat and their families are not being deported yet, I have asked that the craftsmen and garbage collectors also not be deported. . . ."

On July 23, 1942, the Nazis came to him to sign the mass deportation order that would send the Jews of the ghetto to their death in the concentration camps. He refused to sign, choosing instead to commit suicide. He left a note for his colleagues which begged them not to think of him as a coward. "I am helpless, my heart breaks from pain and pity. I can no longer stand this. . . ."

After his death, one of his severest critics wrote of him:

> The first victim of the deportation decree was the president, Adam Czerniakow, who committed suicide by poison in the Judenrat building. . . . His end proves that he worked and tried for the good of his people; that he wanted its welfare and continuity, even though not everything done in his name was praiseworthy. . . . The president, who had a spark of purity in his heart, found the only way out worthy of himself—Suicide! . . . He did not have a good life, but he had a beautiful death. . . . There are those who earn immortality in a single instant.

Ugo Foa, in the Rome Ghetto, kept reassuring the Jews of Rome that they were safe. The Nazis promised protection for the Jews of this ancient city, living in the shadow of the Pope. But the Pope was more concerned with the possibility that the Italians might become Communists than he was about the murder of the Jews. Though Foa was warned about the deportations and gas

An order establishing the Jewish Councils (the Judenrat) as a first step in the "final" solution. Reading this order helps us to understand how difficult the situation was for the "Elders," the Jewish leaders.

The first step toward the final goal must bring all the Jews from the countryside into the larger towns. It is to be carried out at all speed. It is absolutely necessary that Jewish communities of less than 500 people are broken up and concentrated in the nearest towns.

Jewish Council of Elders

1. A Jewish Council of Elders is to be set up in every Jewish community. It is to be made fully responsible in the full sense of the word for the exact and prompt carrying out of all past or current orders.

2. In the case of sabotage of such orders, the severest measures are to be announced to the council.

3. The Jewish councils must undertake a count of the Jews and tell us the result without delay.

4. The Councils of Elders are to be told the dates and time limits, the facilities and finally the routes of the departure. They are then to be made personally responsible for the departure of the Jews from the countryside.

The reason to be given for the concentration of the Jews in the towns is that Jews have been most active in raids and looting activity.

chambers, he kept telling himself and others that the Jews of the Holy City of Rome would be spared.

Important Jews in the community begged Foa to destroy the lists of the thousands of Jews who lived in Rome. He refused to do so. On a Sabbath day, October 16, 1943, the Nazis, aided by the lists that they had taken from Foa's office, rounded up the Jews of Rome and deported them.

Chaim Rumkowski of the Lodz Ghetto was different. It is believed that he sought the leadership of the ghetto, so that he would have power and be important. Through this power, he thought he could gain wealth, and people would look up to him. But this was at the expense of other Jews in the Lodz Ghetto. He was a great organizer, though, and organized workshops, hospitals, and schools. Rumkowski had a sincere liking for little children which, however, did not stop him from leading them to the railroad station to certain death. That day, he said, was the most tragic day of his life, but unlike

The Judenrat Government

Janusz Korczak, about whom you will soon read, he did not go with the young ones. He turned them over to their murderers.

He became very dramatic wearing a long cloak and shining boots, carrying a cane, and always insisting that a gray horse draw his carriage. He permitted no opposition, and allowed no negative or critical writings. He was considered an evil and terrible dictator by those poor Jews of the ghetto. However his ghetto was the best organized and most productive of all the ghettos. Because of this the Lodz Ghetto was the last to be destroyed. The Russian army was stationed across the Vistula River, and remained there for six months. Had they crossed six months earlier to defeat the Nazis, Rumkowski would have been a hero and savior. Instead, when his usefulness to the Nazis was over, he was sent to the gas chamber along with the rest of the Jews of Lodz.

Another leader of a smaller Jewish community was shot because he refused to hand over children, sick, and aged people to the Nazis. "I am no master over human life," he told the Nazis, "I will not give you Jews." In another community, the Nazis demanded that both Jews and non-Jews fulfill a quota for a supposed act of sabotage against them. The non-Jews supplied the quota, but the Jewish leader refused, saying "you may take *me* away, but I am not going to deliver innocent people to their death." He was killed. Many leaders resigned and were killed by the Nazis because they refused to be tools in the hands of the killers.

One desperate leader said: "I must select people for deportation for gassing. If I refuse I'll be shot. This would be the simplest solution for me. But then what happens? The Nazis have said if I die, they will make the selections. That would mean the rabbis, scholars, poets would go into the oven first. . . . I no longer enjoy being alive. If you know a better way than the one I have found, show it to me, and if you don't, tell me: shall I stay or shall I have myself shot?"

These are a few of the leaders who headed Jewish communities during the Nazi period. Some were strong and some were weak, some were greedy and some longed for power. Probably, each tried to do his best.

Things to think about

1 The Jews who became leaders of the *Judenrat* governments were trapped from the start. They knew the Nazis would kill and replace them if they did not follow orders. At the same time, they felt a need to help the Jewish community. In this chapter you have studied some of their reactions. Suppose you were a leader of a ghetto and just learned the truth about the Nazi orders

The Judenrat Government

—that Jews were being sent to their deaths—what would you do? Would you inform the Jewish community?

2 Each leader reacted individually to the problems of deportations and selections. Today the survivors of the Holocaust and historians of the Holocaust still argue which of the leaders were heroes and which of them were cowards. Which of the leaders you studied in this chapter would you consider heroes? Which cowards?

3 Is courage the most important characteristic of a good leader?

six

The Rabbi Leaders

^^^

MOSES Maimonides, the great Jewish medieval scholar and philosopher, said: "If an enemy should tell the head of a Jewish community, hand over a Jew for us to put to death or all of you will die, the person should not be handed over."

During the Holocaust, many community leaders were put into this situation. Some of these community leaders were rabbis. One rabbi said, "If a Jewish community has been condemned to death and there are means of rescuing part of it, the leaders of the community should have the courage to rescue whomever they can." However, other rabbis, when requested to make a selection of those to be sent to their death so the rest of the community could remain alive, abided by the ruling of Maimonides and did not hand over a list. This became an important question for rabbis and community leaders.

During the years the Nazis occupied Europe, millions of people became known by a number instead of a name. Perhaps you have seen a person with a number tatooed on his arm. Perhaps you have wondered what that number meant. Those were the tatoo numbers the Nazis burned into the arms of their prisoners. Each person imprisoned in a concentration camp had a number. Number 187,894 was given to the Rabbi, Dr. Leo Baeck, who had been head of the Jewish community in Berlin, Germany.

On January 27, 1943, at 5:44 in the morning, German SS soldiers came to Rabbi Baeck's home in Berlin, and told him he was being taken to the police station for questioning. Dr. Baeck, who usually arose early in the morning anyway, asked for an hour to put his things in order. Although Nazis usually did not observe the courtesy of informing their prisoners where they were taking them or of giving them time to prepare themselves, they gave him one hour. He wrote a letter to his daughter who was living in London, and made out payments for his gas and electric bills. He was sent to the Theresienstadt concentration camp.

Rabbi Baeck was almost seventy years old when he was sent to Theresienstadt. He was put to work pulling a garbage wagon. He seemed not to mind. This man who had always been a scholar, a teacher, and a rabbi would not let a little thing like pulling a garbage wagon make him bitter. He continued to discuss philosophy and literature with the man hitched next to him as they pulled the garbage.

In Theresienstadt he comforted the sick, attended the dying, and taught the living. Soon after he came to the camp, a Rabbi Beck who was imprisoned there died. Adolf Eichmann, the man who engineered the murder of the 6,000,000 Jews, came to Theresienstadt. There he met Rabbi Baeck. He was very astonished and said, "Herr Baeck, are you still alive? I thought you were dead!"

Rabbi Baeck looked him right in the eye and answered, "You are apparently announcing a future occurrence."

Although Rabbi Baeck realized by 1933 what Adolf Hitler thought about Jews, he felt "as long as there is one Jew left in Germany" he must remain there. He had been invited to come to the United States to be a professor at the Hebrew Union College, but refused. In 1939 he led a group of children out of Germany to England and could have remained with them there, but chose to return to his people.

During this time, Dr. Baeck composed a Yom Kippur prayer for his congregation in Berlin. It was a prayer that spoke of Nazi brutality. He knew that the Nazis had spies in every synagogue, and that many Jews had been sent to death camps for lesser reasons; that torture

A prayer by Dr. Leo Baeck. A man of great courage and a
fine leader, Rabbi Baeck stayed with his people, the Jews
of Berlin, through the entire Holocaust, comforting
and teaching.

*At this hour all Israel stands before its God, who
judges and pardons. Let us in His presence examine
our ways, what we have done and what we have left
undone, where we have been and where we have
failed to be. Let us openly confess our wrongdoings,
declaring, "We have sinned" and in full earnestness
of repentance pray "Forgive us!"*

*We stand before our God. With that same force with
which we have confessed our sins, personal and
collective, let us say that the lies uttered against us,
the false charges made against our faith and its
defenders are hateful. Let us trample these false-
hoods beneath our feet. . . .*

*At this hour all the people of Israel stand before
their God. The prayers, the confidence, and the faith
that are in us are in all Jews on earth. We gaze on
one another in recognition, our eyes lifted up to our
God, and we know our eternity.*

*We are filled with sorrow and pain. Standing in
silence before our God we express what lies on our
souls. May this silent prayer go forth and be heard
above all other sound.*

and death awaited those sent to camps. Yet Rabbi Leo Baeck was a man of great courage and strength. His prayer was recited aloud.

Dr. Baeck knew what was going on in the concentration camps. He spent many sleepless nights trying to decide whether he should tell the Jews what awaited them when they were shipped away. Finally he decided not to. He felt that perhaps some would not be put to death, but rather to hard labor. Why should he cause them the pain of knowing what was to be? It was a difficult decision to make and it is difficult for us to say if it was right or wrong.

At the end of the war, a foreign officer appeared in Theresienstadt and offered to take Dr. Baeck out immediately. The Rabbi refused to be treated as a special case. He had come with the others and would leave with the others. . . .

In September 1943, on the eve of Rosh Hashanah, Rabbi Marcus Melchior, the Chief Rabbi of Denmark, was informed that there was going to be a roundup of the Jewish community by the Nazis. When the Jews came to synagogue that evening, Dr. Melchior informed his congregants of the danger and urged them to flee and hide, explaining that High Holiday services would not be held. He made sure those who were in synagogue would inform those who had not come. In Denmark it was a little easier to hide because the non-Jewish community was willing to help the Jews. In some countries,

the non-Jewish community did everything it could to hinder the Jews from escaping.

In Rome Chief Rabbi Israel Zolli was afraid of the Nazis. He had heard about what was happening, and particularly was afraid of their treatment of rabbis. He pleaded with the head of the Jewish community in Rome, Ugo Foa, to urge the Jews not to assemble for any reason whatsoever. He suggested that they could have services at home, for God is everywhere. He urged Foa to announce that large groups should not congregate in public places. Mr. Foa was very angry with the rabbi and scolded him, saying he should give strength and confidence to his people, and not run away himself. Zolli later turned out to be a traitor to the Jewish people, perhaps the only one among thousands of rabbis.

In 1943 a very large transport of Jews was being sent from France to concentration camps. The Chief Rabbi of France, Isaie Schwartz, went to Vichy, France, then the capital, to protest against this act. The Security Police said it was necessary for the protection of the French Jews to remove those who had come to France from other countries. Rabbi Schwartz argued with the police that the French Jews did not want to be "protected" in such a manner. His argument did not help. Like cattle, the Jews were shipped away.

Rabbi Zvi Koretz was appointed to be head of the Salonika Jewish community in Greece in 1942. He carried out the orders of the Germans to try to convince them that the Jews were loyal and orderly. Many of the survivors of Salonika believe that if Rabbi Koretz had not hurried to carry out German orders, more Greek Jews might have escaped or hidden. On the other hand, the surrounding non-Jewish community in Greece was not friendly to the Jews, so that there was little assistance and few places for a Jew to hide.

The Rabbi did try to urge a large segment of Jews to accept work in Greece rather than submit to deportation to Poland which he suspected meant death. But the Greek Jews had seen how difficult working conditions

The Rabbi Leaders

under the Nazis could be, and most decided to go to Poland.

Rabbis and community leaders were no more or less human than other people. Leading the community meant many fateful decisions. Some rabbis were afraid, some were brave, some made decisions for the community as they saw best. There were those who collaborated, and those who tried not to collaborate.

Things to think about

1 In this chapter, we have read the stories of several rabbis. Each of them reacted differently to the Nazi threats and commands. Is there a special way rabbis should act in times of crisis? Should we expect all rabbis to think and act alike?

2 One of the rabbis' duties is to help Jews to behave in a Jewish way. Was there a Jewish way to behave at the time of the Nazis? Did the Jewish people ever before in history face a threat like the threat of the Nazis? If you had been a rabbi at that time, where might you have turned for wisdom?

3 In the end, all a real leader can do is to set an example for his followers. In the end, all rabbis showed some concern for their communities, for the Jews who looked to them for leadership. And in the end, Adolf Hitler committed suicide instead of taking the responsibility for

having ruined Germany. Hitler deserted and cheated his followers and left them at their enemies' mercy. Are concern and responsibility part of being a leader? Are leaders always brave? Are leaders always right? Do you think that you would make a good leader? Are you careful about the kind of leader that you follow?

seven

The Warsaw Ghetto

‸‸‸

WARSAW is the capital city of Poland. Before 1940 it had a very large Jewish population. Jews lived in Poland before the year 1200. They had settled in Warsaw around 1414, even before Columbus discovered America.

On September 1, 1939, the Germans under Adolf Hitler attacked Poland. Many Jews volunteered to fight in the army with the Poles against the Germans, but they were overwhelmed by superior German military equipment and trained soldiers. By September 28, less than a month later, all Poland had been overrun by the Nazis.

In 1940 a Jewish ghetto was established in Warsaw and a brick wall built around it. The wall was to keep the

The Warsaw Ghetto

Jews inside the ghetto and all others out. The wall enclosed approximately 840 acres. Since one square mile is 640 acres, 840 acres is about one and a third miles square or 24 square blocks. Into this area, where about 160,000 people were originally, somewhere between 330,000 and 500,000 Jews were now forced to live.

Jews were forced to leave homes in other parts of the city and to move into the ghetto. They had no wagons to move furniture and clothing and so took only what

they could carry on their backs or in hand-wagons or baby buggies. Often three and four families were forced to live together in one room.

The Germans did not provide enough food for even half the number of people in the ghetto. The bowl of soup that was eaten was sometimes boiled from straw. It was forbidden to bring food into the ghetto and though some small amounts were smuggled in, many Jews starved to death.

The Warsaw Ghetto

Since the Jews had brought only the clothing they could carry, and since the Nazis forced them to give up fur coats and even coats with fur collars, they had little warm clothing. Although small quantities of coal were smuggled into the ghetto, it was very costly and most Jews could not afford it. Polish winters are long and very cold, and so from lack of warm clothing and heat many Jews froze to death.

Because they were made to live in such crowded conditions, the terrible disease, typhoid, began to spread. There was little water and it was not fit for drinking. Sanitary conditions were very poor. Many Jews in the ghetto died from typhoid, and most were sickened through weakness.

Life was bitter. A few Jews exploited other Jews, a handful thought they would save their lives by working with the Germans, but most of the Jews behaved in a humane fashion, and many even heroically.

Januscz Korczak, the doctor and director of the orphanage in the ghetto; Adam Czerniakow, the leader of the Jewish Council; Emanuel Ringelblum, one of the historians of the ghetto—all were special kinds of heroes. All three could have escaped, but they chose to remain with their people and die with them. In addition to Ringelblum's, at least two other diaries have been found that relate the happenings and daily life of the ghetto.

Mary Berg, the daughter of an American citizen, was imprisoned in the Warsaw Ghetto when she was just sixteen. She began writing her diary even earlier,

Another laughable order is about the First Aid car.

*The Star of David on the car of the Jewish social
self-help, in which the sick are taken to Otwock, is
to be considerably enlarged and, what is most
important, its color must be yellow—"Jew-yellow."*

*It won't take long before we are ordered to paint
our gates, trams, houses, streets, faces, and perhaps
even the sky above us, yellow.*

when she was fifteen, during the siege of the city of
Warsaw. Her diary ends in March 1944, when she was
put on a ship with her mother and father bound for the
United States. In between, because she was an American
citizen, Mary was sent to a prison instead of a concentration camp.

Still another diary was discovered that had been
kept by a man named Chaim A. Kaplan. Chaim Kaplan
was a religious Jew and remained so until his death. His
diary begins on September 1, 1939, and ends in August
1942. Chaim Kaplan describes the ghetto like this: "If
it were said the sun has darkened for us at noon, it

would be true. We will rot within the narrow streets and crooked lanes in which tens of thousands of people wander, idle and full of despair. . . . What good will ten decagrams of coarse bread a week do? There is nowhere to earn a penny, and now a loaf of coarse bread costs three zlotys, a kilo of butter 30 zlotys." (A zloty in that time of inflated prices was approximately what a dollar would be to us.)

Emanuel Ringelblum, the historian, speaks in his diary of attempts to grow food for the ghetto. Zionist youth organizations—whose members became the leaders and the majority of the fighters in the uprising— tried to plant vegetables on tiny patches of land. Small gardens were planted on the places where houses had been burned down. Vegetables were grown on balconies and even rooftops.

In spite of all the filth and starvation, some of the leaders tried to raise the low spirits of the inhabitants of the ghetto. Although schools for children were forbidden, they existed underground on all levels. In back rooms, on long benches, near a table, schoolchildren sat and learned. In time of danger, the children learned to hide their books under their clothes. There were classes and lectures for adults. There were also lectures and classes for medical students; laboratories were established. Theater groups performed plays in Yiddish right up until the time the ghetto was destroyed. Artists, musicians, and writers in the ghetto were encouraged.

Chaim Kaplan writes, "The idea that all Jews are

responsible for each other has stopped being merely a slogan. 'Courtyard committees' have been set up and are taking care of all the residents of the courtyard, even middle-class and wealthy ones. They established food kitchens and a permanent fund for soup kitchens." The ghetto was made up of apartment buildings. Each set of apartments had a courtyard, so many residents used one courtyard. Therefore each group of apartments had its own courtyard committee. Chaim Kaplan ends his paragraph by saying, "When historians come to write the history of the courtyard committees, let them end their chapter with the blessing, 'May the Lord remember them with favor.' "

Kaplan even tells in his diary how Hanukkah was celebrated in 1940. Hanukkah parties were held in every courtyard. "We arranged a celebration in our courtyard for which we charged, and then gave the proceeds toward feeding the poor in our courtyard. There was even a speech full of jokes, scientific and historical talks in Yiddish and Hebrew." He finishes this passage by saying, "At a time like this, there is no better cure than to be a believer in God. Even gentiles are amazed to see our will to live."

From time to time thousands of Jews from other communities were forced into the Warsaw Ghetto, and the Jews living there had to find room for them, and share their meager food supplies with these strangers.

Kaplan wrote, "there is even dancing, although the stomach is empty. It is almost a *mitzvah* to dance. The more one dances, the more it is a sign of his belief in the 'eternity of Israel.' Every dance is a protest against our oppressors."

Kaplan felt that the residents of the ghetto tried their best to assist fellow Jews in misfortune. There was a Self-Aid organization that raised half a million zlotys to support the needy. It was a unity built upon tragedy —this desire and need to help each other.

The Nazi idea of having a little fun was to come into the ghetto to beat up old people, shoot children, and help themselves to anything they wanted. But a time came when Germans dared not come within the ghetto walls, except in large groups, armed with machine guns. They learned to fear and respect a small resistance group that organized to fight. The Jewish Fighter's Organization,

The Warsaw Ghetto

headed by a young man named Mordechai Anilewitz, was responsible for this change.

Things to think about

1 The diaries and notebooks which were found in the area occupied by the Warsaw Ghetto after the war was over tell us much about the life inside the Ghetto walls. Warsaw held the largest concentration of Jews in Europe. Jews banded close together, forming new organizations to help one another, teaching, studying, working, dancing. What ideas and feelings do you think these people shared which kept them civilized even as the Nazis prepared to destroy them? Why did they continue to prepare for the future, even in the death camps?

2 What part did religion play in keeping up the spirits of the people in the Ghetto? Would it have made a difference if the people in the Warsaw Ghetto were not all of one religion?

3 In what ways are ghettos in modern cities like the Warsaw Ghetto? In what ways do they differ? Is there any lesson that the historians of the Warsaw Ghetto taught us that would be useful to people living in ghettos today?

eight

The Boy Who Fought Back

MORDECHAI ANILEWITZ

∿∿∿∿∿∿∿∿∿∿∿∿∿∿∿∿∿∿∿∿∿∿∿∿∿∿∿∿∿∿∿∿∿∿∿∿∿∿

ON a hill at a kibbutz outside of Tel Aviv, Israel, stands a bronze statue of a tall, proud-looking young man, shirt unbuttoned, chest bare. In one hand he clutches a "Molotov cocktail."

This is the statue of Mordechai Anilewitz, and the kibbutz near the statue is named Yad Mordechai. Mordechai Anilewitz taught the world what it means "To die with honor."

When Mordechai was a young boy, it was popular for Polish gentile toughs to attack young Jews—just for fun. Most Jewish youths ran and hid, but not Mordechai. He not only stood up to the bullying Poles, but fought back fiercely. When the toughs saw Mordechai coming, they would detour to stay out of his way. If Mordechai heard shouts for help on the street, he was out in a minute with his youth group to help the victims. He never started a fight, but he never backed down either.

When the Nazis occupied Warsaw and established the ghetto, Mordechai was a young man. He sought ways to help his fellow Jews, and at the end of 1942, he organized a fighting unit. He operated a secret radio station to inform the Jews in the ghetto of what was happening outside. He wrote short, powerful articles in an underground journal called *Against the Stream*. Copies of this journal were found in all corners of the country—far beyond the ghetto walls.

In his youth, as a member of the Zionist youth organization, *Hashomer Hatzair* (The Young Watchman), he became known as "Chaver (friend, comrade) Mordechai." The name stuck to him until he was killed.

Mordechai was convinced that everyone in the ghetto would die at the Nazis' hands. "The question is," he asked, "how shall we die?" And he answered, "We have decided to die in battle." He began organizing all the young and middle-aged people in the ghetto for battle—girls and women, boys and men. He drilled, trained, and obtained weapons, some of which were purchased at enormous cost and smuggled into the ghetto. Grenades were produced by hand, at the rate of about fifty a day.

In January 1943, the Germans rounded up a few hundred Jews for deportation to the death camps. They dragged these unfortunate people to the *Umschlagplatz*, the roundup place in the ghetto where their unfortunate victims were herded into cattle trains to be taken to the concentration camps. This time, Mordechai entered the crowd with his comrades. At a signal, they attacked the Germans. The captured Jews fled; the Germans scattered in confusion, leaving behind their wounded and dead. The young fighters stood their ground. Mordechai, after using up all his ammunition, attacked one Nazi soldier with his bare fists, taking the German's weapons.

The deportations stopped for three months. The Germans were preparing themselves for a terrible battle. But the ghetto fighters were also preparing themselves. Mordechai worked day and night. He was everywhere. He helped dig bunkers with secret tunnels. (A bunker is an underground hiding place with ventilator shafts for air.) There were a number of very large bunkers hidden in the ghetto. Mordechai also helped set up tank-blocks in entrances to buildings. He organized the collection of arms and was in constant contact with comrades on the other side of the ghetto walls. He drew maps of the ghetto with detailed information—every alley and every passageway was marked out for the fighters. To a friend he wrote:

> We don't have a moment's rest. We sleep in our clothes. At every entry to the ghetto we stand on guard day and night. We are making the final preparations. Soon we shall

From the last testament of Mordechai Anilewitz. Anilewitz
wrote this letter when he knew that he was about to die.
Anilewitz and the Ghetto were destroyed by the Germans,
but the letter survived.

*It is now clear to me that what took place exceeded
all hopes. In our opposition to the Germans we did
more than our strength allowed—but now our
forces are waning. We are on the brink of being
wiped out. We forced the Germans to retreat twice
—but they returned stronger than ever. . . . I feel
that great things are happening and that this action
which we have dared to take is of enormous value.
. . . We need many rifles, hand grenades, machineguns, and explosives.*

*I cannot describe the conditions in which the Jews of
the Ghetto are now "living." Only a few exceptional
individuals will be able to survive such suffering.*

*The others will sooner or later die. Their fate is
certain, even though thousands are trying to hide in
cracks and ratholes. It is impossible to light a candle,
for lack of air. Greetings to you who are outside.*

*Perhaps a miracle will occur and we shall see each
other again one of these days. . . . The last wish of
my life has been fulfilled. Jewish self-defense has
become a fact. Jewish resistance and revenge have
really happened. I am happy to have been one of the
first Jewish fighters in the Ghetto. Where will rescue
come from?*

have to separate ourselves from life and go to the place that no one wants to go. But ours is the correct path. We cultivated in our hearts the idea of revolt—this is the path of the Jewish youth—be well, *chaverim.*

On Sunday, April 18, 1943, the leaders of the central ghetto met with Mordechai as chairman. At the end of the meeting, he distributed weapons and baskets of handmade bombs, known as "Molotov cocktails." Some food was distributed, and poison for those fighters who might be caught and did not want to be tortured by the Nazis. Houses were barricaded with furniture and sandbags, pillows were placed on windowsills for support and protection. Finally an all-night watch was set up in the ghetto. It was the eve of the first seder of Passover, and Jews from the Aryan side of Warsaw had sneaked into the ghetto to participate in a seder with the other Jews. On Monday, the Nazis attacked. Because they themselves were afraid to face the fire of the Jews, they sent other groups ahead; first the Jewish police and then German and Ukranian columns. Following these came a squadron of motorcyclists, heavy trucks, infantry, heavy machineguns, ambulances, a field kitchen, field telephones, and 12 panzer (armed) vehicles. On the main streets, they set up tables and benches for headquarters; and they installed telephones on the tables. Full of confidence in their superior strength and weapons, the German column, singing loudly, reached the corners of the two main streets. Suddenly, a hail of Molotov cocktails sent them fleeing in panic, leaving behind their dead and wounded. One tank after another was hit with well-aimed handmade bombs; the men driving them burned alive inside. Panic broke out among the Germans. The Nazi report to headquarters was: "The Jewish resistance was unexpected, unusually strong, and a great surprise."

On April 23, Mordechai Anilewitz wrote to a friend:

> Be well my friend. Perhaps we shall meet again. The main thing is that the dream of my life came true. I was fortunate enough to witness Jewish defense in the ghetto in all its greatness and glory.

The fighting continued, but lacking arms and ammunitions, the Jews grew weaker. On May 8, the Germans found the bunker at 18 Mila Street. This was the main bunker of many fighters, including Mordechai Anilewitz. The Nazis threw poison gas into the bunker and shot all those who came out. Whether Mordechai was killed by the gas, or whether he committed suicide, we shall probably never know.

Most of the fighters were killed, but a few of those who had fought against the Nazis escaped through the sewers and joined some companions in the forests to continue the fight.

The Jews in the ghetto, with their pitiful weapons, held out longer against their Nazi enemies than the Poles had held out when the Germans attacked Poland.

The Boy Who Fought Back

Things to think about

1 Mordechai Anilewitz knew that the revolt of the Warsaw Ghetto would fail. "The question is how shall we die?" he said. "We have decided to die in battle." Why was fighting so important to Mordechai and his followers? Did they want to die?

2 Others in the Ghetto disagreed with Mordechai and his followers. These others felt that help could yet come, that the war might end soon and all would be freed. Some few who did not fight survived even after being sent to concentration camps. Faced with the choice of fighting or following the orders of the Nazis, which choice would you make and why?

3 In truth, we are each responsible for our own decisions. Whenever we are faced by a choice which is important, we must carefully weigh both sides of the choice. Yet much depends on the kind of person that we are at the time the choice is presented. What kind of person was Mordechai Anilewitz? Could he have chosen *not* to fight?

nine

A Leader
in the
Underground

‸‸

VILNA is a city in Lithuania in which a thriving Jewish community had lived for hundreds of years. There the Vilna Gaon, in the 1700's, had been the foremost rabbi of his generation and created a great *yeshiva* for Jewish study. Other yeshivot and schools of Jewish scholarship came into being. The Jews called Vilna the Jerusalem of Europe. Even today, when someone says he attended a yeshiva in Vilna, we expect great learning and wisdom from him. Before the Holocaust, Vilna was a flourishing Jewish community with libraries, theaters, and many Zionist youth organizations.

When the Nazis came to Vilna, the first to suffer were the youth who belonged to these organizations.

73

They reacted to the shock of Nazi brutality by organizing themselves into an underground unit. They called themselves the Joint Defense Committee and included representatives from all the youth organizations. Heading this group was a young man—Itzik Wittenberg, who became known as "Leon" to his comrades in the underground.

The young people soon realized the Nazis' evil intent. The Nazis wanted the Jews to slave until the end of their strength and then be killed. What were they to do? They could try to escape and hide from their killers. They could fight underground in the ghetto or go into the forests and fight along with the partisans. Many felt they should not desert their fellow Jews in the ghetto. After many meetings and discussions, they decided to collect

guns and ammunition, and at the right moment to strike
at the Nazi troops, blow up the ghetto and the Nazi
ammunition dumps, try to flee to the forest with as many
fellow Jews as they could, and join the partisans. Although it was difficult to obtain arms, the first gun was
smuggled into the ghetto in January 1942, and by the
middle of 1943, the Vilna Ghetto possessed a number of
guns and some other weapons. This was accomplished
mainly through the untiring efforts of Wittenberg, who
stole through the Nazi lines in disguise. He was brave
and bold; a real threat to the Nazis who wanted to capture and murder him.

In July 1943, two leaders of the Communist
Committee in Vilna were arrested by the Germans. They
were tortured, and it is thought that one of them told the

From a Yiddish song. The heroism of Itzik Wittenberg
became a legend, a symbol of all that meant courage.

Our foe lies there crouching,
Like a beast of the jungle.
My pistol is ready in hand.
Watch out—the Gestapo!
They're leading a captive
At night—our commander in chief!

Then Itzik spoke to us,
His words were like lightning:
"Don't take any risks for my sake,
Your lives are too precious
To give away lightly."
And proudly he goes to his death!

~~~~~~

Gestapo, the Nazi police, that they were in contact with
Wittenberg and the underground movement.

According to one source, the German officer in
charge of the Vilna district thought that by catching
Wittenberg, he would put an end to the activities of the
underground. He forced the cooperation of the head of
the Jewish Council in Vilna and the Jewish police. Together they managed to capture Wittenberg. But his
comrades in the underground learned of his capture,
attacked the guards who were leading him to prison, and
freed Wittenberg.

A Leader in the Underground

Jacob Gens, the head of the Jewish Council in Vilna, called together the entire ghetto population and told them that Wittenberg was endangering the lives of the people in the ghetto. He told them that the Germans had given an ultimatum: If by six o'clock the next morning, the ghetto did not hand over the underground hero, the Germans would come with tanks and airplanes and destroy the ghetto and everyone within. Many inhabitants of the ghetto agreed that the life of one man was not worth the destruction of the entire ghetto, and asked Wittenberg to give himself up.

The Fighting Force of underground comrades did not think Wittenberg should surrender. The leaders of the Communist group, one faction in the underground, did not want the entire ghetto destroyed because of Wittenberg. The Communist group informed the underground leader of its thinking, but Wittenberg did not agree. Wittenberg said: "It has never yet happened that an organization should by its own will surrender its commander. An organization that does this is doomed to failure." He changed his place of hiding.

Finally the leaders of the Fighting Force were forced by the other groups to change their minds. Reluctantly they told him that they agreed with the decision of the Communist group. He still refused to give himself up, saying the Ghetto was doomed anyway. The three representatives answered that the ghetto population did not believe that all was lost and was not ready for a struggle as yet.

77

A Leader in the Underground

At last Wittenberg accepted the decision and agreed to surrender, but insisted on taking a vial of poison which he hid in his ear. The next day Itzik Wittenberg was dead.

After this the Fighting Force decided to transfer its activities to the forest and many of them escaped the ghetto to join the partisans. But again the Nazis came to the ghetto and demanded the surrender of the families of all those who had gone to the forest. Once again, the fighters were faced with a moral problem—to escape and fight and have their families killed, or to stay and not fight and all be killed sooner or later. Driven to desperation, the Vilna Ghetto erupted. They fought the Nazi army with pitiful weapons until they were all slain. It was a situation that was repeated over and over during the Nazi period and a moral problem that became a terrible burden for those who made the decision.

Things to think about

1 The story of "Leon" is much like other stories of the Holocaust. The Nazis often asked the Jewish community to turn over a troublemaker. If not, they threatened, the entire community would suffer. Imagine that you are a part of the Jewish community of Vilna, asked to surrender Wittenberg to the Nazis. Whose decision should it be? Should the community vote? Should it be the

A Leader in the Underground

decision of the *Judenrat*? Should it be the decision of Wittenberg?

2 What choices did Jacob Gens have when he was faced with that decision? Should a leader risk the lives of all his followers just to protect one of them?

3 Wittenberg was a leader, too. He said: "It has never yet happened that an organization should by its own will surrender its commander. An organization that does this is doomed to failure." He refused to give himself up at first. Then later he changed his mind. Was he right in the first place or in the last? What caused him to change his mind? Why do you think he committed suicide?

ten

Father of
Orphans

JANUSCZ KORCZAK

~~~~~~

SOME time ago, a Jewish physician who had been in the Warsaw Ghetto hospital was asked, "Perhaps you knew Januscz Korczak?"

Softly he answered, "Knew him? Yes, I knew him well. There was only one Januscz Korczak in the whole world—only one man like him."

Januscz Korczak was a pediatrician, a children's doctor. He was also an educator, interested in progressive, modern education. In addition he was a writer of children's stories, and the director of an orphanage. Because he cared for each child in the orphanage as his own, he soon began to be called "Father of Orphans."

In the year 1879, Henryk Goldszmit was born into a

81

Father of Orphans

Jewish home in Warsaw, Poland. When he grew up and began writing stories for children, he took the name Januscz Korczak. This had been the name of a make-believe hero in a Polish novel, and this became Henryk Goldszmit's pen name—and the name we know him by today.

Korczak's father was a lawyer, and in the middle-class home in the large Polish city in which he was brought up, the lad scarcely knew he was Jewish. His father died when he was very young; his childhood was lonely. As he grew older, he supported himself by teaching. In visiting the slums of Warsaw, he became interested in how the poor children were living and how they were being educated. In 1903 he graduated from the University of Warsaw, and continued his studies in medicine, specializing in pediatrics.

Although he could have been the physician of the richest families in Warsaw, he chose to take care of the children of slum families. He was the doctor who accepted "undesirable" house calls which other young physicians refused. He took time to stay and play with his little patients. He cared for many of these children without a fee, or, as he once explained, he took a symbolic kopek, since a "physician who takes no fee does not help the patient."

More and more he became involved in the care and welfare of poor and orphaned children, and finally, in 1911, he gave up his hospital activities and successful private practice to become the head of a large Jewish

From "Januscz Korczak's Last Walk" by Hanna Morkowicz-
Olczakowa. Courage and resistance during the Holocaust
took many forms. The "last walk" was a quiet, but forceful
statement of moral victory.

The day is Wednesday, August 5, 1942, in the
morning. The police close off the street. They
surround the house. Horrible screams: "All Jews—
out!" (in German); and then in Yiddish: "Quickly!
Quickly!" The efficient organization for which the
orphanage is well known can now be seen in
operation. The children, who surprised in the middle
of their breakfast have their normal days' routine
upset at a moment's notice, go down quietly and
line up in fives. . . .

Of all the deeds and creations of Januscz Korczak,
the artist and reformer; of all [his assistant] Stefa
Wilczenska's efforts; of all the games, smiles, and
hopes of two hundred boys and girls—this one last
walk will be remembered forever: because with one
daring leap, it overcame murderous brutality. This
small group under the leadership of Korczak has
received eternal glory. It is a small group, the
members of which are known by name, among the
tens of thousands whose names fate caused to be
forgotten. . . .

Father of Orphans

orphanage in Warsaw. His House of Orphans at 92 Krochmalna Street became famous as one of the first institutions in the world to bring up children in an atmosphere of self-respect, affection, and self-expression. Discipline was based on a set of rules adopted by a committee of children selected by children. Duties were assigned by the children, and a children's "court" judged those who broke the rules. The youngsters even published their own newspaper. With inspiration, insight, and devotion, Korczak and his assistant Stefa showed what could be done under difficult conditions.

He received no salary, and lived in a small, poorly furnished attic room, which he often shared with a child who had to get away from the others, or who needed

quiet for a while. He even did some of the lowly tasks like washing dishes or scrubbing the floor.

The six full-length books he wrote for children have become favorites both in Poland and Israel. In each story, Korczak taught an important principle for good living. Many times he wrote about children who find themselves in positions of responsibility and the things they have to do for the benefit of others.

A children's weekly, which was a supplement to a well-known Polish-Jewish newspaper, and which supported the idea of Palestine becoming a Jewish State, may have had an influence in bringing him back to Judaism. Also many of his students at the orphanage "graduated" and went to Palestine. They corresponded with the doctor. He became interested in that land and traveled twice to Palestine. The second time he spent several weeks with his former students on a kibbutz. The spirit of self-sacrifice, the ideals, and the society built on trust that one person had for another—all this appealed to him.

When the Nazis began pressuring Jews, he became more closely identified with his people. In the fall of 1940, he was told that his orphanage was outside the limits of the ghetto set up by the Nazis. He was ordered to move the children. During the move a sack of potatoes Korczak had obtained with great effort was stolen by the German guards. He went directly to the office of the governor of Warsaw, complaining that those potatoes were for "his children." He was arrested and forced to spend four months in jail. After his release, although his non-Jewish friends begged him to leave the ghetto—and the country—he returned to the children.

On Wednesday morning, September 5, 1942, at the age of 64, Januscz Korczak led "his children" from the Jewish orphanage to the Umschlagplatz. Passersby could not believe their eyes. They saw a procession of singing children dressed in their "best" Sabbath clothes, led by a stately old man carrying a sick child.

The scene was described in these words:

> Today Korczak's orphanage was "evacuated". . . . Korczak refused to stay behind. He would not abandon "his" children. He went with them. And so, a long line formed in front of the orphanage . . . a long procession, children small, rather precocious, emaciated, weak, shriveled, and shrunk . . . no one is crying. Their eyes are turned toward the doctor. He is going with them, so what do they have to be afraid of? They are not alone, they are not abandoned. . . .

Although he knew the truth, he told the children that they were going to sunshine and green fields. At the railroad station, one of the guards watched as the children were told to take off their yellow stars and pile them together. "It was like a field of buttercups," said the guard, sadly. From the railroad station, the children went to Treblinka and to death in the gas chambers.

Father of Orphans

Things to think about

1 Resistance comes in many forms. In the Warsaw Ghetto, resistance meant fighting the battalion of German armed forces. But the word *resistance* has a special meaning when we recall a man like Januscz Korczak. In what ways do you think Korczak resisted the Nazi terror?

2 Was Korczak right to lie to the children about the future?

3 The Jewish religion has always considered the plight of the orphan a special case. Special laws are indicated in the Bible to provide for the widow and the orphan. What was there about the way in which Korczak treated the orphans which made them love him? Do you think that Januscz Korczak was a good leader of children?

eleven

The Doctor Warriors

~~~~~~

DOCTORS are generally considered to be unusual people. Part of the 2,000-year-old Hippocratic Oath taken by medical students receiving their degree, reads: "I swear I will prescribe for the good of my patients according to my ability and judgment and never do harm to anyone. To please no one will I prescribe a deadly drug nor give advice which may cause death. . . ."

The life work of most doctors is to try to heal their patients and ease pain. But during the Holocaust many German doctors did just the opposite. In concentration camps they performed all kinds of cruel medical experiments. Many of the unfortunate people who were

The Doctor Warriors

"operated" on were Jewish. Instead of using their knowledge to heal, the Nazi doctors destroyed people.

The Jewish doctors in the ghettos, in the camps, and in the forests played an important part in trying to preserve life. The ghettos were overcrowded, had no running water, sanitary facilities, or electricity. Can you imagine how hospitals could function under such conditions?

The Doctor Warriors

In the Warsaw Ghetto, in 1942, Dr. Israel Milejkowski said to his fellow physicians: "My friends, your fate is the fate of the community. Slavery, starvation, expulsion, hang over all our heads. But in continuing your work you will give one answer to the Nazi murderers . . . and remember, not all of us shall perish."

In the Vilna Ghetto doctors worked together to set up hospitals, first-aid stations, rooms for child and baby care, and dispensaries. Innoculations were given against the diseases that affect people when they are forced to live together in overcrowded, unhealthy conditions. A system of disinfecting or sterilizing rooms began. Doctors organized public baths and laundries. Their task seemed hopeless, but they kept trying.

Jewish doctors in France organized a secret network for rescuing children, but many of these brave doctors were caught and murdered. In the death camps, Jewish doctors tried to hide their profession from the Nazis because they knew the Nazis would force them to do terrible and illegal acts. They preferred to dig ditches and to work in factories and even to starve, rather than to admit they were doctors. Some, however, who were well-known were forced to serve as doctors. Many of these men and women risked their lives in order to obtain medicine for sick prisoners. Others sat up all night, trying to prepare substitute remedies from herbs to ease the suffering of the sick people in the camps.

Doctors fled to the forest to fight the Nazis and

From a study by Dr. Mordecai Lenski. Doctors during the
Holocaust worked under terrible conditions. The Nazis
supplied them with very little medicine and the rapid spread
of disease supplied them with very little hope. Yet they
carried on, against all odds, resisting the Nazis with their
knowledge and skills alone.

*From a study of disease among Jews in the Warsaw
Ghetto, it appears that the Nazi authorities were to
blame for the unchecked spread of diseases: typhus,
tuberculosis, dysentery, and starvation. The Nazis
reaped a rich harvest of death among the Jews of
Warsaw through the spread of diseases caused by
conditions of overcrowding and lack of food in the
Ghetto. During three years from September 1939 to
September 1942, 80,000 persons died of disease and
of these 18,000 died of starvation.*

joined other men and women hidden there. Some helped
as physicians and some fought. One of the bravest
and best known of these fighter-physicians was Dr.
Yehezkiel Atlas. Dr. Atlas was born in Poland in 1910
and received a fine Jewish education and a good general
education. But he was not permitted to study medicine
in Poland unless he converted to Christianity. This he
refused to do, so he left Poland and went to Italy to
study. There he received his degree in 1939 and returned
to Poland.

92

The Doctor Warriors

In 1942 the ghetto in which he lived was destroyed by the Nazis. All the Jews of the town, including his mother, father, and sister were taken to the marketplace, shot, and their bodies dumped into a mass grave.

Because the Germans needed doctors, they saved Atlas, sending him to a Polish village to become the physician there. He tended the peasants with care and kindness. From them he learned that some Russian soldiers and Jews were hidden in the nearby forests. Dr. Atlas was able to contact a small band of these refugees. He brought them food, took care of their wounds, and even obtained ammunition for them.

When the thin, young, handsome doctor realized he could accomplish nothing more in the village, he joined the group in the forest. He became a symbol of heroism to these ragged fighters, known as partisans. He organized them into several separate units. When the call "Dr. Atlas has come" was heard there was great excitement, and when he appeared wearing his revolver in his belt, dressed in a peasant shirt and high Russian boots, the partisans would shout for joy.

The first objective of Dr. Atlas was to attack the Germans in the town of Dereczyn, where the Nazis had recently murdered hundreds of Jews. Dr. Atlas fought at the head of his platoon, and all the Jewish forest fighters showed great bravery. They drove the Germans out of the town, took possession of it, and on the mass grave of the recently murdered Jews, shot 44 German Nazis.

Atlas led his followers on many dangerous raids,

securing food and ammunition, dynamiting bridges and trains. Because they showed so much courage, the group soon began to pose a nasty threat to the Nazis. The Germans decided to launch a fierce counter attack against the partisans. They brought thousands of heavily armed German troops to fight the small remnant of ill-clothed, ill-fed, poorly armed men in the forest. In the battle, Dr. Atlas was mortally wounded. His last words were: "Pay no attention to me. Go on fighting!"

The Partisans wept for their fallen leader, but heeding his words they continued fighting until the end of the war.

Things to think about

1 Dr. Atlas faced a moral dilemma. He was a trained doctor, who had pledged himself to save the lives of others. Yet he became a killer, intent on destroying the Nazi troops. Do you think that a doctor should be a peaceful individual no matter what; or do you think that Dr. Atlas was right in becoming a partisan?

2 Dr. Atlas might have argued that by killing the Nazi soldiers, he was doing his part to save lives. Just as a doctor sometimes cuts off a patient's arm or leg to save the patient, the doctor might argue that to save the human race it was necessary to destroy the Nazi "disease." What is true about this argument? What is false?

The Doctor Warriors

3 All through the war, in whatever situations and places they found themselves, Jewish doctors and nurses continued to try to help the sick and the dying. Do you think that it made any difference that these doctors and nurses were Jewish? Did it make any difference that their patients were Jewish? How did the behavior of the Jewish doctors differ from that of the Nazi doctors mentioned in the chapter?

twelve

Women Fighters

MEN, women, and children performed many individual and collective acts of resistance during the Nazi
occupation of Europe. Each in their own way played a
heroic part. But the heroism of the women was especially
outstanding. Young girls and women fought with guns
and homemade bombs; they sloshed through the filth of
the sewers guiding people to the "other side of the wall."
They behaved heroically in ghettos, camps, and forests;
and when there was no other way, they resisted pas-
sively. One Nazi grudgingly reported how courageous
an old white-haired woman behaved as she stood beside
a death pit, holding a year old baby in her arms, singing
him a song, and tickling him as he gurgled with pleasure.

Women Fighters

She could have run around, screaming, and tearing her hair, making the child's last moments a horrible nightmare, but she chose to end her life and his with dignity, no matter how much pain she felt in her heart.

Women as well as men were instrumental in making decisions about underground resistance. In the Bialystok Ghetto, the records of a meeting show the names Sara, Fanya, Yocheved, Zippora, and Ethel—girls whose last names we shall probably never know. All played a part in making the decision that the Bialystok Ghetto would resist. When the Germans came, the ghetto fighters, men and women, stood their ground bravely.

Nuta Teitelboim, a young Jewish woman from Warsaw, blonde and blue-eyed, was "wanted" by the Gestapo. She was one of the most fearless fighters in the ghetto and organized a woman's detachment in the ghetto. Later she fought heroically in the uprising. Known as "Little Wanda with the Braids," she blew up cafés where German soldiers were drinking, derailed trains, and carried out daring acts of sabotage against the Nazis even in broad daylight.

Dr. Anna Broide Heller gave medical attention to homeless children of the ghetto; food and baths were given to them by other women. Some of them remade their tattered rags so that the children would have clothes just a little longer.

Women Fighters

A long list of women who worked on or distributed underground newspapers include Sonia Madesker, Bela Chazan, Tosia Altman, Feigele Milstein, Rivka Karpinkes, Rushka Zilber. And there was Frumka Plotnicki, who brought money from Warsaw to Vilna, along with news about the Treblinka death camp. Lisa Magun was active in the Vilna underground and knew many of the underground's secrets. She was caught and tortured, but smuggled a message out of prison that the United Partisan Organization should not worry. She would not betray them. She was so beloved, they later used "Lisa calls," as their password. Vitka Kempner was sent out on reconnaissance missions and blew up German transports, killing as many as 200 soldiers at one time.

Women Fighters

From a report by General Stroop, the German general in charge of murdering the Jews of the Warsaw Ghetto, we read:

> During the armed resistance, the women belonging to the battle groups were equipped the same as the men. Not infrequently, these women fired pistols with both hands. It happened time and again that these women had pistols or hand grenades (Polish "Pineapples") concealed in their underclothes—up to the last moment—to use against the men of the SS.

Vladka, a teen-age girl, was able to live outside the ghetto walls because of her non-Jewish appearance. She was given the responsibility of smuggling dynamite into the ghetto, which she hid in greasy packages made to look like butter packets. Vladka was one of the few lucky ones who was not caught.

Zofia Yamaika became an underground leader, escaped to the forest, was caught and put on a train to Treblinka, jumped from the train, pretended she was dead, and finally returned to Warsaw. In Warsaw she worked on an underground paper, was captured again, and put into a German prison. She was finally allowed to go free, and went once more into the forest. Her group was attacked by 300 Germans, and she and two Poles covered the retreat of the Polish partisan unit. Zofia manned the machinegun, and although the three were killed, even Germans praised her bravery.

Malka Zdrojewicz's memories were not the exception: women and men resisted the Nazis at every turn. It was not unusual for the Germans to line Jews up before a firing squad, kill some, and lead the rest off to the camps.

In the brush factory there was an organized group of boys and girls. There was an arms cache under my bed as well. Some time later I gave up my work at the brush factory and so did the others. We went to a neutral place in the Ghetto area and climbed down into the underground sewers. Through them, we girls used to carry arms into the Ghetto; and we hid them in our boots. During the Ghetto uprising, we hurled Molotov cocktails at the Germans.

The Germans beat us up badly and lined us up to be executed by a firing squad. Suddenly, I felt a heavy blow on my head and at the same instant I heard shots. Blumka fell dead on the spot. Rachela and I, together with the others, were driven to the Umschlagplatz. They later took us to Maidanek (a concentration camp).

Jewish women who were imprisoned in labor and death camps also practiced a form of resistance. Many of them observed the holidays the best way they could, lighting Sabbath candles made from a scooped-out potato filled with margarine and a rag wick. *Yahrzeit* candles to commemorate the dead were made the same

the female oversee

way. Many of the women gave their lives for *kashruth* and chose hunger and suffering rather than eat forbidden food. Some refused to work on the Sabbath, suffering blows and torments because they would not do what they considered a sin.

In one camp, women had to prepare an area for the army on Rosh Hashanah. While they dug trenches they prayed, stationing a guard at the front of each trench to warn them if the labor supervisor should come. On Passover, some women ate nothing but a basket of raw

carrots or cooked mashed potatoes and one block even managed to hold a seder which about 300 women attended, singing songs from the *Haggadah* around an empty table.

Hundreds of women doctors appear on lists of Polish Jews who were murdered, including Maria Reiter, a pediatrician; Netty Bahr, an internist; Fryderyka Ameisen-Distler, a dermatologist; Sara Alterman, a gynecologist; and Rachela Wajsberg, a general practitioner.

Women Fighters

Zivia Lubetkin, one of the few survivors of the Warsaw Ghetto uprising, tells of beginning of the revolt:

> The young men and women who had been waiting for this moment for months, the moment when they would shoot back at the Germans, were overjoyed. I was standing in an attic when I saw thousands of Germans armed with machine-guns surrounding the ghetto. And we, some twenty young men and women had a revolver, a grenade, and some home-made bombs that had to be lit with matches. It must have been a strange sight to see us happily standing up against the heavily armed enemy—happy because we knew their end would come. . . .

Hanka was another girl fighter. She was sent from Lemberg, not yet under Nazi control, to the Warsaw Ghetto to warn them of what was coming. She had to swim through an icy lake in order to smuggle herself across the border. When she stepped into the freezing water, she lost her nerve and returned to Lemberg. Two days later she tried again, steeled her nerve and swam the icy water. Then she made her way to Warsaw, to warn the Jews there.

Reyne, a typically Polish-looking lass, was very useful in smuggling arms. The SS man who tried to flirt with her never dreamed she was Jewish, carrying a pistol in her basket of vegetables. Meta was another Aryan-looking girl who secured a job as a typist in Gestapo headquarters in Paris. There she was able to

obtain valuable information and the document forms
needed by Jews who had to pose as non-Jews.

Lia was a French beauty and a faithful rescue
worker in Vichy France. She carried funds, documents,
or weapons to those who were hidden. She was an excellent bicyclist and when she carried something particularly dangerous, she would ride swiftly. If she had
to pass a policeman, she would let go of the handlebars
and skim by, smiling sweetly at him. They never suspected she was a Jewish resistance worker.

Chaika Grossman, another of the heroines of the
Bialystok uprising, writes: ". . . the true heroes of a
nation are small people, almost unknown. . . . I recall
the memory of the daughters of Israel who fell heroically
on the battlefield—Lonka, Tosia, Frumka, and many
others. . . ."

Rushka was one of the forest fighters who often
dynamited railroad tracks. One winter day she fell into
a pond. When her clothes froze on her, her companions
suggested she return to camp. But though she was completely covered with ice, she continued with the rest.

One girl journeyed from the woods into Vilna
seventeen times to find groups of Jews who might still
be hiding in the ruins of the ghetto and so that they
could be led to the forest.

Women Fighters

Mala Zimetbaum and Rosa Robota were two young ladies imprisoned in Auschwitz, one of the worst death camps. Both were involved in underground activities there. Both were caught, tortured, and murdered by their Nazi captors, but neither would give any information.

These were but a few of the Jewish heroines. Some were young girls—many of them in their teens—some were middle-aged women, and some were old, but they felt they had a mission and they accomplished it, quietly and bravely.

Things to think about

1 Men and women fighters in the resistance stood side by side on the battlefield. Decisions of whether or not to fight the Germans were made jointly. In all this time, the question of whether women had equal rights or not did not arise. Why?

2 Some jobs were better done by a woman than by a man. From the chapter, can you choose those women who served in tasks which a man would find extremely difficult, if not impossible?

3 The kind of resistance practiced by the women imprisoned in labor and death camps had to do with ritual laws such as lighting Sabbath candles, keeping *kashrut*

(the dietary laws), and observing the holidays. Judaism teaches us that such laws may be broken if it means saving one's life. Yet these women, who were living in constant fear of death, refused to break the laws. Imagine interviewing one of these women. What reasons would she give for keeping the laws even when Judaism permits her to break them?

thirteen

The Underground Press

‸‸

HAVE you ever really thought about your newspaper? It is delivered each morning to the house. You read it, throw it away, or recycle it. Perhaps we worry about the news, but have you ever wondered how a paper is published? Type, presses, typesetting equipment, copy paper, dummy sheets, paper cutters, typewriters, ink and paper, are just a few of the things needed. Someone has to get the news, write copy, edit and correct it, set the type, and run the presses. Needed, above all, is freedom to move about, freedom to receive the latest news, space to set up machinery, freedom to run the presses day or night, and freedom to distribute the finished newspapers.

When we read the following sentence, we feel it

109

must have been written at a time when there was a great deal of freedom: "Publications have multiplied like mushrooms after the rain." We may guess it was written when competition among newspapermen was strong, and when many people purchased many different papers. But it is not so. The sentence was written by Emanuel Ringelblum, one of the historians of the Warsaw Ghetto during the Nazi occupation, between 1939 and 1944, the year in which he was killed.

How could it be that during the Nazi occupation "publications multiplied like mushrooms after the rain"? Jews were being forced into ghettos, murdered in the streets, transported to death camps. There was little food, no warm clothing, no fuel. Terror was all about—how could the Jews concentrate on newspapers?

In Vilna, a city in Poland, during the first weeks of the Nazi occupation, there were no newspapers. Then, a German-Polish paper appeared, published by the Polish, full of anti-Semitic articles. It angered the Jews of Vilna. They wanted to publish their own paper, but it was not allowed. They were forced into a ghetto in 1941 where, in January 1942, a United Partisan Organization was established. Isaac Kowalski, a printer and writer, was one of those in the ghetto. He asked the UPO to give him permission to organize a secret press. The Organization agreed, but did not know where to get all the necessary equipment and supplies. Isaac managed to get a job in a German printing shop, the Aushra press. At lunchtime, when one of the shop exits was open, Isaac would go to the exit with type in his pockets and lunch box, turn the type over to a friend who always gave him another lunch box—exactly like the first. Isaac then would go back into the plant and innocently eat his lunch.

Three months later, after many narrow escapes, enough type was assembled to start a paper. Isaac's "outside" man was a Pole by the name of Jan Pzewalski. Now they had type, but where to get a press? Isaac found a small, worn-out handpress in the typesetting room. Within a few days, the press was taken apart and smuggled out of the printshop in pieces. After a day's work at the German press, Isaac stayed up all night preparing the illegal newspaper with Jan and Mrs. Pzewalski. The first edition of the paper, *The Fatherland Front*, made a strong impression on those who read it. The Gestapo tried desperately to find where the paper was being printed, and by whom. When the ghetto was destroyed, Isaac Kowalski, together with other Jewish fighters, went to the forest. He brought the press with him, and when the war was over, returned to Vilna once again, bringing the underground press equipment with him.

Vilna was not the only city where there was an underground press. Bernard Goldstein writes in his Warsaw Ghetto memoirs about the illegal press in that city:

> Every Jewish printing plant, including the smallest, had been taken away by the Germans. Our underground press,

From the book by Isaac Kowalski, *A Secret Press in Nazi Europe*. To print the truth always takes courage, but during the Holocaust, it could lead to torture and death.

At one of the meetings of the U.P.O. [United Partisan Organization], I submitted my project to organize a secret press that would print a newspaper for the non-Jewish population . . . after several meetings, I was allowed to go ahead.

The main question was: Where to get type, printing presses, etc. One way was to smuggle into a German printshop and take out what was needed. How could this be done? I decided to call on an old friend, a Lithuanian who headed the German government press, Aushra, to let me work in the plant.

The paper was published in Polish and we appeared as Polish patriots and told what the Germans were doing to the Polish people, including what was being done to murder Jews. We suggested that it was the Polish patriotic duty to help save Jews and give them protection. Whoever betrayed the Jews to the Gestapo was committing a national betrayal . . . Our announcements were published over the signature of the Association of Polish Patriots.

Our paper had an influence among the Polish people who felt this friendly attitude to the Jews was the official policy of the Polish underground. They never dreamed the paper came to light because of the initiative of a Jew and that it was published almost entirely by Jews.

therefore, consisted of two mimeograph machines, which had been removed from certain offices and hidden. After the small supply of ink, paper and stencils had been used, we acquired new supplies, but with great difficulty. We worked in constant fear that if copies of our paper fell into the hands of the Germans, they would be able to track us down through discovering our sources for paper or ink.

For safety, the editorial work and the actual printing were separated. One person was the contact between the two. Distribution was also separate from printing. If any distributor fell into Nazi hands, he could not, even if he was tortured, endanger the plant.

Morizi Orzech, one of the heroes of the Warsaw Ghetto, returned to Warsaw from a German prison in April 1940. He insisted that we issue a Polish paper to keep the Poles informed of what Jews were thinking, doing and living through. He was a talented writer and became the principal editor for Jewish and Polish papers and bulletins. He urged us to fight against the Germans for a better world.

One of the Jews in the Warsaw Ghetto was sent out to learn what was really happening to Jews after being deported, although it was already suspected that they were being sent to their death. Zalman Freydrich was chosen for this errand. In a town near the village of Treblinka, he learned the truth about the Treblinka camp, the freight and cattle cars packed with Jews, the "showers" that were really gas chambers. Freydrich returned to Warsaw with this information, and based on this, a special edition of *Storm*, one of the underground papers, was issued with a description of what was happening and a warning: "Do not be deceived. . . . You are being taken to death and extermination. . . . Do not give yourselves voluntarily into the hands of your executioners!"

In Warsaw, there were three main Jewish political groups. The underground press played an important part in each. The function of the press was to strengthen Jewish resistance and stamina in the face of the terrible persecution. The press also tried to give some hope, that in spite of persecution, they could hold out and would yet live to see their enemies overcome. *The Young Guard* encouraged the youth to continue the fight, but not to neglect education. Another youth publication, *Flames*, and *El Al* (Upwards) also urged continuation of study and resistance. *El Al* said: "We have not gone and shall not go willingly to slaughter. . . . despite the ghetto, despite our misery, we shall raise our heads high and look ahead. . . . In spite of everything our motto remains: Scouts—upwards!"

Against the Stream was a paper for elderly people, issued monthly in Hebrew, Yiddish, and Polish. *The Dawn, Before Spring, The Spark*, and *Ferment* were others. In addition to these, a three-page daily bulletin was issued with news from various fronts. The news came from a radio hidden in the lodgings of Mordechai Anilewitz. *Dror* (Liberty) was an important publication in Yiddish and Polish, and *Bulletin, Our Way, Stamina, The Call of the Youth, Torches*, and *Our Mottos*, were a few of the youth publications. *Shaviv* (Spark), the illegal

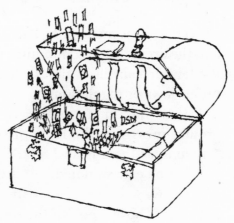

monthly of one of the youth organizations, was published in Hebrew and *Our Hope* in Yiddish.

Some of these papers were smuggled even into the
concentration camps. Many of the "smugglers" were
girls, who carried illegal publications to far-off places in
spite of the risk involved. Editors, printers, and distribu-
tors of these illegal papers were mainly leaders and
spokesmen of the underground who practiced what they
preached.

Between 300 and 500 copies of the various papers
were published; and about twenty persons read each
copy, passing it from one to another. Great care was
taken. Still many people connected with the newspapers
were arrested and murdered.

The papers told of life in the camps; the reactions
of the Jewish masses; reports of sabotage, resistance, and
struggle; economic conditions; accounts of bravery;
sometimes poetry; and calls for revenge. The masses
were alerted to the true nature of the Jewish police, some

115

The Underground Press

of whom in normal times had been thieves, smugglers, and the dregs of the community. They also wrote against the Jewish councils at times when the councils instituted unfair laws or regulations against the Jews in the ghetto.

One important subject discussed in the underground press was the hope of settling in *Eretz Yisrael*. "As long as there is an Eretz Yisrael, the Jewish people will not be exterminated," said *Our Path*, in May 1942.

So we see that the written word is of great importance. Those who put the undeground press together in each ghetto took great risks. Papers were written and published at the cost of many lives. The people who worked on the press were the quiet heroes. They did not carry guns, but used their pens as weapons against the Nazi warlords.

Things to think about

1 Stealing a press one piece at a time, a set of type a few pieces at a time, and paper and ink were only the first problems faced by the Jews who wished to publish underground newspapers. In addition, they had to gather news. From what you have read in this book and what you already know, what kind of news did the Jews in the ghettos need to read? How was the news gathered and by whom?

The Underground Press

2 The Gestapo, the Nazi secret police, spent much time and effort in trying to track down the hiding places of presses printing underground newspapers. They worked tirelessly to find the editors and the writers; even to stop Jews from smuggling the papers in and out of the Ghetto. Why do you think the Gestapo was so afraid of the little underground newspapers? What makes a newspaper dangerous?

3 In our country the freedom of the press is guaranteed by law. In the light of what you know about the Holocaust, do you agree with our First Amendment to the Constitution? Do you feel that the freedom of the press is important? Is it better to have a free press or an underground press? To which kind of press do people pay more attention? Which kind is better at reporting the truth?

fourteen

A "Model" Concentration Camp

THERESIENSTADT

ONE of the things that Adolf Hitler did to achieve his "final solution" to rid Europe of its Jews, was to establish concentration camps. "Concentration" means bringing together; and in these camps he brought together Jews from all over Europe—rich and poor, sick and well, young and old.

In some of the camps gas chambers were constructed. The German guards would tell the Jewish prisoners they were going to have a shower. They would make the Jews take off all their clothing, shove them into the huge chambers, and lock the doors. Then they turned on the gas and murdered hundreds of people—all at once. Babies, children, old men and women—everyone was

119

gassed. There was no place to bury all these people, so the bodies were burned. In some camps the Germans built crematoriums—ovens where they could burn hundreds of bodies at one time. Auschwitz, Sobibor, Treblinka, Maidanek were the names of four particularly terrible concentration camps.

Night and day, smoke came from the camps with the horrible odor of burning bodies. Yet the people who lived near the camps paid no attention. They lived in neat little white houses, with neat little lawns and blossoming flowers and pretended they could not see, hear, or smell what was happening. They tried not to notice the hundreds of cattle trains filled with thousands

of starved, tortured, and smothering people that passed through their towns. They did not notice—or did they?

Another concentration camp was Theresienstadt. The village of Terezin or Theresienstadt in Czechoslovakia was chosen by the Nazis as the spot for a "special" concentration camp. Because Terezin was a fortress town enclosed by a wall, they felt it would be simple to guard. It even had its own built-in isolated stone building that could be used as a prison, and its own nearby railway station from which transports of people could be sent to the gas chambers of Auschwitz.

Rumors were spread by the Nazis that it would be an old folk's home, a sort of resort for privileged Jews. The Nazi propaganda was good. Some Jews even paid to be sent to Theresienstadt because they believed the Nazi lies.

Hitler decided that Terezin would become the model camp, the camp he would show to the Red Cross. The surroundings were beautiful. It was built on green meadows and nearby were fruit trees, tall poplars, and rolling hills which almost looked blue in the distance. Here the Germans took the Red Cross on a tour and said, "See, our prisoners do not have it so bad. Even the food is good, taste it for yourself." The Red Cross, of course, did not know that the food they ate was not the food served to prisoners. The menu of the Jews in Terezin was always the same; bread and unsweetened, black, fake coffee for breakfast; watery soup for lunch; soup and bread for dinner. In fact a painting called

A "Model" Concentration Camp

"Hunger" by one of the artists, which showed the Jews looking for food in garbage cans, was cause for all the artists of Terezin to be tortured and beaten and finally murdered. But the Red Cross did not see this. The Nazis showed them how clean Terezin was. They did not show them the filthy barracks with the sick, dying, and dead prisoners. The Nazis cleverly painted the fronts of the buildings and showed the Red Cross a store where prisoners could buy such things as fresh bread and vegetables. It was the first and last time that these foods were in Terezin. It was all phony. The Red Cross did not know that Terezin was the stopping-off place for the Jews who were going to be slaughtered. They did not know that an entire hospital ward of tuberculosis patients had been sent to the gas chambers, so they would not be seen during the Red Cross visit in 1944. The visitors were not shown the storehouses of jewels and goods stolen from Jews who came to Terezin. And, of course, they were not taken to death camps like Auschwitz, Treblinka, and Maidanek where there were gas chambers and crematoriums.

Many artists were shipped to Terezin. For a time they were allowed to work as draftsmen and in similar jobs. But when they began sketching what they saw around them, they were beaten and tortured. Most of them were imprisoned and then sent on to be murdered at Auschwitz. However the pictures that these artists produced survived and tell us better than words how horrible life was in Terezin. The artists fought against

A memory of one of the members of the "Helping Hand."
The "model" concentration camp was made up mostly of the
very young and the very old. Helping one another was a way
of life for those imprisoned in Theresienstadt. The "Helping
Hand" was a kind of very serious scouting for the young
people, as this document shows.

*We gave a lot of thought to how we could not only
be of assistance to the old people, but also bring
them some joy. We looked through the card index
and found out the birthdays of the old people who
were alone and on these days the scouts would bring
them presents they had made or received themselves
—a few flowers, a plaited loaf of bread, or cake they
had saved from their rations; they sang songs for
them and—in short—arranged a small party. The
old people were extremely happy and thankful that
someone had paid attention to them. . . .*

*But we were not satisfied with doing just this. We
looked for ways of doing more. We set up dramatic
troupes, which on special occasions would put on
shows in the grounds of the old and handicapped
peoples' houses. . . . Because it was forbidden to
pick flowers from the garden, the children would
bring them, hidden under their clothes, to the old
people. The old people, who were unable to believe
that kindness still existed in the world, wept and
when we had to leave them we would hear calls from
the beds packed close to each other, "Come back
again soon."*

A "Model" Concentration Camp

the Nazis—not with guns and fists, but rather, like the writers in the underground press, with pen and ink.

The greatest tragedy of Terezin surrounded the children. Thousands of children were brought there. They had been exposed to inhuman experiences in the towns from which they came. They had been expelled from school because they were Jewish; they had the Star of David sewn on their garments. They were not allowed to play in gardens or streets, only in cemeteries. Can you imagine playing in a cemetery? Many had seen their parents murdered and had been beaten themselves.

A few children in this camp lived with their parents, but most were orphans and were housed together in huge barracks, 20 to 30 children in a room. The Jewish officials of Theresienstadt arranged this.

A school was immediately organized, classes being held in the same room where the children slept and ate. There were few books, and teachers were constantly changed, as some were put to death. But most of the children received some education.

The older children, from the age of fourteen, had to work, sometimes in the fields, building roads, digging ditches, or cleaning barracks. They worked long hours at back-breaking work. But the younger ones secretly studied and drew pictures—on all kinds of scraps of paper.

The children saw bread being carried in funeral carts, and humans harnessed to pull them; people murdered; people dying from starvation and illness.

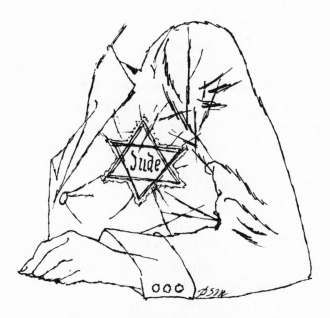

They drew these things into their pictures and wrote about them in their poetry. Sometimes they remembered pleasant things from the time before Hitler, and tried to look outside of the camp to the green meadows and hills.

Occasionally the children were allowed to play in the barracks. Sometimes they were permitted a breath of fresh air. But they all seemed to know, even better than their parents, that they had been selected for death, sooner or later. This, too, showed in their drawings and in their poetry.

Sometimes children stayed at Terezin three months, sometimes half a year, and once in a while a little longer, if they were lucky. More than 15,000 children stopped off at Terezin for a short time. Of this number only about 150 lived.

All of this seems like something impossible to believe, like a cruel fairy tale about evil witches. Although the ashes of these children have long since become dust in the air around Auschwitz, some of their drawings and poems still exist. Many are in a beautiful book called *I Never Saw Another Butterfly*. Here are two of them:

THE BUTTERFLY
>   The last, the very last,
>   So richly, brightly, dazzingly yellow.
>   Perhaps if the sun's tears would sing.
>   against a white stone . . .
>   Such, such a yellow
>   Is carried lightly 'way up high.
>   It went away I'm sure because it wished to
>   kiss the world goodbye.
>   For seven weeks I've lived in here.
>   Penned up inside this ghetto
>   But I have found my people here.
>   The dandelions call to me
>   And the white chestnut candles in the court.
>   Only I never saw another butterfly.

>   That butterfly was the last one.
>   Butterflies don't live in here,
>   in the ghetto.

A "Model" Concentration Camp

Pavel Friedman, the author of this poem, was sent to Terezin on April 26, 1942. He died in Auschwitz, on September 29, 1944.

FEAR

    Today the ghetto knows a different fear
    Close in its grip, death wields an icy scythe.
    An evil sickness spreads a terror in its wake,
    The victims of its shadow weep and writhe.

    Today a father's heartbeat tells his fright
    And mothers bend their heads into their hands.
    Now children choke and die with typhus here,
    A bitter tax is taken from their banks.

    My heart still beats inside my breast
    While friends depart for other worlds.
    Perhaps it's better—who can say?
    Than watching this, to die today?

    No, no my God, we want to live!
    Not watch our numbers melt away.
    We want to have a better world,
    We want to work—we must not die!

Eva Pickova wrote this poem. She was born May 15, 1929, sent to Terezin April 16, 1942, and murdered in

A "Model" Concentration Camp

Auschwitz in 1943. She was about twelve years old when she wrote her poem.

These are just two of the poems of children who were taken from their parents, sent to Terezin, and then to Auschwitz to be murdered. These children drew and wrote poetry just like you. They liked pretty things and springtime; they had the same hopes and dreams as you. They played games, sang songs, and danced dances. Maybe, among these lovely children who were put to death—only because they were Jewish—were those who would have conquered disease, written music or poetry, or brought the world closer to peace. Because they died, we are all poorer.

Things to think about

1 Even in the concentration camps, the Jews still continued to struggle for "normal" life. Artists continued to sketch and draw and improve their art. Schools were organized for the children. Even Judaism was taught. What qualities or feelings do we all have that make us strong when times are hard? What makes us struggle to be "normal"?

2 How do you feel when you read the poem, "The Butterfly"? What is there about a butterfly which makes it seem so precious? Is it really a butterfly that Pavel is writing about in the poem?

A "Model" Concentration Camp

3 If Hitler truly believed that he was doing the right thing in killing the Jews, why would he set up a "model" concentration camp? If Hitler truly believed the world "did not care" what happened to the Jews, why did he not show the Red Cross the true concentration camps? And why, when the Germans began to lose the war, did they try to cover up the concentration camp murders by hurriedly digging mass graves? Could they truly have believed that murdering human beings was all right as long as they were Jews?

fifteen

Passover in a Concentration Camp*

~~~~~~

IN America, we open our Passover Haggadah and begin, "Lo, this is the bread of affliction. . . ." We eat matzoth-ball soup, haroset, matzoth, and all the other wonderful foods to celebrate our Festival of Freedom. We may recall the hard tasks that the Jews were forced to perform in the land of Egypt at the time of Moses, but Jews in other times had hard taskmasters too. During the Holocaust, Jews were forced to perform hard labor, get along with almost no food or sleep, and live in filthy crowded conditions. The Nazis thought nothing of beating, torturing, and murdering Jews. Nazi guards

* Excerpted from a book by S. B. Unsdorfer, *The Yellow Star*, published by Thomas Yoseloff (with the publisher's permission).

131

would take a baby out f its mother's arms, smash the baby's head against a wall—and then go home to play with his own children.

Out of this nightmare came a Haggadah and matzoth. This story is told in the words of one who believed in the sun even when it was not shining, and in God—even when He was silent.

"Knowledge of the approach of Purim and Passover gave us some hope and courage. I approached Schiff, one of the prisoners who worked in the office, and asked him to 'organize' some paper from the office so that I would be able to write a Haggadah for Passover. Schiff gave me some discarded, odd pieces of paper, most of which had drawings of fighter aircraft on the back.

"Each day when I returned to my bunk from a night of work, I spent an hour on my Haggadah. Writing from memory the story of the Exodus of the Jews from Egypt was a worthwhile task. It helped keep my mind off our terrible tragedy and worries about the future. Even during working hours I tried to direct my attention to passages of the Haggadah that required writing. Happy memories were brought back to my mind, of my childhood, and of seder nights at home, when I sat at our table listening excitedly and attentively to Father's recital of the Haggadah which he always did so beautifully and inspiringly.

"Indeed, this work served as a source of great courage and hope for me. It was a reminder that our people have gone through many difficult and tragic experiences in our long history, and have been freed each time, by the will of God, from bondage and slavery. How wise, I thought, of our great rabbis of the past to command that the stories of Passover and Purim be repeated each year, and thus remain alive among the Jewish people. Where would we have gained the courage and strength to survive all our sufferings, were it not for our great and historic past?

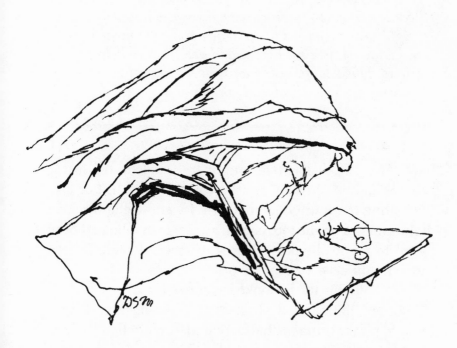

From *Notes from the Warsaw Ghetto* by Emanuel Ringelblum. The Jews in the Ghetto were disturbed by the lack of matzoth for Passover. They did not realize how much worse it would be when they would reach the concentration camps. Yet, wherever Jews were when the holiday of Passover came, they yearned for matzoth, the symbol of freedom.

April 17, 1941. There were fearful scenes in the office of the refugee organization on the eve of the Passover holiday. A crowd of 7–8,000 refugees gathered, waiting for matzoth and other packages. People applied to receive free packages whose neighbors considered them to be persons of means, and who a short time before had been able to help others. The disappointment of those who could not receive packages is indescribable.

"Yes, I felt Passover ought to be celebrated in the camp, and not just by reciting the Haggadah, but also by eating the traditional matzoth. I went to the foreman who worked on the tool bench, a quiet man who had been kind to me in the past. 'Herr Overseer,' I said, 'I want to ask you a very great favor.'

" 'What is it?' he looked surprised.

" 'Nothing dreadful,' I assured him hastily. 'I want you to please bring me half a pound of plain flour, which I need badly. I beg you.'

134

Passover in a Concentration Camp

" 'Flour? What the devil for? Birthday cake?' he smiled sarcastically.

" 'For a purely religious purpose,' I explained. 'No one will ever know it came from you. There is no one else I can turn to.'

"He looked cautious. 'Things are hard nowadays, the guards are strict in their inspections, and the atmosphere is tense. I can't promise.'

"What he said was true. Besides the raw material and transportation difficulties, ever-increasing air-raid alarms reduced our working time to a few hours per shift. We knew that within a matter of weeks, or possibly days, great changes would take place. The factory would have to close, and we would either be liberated or transported elsewhere to be killed. At the back of our minds we hoped we would still be at Nieder-Orschel when the first American tank bulldozed its way into the village.

"On Saturday morning, just before Passover, the civilian employees of the camp collected their personal belongings, since they were leaving camp because of lack of work. In the rush, the friendly overseer came to me as I did the final cleaning of my machine.

"He pushed a small bag of flour into my pocket and whispered: 'We shan't be coming here any more. I brought you the flour and good luck.'

"I was pleased. 'If we are to get the matzoth made,' I said to my friend, Benzi, who was our leader, 'it must be done this evening immediately after the end of the Sabbath, otherwise we shall have no fire for baking.'

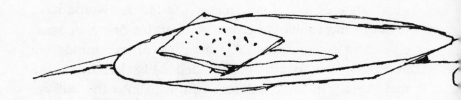

"So at the end of the Sabbath, Grunwald, Fischof, and I sneaked out of the barrack and into the smithy's workshop. Fischof worked desperately at the bellows to liven the dying embers. Grunwald worked hastily on the dough, while I cleaned up a dirty tin plate to serve as a platter.

"Within half an hour, three tiny round matzoth were taking shape and color, accompanied by our happy murmur that these matzoth were being prepared for the sake of God and His Commandments.

136

"Nothing was as soothing and satisfying as the knowledge that even in this God-forsaken death camp, where the value of a cigarette was greater than a life— even here, three little matzoth had been baked in preparation of the forthcoming Passover festival.

"There were tears in the eyes of every one of the eighty inmates in Room 10, when after nightfall on Wednesday, March 28, 1945, I opened my little hand-written Haggadah, lifted up the three little matzoth, and recited the first chapter, beginning with the familiar opening words 'Lo, this is the bread of affliction which our forefathers ate in the land of Egypt. Let all who are hungry come and eat, let all needy come and feast with us! This year we are here, next year we may be in Jerusalem. This year we are slaves, next year we shall be free men!'

"Everyone came to our table. Rabbi Domany, a little old man from Hungary who lived in the next room, was asked to sit at the head of the table and conduct the seder. I read the passages from the Haggadah as loudly as I dared, and the rest followed in a whisper. Then, raising the rusty cup of black coffee which he had saved from the morning in place of the traditional cup of red wine, Rabbi Domany called out in a tear-choked voice the words of the Haggadah:

> And it is this promise which has stood by our ancestors and by us. For it was not just one person who rose up against us to destroy us, but in every generation men rise against us. But the Holy One, blessed be He, delivers us from their hand.

"How true were the words that evening. Never before have so many men at one and the same time been so overawed in their trust of Almighty God as on that evening in Room 10 at Nieder-Orschel; never before was there such a truly solemn seder service; never before was there such longing for God and His protective arm."

Passover in a Concentration Camp

Things to think about

1 When all books had been taken away, S. B. Unsdorfer was still able to "write" a Haggadah. If all books were taken from you, what stories would you be able to write from memory? If you could have only two sheets of paper, which story would you write down to share with your friends? Why would you choose that story above all the rest? Why did Unsdorfer choose the Haggadah?

2 Reading the story of the baking of the matzoth might remind you of how the presses were built for the underground newspapers. Do you think the baking of the matzoth was a kind of resistance? Was the Passover seder a kind of resistance?

3 What special meaning did the holiday of Passover hold for these imprisoned Jews? Why do you think that they had not lost their faith?

sixteen

Danish Rescue

~~~~~~

THE Germans met very little resistance in their occupation of European countries. But two, Holland and Denmark, both tiny countries, caused the Germans the most trouble. Denmark's resistance was unique and especially effective. The Danes protected, hid, and saved 98.5 percent of their Jewish population, which numbered 8,000.

One of the most effective underground groups involved in anti-Nazi activities and in saving Jews was located in the town of Elsinore. Danes from all walks of life participated in this underground ring. Borge Ronne, a newspaper correspondent; Erlin Kiaer, a bookbinder; Thomond Larsen, a detective; Ove Bruhn, a bookkeeper;

and Jorgens Gersfelt, a physician, gathered together as the center of the underground. Like most Danes, they were disturbed when Denmark gave in to Germany in 1940 without firing one shot. But in 1943, when the Germans decided to round up all Denmark's Jews and send them to death camps, the Danes cooperated to save their Jewish neighbors. Danes disliked the Germans from previous encounters with them. Also, they did not regard Jews as separate people, but rather as Danes. It was not a written or voted decision. It was just something that happened.

The "Elsinore Sewing Club" was the name of the underground fighters' group, and it became an important center for saving Jewish lives. Each man in the group had a special job. When children were hidden, or taken on boats, Dr. Gersfelt was charged with keeping the younger ones quiet. Sleeping pills wore off too soon. So, although he was afraid of injecting narcotics (not knowing the exact amounts he should use and what would be the effect on the children), he was forced to do so in order to get the children past the German checkpoints. He waited anxiously for news of the first transport to Sweden, to hear how the injected children had fared. When he found they arrived in good health, he injected others without hesitation. As a physician, he also had an extra gas ration and was able to serve as a driver.

Because Elsinore was separated from Sweden by a waterway only two and one-half miles wide, it was the

Proclamation of the Danish Freedom Council. Early on, the Danish people realized that a threat to the freedom of the Jews was a threat to the freedom of all Denmark. In this brave northern country, resistance became an everyday way of life during the Nazi occupation.

The Danish Freedom Council condemns the pogroms the Germans have set in motion against the Jews in our country. Among the Danish people the Jews are not a special class but are citizens to exactly the same degree as all other Danes. . . . We Danes know that the whole population stands behind resistance to the German oppressors. The Council calls on the Danish population to help in every way possible those Jewish fellow-citizens who have not yet succeeded in escaping abroad. Every Dane who renders help to the Germans in their persecution of human beings is a traitor and will be punished as such when Germany is defeated.

best place for the refugees to cross. Mostly the group used fishing boats, even purchasing two boats for this purpose. Kiaer manned the boats and took so many Jews over he became known as the "Danish Pimpernel," and was hunted by the Nazis. Kiaer was finally captured and tortured, but never revealed any information.

An entire Danish uprising began the morning of Friday, September 30, 1943. It was the day before Rosh

143

Danish Rescue

Hashanah and Rabbi Marcus Melchior, Chief Rabbi of Denmark, stood before about 150 members of his synagogue in Copenhagen. He warned them that he had word that on the next day the Germans were planning to raid all Jewish homes and ship the Jews to concentration camps. He urged those present to contact everyone they knew who was Jewish, to contact Christian friends and urge them to report the dreadful news to their Jewish friends. This had to be done immediately, so that by night all the Jews would be in hiding.

Rabbi Melchior was married and had five children. No one person could hide such a large family, so the Rabbi decided they would have to separate. He was also worried about where to hide the precious ritual objects such as the Torah scrolls and the prayerbooks. He called on his friend, Pastor Hans Kildeby, who lived 60 miles south of Copenhagen. The Pastor insisted the whole family come to him. Then Melchior contacted another Lutheran minister in Copenhagen, who agreed to hide the ritual objects in the basement of his church.

Much of the Danish behavior was spontaneous. On the day of the secret announcement, a young ambulance driver was told of the trouble. He took a phonebook, circled all the Jewish names, and drove through the entire city warning these people. When some became frantic, not knowing where they could hide, he put them into his ambulance and drove them to Bispebjerg Hospital, where he knew Dr. Karl Køster would hide them.

Danish Rescue

When questioned why he had done this, he said, "What else could I do?"

Professor Richard Ege, now a biochemist at the Rockefeller Institute, when asked why he had hidden so many Jews in his building, said "It was a natural reaction to want to help good friends." And his wife said, "It was exactly the same as seeing a neighbor's house on fire. Naturally you want to do something about it." One pastor said "I would rather die with the Jews, than live with the Nazis."

The Jews could not hide forever. But where could they go? Neutral Sweden seemed to be the logical place for them, but would Sweden agree? Who could convince the authorities in that country? The Nobel Prize winner, Niels Bohr, was one of the two most famous nuclear physicists in the world (Albert Einstein was the other). On September 30, he was smuggled out of Denmark into Sweden. Upon arrival, Bohr was told he would have to go to London to be safe from the Nazis. He refused.

He would not leave Sweden, Bohr said, until he could speak with the Swedish foreign minister. In Stockholm, he told the foreign minister he could not leave until Sweden opened her doors for the Jewish refugees. The Minister was uncooperative. Bohr became angry and insisted on seeing King Gustav. After meeting with the King, he was assured that Sweden would accept the Jews. Bohr then asked that Sweden announce its decision on the front pages of its newspapers and in a radio broadcast to Denmark. After the broadcast, Bohr left for England, and from there, went to the United States.

Mogens Staffeldt owned a bookstore. The Nazis took over the entire building in which the bookstore was housed. Mr. Staffeldt moved across the street. Here a very active underground group met, and it was decided that the empty back room would be used as a collection point for refugees before taking them to the boats. If a certain book of poems was in the window, it meant the coast was clear for the refugees. However, if the book was absent, it meant that Jews should not enter.

The men in the underground praised the Jews. "They were very frightened," they said, "but courageous and often noble. If there was not enough room in a boat, there was trouble—not because each wanted to go, but because each adult male insisted on staying behind. One elderly Jew said, 'I'm seventy. Why should I go? Maybe I'll die next year. This man is forty—let him go.' " About 600 Jews were saved through the efforts of the bookstore group.

The people of Denmark sacrificed themselves in order to save fellow human beings from death. If you ever hear the Danish national anthem beginning with the words: "It is a lovely land," you can believe it.

Things to think about

1 In 1943 when the Germans prepared to round up Jews living in Denmark, the Danish people united to save

Danish Rescue

their Jewish neighbors. The great majority of the nation banded together in this effort. From what you know of history in general and of Jewish history—consider the governments, religious beliefs, and ways of life—why do you think the Danish people acted differently from the Polish people or the people of Russia?

2 Germany was not the only nation which set up concentration camps. During World War II, the United States established concentration camps for some of its own citizens, the Japanese Americans. And the British established concentration camps for Jews who were caught trying to enter Palestine illegally. Of course there were differences between these concentration camps and those of the Nazis. What were the differences? Do you think that living in a country of freedom like the United States or Britain should give us a respect for the freedoms of other people? (If you do not know about the concentration camps in the United States during World War II, ask your teacher to help you locate information.)

3 After leaving Sweden, Niels Bohr made his way to the United States. He worked in Los Alamos, New Mexico, helping the USA to develop the atomic bomb. In 1945, when the war was over, Bohr returned to Copenhagen to take up his position as a college professor. Was Bohr wrong when he demanded that the king of Sweden protect the Jewish people? Was Bohr wrong in helping with the design of the atomic bomb? What events made it possible for Niels Bohr to have done two things so opposite from one another?

seventeen

The Righteous Gentiles

JOOP WESTERWILL

~~~~~~

IN Jewish writings it is said, "The righteous among the Gentiles will have a place in the world to come." In Israel today, on the Mount of Remembrance, outside Jerusalem, near Yad VaShem, the memorial building to the Six Million, there is a garden. In this garden are planted trees honoring those righteous non-Jews who helped Jews during the Nazi period. Each tree in the Garden of the Righteous Gentiles bears a plaque telling about the person in whose memory or honor the tree is planted. One tree is planted in memory of a Dutchman— Joop Westerwill, a courageous, noble man, who assisted hundreds of Jewish children and teenagers escape the Nazi Holocaust.

The Righteous Gentiles

The Dutch people have a deep-rooted sense of moral justice and desire for freedom, and to Joop these values meant more than life itself. He was a teacher at Werkplats, a progressive school in Rotterdam, Holland. When Germany invaded Holland and took over the government, Joop was approached by some young Jews to help hide and assist in the escape of Jewish children. "My friends," he said, "I have been expecting this call for a long time. I have been waiting and hoping for it. In my work with the children at school, I felt I had reached a dead end. When one tries to teach in the face of this humiliation to humanity, it is impossible. I cannot teach children even the simplest things."

The Righteous Gentiles

Short, with a bright look, smiling eyes, wavy brown hair, and lots of energy, Joop was very clever. Although he was religious he was always rebellious, and even when young stood up for the underdog.

As a young man, he was inducted into the Dutch army, but since he opposed war and became the first conscientious objector in the Dutch forces, he was expelled from Indonesia where he had been forced to serve. He also refused to pay certain taxes because they were being used for military purposes and had many clashes with the authorities because of his devotion to peace.

When the Nazis took over the Netherlands, Joop decided he would do everything he could to help the Jews. He rented apartments in his own name and allowed Jewish families to live in them. At times, he had three apartments in his name, filled with Jews trying to escape deportation. Once he wrote that he would have liked to be Jewish. "You Jews have a cultural life for yourself. You are really unique and have the highest regard for human values, because in the face of all the persecution and shame the Nazis heap upon you, you can still hold your head up high and instill culture in yourselves and your children."

He always encouraged Jewish children in hiding to continue their studies. One time, two of his boys escaping over the border were caught by the police, who thought they were smugglers. The guards found only books in their luggage, let them go, and even warned them that nearby was a Nazi patrol. Joop once had to

Joop Westerwill's last letter. When the Dutch underground
worker was finally caught by the Nazis, he continued
resisting in the only way possible: by standing firm.

*. . . This morning they informed me that they were
going to call me up before a military court. Did I
wish to write a farewell letter to my wife? When I
began it they again interrupted me for questioning.
At the moment I have a little rest. But on Monday
the same thing [torture] awaits me. You know I
shall not give anyone away. Of that I am certain.
Suicide? No, I want to stand firm. . . . Best wishes
to you all, perhaps for a long time. If we do not meet
again, I hope what we did together will remain a
sacred memory for life. God bless you. Joop.*

hide some children on the Sabbath. He apologized for
having to divide money, food, and clothing on that day.
But he reminded the religious children that they must
try to stay alive and that the beauty of Judaism is its
positive attitude toward life.

Joop and his Jewish friends from *Aliyat Ha-Noar*
(Youth Aliya) went back and forth from Holland and
France into Spain, danger at their heels every step of the
way. Many discussions were held on these trips, and
Joop often said after Germany was defeated, he, his

152

wife, and four children would go to Palestine and settle on a kibbutz. Although these discussions were always held when the group was in danger, the topic of discussion was always tomorrow, never yesterday. Joop always looked ahead.

He took one group to the Spanish border in 1944. Although the children were tired, frightened, dirty, and cold, he spoke to them one last time. And they remembered his words long after he left them, and even today they are inspired when they think of what he said. He told them that in *Eretz Yisrael* they must build a new life based on freedom and justice, and 'that it should be a model to the world.' He asked that they remember their friends who fell along the way, and build a monument to them. One child who survived, Sophie Nussbaum, said later, "I'll never forget him. In those dark days, he was the only spark of humanity."

For twenty months, Joop managed to involve dozens of Dutch families in the lifesaving task. For twenty months he was a tremendous inspiration. Weeks went by when he slept only two hours a night, and by day continued his work as principal of the school. Each time he escorted a group of children to the border, the tired man with the shaggy hair would have a bright smile, a good word for them, and then would turn and go back— alone.

On March 11, 1944, Joop was captured by the Nazis while trying to smuggle two girls into France. Taken to jail, he was constantly beaten and tortured, but would

153

give no information. To those outside, he wrote notes urging care for the hidden children. And when he was in solitary confinement, he taught songs and gave lectures to the others in near-by cells.

His friends tried to get his release and then to arrange for his escape. In August 1944, he was shot by the Nazis. His last note said, "If we do not meet again, I hope that what we did together will remain a sacred memory for life. God bless you."

Things to think about

1 Stories were told after the war was over of Jewish mothers who had left their young children with a Catholic nun or with a priest, and when the parents returned they found that the children had been taught to be Catholic and to forget their Judaism. Joop Westerwill, on the other hand, showed a deep respect for the religion of the Jewish children he helped. Is it easy to respect another person's beliefs without wanting to change them if they do not agree with our own? What reasons could the Catholics who converted Jewish children give for their actions? What reasons could Joop Westerwill give for his?

2 To help the Jews, Joop Westerwill gave up everything; he turned all his efforts to this one cause. From the story

154

you have just read of his life, what ideals did he have which made him a good teacher? Did he ever really stop teaching?

3 Do you think that Joop Westerwill should be considered a Dutch national hero?

eighteen

The Lady with the Stamps

∿∿∿

THE word "propaganda" means an organized effort to spread particular ideas or beliefs to the public. When used in politics, propaganda often presents only half the truth. A group or government may tell only those facts which make its side seem completely right and its enemies completely wrong. At its worst, propaganda can be the spreading of ugly lies to stir up hatred against a group of people.

This is the kind of propaganda the Nazis used against the Jews. They tried to represent the Jews as subhuman so that non-Jews might feel free to treat them inhumanly. Posters and cartoons were drawn showing the Jews as monsters, murderers, and thieves. Photos

157

were also prepared to show the Jew in an evil light. In order to produce these photos, two different negatives were combined. They showed the "subhuman" Jews as capitalists planning to dominate the world. How this could be done by subhumans is not clear, but the Nazis cared nothing for reason, and most of those who came to see the exhibit did not think. The Nazis also accused the Jews of being the force behind the Communist movement. All the troubles facing Germany at that time were blamed on Jews and Communists.

There were Germans who understood that the propaganda was a series of lies dreamed up by sick minds. But only a few people realized how dangerous these lies were. The propaganda taught that all the problems in Germany were due to Jews; to eliminate the problems, Germans had only to eliminate the Jews. Thus the way was prepared for the mass murder of the Jewish people.

One person who immediately realized the danger of this kind of Nazi anti-Semitism was Mrs. Irene Harand. She was a lovely, dark-haired Christian lady who lived in Vienna. When Hitler's followers first began abusing the Jews in 1933, she wrote a book exposing the evils of anti-Semitism. It was directed to "those in Germany who have not lost every feeling of shame." In September 1933, she began publishing a newspaper called *Gerechtigreit* (Justice). Across the top of the front page was written: "I am fighting anti-Semitism because it defiles our Christianity." The cost of producing this

The Lady with the Stamps

paper was paid by Mrs. Harand herself. When she ran out of money, she pawned all her jewelry in order to be able to go on with the fight.

In 1934, she formed the "World Organization Against Racial Hatred and Human Misery," which came to be known as the Harand Movement, and at one time boasted 40,000 members.

One of her most effective weapons against anti-Semitism was a series of colorful stamps. The first set of stamps was issued in October 1937. Each bore the picture of a famous Jew who had made an outstanding contribution to humanity. Some of those represented were: Paul Ehrlich, the scientist; Heinrich Hertz and Robert Lieben, pioneers in developing wireless telegraphy; Baruch Spinoza, philosopher; Benjamin Disraeli, English Prime Minister. One issue of stamps gave facts

The Lady with the Stamps

regarding Jewish contributions to Germany during World War I. Still another showed a photo of Mrs. Harand herself, who by this time, had become a symbol of freedom in the hate-ridden world of Europe. These stamps were pasted on letters right next to the regular postage stamp and widely circulated throughout Europe.

In November 1937, the Nazis gathered together all their anti-Semitic propaganda for an exhibit in Munich, Germany. This became a traveling exhibit which was later shown in other German and Austrian cities. It was called "The Eternal Jew." A poster with the same title showed an evil-looking old man with money spilling from one hand and the sign of the Communist party on his arm. Thousands came to view this exhibit. School children were brought to the exhibit by their teachers who wanted to make sure they saw it.

The anti-Semites were pleased to see the Jews shown in such a terrible light. But some other people were so disgusted by the exhibit that they wanted to take action against it. But there were few to turn to and Mrs. Harand was one of the few.

When the Munich exhibition opened, Mrs. Harand immediately issued a new set of stamps with the inscription "The Harand Movement of Vienna Answers the Munich Exhibition 'The Eternal Jew.'"

One night, two sailors who worked on the Danube River knocked on Mrs. Harand's door. "We have come for some stamps," they told her. "That exhibit in Munich

A personal statement by Irene Harand. Mrs. Harand's stamp
campaign made her the sworn enemy of the Nazi Party.
In her quiet way, she helped to force truth to shine in the
darkest corners of Nazi-controlled Europe.

*Today is the 25th anniversary of the unbelievably
inhumane day of November 10, 1938 (Kristallnacht) when Hitler's hordes in Germany began
the rounding up of thousands and thousands of
perfectly innocent and decent human beings to
throw them into concentration camps. The only
"crime" of these people was that they were born
Jews . . . and the whole world looked on . . . I,
myself, was only carrying the flag. Without my
followers none would have noticed.*

is a disgrace to civilized human beings. We felt we had
to do something."

She quickly let them in. The three spoke in hurried
whispers, for already the Harand Movement had become
a threat to the Nazis, and Mrs. Harand was in danger of
being arrested. The sailors explained how they planned
to use the stamps. "We are going back to Munich to-
night. We will paste them on the walls of the exhibition
hall. Though they are small, hundreds of people will see
them before they are discovered and removed by the
authorities."

161

The Lady with the Stamps

"Where will you hide them?" she asked. "You will be killed if you are caught."

The younger of the sailors took off his shoe and turned it over. He swung the rubber heel to one side. Inside was a hollow place where the stamps could be hidden. Mrs. Harand immediately took dozens of stamps and made them into tiny bundles. The sailors hid them in their heels and went back into the night. A few days later in Munich, tiny pictures of great Jewish scientists, scholars, and artists appeared next to the posters and pictures of imaginary Jewish villains.

In 1938, when the Nazis took over Austria, Mrs. Harand was seventh on the list of people they planned to execute. Fortunately she was in England on a speaking tour at the time. She never returned to her homeland, but continued her battle against the Nazis until the end of the war.

Mrs. Harand now lives in the United States. On November 10, 1964, she made this statement:

> Today is the twenty-fifth anniversary of the unbelievably inhumane day of November 10, 1938 (Kristallnacht) * when Hitler's hordes in Germany began the rounding up of thousands and thousands of perfectly innocent and decent human beings to throw them into concentration camps. The only "crime" of these people was that they were born Jews . . . and the whole world looked on . . . I, myself, was only carrying the flag. Without my followers none would have noticed.

* Kristallnacht occurred in Austria too and they commemorate it on November 10 instead of November 9.

The Lady with the Stamps

Things to think about

1 First Mrs. Harand wrote a book, then she tried to attack the German lies through a newspaper, but the most effective weapon she tried was the stamp. Why were the stamps so effective when the book and the newspaper failed?

2 Why were the Germans so anxious to execute Mrs. Harand? What did they have to fear from the small stamps that Mrs. Harand made? Or was it the ideas behind the stamps that the Germans were so afraid of?

3 From your study so far this year, can you list several different types of heroes? Can you make a list showing examples of each different type from among the people you have studied in this book? Which of these heroes deserve to be on a stamp?

nineteen

Rescue from the Sky

~~~~~~

AS the Nazis closed in on them, the Jews of Europe looked desperately for help. They looked to their Gentile neighbors. They looked to the resistance fighters of the occupied countries. They looked to the Allies. They found no hands outstretched to help them.

Finally, near the end of the war, more and more of the trapped Jews turned their eyes away from the indifference about them, and looked toward the heavens.

And help came to them from the skies. It came in the form of the *tzanchanim*—young Jewish parachutists from the Jewish community of Palestine.

The tzanchanim consisted of 32 men and women who volunteered to serve the British by parachuting be-

165

hind enemy lines, where they were to do their utmost to disable the enemy. They blew up railroad tracks, bridges, and munition plants; they were also anxious to establish contact and help the remaining Jewish communities survive and individuals to escape.

The Jews of Palestine were ideal for this kind of mission. Many of them had been born in European countries, knew the land, and spoke European languages as their mother tongues. And they were completely dedicated to the Allied cause.

The job of selecting and training the tzanchanim went to Enzo Sereni, an Italian Jew who had emigrated to Eretz Yisrael in 1926, where he had helped build Givat Brenner, today one of the largest kibbutzim in Israel.

Even before Hitler came to power, Enzo recognized the true nature of Nazi anti-Semitism. During a visit to Germany in 1929 as a delegate of the *Hechalutz* (Pioneer) movement, he warned the Jewish communities that they were sitting on a volcano. Hundreds of Jews were moved by his message and by his enthusiasm for Zionism. Inspired, they emigrated to Palestine. In 1933, he returned to Nazi Germany and then went on to Italy, France, Holland, and Norway to alert and rescue more of his people.

In 1940 he enlisted in the British secret service. At the same time he was a member of the Jewish underground in Palestine. In 1944 he was asked to train the tzanchanim. After choosing the team to be trained, Enzo himself enlisted. His best friend asked why he endangered himself, especially since he was by far the oldest in the group. "Voices," he answered, "voices of my brothers crying from death wagons, gas chambers, and mass graves fill my heart. . . ."

Headquarters for the parachutists' training program was Cairo. The young men and women had to know by heart the names of the Jewish underground leaders and their identifying features. They had to know how to drive and how to use a wireless. They learned to handle explosives. They memorized a special code, and, of course, they practiced parachuting from airplanes.

Some were sent to Italy and waited there for their assignment. Enzo was with them. While Enzo waited, he received a letter from his small son, Daniel, who wrote: "*Abba*, it is not important if you die. The important thing is to die like a hero." Enzo went to the airport in Bari, Italy, with each group and as he looked over his tzanchanim, he thought, "Eretz Yisrael is not forsaken if she has children such as these."

Wherever they went, the parachutists were treated as heroes. For the poor Jews enclosed in ghettos, hiding in forests, and imprisoned in death camps, it seemed like a miracle that these people had come to help. Free Jews from a free Eretz Yisrael risked their lives to help their brothers in Europe.

Enzo's turn to parachute came on May 15, 1944,

167

but the mission turned into a disaster. The pilot lost his
way and Enzo parachuted into a German camp. He was
immediately captured by the Germans and taken to
Dachau, a death camp, where he was tortured horribly.
But he revealed nothing, and finally the Nazis murdered
him.

Fourteen months after Enzo's death a ship bearing
his name docked in Haifa harbor, proudly flying the
blue and white Jewish flag. Palestine was still under
the rule of Britain who would not allow Jews to enter the
land. But this ship carried a precious cargo that Enzo
would have been proud of—a thousand "illegal" refugees, smuggled into the harbor.

168

Rescue from the Sky

Years later, at a memorial meeting for Enzo, one of Israel's leaders said of him: "If Abraham had founded the Jewish nation only for the sake of Enzo Chayim Sereni, it would have been reason enough."

Another parachutist from Palestine who gave her life to the cause was Chana Senesh—pioneer, poetess, and parachutist. Chana was born in Budapest, Hungary, into a wealthy and prominent Hungarian Jewish family which had grown away from Judaism. At seventeen, Chana became interested in Zionism. She learned Hebrew and decided to settle in Eretz Yisrael. She was accepted at an agricultural school in Palestine and then applied for a certificate to leave Hungary.

Ten days after her eighteenth birthday, she received the certificate. Three months later, she arrived. First she trained on a farm for her agricultural career. Then she settled on a kibbutz called S'doth Yam, which was a new, struggling settlement near Caesaria. She hardly missed her easy, luxurious life in Hungary, or the elegant parties or beautiful clothes and fine food. She only missed her mother.

Chana Senesh was a poetess. She saw everything— her own life, the sacrifice her mother made in allowing her to leave Hungary, and the country which she adopted as her own—with a poet's sensitivity. Little by little she learned Hebrew well enough to write her poetry in it. One beautiful poem said:

Rescue from the Sky

My God: these should never end:
the sand and the sea,
the sound of water,
the thunder of heaven,
the prayers of man.

When she was chosen to be a parachutist she wrote
in her diary "To leave this land and freedom? I would
like to fill my lungs with the fresh air of Eretz Yisrael,
which I will be able to breathe in the choking atmosphere
of Europe, and to give it to those who have been denied
the taste of freedom. . . ." Then she wrote:

To die—young—to die—No, I did not wish it
I love the warm sun,
And I did not want destruction, war. . . .

But if I am commanded to live today
In a stream of blood; amid terrible havoc,
I will say, Blessed be the Name for the privilege,
To live, and when the hour comes to die—
On your soil, my country, my Homeland.

Together with her companions, she parachuted into
Yugoslavia and slowly made her way to the border of
Hungary. Meantime Hungary was invaded by the Nazis.
But Chana continued her assignment.

After many days of travel through forests and
villages, she succeeded in crossing the border, but was

170

almost immediately captured by Hungarian police. She was tied, and whipped on the palms of her hands and the soles of her feet for hours. The Nazis wanted the secret radio code, but Chana knew its importance and would not reveal it, not even under terrible torture.

Then came the worst punishment of all. The Nazis located her mother and brought her to jail. They told Chana if she did not reveal the code, Mrs. Senesh would be tortured and killed. Still Chana kept the secret. Finally they let her mother go.

Joel Nusbacher, also in Chana's group, was captured and imprisoned in the same jail with Chana. He soon discovered she was there, for everyone spoke of her with reverence and love. "Even in the police wagon she raised our spirits as she told of Eretz Yisrael," said one prisoner. Chana was three floors above Joel, in solitary confinement, but Joel cleverly invented a system of "talking" to her with mirrors. Chana also invented a system of "talking." She made large letters from paper, with which she formed words and sentences. From morning till night the prisoners watched Chana's window as she "lectured" to them on Eretz Yisrael and life in the kibbutz.

The guards even supplied her with bits of paper. From these she made small puppets. Then her window became a "theater" as well as a lecture hall. Finally, after two months, Chana was transferred to a large cell. First she conducted exercises for everyone. Then she led discussions, especially about Israel. She taught two Polish children who had spent most of their lives in prison to read and write, and rewarded them for good efforts with paper dolls she herself made.

Chana and Joel were finally transferred to another jail in Budapest. Here Chana was put on trial and pleaded guilty. But at the end of the trial, she accused those in the courtroom, as well as all the Nazis and Hungarians who cooperated with the Nazis, of horrible deeds and murderous acts.

On a gray and rainy day in November 1944, the Hungarian prosecutor entered Chana's cell, number 13. She looked up as he asked, "Chana Senesh, you are condemned to death. Will you plead for mercy?"

"Mercy from you? No, I beg no mercy from the hands of hangmen."

"Then you may write farewell letters, for in an hour you will be shot."

Chana wrote two letters, one to her mother and the other to Joel. To Joel, she wrote, "Continue—never retreat—carry the battle to the day of freedom!"

The hour was up. Chana was led to the courtyard, her hands tied to a pillar. A Nazi tried to put a blindfold on her eyes, but she refused to allow it.

Chana wrote a poem which begins:

Blessed is the match consumed in kindling a flame.
Blessed is the heart with strength to stop its beating
    for honor's sake.

172

Rescue from the Sky

Chana herself was the blessed match who kindled a flame in her people that will remain lighted forever.

Things to think about

1 Really the parachutists' mission was very unsuccessful, yet their heroism has been remembered and commemorated. Is a person a hero only if he is successful? Was Chana Senesh a heroine? Why? What qualities did she have and what actions did she take which made her a heroine whether or not she was successful in her mission?

2 Even though the mission was unsuccessful, many Jews suffering under the Nazi oppression gained hope from the legend of the Israelis who had come to help. Do you think that the parachutists were afraid? What does the word "courage" mean? Can we give courage to others through being courageous ourselves?

3 Enzo Sereni's daughter was once asked, "Why did your father volunteer at his age"? She answered, "How could he look me in the face if he sent others to their death, but did not volunteer himself"? Do you think that her statement was right? How would you answer if your father had been Enzo Sereni? If you were Enzo Sereni?

twenty

Youth Aliyah and Aliyah Bet

IN 1932 some German teenagers came to the home of Recha Freier in Berlin. They had been fired from their jobs because they were Jewish. Mrs. Freier became very upset over this incident and tried to help them. But the general Jewish community in Germany felt this anti-Semitism would soon blow over and Adolf Hitler would fade into history.

Mrs. Freier did not feel this way. She was very worried about things that were happening in Germany. She felt one way to help was to pave the way for the boys to go to Palestine and work on a kibbutz. This plan would help both the Jewish youngsters in Germany and the struggling Jewish community in Palestine. Most of

175

the Zionists in Germany laughed at her plan, but a few thought it was a good idea. Mrs. Freier didn't give up and finally, at the beginning of 1933, a committee was formed and a meeting was held. The group was given a name—"Aid Committee for Jewish Youth," better known to everyone as Youth Aliyah. Aliyah means to "go up" to Israel, or Palestine (as it was called then). In Eretz Yisrael, the person who directed the Youth Aliyah organization was Henrietta Szold. Youth Aliyah was established January 30, 1933, the exact day that the Nazis took office in Germany.

Through the efforts of Youth Aliyah, thousands of Jewish youngsters were saved from certain death during the Nazi period. In Israel today, "graduates" of Youth Aliyah can be found in important posts all over the country—in the army, on kibbutzim, and in the government. One of these famous young men, who lost his entire family in Europe, is Yossi Stern, the Israeli artist.

Yossi was born in Hungary in 1923, and at the age of ten moved with his family to Budapest, capital of Hungary. Yossi's family was not much interested in being Jewish. They were Hungarians first, and gave their children no Jewish education, nor did they attend synagogue.

Yossi was a boy scout. When he was thirteen, he became the head of his troop. He loved scouting. One day, a letter came from the Hungarian government addressed to the scoutmaster. Yossi read it. It said: "From now on, no Jews are allowed to wear the uniform of the boy scouts or participate in their activities." After Yossi finished reading the letter out loud, he stepped out of the room, changed his uniform for his street clothing, and left. No one stopped him; no one cared.

Scouting had been very important to him. Losing it left him lonely and unhappy. He turned to some of his Jewish acquaintances. One day one of his Jewish friends said, "Yossi, come join our Zionist youth group."

"What do I know about Zionism or Judaism? I know I was born a Jew, but I don't even know what Jew means. I know that many people hate us and that there are many laws keeping us from doing the things we want to do. But I really don't understand it all."

"We will teach you," answered his friend. He gave Yossi a book, *The Jewish State*, by Theodor Herzl. "You see," said his friend, "Theodor Herzl once knew nothing about Judaism either, and look at what a great Jew he became."

Yossi read the book. Then he read other books that were given to him by Jewish friends. He thought about how he felt when he had read the letter to his scout troop. Though he had believed the other scouts who were not Jewish were his friends, not one word had been said by them in his behalf. Were they really his friends? Or were these Jewish boys his real friends? They were Jews. They were brothers. It sounded odd. My Jewish brothers. But each time he said it, it made more sense. And the books made sense. Theodor Herzl, who had been a Jew like himself, an uninterested Jew, also made sense. "A

177

land of our own where the authorities cannot say, 'take off your scout uniform, Jew!' " That made sense.

So Yossi gradually became a Zionist. He was the only Zionist in his family. His uncles sarcastically called him "the preacher." They were amused. "Anti-Semitism is a fashion now," they said, "but there will never be real anti-Semitism in Hungary." It seemed the grown-ups knew less about what was happening in Europe than did the young people. Even when Czechoslovakia was taken over by Nazi Germany, they gave a thousand reasons why anti-Semitism would never take root in Hungary.

In spite of his family, Yossi kept on with his Jewish studies. And together with his Jewish friends, he talked about how to escape from Hungary. One day one of his friends called him. "Yossi, now is your only chance. You know about Aliyah Bet. You know legally we are not permitted into Eretz Yisrael, so we have to enter illegally. Aliyah Bet is the organization helping with this illegal immigration. Now is the time to save our lives. Come with us, Yossi." He continued, "One ship will have 100 places on it. No one, not even your relatives, must know you are leaving. You can't even say goodbye. You must meet us after midnight."

Yossi immediately decided to go. Things in Hungary were getting worse and worse for the Jews. He feared for the lives of his family but there was no way he could convince them of the danger, so he decided to leave alone. He told no one of his decision. Under the

From *Come from the Four Winds*. Arye was not unlike other
Jewish children whose lives were torn from their everyday
world of school and play and changed overnight by the
effects of the Holocaust. Thanks to Youth Aliyah, however,
Arye was one of the lucky ones who survived.

*Arye's farming experience dates from his Hakhshara
(preparation) days on a Youth Aliyah training farm
(in Germany) where he had gone early in 1939, at
the age of fifteen. His father, a . . . bank official,
had been dismissed by his Nazi employer; and Arye
had been expelled from the . . . school he had
attended. . . . One of his fellow students had been
the stepson of Dr. Joseph Goebbels, Hitler's . . .
minister of propaganda.*

*"The farmers around the place couldn't get over
seeing Jewish boys actually working on the land,"
Arye recalled.*

cover of night, he slipped out of the house with a tiny
bundle. He boarded a boat at the appointed spot after
midnight. The boat was going to Rumania and was very
crowded. Yossi slept on a ledge on the deck. The motor
was beneath him, so even though the weather was quite
cold and there was snow all about the deck, the heat of
the motor kept him warm. The ship sailed down the
Danube, but downstream the Danube River became
frozen. They were forced to remain in Galatz, a seaport

in Romania. The passengers were placed on huge rafts caught in the ice and frozen in place. Romanian Jewry supplied them with food and lumber and warm clothing. They built roofs with the lumber for the rafts. They remained in the frozen river for three months. Finally the river began to thaw, and one night they received news that a Turkish coal ship was coming to take them to Palestine.

In the middle of the night, Yossi, along with many others, climbed aboard the small boat and went to the side of the Turkish ship—the *Zacharia*—an Aliyah Bet ship. When it was his turn to climb onto ship, he became frightened. He glanced down as he put one foot on the crude rope ladder. Beneath him was pitch-black water— above him pitch-black night. He tightly clutched the little bag which he had brought from home. He was frightened. He was afraid he might fall into the water and drown. Should he throw the pack away? Then it would be easier to climb. While these thoughts raced through his mind, he was climbing rung by rung without realizing it. Someone below hissed, "Hurry up, we must be loaded soon. It will be light before we know it." He was close to the top and someone reached out and firmly took hold of his hands and his pack, helping him onto the deck of the ship. Once on board, he found 2,000 people—and coal—and the friend who had helped him aboard. This is someone with whom Yossi is still close. The ship was loaded and it went out into the open sea through the Bosporus to Turkey. Life on shipboard

was interesting. Though it was crowded, it was organized like a minature Jewish community. The Jews from
Vienna even formed a cabaret and added some enjoy-
ment for the people.

As they approached Israel, they were sighted and
captured by a British boat. The British, cooperating with
the Arabs, tried to prevent Jewish immigration into
Palestine. They threatened to send this ship back to
Romania. This time the British put the ship's passengers
into a camp in Palestine, a camp surrounded by barbed
wire. Yossi was herded with the others into the camp.
It was not pleasant, but it was better than being sent
back to Europe.

Each one was given special chores. Yossi had always
done a little sketching. After his chores he would collect
all the odd scraps of paper he could find, and with the
stump of a pencil do some sketching.

After several months this group of Jews was freed
and Youth Aliyah found Yossi a job picking fruit. From
that job, he went to building houses. But he always
continued sketching. When the leaders of Youth Aliyah
saw his artwork, they arranged for him to study at
Bezalel (the art school in Jerusalem) on a Youth Aliyah
scholarship. He was so talented that he graduated from
there in three years instead of four, and won an important art award. He also was hired immediately by the
school as an art instructor.

Yossi loves Israel, and especially Jerusalem. He says
"Art is a form of communication—storytelling—and I

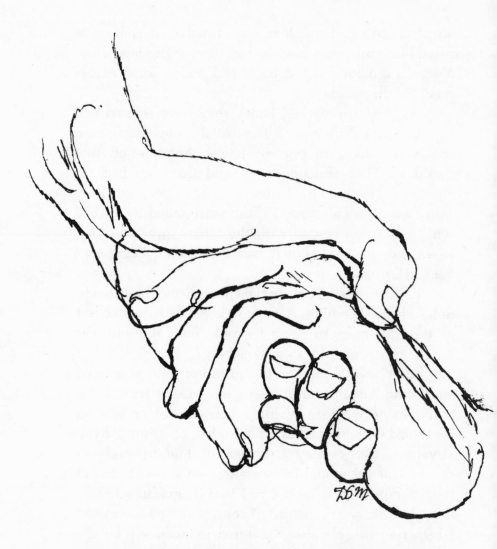

want to express the warm feeling I have for my country
and my people. There are a thousand faces to this country and a thousand faces of my people. I love Jerusalem's

hills. I am not happy when I am in flat country. Jerusalem is so full of history that everything here becomes symbolic. A simple beggar looks like Job from the Bible. Figures in the marketplace look like Kohelet. Nowhere else in the world is the Bible so brought to life as here. One miracle follows another." He can't stop telling about Jerusalem. "Every time I see the Gates (of the Old City) it is a miracle. I don't take this sight for granted. I am still a newcomer after thirty years. Everything is still fresh to me. I have not become used to it. Every day in Jerusalem is a holiday."

Yossi is one of thousands who escaped from Europe with the help of Youth Aliyah. Each one tells a different, exciting, and often tragic tale.

Things to think about

1 Even before she began to lead the work of Youth Aliyah in Palestine, Henrietta Szold had already accomplished more than most people accomplish in a lifetime. She was born in Baltimore, the daughter of a rabbi. In 1877, after graduating from high school, she began to teach classes in "Americanization" to European immigrants to the United States.

In 1892 she became an editor and secretary for the Jewish Publication Society of America. One of her major accomplishments was the translation of Louis Ginzberg's famous *The Legends of the Jews* from the original German. Her English translation fills six thick volumes and took Henrietta Szold twenty-seven years to complete.

Of course, she was doing much more during that same time. She first visited Palestine in 1909. She discovered a great need for medical services in Palestine. The country was ravaged by malaria. There was no medical care for mothers and children. Her loyalty to Judaism led her to devote her whole life to the cause of Zionism, the rebuilding of the Jewish State in the Holy Land. To combat the dreadful lack of sanitation and medical facilities in the Holy Land, in 1912 she founded the American women's organization, Hadassah, of which she was president from 1912 to 1926. Concerned with Jewish youth, she established ties between the Hadassah youth organization, Young Judaea, and the Israeli youth organization *Hatzofim*.

From 1920 on, Henrietta Szold lived in *Eretz Yisrael*, directing the work of the medical organization she founded. The small clinics that she and her coworkers established became the great Hadassah hospitals in Jerusalem, among the world's finest medical institutions.

In 1933, as conditions in Germany worsened for the Jews, Henrietta Szold took up leadership in the work of a small organization known as Youth Aliyah. The organization grew as the threats of the Nazis deepened. Until her death in 1945, Henrietta Szold devoted herself to aiding the thousands of children brought to Israel from Europe, saved from the Holocaust.

Reading the story of one of the youngsters that she helped, Yossi Stern, the Israeli artist, we can see the kind of monument that Henrietta Szold built for herself through her work.

From her life story, what concerns do you think were most important to Henrietta Szold? Which of the organizations she helped to form are still in existence today? Have the ideas and goals of these organizations changed?

2 Look up the word "Zionism" in any encyclopedia. What exactly is a "Zionist"? Why did Yossi Stern finally become a Zionist? Is everyone who lives in the State of Israel a Zionist? Is it possible to be a Zionist without living in Israel? Is it possible to be a Zionist without being Jewish?

twenty-one

Hunted and Hunters

SOMETIMES a murderer is caught by a most peculiar twist of fate—or by a strange set of circumstances— or by a little slip, when he is sure he is safe from harm.

Such a man was Adolf Eichmann. It was he who engineered the murder of the six million Jews. It was to be the "final solution" of the Jewish problem, for with the murder of all the Jews—which was what the Nazis hoped to achieve—there would be no more Jewish "problem."

Eichmann was cruel and inhuman, although he appeared to be normal. One example of his cruelty was an occurrence in Prague when Eichmann summoned the president of the Jewish community and said to him:

"The Jews must go—but fast!" The president replied that Jews had lived in Prague for 1100 years and were indigenous (native to the country). Eichmann began screaming, "Indigenous? I'll show you!" The next day, the first shipment of Jews left for a concentration camp, never to return.

After the war, in 1945, when it became known who the main executioner of the Jews was, serious attempts were made to find him. First it was thought he had committed suicide. But at the Nuremberg trials, one of the Nazis who took the stand expressed the belief that Eichmann was still alive. The Nazi, Captain Dieter Wisliceny, stated that Eichmann once said, "I will leap laughing into the grave because the feeling that I had the death of five million people on my conscience would be, for me, a source of extraordinary satisfaction." Eichmann had engineered the murder of 73 percent of the Jewish population of Europe by the time the war was over.

In 1947 Eichmann's wife wanted him declared dead. Once this was done, his name would be taken off the "wanted" list of Nazi criminals. Simon Wiesenthal, one of the men indirectly responsible for his capture, found out about this. Wiesenthal discovered that the man who had declared Eichmann dead was his brother-in-law, and that in all likelihood, the whole thing was a fraud. Eichmann's wife was called into court and severely scolded by the judge and the case was dismissed. Eichmann was still listed as alive.

Hunted and Hunters

The facts in the Eichmann case were pieced together slowly and tediously, like the pieces in a jigsaw puzzle. Eichmann was discovered to have been in various places after the war. One of these places was Altaussee in Austria, where his family lived. He fled from Austria and voluntarily hid in an American internment camp. When things got too hot there, he ran away and hid in various places, finally leaving Europe. In most places he hid, he was protected by groups of pro-Nazis, and people who knew him when he was important. These men were paid well to protect the Nazi criminals and to sneak them out of Europe. In 1952 it was discovered that Frau Eichmann and her sons had disappeared from Austria.

Simon Wiesenthal, who still makes it his business to hunt Nazi criminals, could not sleep. When he went to his doctor, the doctor suggested he take up a hobby—stamp collecting, perhaps. Mr. Wiesenthal decided to do this. Late in 1953, the "hunter" met an old Austrian baron and was invited to his beautiful home. The baron, who was also a stamp collector, showed Mr. Wiesenthal his collection. Over wine they talked and looked at stamps and the baron listened to Mr. Wiesenthal tell about the work he was doing. The baron was shocked that some "big" Nazis were back at important jobs and no one seemed to care. Then he arose, opened a drawer, and mentioned a friend in Argentina, a former German lieutenant-colonel, who was known as an anti-Nazi. Because of this he had fled, during the war, to Argen-

From *The Murders Among Us* by Simon Wiesenthal.
Wiesenthal had tracked Eichmann for nearly sixteen years
without ever seeing him. The Eichmann trial focused the
world's attention on the Holocaust. Television and news
coverage brought the full truth to millions who had never
before heard it.

I saw Adolf Eichmann for the first time on the open-
ing day of his trial in the courtroom in Jerusalem. For
nearly sixteen years I had thought of him practically
every day and every night. In my mind I had built
up an image of a demon, a superman. Instead I saw
a small, plain, shabby fellow in a glass cell between
two Israeli policemen; they looked more colorful and
interesting than he did. Everything about Eichmann
seemed drawn with charcoal: his grayish face, his
balding head, his clothes. There was nothing demon-
like about him; he looked like a bookkeeper who is
afraid to ask for a raise. Something seemed com-
pletely wrong, and I kept thinking about it. . . .
Suddenly I knew what it was. In my mind I'd always
seen Eichmann, commander of life and death. But
the Eichmann I now saw did not wear the uniform of
terror and murder. Dressed in a cheap dark suit, he
seemed a cardboard figure, empty, and two-
dimensional.

tina. "I just received this letter," said the baron. "I had asked the lieutenant-colonel if he met any of our old comrades down there. He wrote back, among other things, 'Imagine whom I recently saw—and even had to talk to twice: *dieses elende schwein*, Eichmann [this awful swine, Eichmann] who killed the Jews. He lives near Buenos Aires and works for a water company.'"

The baron continued, "How do you like that? Some of the worst criminals got away."

Mr. Wiesenthal returned to his hotel room. Although he was very excited about his discovery, he realized that as a private investigator his work was done. It would be necessary now for the Israeli government to take over. However, nothing happened because there simply was no money for such an extensive manhunt by the Israeli government.

In 1959 the hunt was picked up again, and it was discovered that Adolf Eichmann was still living on the outskirts of Buenos Aires, Argentina, working in the Mercedes-Benz factory. He had changed his name to Ricardo Klement.

Three young Israelis took over the detective job now. They rented a room near Eichmann's home where they could keep watch on the Nazi's movements. To be sure that he was the right man, they took photographs of Eichmann with a camera hidden in the lock of a briefcase. They followed him to and from work so that they knew—down to the second—when he got on a bus, when he got off, how long it took him to walk home

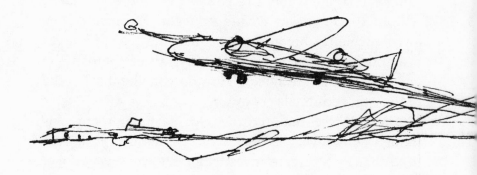

from the bus, and so forth. They decided that when they captured him, the only way to get Eichmann out of Argentina would be by charter plane. It was obvious that neither his family nor the authorities in Argentina must know anything about the kidnapping. The date decided upon was May 11, 1959.

On that day the kidnap car stopped by the side of the main highway which Eichmann had to pass on his way home. One of the Israelis opened the hood of the car as though to fix the engine. The second Israeli was to ask Eichmann a question and then the two of them would overpower him. That was the plan. But when Eichmann appeared, he thrust his hand into his pocket as though he had a gun. The kidnappers were surprised.

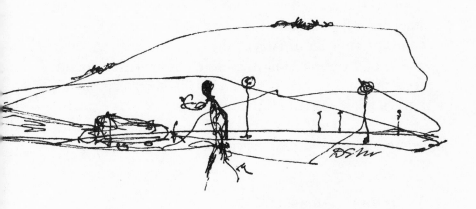

One, who was a judo expert, grabbed Eichmann and tumbled with him into a nearby ditch. Eichmann began screaming. But luck was with the Israelis. No one bothered to stop. Eichmann was bundled into the floor of the car and off they went. The entire kidnapping procedure had taken only 27 seconds. Eichmann was taken to an isolated house which had been selected beforehand. His first words were: "I am Adolf Eichmann and I know I am in the hands of Israelis."

The fifteen-year hunt was over. But Eichmann was still not out of Argentina. On the evening of departure, Eichmann was given drugged coffee. While he slept, they dressed him and took him to the airplane. He appeared to be an elderly, wealthy, but ill traveler. Everything was done to show that this was, indeed, the case. He was brought to the airport in an elegant limousine with a "chauffeur"—one of the Israelis, of course.

On May 23, 1959, a special meeting was called in Israel of the parliament, the *Knesset*. David Ben Gurion, the prime minister of Israel, stood up. He said, "A short time ago, an important Nazi war criminal was found. He is under arrest in Israel and will shortly be put on trial. His name is Adolf Eichmann."

After a long trial in Israel, Eichmann was condemned to die and was executed.

Things to think about

1 The State of Israel has no capital punishment—criminals are not put to death even for the crime of murder. With one exception: A special law was passed so that Nazi war criminals who had been tried and proven guilty of genocide could be executed for their crimes.

Even so, when Eichmann was tried and proved guilty, many felt that he should not be put to death. The subject was widely debated. Which side would you have taken? Here is the subject in the form of a debate question:

> RESOLVED: The Nazi war criminal, Adolf Eichmann, although tried and proved guilty, should not be executed.

2 Eichmann was very loyal to Hitler. At his trial, Eichmann claimed that he was only following orders when he worked on the destruction of the Jews of Europe. Yet the evidence presented by Gideon Hausner, Israel's prosecuting attorney, proved otherwise. In truth, Eichmann often went far beyond the orders of his superiors. Eichmann had become a "fanatic." Look up the word "fanatic" in a dictionary. Can it be good to be a fanatic? When? Are any of the people we have considered in this book fanatics? Which? In what way?

twenty-two

A Unique
World Court

THE NUREMBERG TRIAL

IN the brightly lighted courtroom of the Palace of Justice of Nuremberg, Germany, Lord Justice Geoffrey Lawrence of Great Britain opened the First International Military Tribunal, in the fall of 1945. "The trial which is now about to begin is unique in the history of jurisprudence [system of laws] of the world, and it is of supreme importance to millions of people all over the globe."

Four countries participated in this trial: Great Britain, France, Russia, and the United States. Fifty-two leading judges from these four countries made up the prosecution counsel. (The prosecution is that group which accuses someone of a crime; the defendant is that person or persons being accused of a crime.)

A Unique World Court

Eight men clothed in judge's robes sat on the high bench of the courtroom. Lord Lawrence represented Great Britain; Frances Biddle, the United States; Henri Donnedieu de Vabres, France; and Major General I. T. Nikitchenko, the Soviet Union. There were also four alternate judges, one from each country. Behind this group hung the flags of their nations.

This international court, the first in history, was trying twenty-one men who had occupied important positions in the government of Nazi Germany. These twenty-one men were being tried as major criminals. The proceedings of this trial lasted 216 days and 17,000 pages of testimony were written. No trial in all history ever required such long, involved preparations as this International Military Tribunal.

Nuremberg was chosen as the site of the Tribunal, partly because this ancient city had once been the setting for enormous Nazi rallies. It seemed fitting that the deeds of the Nazis should be revealed here for all the world to hear.

Since the city was practically in ruins, it had to be rebuilt for the trial; the Grand Hotel and the Guest House, Nuremberg's two leading inns, were among the first buildings to be made livable. The judges, attorneys, and others connected with the trial stayed in them.

The courtroom, too, was remodeled. There was room for 250 seats for the press, a gallery to accommodate about one hundred visitors, a glass booth for pho-

tographers, and on one side of the room, a large screen on which films could be shown. It was used frequently.

Everyone present was provided with headsets. Each set had a small dial, like that on a telephone. This allowed the wearer to listen to the trial proceedings which were translated simultaneously in English, Russian, French, or German. This was the most carefully recorded trial of all time. Court reporters and stenographers took careful notes and all proceedings were recorded on tapes and film.

Oddly enough, Germany supplied most of the damning evidence against itself, a complete account of its horrible crimes. Nearly three thousand tons of docu-

A Unique World Court

ments were found written by Nazi leaders. The Germans kept written records of each tiny detail of their beastly crimes. Even 5,000 German photo negatives were found giving pictorial evidence of the Nazis' actions in ghettoizing the Jews, shipping Jews via cattle cars, crowding Jews into concentration and death camps, gassing Jews to death, burning Jewish bodies, and digging mass graves to hide the remains.

The men on trial were allowed to have their own lawyers. They employed 49: forty of their own and nine which were appointed by the court.

Since it was a public trial, news coverage was very important. It was felt that the defendants should not only be brought to justice, but that people all over the world should know the horror of their crimes so that they would never happen again.

The defendants were charged on four counts:

1. A plot to seize power and establish a totalitarian government to rule by force;
2. Crimes against peace;
3. Violation of the laws of war, of international agreements;
4. Crimes against humanity, including use of concentration camps, use of torture, and deliberate murder of civilians.

The Nazis had violated all existing treaties and international law.

Frequently prisoners captured by the Nazis were forced to march until they collapsed. They were stabbed with bayonets, struck with rifle butts, and whipped by sentries. One loaf of bread was distributed to 35 men.

A Unique World Court

American prisoners were starved and beaten. On Christmas 1944 at one concentration camp, prisoners were hung from a lighted Christmas tree. A doctor testified that he had been forced to remove skin from the dead to be used for lampshades.

A new word was invented: genocide, meaning the systematic killing of an entire nation of people. In Maidanek, one concentration camp, about 1,500,000 persons were killed; in Auschwitz about 4,000,000. In Babi Yar, near Kiev, Russia, over 100,000 people were shot.

In the prisoner's dock, Goering, Ribbentrop, and Hess, three of the men on trial, found the proceedings amusing. Their smiles and smirks stopped, though, when a documentary film on Nazi concentration camps as found by American troops was shown: piles of dead . . . the ovens at Buchenwald . . . men in striped prison suits, looking more like skeletons than human beings.

The French prosecution began on January 17:

> France, who was systematically plundered and ruined; France, so many of whose sons were tortured and murdered in the jails of the Gestapo or in their concentration camps . . . asks you above all in the name of the heroic martyrs of the Resistance . . . that justice be done.

On February 8, General Rudenko, of the Soviet Union, began his prosecution:

> When entire regions of flourishing countryside were

201

turned into desert and soil drenched with the blood of those murdered, it was the work of their hands (the defendants). . . . In the name of the sacred memory of millions of innocent victims of the fascist terror . . . may justice be done.

The defense of all the Germans was that they knew nothing of what was going on in the concentration camps. All the defendants lied outrageously.

From beginning to end, the military trials were the subject of much debate and discussion. Some said it would have been better to shoot the war criminals and have it over with. Some judges questioned the legality of this court—could an international court be a true court of law since there was no world state in existence?

However the Nuremberg Trial marked a milestone in legal history. Lieutenant-commander Whitney Harris, of the United States counsel, said: "The most significant thing about Nuremberg is that it happened."

Not one person who can read will ever be able to say that these crimes and atrocities have been exaggerated. They are all on the record—for anyone to read.

Things to think about

1 Most of those on trial at Nuremberg claimed that they were only "following orders." Can a person be excused for doing the wrong thing because he is following orders? In training soldiers for an army, countries very often teach their men to obey orders without question-

From the opening speech presented by Justice Robert
Jackson, chief counsel for the United States of America.
Although the Nuremberg trials were very important, much
of the truth about what happened to the Jews of Europe was
not yet fully realized at the time of the trials. Only later as
all the evidence was pieced together did a full picture emerge,
a full understanding of the Holocaust.

*May it please your Honors, the privilege of opening
the first trial in history for crimes against the peace
of the world imposes a grave responsibility. The
wrongs which we seek to condemn and punish have
been so calculated, so malignant and devastating,
that civilization cannot tolerate their being ignored
because it cannot survive their being repeated.*

ing. Is this possible? Is it right? When must a soldier
think for himself?

2 The trial at Nuremberg was the first of its kind in
world history. The Nazis were charged with crimes
against humanity. In addition to attempting to destroy
the Jewish people, the Nazis had almost totally destroyed
the Gypsies, had attempted to murder all who disagreed
with them politically, and had destroyed or confiscated
personal property and land. But only a few Nazi leaders
were actually tried. Many others who were responsible
escaped without any punishment whatever. Was Nuremberg a fair trial in your opinion?

A Unique World Court

3 The word "genocide" has been used to describe the suffering in Biafra, the slow and methodical murder of blacks in Nigeria, and the terrible treatment of native Indians in some South American countries. How did the Nuremberg trials affect these places? Should trials have been held for those who participated in these wars and persecutions? How did the Nuremberg trials affect the founding of the United Nations? What is the United Nations' stand on genocide? Do you think genocide is really possible today?

Bibliography

~~~~~~

Adon, D. & P.: SEVEN WHO FELL, Palestine Pioneer Library.

Barkai, M.: THE FIGHTING GHETTOS, J. B. Lippincott Company, 1962.

Bauer, Yehuda: FLIGHT AND RESCUE: BRICHA, Random House Inc., 1970.

Bauminger, A.: ROLL OF HONOR, Yad V'Shem, 1970.

Berg, Mary: WARSAW GHETTO, L. B. Fischer, 1945.

CHARLOTTE: A DIARY: Harcourt, Brace & World, 1963.

THE DIARY OF ANNE FRANK, Doubleday & Company, 1952.

Donat, A.: THE HOLOCAUST KINGDOM, Holt, Rinehart and Winston, 1963.

EXTERMINATION AND RESISTANCE, Ghetto Fighters' House, Israel, 1958.

Falstein, L. (ed.): MARTYRDOM OF JEWISH PHYSICIANS IN POLAND, Exposition Press, 1963.

Flender, H.: RESCUE IN DENMARK, Simon and Schuster, Inc., 1963.

Flinker, Moshe: YOUNG MOSHE'S DIARY, Yad V'Shem, 1965.

Friedlander, A.: OUT OF THE WHIRLWIND, Union of American Hebrew Congregations, 1968.

————.: LEO BAECK, TEACHER OF THERESIENSTADT, Holt, Rinehart and Winston, 1968.

Friedman, Tuviah: THE HUNTER, MacFadden Books, 1961.

Glatstein, Knox and Margoshes (eds.): ANTHOLOGY OF HOLOCAUST LITERATURE, Jewish Publication Society, 1968.

Goldstein, Bernard: THE STARS BEAR WITNESS, Viking Press, 1949.

Hausner, Gideon: JUSTICE IN JERUSALEM, Harper, 1968.

Hilberg, R.: DESTRUCTION OF EUROPEAN JEWRY, Quadrangle Books, 1961.

————.: DOCUMENTS OF DESTRUCTION, Quadrangle Books, 1971.

I NEVER SAW ANOTHER BUTTERFLY, McGraw-Hill & Company, 1964.

Kaplan, C.: SCROLL OF AGONY, The Macmillan Company, 1965.

Katz, Robert: DEATH IN ROME, The Macmillan Company, 1967.

————.: BLACK SABBATH, The Macmillan Company, 1969.

Bibliography

Katznelson, Y.: VITTEL DIARY, Ghetto Fighters' House.

Kowalski, I.: A SECRET PRESS IN NAZI EUROPE, Central Guide Publishers, 1969.

Levin, N.: THE HOLOCAUST, Thomas Y. Crowell Company, 1968.

MASSACRE OF EUROPEAN JEWRY, Hashomer Hatzair, 1963.

Meed, Vladka: ON BOTH SIDES OF THE WALL, Workmen's Circle and Ghetto Fighters' Kibbutz, 1973.

Morse, A.: WHILE SIX MILLION DIED, Random House, Inc., 1968.

Ringelblum, E.: NOTES FROM THE WARSAW GHETTO, McGraw-Hill & Company, 1958.

Shabbatai, K.: AS SHEEP TO THE SLAUGHTER? World Federation of Bergen-Belsen Survivors, 1963.

Shirer, William: THE RISE AND FALL OF THE THIRD REICH, Random House, Inc., 1961.

Silverman, Lena Kuchler: ONE HUNDRED CHILDREN, Doubleday & Company, 1961.

Suhl, Yuri: THEY FOUGHT BACK, Crown Publishers, 1967.

Syrkin, Marie: BLESSED IS THE MATCH, Alfred A. Knopf, 1947.

Tenenbaum, J.: UNDERGROUND, Philosophical Library, 1952.

Tushnet, L.: TO DIE WITH HONOR, Citadel Press, 1965.

Trunk, Isaiah: JUDENRAT, The Macmillan Company, 1972.

Unsdorfer, S. D.: THE YELLOW STAR, Thomas Yoseloff, 1961.

Yad V'Shem: JEWISH RESISTANCE DURING THE HOLOCAUST, 1968.

Yahill, L.: RESCUE OF DANISH JEWRY, Jewish Publication Society, 1969.

Magazines and Articles

Bloom, Sol, "Director of the Lodz Ghetto," in N. Podhoretz (ed.), *The Commentary Reader*, Atheneum, 1966.

Brody, R., "Six Million and Two," *Reconstructionist Magazine*.

Bibliography

Grossman, C., "Revolt in the Ghetto," *Youth and Nation*, March–April 1951.

——., "Mordecai Anilewitz," *Youth and Nation*, April 1951.

Handlin, O., "Jewish Resistance to the Nazis," *American Jewish Historical Quarterly*, January 1969.

"Impact of the Holocaust," *Jewish Digest*, Educational Series.

Jewish Heritage, Entire issue, Spring 1968.

Jewish Heritage, Summer 1965.

Klein, S., "Ghetto of Piotrkow in the Holocaust," *Jerusalem Post*, April 1969.

Knox, Israel, "The Valiant Ones," Workmen's Circle *Call*, March 1968.

Oleiski, J., "The Kovno Ghetto," *ORT Reporter*, March/April, 1971.

Shamir, Y., "Commander of the Ghetto Revolt," *Youth and Nation*, June 1946.

Yad V'Shem Studies, 1957–1967.

Yad V'Shem Bulletins, 1962–1968.

Sources

The author and publisher would like to acknowledge and indicate the sources of the documents used in The Holocaust:

In Chapter 1, Houghton Mifflin Company for Ralph Manheim, tr., Adolf Hitler, *Mein Kampf*, 1943, page 285.

In Chapters 2, 3, and 5, Bantam Books for Susan Sweet, tr., Gerhard Schoenberner, *The Yellow Star*, 1969, pages 20, 148, and 41.

In Chapters 4 and 22, Harper and Brothers, Harwood L. Childs, tr., *The Nazi Primer*, 1938, page 13, and Gideon Hausner, *Justice in Jerusalem*, 1968.

In Chapters 6, 7, 11, and 14, *Yad Vashem Studies*, Volumes VI, VII, III, and VII, 1967, 1968 and 1959, pages 132–133, 177 [from Ringelblum's unpublished notes, dated June 1942], 293, and 123.

In Chapters 8 and 10, World Hashomer Hatzair, *The Massacre of European Jewry*, 1963, pages 198–99 and 175 ["Januscz Korczak's Last Walk," by Hanna Morkowicz-Olczakowa].

In Chapters 9 and 13, Central Guide Publishers, E. Zweig, tr., Isaac Kowalski, *A Secret Press in Nazi Europe*, 1969, pages 104–05.

In Chapters 12 and 19, *Yad Vashem Bulletin*, Numbers 22 and 13, May 1968 and October 1963, pages 37 and 69.

In Chapters 15 and 21, McGraw-Hill, Inc., Jacob Sloan, ed., Emanuel Ringelblum, *Notes from the Warsaw Ghetto*, 1958, page 154, and Joseph Wechsberg, tr., Simon Wiesenthal, *The Murderers Among Us*, 1967, page 96.

In Chapter 16, Jewish Publication Society, Morris Gradel, tr., Leni Yahill, *The Rescue of Danish Jewry*, 1969, page 229.

In Chapter 17, Ghetto Fighter's House, *Extermination and Resistance*, 1958, page 178.

209

Sources

In Chapter 18, *Statement*, 10 November, 1964. [*Kristallnacht* occurred in Austria on November 10 instead of November 9.]

In Chapter 20, Herzl Press, Chasya Pincus, *Come from the Four Winds*, 1970, page 50.

THE POTATO
Evolution, Biodiversity and
Genetic Resources

THE POTATO
Evolution, Biodiversity and Genetic Resources

J.G. HAWKES

Smithsonian Institution Press
Washington, D.C.

First published in the United States in 1990 by
Smithsonian Institution Press

Library of Congress Catalog Number
  89-63527

ISBN 0-87474-465-2

CONTENTS

PREFACE

Breeders and other scientists who work on potatoes have generally found the diversity of related wild species both puzzling and frustrating. The diversity of the cultivated South American potatoes is also not very easy to understand.

Why should this be? Is it due to the perversity of taxonomists who insist on recognizing too many small species, when fewer larger ones might be simpler; or is there something intrinsically difficult in the group itself? The answer on the whole lies in the latter explanation. The species seem to be young, actively evolving and with rather imprecise boundaries between them, as will be shown more clearly in Chapter 5.

There is no doubt that potatoes are unique among crop plants in possessing a very large range of biological diversity *outside* the crop itself. Not even wheat, sweet potatoes or yams (*Dioscorea*) can approach the potato in this respect.

In order to help potato researchers to understand and utilize their materials more effectively, I was asked some 35 years ago by Dr J.W. Gregor, Director of the Scottish Plant Breeding Station at Edinburgh, to write a simplified 'Revision of the Tuber-bearing Solanums'. I agreed to do this, and published the first edition in 1956 as an occasional paper in the Annual Report of the Scottish Plant Breeding Station for that year.

In that first edition I tried to justify (as I shall do in the present one) the need for bringing together information from descriptions in often very obscure journals and making decisions on species that had often been described as distinct when really they were merely forms of previously established ones. I also included keys for identification and short descriptions.

The work was well received and I was encouraged to write a second edition in 1963 in Dr Gregor's new series entitled the Scottish Plant Breeding Station Record. This new edition was needed in that I had meanwhile collected and studied wild potatoes in the USA, Mexico and Central America in 1958 and had begun to understand much more clearly the eco-geographical patterns of diversity than I did in 1956. I had also been studying and collecting the wild species of Argentina and neighbouring countries in collaboration with J.P. Hjerting of Copenhagen. This, also, gave me greater insight into taxonomic problems.

Meanwhile D.S. Correll had published his very fine monograph of the whole group in 1962 and I was thus able to incorporate his results into my second edition, as well as those of C.M. Ochoa, who monographed the Peruvian species in the same year.

There has unfortunately been a very large gap between the second and third editions; yet much has been accomplished in that period. Thus, my colleague J.P. Hjerting and I have studied, collected and monographed the potatoes of Argentina, Bolivia, Brazil, Paraguay and Uruguay (Hawkes and Hjerting 1969, 1989). I have gained a greater insight into the potatoes of Peru and Mexico, and my colleague C.M. Ochoa has described very many new species in South America, particularly from his native country, Peru.

The foundation of the International Potato Center (CIP) at Lima, Peru in 1972 has widened the perspective of all potato scientists and shown us a very great deal more of the diversity of wild and cultivated potatoes than was ever before realized. Many germplasm collecting expeditions have been supported by CIP, thus helping us to understand much more clearly the nature of many of the wild potatoes about which we formerly knew very little.

To conclude this Preface I should like to thank the CIP Director, Richard L. Sawyer, and many of his staff for the study facilities made available to me at CIP, particularly concerning the living collections of cultivated potatoes at the Huancayo field station.

I am also most grateful to Roger Rowe and Robert Hanneman (former Directors) and John Bamberg (present Director) of the Potato Introduction Station at Sturgeon Bay, Wisconsin, USA, for inviting me to work there on many occasions. My thanks also go to other staff members, particularly Roman Ross, David Spooner and Jean Smejkal for their invaluable help during my visits.

Thanks are due also to the Directors and Curators of the many herbaria who provided facilities for study and sent specimens on loan, particularly the Royal Botanic Gardens, Kew, the British Museum, the US National Herbarium at Washington, the Missouri Botanical Garden at St Louis, and the Botanical Garden at Copenhagen. I also wish to express my thanks to Jean Dowling for drawing Figs 1.3 and 1.4, and to Carl Burness for drawing Figs 1.1, 1.2, 5.2 and 5.3.

Finally, my grateful thanks go to J.P. Hjerting for checking the text, and particularly the taxonomic section (Chapter 6); to Mrs Janet Jones for typing the Glossary and the Bibliography; and to my secretary, Lucille Francois, for her patience in setting the whole of the rest of the text on to a word processor.

J.G. Hawkes
Birmingham, 1989

INTRODUCTION

The potato as a world crop

It may come as a surprise to many people to learn that the potato is very widely grown on a world scale and ranks fourth in food production, following wheat, maize and rice (Table 1.1). Of the root crops it easily tops the list, followed by cassava, sweet potatoes and yams in that order. It is also interesting to note that world potato production exceeds that of many cereals, such as barley, sorghum, millets, rye and oats.

The greatest potato production per country is in the USSR (73,000 kilotonnes). This is followed by China (45,528 kt), Poland (36,546 kt), USA (18,331 kt), India (12,642 kt), and the German Democratic Republic (11,500 kt), with the Federal Republic of Germany, France and the UK fluctuating around 7,000–8,000 kt (FAO, 1985). It should be noted that only one of the large producers is a developing country – India. Nevertheless, the potato is being adopted more and more in developing countries, as reports from the International Potato Center (CIP) show. In fact, CIP is breeding potatoes specially for countries in the humid tropics because of the interest shown in this crop for such conditions.

Although the potato can compete favourably with wheat, maize and rice in terms of total production, in protein content it does not do so well. Nevertheless, in terms of production value per hectare per day in developing countries, the potato does better than rice and wheat for edible energy and is only a little way behind wheat for edible protein, as shown in Table 1.2.

As principal food crops the potato and the sweet potato perform remarkably well in total production value in developing countries, though in this they lag considerably behind rice and wheat, but less so behind maize (Table 1.3).

Thus, potatoes are clearly a crop of considerable world importance, fourth in world production and of high nutritive value.

Table 1.1 World production of major
starch crops (cereals and tubers) for
1985 in metric tons (000)

Wheat	510,029
Maize	490,155
Rice	465,970
Potato	299,132
Barley	178,004
Cassava	136,532
Sweet potato	111,438
Sorghum	77,452
Millets	31,559
Rye	29,567
Yams	25,860
Oats	25,747

(FAO Production Yearbook **39**, 1985.)

Table 1.2 The ten food crops with the highest production value per hectare per
day in developing countries

Crop	Growth duration (days)	Dry matter (kg/ha/ day)	Edible energy (000 kcal/ ha/day)	Edible protein (kg/ha/ day)	Production value $/ha/day
Cabbages	110	12	29	1.6	27.50
Tomatoes	125	8	25	1.3	25.30
Potatoes	130	18	54	1.5	12.60
Yams	180	14	47	1.0	8.80
Sweet potatoes	180	22	70	1.0	6.70
Rice, paddy	145	18	49	0.9	3.40
Groundnuts in shell	115	8	36	1.7	2.60
Wheat	115	14	40	1.6	2.30
Lentils	105	6	23	1.6	2.30
Cassava	272	13	27	0.1	2.20

(From D.E. Horton, *SPAN* **30**(3), 116.)

Solanaceae relatives

The potato that we know as an important world crop is a single species,
Solanum tuberosum, belonging to the plant family Solanaceae. Other well-
known crops in that family are the tomato (*Lycopersicon esculentum*), the
egg-plant (*S. melongena*), various species of chili peppers (*Capsicum*) and
tobacco (*Nicotiana tabacum*). Many alkaloid drug plants belong here also,

Table 1.3 Value of production of ten principal food crops in all developing countries

	Number of producing countries	Production metric tons (000,000)	Producer price ($/t)	Value (billion $)
Rice	97	383	170	65
Wheat	69	162	148	24
Maize	119	154	119	18
Potatoes	95	91	142	13
Sweet potatoes	100	137	89	12
Cassava	95	127	70	9
Bananas and plantains	119	62	107	7
Sorghum	69	44	123	5
Groundnuts	92	17	297	5
Millets	53	27	144	4

(From D.E. Horton and H. Fano, *Potato Atlas*, CIP, 1985.)

such as *Atropa, Hyoscyamus, Scopolia* and *Mandragora*; and ornamentals in the genera *Petunia, Nicotiana* and *Schizanthus*. Finally, there is a whole range of tropical fruits such as pepino (*S. muricatum*), lulu or naranjilla (*S. quitoense*), tree tomato (*Cyphomandra betacea*) and husk tomato (*Physalis* species).

Cultivated potato species

Seven cultivated species of the potato are now recognized, occurring in a range of chromosome numbers, from 24 (diploid), 36 (triploid), 48 (tetraploid) to 60 (pentaploid). These are shown in Appendix II and will be discussed in more detail in Chapter 4. *Solanum tuberosum* is tetraploid, and as we mentioned above, has a world-wide distribution in the form of its subspecies *tuberosum*. It has another subspecies, *andigena*, cultivated in the Andes of South America, whilst subspecies *tuberosum* has also been grown in southern Chile, probably for several millenia. The other cultivated potatoes (diploids, triploids and pentaploids) are restricted to the high Andes of an area stretching approximately from central Peru to central Bolivia. One of the diploids, *S. phureja*, proves the exception to this rule, and it spread even in pre-Spanish days northwards from central Peru to Ecuador, Colombia and Venezuela (see Figs 1.1 and 1.2). All these species, and particularly *S. tuberosum* subsp. *andigena*, occur in a vast range of forms, with a diversity of flower colours and tuber shapes, colours and patterning vastly greater than those of the common potato, *S. tuberosum* subsp. *tuberosum*, in Europe, North America and elsewhere (other than South America).

Fig. 1.1 Distribution of diploid cultivated potato species.

○ S. tuberosum subsp. *tuberosum*   ⬭ S. tuberosum subsp. *andigena*

○ S. chaucha, S. juzepczukii, S. curtilobum

Fig. 1.2 Distribution of triploid, tetraploid and pentaploid cultivated potato species.

Wild potato species

The biological diversity of potatoes is not by any means confined to the cultivated species. Related to them are many highly complex groups of wild species, a few of which gave rise to the cultivated ones, as we shall see in Chapters 5 and 6. It seems certain, in fact, that the potato possesses more related wild species than any other crop plant. Thus 235 species are now recognized, of which seven are cultivated and 228 are wild.

These wild species, which, together with the cultivated ones, are described in detail in Chapter 6, are very widely distributed through much of the

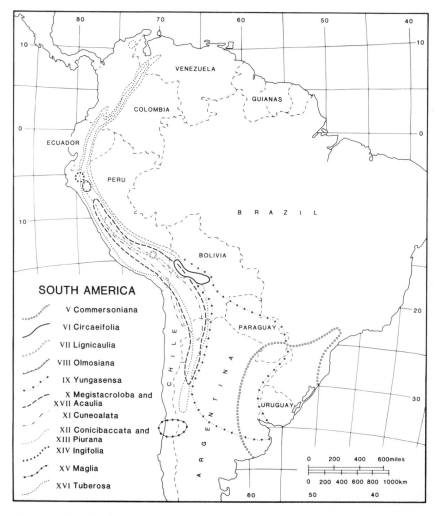

Fig. 1.3 Distribution of wild potato series in South America.

Americas, from south-west USA (states of Nebraska, Colorado, Utah, Arizona, New Mexico and Texas), into nearly every state of Mexico and thence to Guatemala, Honduras, Costa Rica and Panamá. In South America they occur in every country apart from the Guianas, but are chiefly found in the Andes of Venezuela, Colombia, Ecuador, Peru, Bolivia and Argentina. They also occur on the Peruvian desert coast, in central to southern Chile, on the plains of Argentina, Paraguay and Uruguay, and also in south-east Brazil. Two clear centres of diversity can be recognized: one in central Mexico and the second in the high Andes from Peru through Bolivia to north-west Argentina (Figs 1.3, 1.4).

No single wild potato species extends throughout the total geographical area described above, but some are remarkably widespread, such as *S. colombianum*, *S. acaule* and *S. chacoense*. Other species may be restricted to limited areas and ecological zones.

Wild potato diversity

The wide geographical distribution of wild potatoes indicates a wide range of ecological diversity and thus a range of adaptation to extremes of temperature and humidity far surpassing that of the cultivated species. Thus some species, such as *S. acaule* and *S. megistacrolobum*, can withstand sub-zero temperatures; others, such as *S. berthaultii*, *S. neocardenasii* and *S. gracilifrons* are adapted to hot, dry, semi-desert conditions; yet others grow in subtropical to temperate mountain rain forest with very high humidity. In Mexico and the USA many species inhabit pine and fir (*Abies*) forests, whilst pine-oak forest is a common wild potato habitat in Mexico. In South America, where pines are not native, potatoes are often found in *Podocarpus-Alnus* woodlands. Lower down, other species inhabit *Prosopis* summer-green woodland and in drier habitats are found among opuntias and columnar cacti.

Medium altitude habitats are commonly adopted in Mexico and the USA where scrub pine and Juniper are common and in seasonally dry regions of cactus and drought-resistant shrubs.

In the Andes of South America very high altitude species are encountered, in regions from 3,500–4,500 m or more, on the windswept drier puna vegetation to the south of central Peru and the jalca or páramo vegetation from northern Peru into Ecuador and Colombia. In fact, apart from the lowland tropical rain forest, wild potato species seem to have penetrated into nearly every natural habitat and a number of artificial or man-made habitats also. Thus many, such as *S. sparsipilum* and *S. chacoense*, are commonly found in cultivated fields. Perhaps the most curious wild potato of all, though, is the normally epiphytic *S. morelliforme*, which selects mossy branches of oak trees as its natural habitat.

In addition to the physiological diversity of wild potatoes from an ecological and phytogeographical viewpoint, wild potatoes exhibit a wide diversity of resistance to fungal, bacterial and virus diseases, as well as to insect, arachnid and nematode pests (see Chapter 7 and Hawkes and

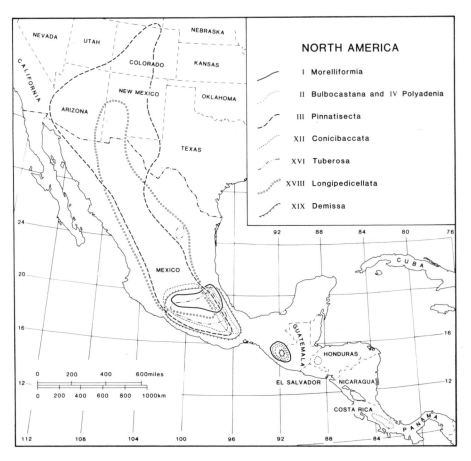

Fig. 1.4 Distribution of wild potato series in North and Central America.

Hjerting 1969, 1989). Some also possess high dry-matter content in the tubers, though most have watery tubers that often contain unacceptably high alkaloid contents. Wild potatoes are sometimes eaten by Indians when no other food is available, but do not generally form a regular article of diet except for a much esteemed Mexican potato (*S. cardiophyllum* subsp. *ehrenbergii*) that commands a higher price per unit of weight than the cultivated potato itself.

In their morphology, many wild potatoes resemble a small and more delicate version of the cultivated potato. Indeed, they were often considered as naturalized escapes from cultivation, or even if truly wild were sometimes thought of as belonging to the same species as the cultivated ones. Yet many are completely distinct, such as the simple-leaved *S. morelliforme*, *S. clarum* and *S. bulbocastanum* from Mexico, which lack the divided leaf typical of the cultivated and many wild species. Others possess very narrow leaflets or leaf lobes (*S. gracilifrons*, *S. infundibuliforme*, etc.), whilst yet others have large terminal leaflets and much smaller lateral ones (*S. microdontum*, etc.). Although the corolla of the cultivated potatoes is rotate (wheel-shaped) or pentagonal, many wild species possess stellate (star-shaped) corollas. Most possess globular berries but some have long conical ones. The variety seems to be endless.

This morphological diversity, whilst interesting as such, especially to the taxonomist, is far outweighed by the potential economic importance of this group in providing useful characters of interest to potato breeders (Chapter 7). Thus the knowledge of such characters in certain species, or the hope that useful features might be found in hitherto almost unknown species, has been a great incentive to their exploration and collection in the form of tubers and seeds. A study of living collections has helped to unravel relationships by means of cytological and crossability investigations (Chapter 4), thus leading to some general ideas on their evolution (Chapter 5), and to the origin and evolution of the cultivated potatoes themselves.

Potato pre-history and introduction into Europe

Biological data give us considerable understanding as to the ancestry and place of origin of the potato as a cultivated plant, but tell us little about the time at which it was cultivated and the extent to which it spread. These matters are discussed in Chapter 2, going back in time through Peruvian coastal ceramic cultures, into the pre-ceramic period as far ago as 7000 BP (before present).

As most people know, the New World was not discovered until 1492, and Columbus began by making landfall on certain Caribbean Islands, believing that he had arrived at the East Indies. Hence the general name of 'Indians' for the original inhabitants of North and South America. Mexico was conquered by Cortés in 1519, but no cultivated potatoes existed there, and although plenty of wild species grew in Mexico they seem to have been of no interest to the Aztecs or any of the other indigenous peoples of that country. Similarly, what is now Brazil was an area without cultivated potatoes, and the wild species were found only in the south-eastern region.

Pizarro and his men were probably the first Spaniards actually to see potatoes when they climbed up to Cajamarca in what is now northern Peru. This was in 1533, the year that the conquest of the Incas was effected. Alas, no written records of potato sightings exist for that expedition.

Spanish exploration in the Andes of Colombia gives the date of 1537 for a first recorded sighting (Castellanos 1886), whilst wild potatoes were first mentioned by Cobo (1890, written 1650) (see Chapter 2).

By great misfortune, we have no contemporary account of the introduction of the potato into Europe. Nevertheless, there is much information on its progress through Europe in the late sixteenth and early seventeenth centuries, and an account of this is given in Chapter 3, showing early illustrations and indicating also its spread to other parts of the world.

THE ORIGIN AND FIRST HOME OF THE POTATO

Ancient origins

The potato is one of mankind's ancient cultivated plants. It is undoubtedly of New World origin, having been brought to Europe in the late sixteenth century some years after the discovery and conquest of Peru. Some controversy still exists as to whether there was a single area of domestication in the central Andes or whether there was a second independent one in Chile. At one time Virginia in North America was a strong contender for the honour of being the original home of the potato, but this hypothesis is no longer acceptable.

At the time of the Spanish conquest of the Americas contemporary accounts attest to the fact that the potato was widely distributed throughout the Andes, from Colombia to Peru and also in southern Chile. We shall deal with the evidence for this later, but it should be mentioned that indigenous potatoes are grown in the Andes at very high altitudes (*c.* 2,800–4,500 m), and can be grown at or near sea level only in southern Chile where the cool, temperate climate echoes the cold windswept valleys and plateaux of the high Andes.

Archaeologists and art historians have long been amazed at the fine artistic ability and wide variety of design of the peoples who inhabited the river oases of the Peruvian coastal deserts. The ceramics, textile weaving and jewellery were outstanding. No less worthy of comment is the extraordinary agricultural development in the Peruvian highlands. The terraces on which the inhabitants must have grown their crops of maize, potatoes and other food plant are most spectacular, built frequently of dressed stone, finished to a high degree of perfection (Fig. 2.1).

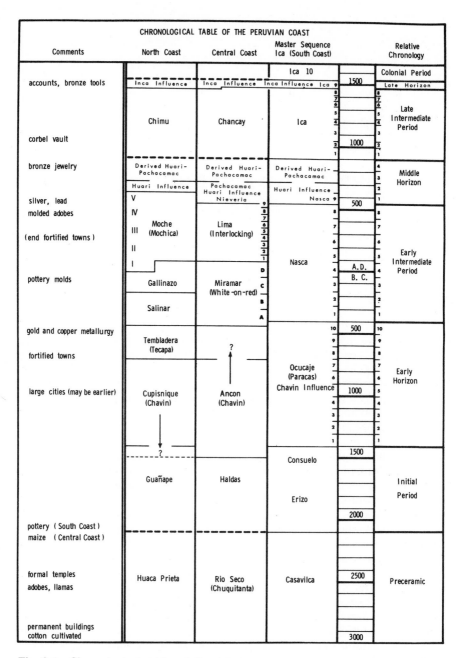

Fig. 2.1 Chronological table of Peruvian coastal cultures. (From Rowe and Menzel (1967) reproduced by kind permission of the authors and Peek Publications, Palo Alto, California, USA.)

Ceramics

The ceramics of the peoples who inhabited the river oases of the Peruvian coastal deserts have been retrieved from burial sites where the mummified bodies were interred, with earthenware, textiles and metal work. The Moche peoples in the north (*c.* AD 1–600) and the Nazca peoples in the south (*c.* 400 BC to AD 550), both of the Early Intermediate Period, as well as the northern Chimu peoples (*c.* AD 900–1450) of the Late Intermediate Period (Fig. 2.1), created large quantities of ceramics, often modelled and painted, in the form of many species of animals, fish, birds and food plants. Natural objects, as well as various kinds of human activities were also shown, such as battle scenes and farming processes. Human beings with apparent diseases or mutilations of the nose and mouth, or lacking parts of their limbs, were sometimes depicted. In certain pots, plant motifs were combined with human or animal heads or bodies. This sort of combination of humans and potatoes attracted the attention of R.N. Salaman (1939, 1949), who was particularly interested in vessels depicting potato tubers and facial mutilations. Salaman thought that, in the human/potato pot, because the cutting back of the lips enlarged the mouth and brought the teeth into prominence, this could be likened to potato eyes with large sprouts. This, by sympathetic magic, would be expected to ensure a larger yield, and so, in Salaman's words: 'The god [was] both strengthened and instructed, and the people eventually saved.'

Salaman had supposed that very large numbers of potato pots were made, but this is not so. In fact, they are quite uncommon. Also, not more than one or two vessels exhibited facial mutilations combined with potato tubers (Fig. 2.2). In nearly all cases they appeared quite separately. It thus seems that Salaman's hypothesis is almost certainly unsustainable. Mutilations may have been some form of punishment or an attempt to cure a particular disease; and the potters, who seemed to have copied everything around them, copied these too. They were also given to flights of fancy, combining human, animal and bird features in various combinations.

Potato pots were rare, as we have said. This was possibly due to the fact that the Peruvian coast where nearly all this pottery was made is extremely warm, too hot for potato cultivation. The coastal peoples must therefore have obtained tubers by trade with highland tribes in the Andes nearby. It seems rather unlikely therefore that they would have practised a form of sympathetic magic on a crop which they did not in fact cultivate.

The really interesting vessels (Figs 2.3–2.5), which we have been discussing above, are all Moche culture from the northern Peruvian coast. The more or less contemporaneous Nazca culture from the southern coast and the later Chancay from the central coast (*c.* AD 900–1500) showed no representation of potatoes.

The one notable exception to the lack of potato representations in the ceramics of the southern Peruvian coast is a series of ceremonial urns of Huari or Pacheco style (Middle Horizon), dated to about AD 650–700, from the Nazca valley. These were about 3 ft (0.9 m) high and had apparently contained offerings of food, having later been broken

Fig. 2.2 Moche pot conbining human and potato themes, the human nose and mouth showing mutilations. The potato seems to be sprouting and the human hand is holding a digging stick. (Negative: R.N. Salaman collection.)

ceremonially before being buried. Figure 2.6 shows a part of one of these urns depicting a potato plant with stems, leaves, stolons, and tubers.

Certain of these urns depict deities or cult figures, holding what may be ceremonial staffs of office. At the ends of these staffs plant motifs are often depicted, or heads of snakes or condors. However, Christiansen (1967) claimed to have found such a figure holding branches, on which flowers were shown above and potato tubers below. This figure he called the 'God

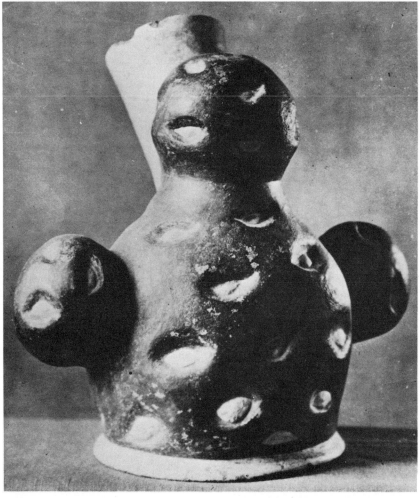

Fig. 2.3 Moche potato pot showing the stylized attributes of a human figure. (Courtesy of the National Anthropological and Archaeological Museum, Lima, Peru.)

Fig. 2.4   Moche potato pot from Trujillo, Peru. (Photo: J. Bryan.)

of the Potato Harvest'. It has been adopted as a logo by the International Potato Center (CIP 1973). Unfortunately, no one but Christiansen has been able to find the original on which he bases his assertion.

Potato vessels were also made by the Chimu peoples on the north coast much later than Moche (Fig. 2.7), but were not of such great interest as the latter. They continued to make such pottery after the Inca conquest, the vessels changing again and becoming generally known by archaeologists as Chimu-Inca (Fig. 2.8).

Plant remains

None of the potato ceramics date back with certainty to before the Christian era. To find earlier evidence we must go back to excavated food plant remains, either from graves and food stores or from rubbish heaps. The materials were often preserved in the form of freeze-dried potatoes, known as chuño, or as partly cooked remains discarded in rubbish heaps. The freeze-dried method of chuño production can only be carried out on the high, cold mountains, but the process is very ancient, was known to the Moche peoples (Fig. 2.9), and has carried on to the present day.

Fig. 2.5 Moche potato pot combined with a human figure. Note that a face is also discernible by reversing the picture. (Courtesy of the National Anthropological and Archaeological Museum, Lima, Peru.)

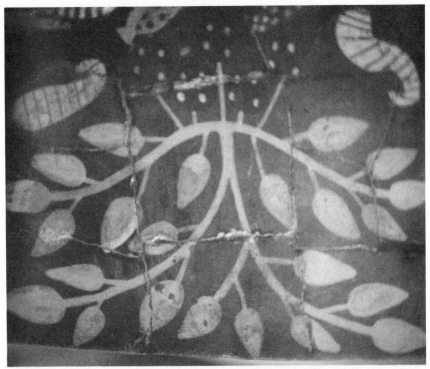

Fig. 2.6 A potato plant with leaves, stems, stolons, and tubers shown on a Huari urn, Robles Mojo style (Middle Horizon). (Photo: Carlos Arbizu.)

Ancient food remains from Ancón-Chillón, just north of Lima, were excavated by Moseley (1975) and examined by Martins-Farias (1976) by phase-contrast and scanning electron microscopy (SEM). Potatoes, manioc and sweet potatoes were established for 4500 BP. Martins-Farias also examined materials excavated by Engel (Engel 1970a, 1970b, 1984) from the high Chilca canyon, south of Lima. Although dated from context materials by Engel at probably 10000 BP, recent verification by the Oxford Radiocarbon Accelerator dated the actual tubers to about 7000 BP. Potato remains have also been mentioned by Ugent *et al.* (1982) for Casma on the north coast, dated between 4000 BP and 3500 BP, using phase contrast and SEM techniques. These materials from all the reported sites would be pre-ceramic, and we therefore must conclude that the potatoes were baked or cooked in an earth oven on hot stones, possibly even cooked in gourds, though this seems less likely. Ugent *et al.* also report (1987) wild potato remains from southern Chile, dated to 13000 BP, long before the beginnings of agriculture. Ugent equates these with the wild potato *S. maglia*, but this is impossible, since *S. maglia* does not occur anywhere near the site described, but is confined to the region of Valparaiso, 600 miles to the north and in a completely different phytogeographical zone. Nevertheless,

Fig. 2.7 Chimu (or Chimu-Inca) black-ware potato pot. (Photo: R.N. Salaman collection.)

Fig. 2.8 Chimu-Inca double whistling potato pot, with a small figure of (possibly) a potter on the left-hand spout. (Photo: J.G.H.)

it is certain that some sort of wild potato was being eaten at that time. However, although several of the older authors confused *S. maglia* with *S. tuberosum*, these two species have been latterly considered as quite distinct, except by Ugent himself (Ugent *et al.* 1987).

To sum up the preceding paragraphs, we can see clearly that the potato is an ancient domesticate, having been cultivated from at least 7000 BP, and preserved at various sites on the coast of Peru. The lack of cultivation evidence in highland sites, apart from the Engel material at 7000 BP, probably indicates merely that preservation conditions were in general not appropriate in such high, wet regions, whilst on the desert coast preservation conditions were ideal. Ceramics also indicate that the potato was widely known from the beginning of the Christian era, as we have seen.

Historical accounts

Evidence of the potato in historical records from the time of the conquest is quite frequent, though it is difficult to know which of the Spanish Conquerors was the first to see the potato. However, in 1536 an expedition led

Fig. 2.9 Moche pot representing two tubers of Tunta (a type of chuño). (Negative: R.N. Salaman collection.)

by Jiménez de Quesada set out southwards from Santa Marta on the Caribbean coast of what is now Colombia. In 1537 they climbed up the valley of the Opón river out of the valley of the Río Magdalena. Here, in the Valle de la Grita in the modern province of Vélez, they saw potatoes. This first recorded glimpse of such an important crop was written down by a companion of Quesada's. The best account known to us, however, is by Juan de Catellanos (Elegías) finished in 1601 but not published until 1886, and written at second hand. The account is a good one and is worth quoting (my translation – Hawkes, 1967).

The houses [of the Indians] were all stocked with maize, beans and truffles [= potatoes], spherical roots which are sown and produce a stem with its branches and leaves, and some flowers, although few, of a soft purple colour; and to the roots of this same plant, which is about 3 palms high [= 60 cm], they are attached under the earth, and are the size of an egg more or less, some round and some elongated; they are white and purple and yellow, floury roots of good flavour, a delicacy to the Indians and a dainty dish even for the Spaniards.

Another good description, and better known than the Castellanos one, was that of Pedro Cieza de León, who was in the region of Pasto and Popayán, in the south of the modern state of Colombia, and also at Quito, the capital of the present Ecuador. Cieza's book was first published in Seville in 1553, but his description is not so detailed as that of Castellanos:

Of provisions, besides maize, there are two other products which form the principal food of these Indians. One is called potato, and is a kind of earth nut, which, after it has been boiled, is as tender as a cooked chestnut, but it has no more skin than a truffle, and it grows under the earth in the same way. (Translation by Sir Clements Markham.)

The honour of publishing the first account of the potato, however, goes to Francisco López de Gómara, who in 1552 published his *Historia General de las Indias*. Speaking of the high regions of southern Peru, then known as the Collao and including parts of what is now included in Bolivia, he states: 'Men live in the Collao for a hundred years or more; they lack maize and eat certain roots similar to truffles which they call papas.'

Many other early accounts of the potato are known, especially that of José de Acosta (1590) who speaks about the dried potato product, chuño, referred to above.

The potato in Chile was not known to Europeans until after its discovery in 1535. Chile was conquered many years after this and the first mention is by Sir Francis Drake who records that he obtained potatoes by barter from the Indians of the island of Moche (off the Chilean coast at about latitude 38°S) in 1578, during his voyage round the world (Drake, 1628). These potatoes, incidentally, could not have been the ones introduced into Europe at about that time, since Drake did not return until 1580, by which time the tubers would certainly have died.

Agricultural practices involving the potato were not dealt with in any detail by the chroniclers with one notable exception. This was Felipe Guamán Poma de Ayala, who wrote a curiously naïve but remarkably compelling work from 1583 to 1613, entitled 'Neuva corónica y buen

11043V

TRAVAXA
HAILLI CHACRAIAPVIC VI

pacha · agosto yapuy quilla

labrador

ayau hay lli yau ayau hay llivau
ayau hay lli yau ayau hay lliyau
chaymi ya chaymi palli

ahaylli

ahaylli

agosto — hacra yapuy
agosto

Fig. 2.10 Foot-ploughing in ancient Peru at the time of the Spanish conquest.
(Felipe Guamán Poma de Ayala (1936); late sixteenth to early seventeenth century
manuscript, reproduced by kind permission of the Institut d'Ethnologie, Paris.)

Fig. 2.11 Digging with a foot-plough and planting potato tubers, December. (Source as for Fig. 2.10.)

1099

Fig. 2.12 Potatoes and maize being not very well guarded from thieves, February. (Source as for Fig. 2.10.)

Fig. 2.13 Potato harvesting with foot-plough and hoe, June. (Source as for Fig. 2.10.)

gobierno' on the Incas and their history and customs. This was never published by the author and lies at present in the Royal Library at Copenhagen. A facsimile edition was published by P. Rivet in 1936.

Poma de Ayala's pictures of foot-ploughing, potato planting, cultivation and harvesting are shown in Figs 2.10 to 2.13.

Inca keros

Yet another point is worth mentioning before we leave the potato in its native land. This concerns some immediately post-conquest depiction of potatoes and other plants on the traditional Inca lacquered wooden beakers or 'keros'. Pre-conquest keros were decorated mostly with geometrical patterns, whilst rather later, when Spanish rule had been well established, the keros bore obviously Spanish motifs. For a short period they were ornamented with personages and flowers, most of which can be easily identified (Vargas, 1981). One particular kero is outstanding – the so-called 'great kero' of Cuzco. Two panels are of particular interest here. The first shows potato cultural practices and the usual libations of chicha (maize beer) during agricultural ceremonies (Fig. 2.14). The second shows

Fig. 2.14   Great Kero, Cuzco. Potato cultural practices on the left; two types of pepper on the right. (Photo: C. Vargas.)

Fig. 2.15 Great Kero, Cuzco. *Oxalis tuberosa* and potato plants in the centre. *Ullucus tuberosus* on the right. The *Oxalis* and *Ullucus* are also domesticated Andean tuber plants. (Photo: C. Vargas.)

an actual potato plant with tubers, and above it a plant of *Oxalis tuberosa* or 'Oca' (Fig. 2.15).

Potato names

To sum up this chapter, we can see clearly that the potato was a very widespread crop in the Andes and in Chile at the time of the Spanish discovery and conquest. Further information on native names bears this out. In Colombia the name for the potato in the now dead Chibcha language was *Iomza*, *Iomy* or *Iomuy*; in Quechua, the language of the Incas, it was *Papa*, a name now spread by the Spaniards throughout the Spanish-speaking regions, but not in Europe; in Aymará, in the region of Lake Titicaca and La Paz it was *Amka* or *Choque*; and in the Araucanian language of southern Chile it was *Poñi*. Other names used by tribes conquered by the Incas are also known (Hawkes 1967). Such a range of distinct words argue strongly for a very ancient origin and wide distribution in South America. In Central America and Mexico, although wild species are native to these regions, the cultivated potato seems to have been a comparatively recent, post-Columbian, introduction.

THE SPREAD OF THE POTATO ROUND THE WORLD

Early introduction

It is a generally accepted fact that the potato arrived in Europe some time towards the end of the sixteenth century. Nevertheless, the exact time of its introduction and the details of its arrival remain obscure and will probably never be fully elucidated.

We know that neither Raleigh nor Drake brought the potato to Europe, but these legends die hard and are still quoted, since we have no name to put in their place. Raleigh saw potatoes off the coast of Venezuela but these were undoubtedly sweet potatoes, and even if they had not been, there is no evidence that Raleigh brought potatoes to England. Raleigh *may* have been instrumental in potatoes being taken to Ireland in the mid-seventeenth century, as Sir Robert Southwell (1693) indicated when President of the Royal Society: 'The President related that his Grandfather brought potatoes into Ireland who had them from Sir Walter Rawleigh after his return from Virginia.'

This statement is evidently the beginning of the Raleigh legend, but it clearly does *not* say that Raleigh had brought potatoes from Virginia, only that he had given them to Southwell's grandfather (see Salaman 1985, 153–8). In fact, as Salaman points out, Raleigh was never in Virginia and the potatoes he gave to Southwell's grandfather might well have been acquired in England.

Drake, it is recorded, saw potatoes in Chile (see p. 22), but could not have brought them to England from that source, as we shall see later.

All the evidence points, however, to two early introductions of the potato into Europe. The first was into Spain in about 1570 and the second into England between 1588 and 1593, with a strong suggestion that 1590 might have been the actual year.

What, then, is the evidence? To follow the argument more easily reference can be made to the chronological sequence shown in Table 3.1.

Table 3.1 The potato in Europe: chronological table of early records and
descriptions

1564	Clusius visited Spain. No mention of potato.
1570	Potato brought to Spain probably at about this time (according to Salaman, 1937, and Laufer, 1938).
1573	Potato being bought in Seville for consumption at La Sangre Hospital.
1576	Clusius: *Rariorum aliquot stirpium per Hispanias.* (No mention of potato.)
1581	Clusius visited Sir Francis Drake, James Garret and others in England. No mention of potato.
1582	Clusius published work on some of Drake's plants. Potato not mentioned.
1586	Drake brought back Raleigh's colonists from Roanoke, Virginia.
1587	Philippe de Sivry, Prefect of Mons in Belgium received potato from a friend of the Pontifical Ambassador.
1588	Clusius received two tubers and a fruit of the potato at Vienna from Philippe de Sivry.
1588	T. Hariot: *A briefe and true report of the new found land of Virginia.* (No mention of potato.)
1589	Clusius received a watercolour painting of the potato from Philippe de Sivry.
1590	Caspar Bauhin received a coloured illustration from Dr L. Scholtz of Breslau. He added an illustration of his own and sent them both to Clusius.
1588 } 1593 }	James Garret of London sent drawing of potato to Clusius in Frankfurt.
1596	J. Gerard: *Catalogue.* (Papus orbiculatus.)
1596	Caspar Bauhin: *Phytopinax.* (Pappar Hispanorum; Solanum tuberosum.)
1597	J. Gerard: *The Herball.* (Battata Virginiana siue Virginianorum; Pappus.)
1598	Caspar Bauhin (in Matthiolus) *Opera omnia.* (Solanum tuberosum esculentum; Pappar Hispanorum or Indorum.)
1599	J. Gerard: *Catalogue.* Second edition. (Papus orbiculatus; Bastard Potatoes.)
1601	Clusius: *Rariorum plantarum historia.* (Arachidna; Papas Peruanorum.)
1620	Caspar Bauhin: *Prodromus theatri botanici.* (Solanum tuberosum esculentum; Openauk; Papas.)
1623	Caspar Bauhin: *Pinax Theatri botanici.* (Solanum tuberosum esculentum.)
1623	Father Magazzini de Vallombrosa: *Dell'Agricoltura toscana.*
1629	J. Parkinson: *Paradisi in sole paradisus terrestris.* (Papas seu Battatas Virginianorum.)
1633	J. Gerard: *The Herball.* Second edition, by Thomas Johnson.
1636	J. Gerard: *The Herball.* Third edition, by Thomas Johnson.
1640	J. Parkinson: *Theatrum botanicum.* (Pappas sive Battatas; Virginia potatoes.)
1644	R. Dodoens: *Cruydt-Boeck.* (Papas; Taratuffoli; Papas Peruanorum; Openauck.)
1651	J. Bauhin: *Historia plantarum universalis.* (Papas; Openauk, etc.)

The central figure in the spread of the potato through Germany, the Low Countries, France and Switzerland was the herbalist Charles d'Ecluse, or Clusius, as he is generally called. He recounts (1601) that whilst at Vienna he was sent two tubers and a fruit in 1588 from Philippe de Sivry, Prefect of Mons, in Belgium, who in turn had received them from a friend of the Papal Legate in Belgium in 1587. In 1589 de Sivry also sent Clusius a water-colour painting, executed in 1588 (Fig. 3.1). Clusius was also given a drawing from James Garrett of London, between 1588 and 1593 and two drawings from the Swiss botanist, Caspar Bauhin shortly after 1590. It is clear that the potato was becoming well-known to botanists and herbalists in the late sixteenth century and that the Garrett drawing was taken from the second potato introduction – the one that came into the possession of John Gerard, of whom more later.

The first botanical description of the potato was that of Caspar Bauhin in 1596 (*Phytopinax*), and it was Bauhin who pre-dated Linnaeus by something like a century and a half by naming the potato *Solanum tuberosum*. Unfortunately, in his later publications Bauhin adopted a trinomial: *Solanum tuberosum esculentum*.

The first printed illustration was that of the Englishman, John Gerard, in his *Herball* of 1597 (Figs 3.2, 3.3), followed closely by that of Bauhin (in Matthiolus) in 1598 (Fig. 3.4) and Clusius in 1601 (Fig. 3.5). At this time the potato in Europe was becoming well-known. We must now look at the evidence for the times and places of its introductions.

Clusius' potato donated by Philippe de Sivry indicated that it came to him from Italy, because of the papal source and the Italian name *Tara-touffli* given to it. Evidently the potato was known in Italy before 1587, since Father Magazzini de Vallombrosa in his book published posthumously in 1623 says that potatoes were grown at Vallombrosa and were brought there by the Carmelite Friars from Spain and Portugal. We can readily believe that the potato in Europe must first have come to Spain, since the Spaniards controlled all trade from their American colonies. Having become established in Spain it quickly spread to Portugal and to Italy.

We know that the potato was not known in Spain by 1564, since otherwise Clusius would have seen it during his visit in that year (Clusius 1576) (see Table 3.1). However, a reference by Professor E. Hamilton (1934, quoted by Salaman 1937) states that the Hospital de la Sangre at Seville bought potatoes in 1576 as part of their housekeeping. Salaman was given evidence by Hamilton, also, that potatoes were being bought by the Hospital de la Sangre in 1573 and in the last quarter of the year, indicating that they were harvested in Spain and not imported. Since they would need to have been grown for some years previously in order to build up stocks, Salaman considered that about 1570 (and not as early as 1564) would be a reasonable date for their first introduction into Spain. This seems to be a convincing argument, always assuming that the records of the Hospital de la Sangre were referring to the *Solanum* potato and not to the *Ipomoea* sweet potato. Unfortunately, Hamilton did not quote or show a reproduction from the original records of the Hospital and the doubt just expressed cannot therefore be resolved until the manuscripts are rechecked.

Fig. 3.1 Water-colour painting of part of a potato plant and tubers, sent to Clusius in 1589 by Philippe de Sivry, Prefect of Mons. The small inscription reads: 'Taratouffli à Phillipe de Sivry acceptum Viennae 26 Januarij 1588. Papas Peruänum Petri Ciecae'. This was clearly written by Clusius after receiving the painting. (Courtesy of the Plantin Museum, Antwerp.)

Fig. 3.2 Portrait of John Gerard as a frontispiece to the first edition of his *Herball* of 1597 (but here dated 1598), showing the author with a potato spray in his left hand.

Thus we can conclude only that the potato probably arrived in Spain between 1565 and 1573; we do not know who brought it or from what part of South America. Probably it was brought to Spain as something of no consequence, in ships' stores or as a curiosity brought home by a returning colonist or administrator.

We must now refer to John Gerard's potato in England. It seems clear that this was not the material from Clusius. Gerard in his garden lists or *Catalogues* of 1596 and 1599 calls it 'Papus orbiculatus'. This shows that

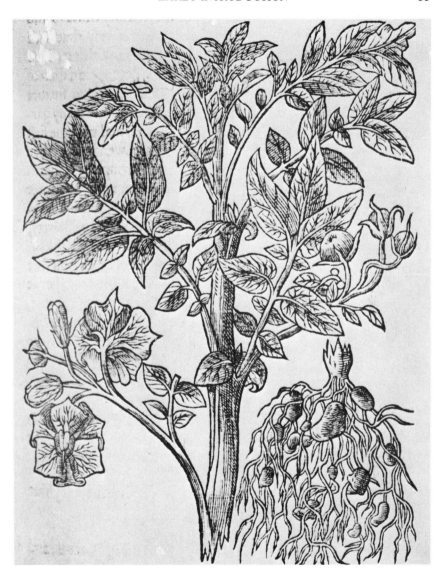

Fig. 3.3 John Gerard's illustration of the potato in the first edition of his *Herball* (1597). This is the first potato picture to be published. Note the small tubers and abundant roots and stolons (not distinguished from each other), which indicate a short-day adapted plant grown in the long summer days of England.

Gerard knew the South American name 'papa', even though he did not get the spelling right, and it would seem probable that he obtained this name from Clusius. However, Gerard also thought that the potato came from Virginia in what is now the United States of America, and thereby opened a hornets' nest which has not even now been completely sealed. Gerard reports as follows: 'It groweth naturally in America where it was first

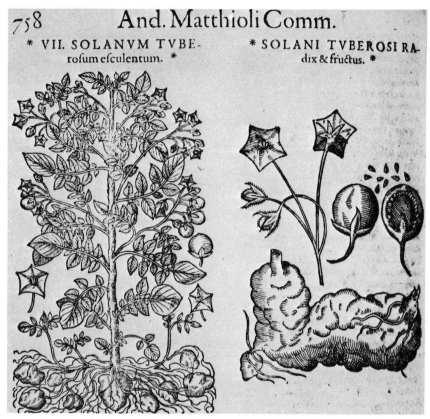

Fig. 3.4 Caspar Bauhin's illustration of the potato (in Matthiolus, 1598). Again, the picture shows the growth of a short-day plant grown in long-day conditions. The tuber in bottom right is probably a Jerusalem artichoke.

observed, as reporteth *C. Clusius*, since which time I have received rootes hereof from Virginia, otherwise called Noremberga, which grow and prosper in my garden as in their own native country.' Concerning South America, Gerard is referring to Clusius' mention of Pedro Cieza de León's description that was quoted in Chapter 2. Evidently Gerard genuinely believed that the potato also occurred in Virginia, no doubt the colony that Raleigh founded in 1584. No potatoes were found there by the scientist Thomas Hariot, who was brought back with the unsuccessful colonists in 1586 by Sir Francis Drake (Quinn 1955). Note that both Raleigh and Drake are involved here in some way, but not to the extent of bringing potatoes from Virginia to England. Thomas Hariot (1588) does not mention potatoes growing in Virginia, even though he describes the Openauk (*Apios americana* – a member of the pea and bean family).

How did Gerard make this mistake? Salaman (1949) takes up the point made by Wight (1916) to the effect that if potatoes arrived from Virginia in

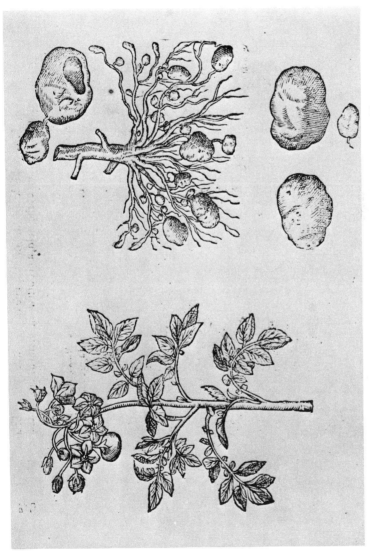

Fig. 3.5 Clusius's illustration of the potato published in *Rariorum Plantarum Historia* (1601). This makes a clear distinction between roots and tubers, and shows a tuber damaged by a fungal or insect parasite.

1586 they must have already been on Drake's ships and that Drake acquired them in the West Indies, perhaps from the sack of Cartagena on the coast of what is now Colombia.

Let us refer again to Gerard's statement 'It groweth naturally in America [which at that time was *South* America], where it was first discovered, as reporteth C. *Clusius*'. How did he know this? Clusius did not publish until 1601 and Gerard's account was published in 1597. It would seem that James Garrett was the link here, whom Clusius mentions as having given him a drawing between 1588 and 1593. It could therefore have been Garrett who passed the information to Gerard about its name, 'papas', and place of origin, 'America', and this limits the arrival of the potato in England from 1588 to 1593 – a period of six years. But this means that Salaman and others cannot have been right in assuming that Gerard received his potatos in 1586 with the returning colonists. (If the reader at this point is thoroughly confused, might I refer him to my more detailed account of the history of the potato in 1967!)

As we have seen, Drake received potatoes by barter in 1578 in Chile but he did not return to England until 1580, and although Clusius visited Drake in 1581 and published in 1582 on some of Drake's plants, he made no mention of the potato (Table 3.1). However, other voyages set out for Virginia, and one of these was partly financed by Gerard in 1590. It was perhaps this ship which, after having taken various Spanish 'prize ships', called at Virginia on the way home, having taken potatoes along with treasure. (Details from Miss Mary Edmond, quoted by Hawkes (1967) 260–1 and 364–5.)

This is all the evidence we have, but certainly 1590 sounds a very likely date for the arrival of the potato in England.

Place of origin

There are two contending theories as to what part of South America the European potato came from. Juzepczuk and Bukasov (1929) believed that it came from Chile because Chilean potatoes, which were adapted to form tubers in the long days of southern latitudes, would have immediately adapted to the similar day length of Europe. Salaman (1946) contested this, stating that the length of time and the number of transhipments needed to get a potato from Chile to Spain would have resulted in the death of any tubers so transported. He further makes the point that the first journey direct from Chile to Europe via the Straits of Magellan was not made until 1579, by which time the potato was already known in Europe. Salaman (1946, 1954) states that it would have been easier for potatoes to have been sent to Europe from Peru or the north coast of what is now Colombia, particularly from the port of Cartagena.

Such potatoes would be 'short-day adapted', able to tuberize only under 12-hour day length or less. Interestingly, we find that the first European potatoes were of this type, forming tubers in November and December, and thus able to grow only in the milder regions of Spain, Italy, southern

France, Ireland, etc. (Salaman and Hawkes 1949). Furthermore, the earliest herbarium specimen of the potato known to us, that of Caspar Bauhin, made in about 1620, is an obvious specimen of subsp. *andigena* from the Andes and not of subsp. *tuberosum* from Chile. The old woodcuts (Figs 3.3, 3.4, 3.5) tell the same story, even though they are conventionally fitted into a rectangular space. There are many inflorescences, many small tubers and occasional shoots (soboles) growing up above the ground from the stolons. These features are what happens to modern subsp. *andigena* when brought to England. There seems to be, therefore, very little doubt that the first European potatoes were short-day adapted subsp. *andigena* varieties from the Andes and very probably from Colombia.

Further spread in Europe

We have seen that the potato was commonly grown in Spain and Italy by the late sixteenth century. Bauhin sent potatos to France by about 1600 and they were widely grown there by the mid-seventeenth century. However, there was considerable resistance to their cultivation by all but the poorest people until Parmentier popularized them in 1773.

The Slavic nations received their potatoes from Germany, since their words are derived from German ones, such as *Kartoffel*, *Grundbirne*, etc. It seems that the general adoption in eastern Europe was late eighteenth to early nineteenth century when the adaptation to short day length had been bred out of them. Even in the milder winter climate of England potatoes did not become universally grown until the mid-eighteenth to early nineteenth centuries. However, the much milder climate of south-west Ireland allowed potatoes to be grown there in the early seventeenth century, as we have already mentioned.

From Scotland the potato was said to have been taken to Norway and thence to Sweden and Denmark, also by the mid-eighteenth century, though potatoes in southern Denmark certainly came from Germany.

The potato was completely unknown in North America until the early seventeenth century, and, as we have seen, there is absolutely no evidence to support Gerard's account of its being native to Virginia. Potatoes in the North American colonies were first received from Bermuda in 1621, where they had been grown after an initial importation from England in 1613. No records exist of importations from South America until Goodrich obtained his varieties from Panamá (see Chapter 7).

Potatoes were said to have been taken to India and to China by British missionaries in the late seventeenth century and were known in Japan and parts of Africa by about the same period. In New Zealand they appeared in 1769 (Yen 1961/2) and were adopted by the Maoris by 1840, who were conversant with sweet potato cultivation.

Finally, Zubeldia *et al.* (1955) have shown that potatoes were directly introduced to the Canary Isles from Peru in about 1622. These potatoes were *S. tuberosum* subsp. *andigena* and still remain very close to that subspecies at the present time.

CHAPTER 4

POTATO CYTOLOGY AND
REPRODUCTIVE BIOLOGY

Cytology – ploidy levels

The presence of polyploidy in wild potatoes, with a base number of 12, was established over 60 years ago by Smith (1927) and by Vilmorin and Simonet (1927). Polyploidy in cultivated potatoes was demonstrated also by Rybin (1930), who was the first to show that *S. tuberosum* formed only a part of a series extending from diploid to pentaploid. (See Appendix II.) Many later workers showed that there was not one but several polyploid series in wild potatoes, which had evidently evolved independently.

Despite the obvious presence of polyploids in the tuberous *Solanum* species the majority (some 75 per cent) are in fact diploid, though quite a large number of tetraploids and some hexaploids also occur (Tables 4.1 and 4.2). In fact, some series (*Acaulia, Longipedicellata*) are mainly tetraploid, some are mixtures of diploid, tetraploid and hexaploid (*Conicibaccata, Tuberosa*) and one (*Demissa*) is mainly hexaploid.

Triploid potato species are normally derived from spontaneous crosses between diploid and tetraploid species. Pentaploid species are either tetraploid crossed with hexaploid species (*S. curtilobum* and *S. edinense*, for instance) or diploids crossed with hexaploids in which an 'unreduced' or 2n gamete from the diploid parent has functioned. These triploids and pentaploids are highly sterile and are maintained entirely by vegetative propagation.

A curious phenomenon with potatoes is the presence of triploid cyto-types in an otherwise diploid species (Tarn and Hawkes 1986). Such triploids are presumed to have been derived from the union of normal and 2n gametes; they, also, are maintained by vegetative reproduction and occur chiefly in areas favourable to the long-continued establishment of a potato in a particular area. Moreover, in some species, such as *S. maglia* and *S. calvescens*, the triploids are extremely common, whilst the diploids

Table 4.1 Numbers and percentages of wild and cultivated potato species at various ploidy levels

Ploidy level	Numbers	Percentage
2x	129	73
3x	7	4
4x	27	15
5x	3	2
6x	10	6
	Total 176	

Notes:
(1) Series *Etuberosa* and *Juglandifolia* are not included.
(2) Chromosome numbers not available for all species, since some are known as herbarium specimens only.
(3) Triploid and pentaploid cytotypes of normally diploid and tetraploid species respectively are not included.
(4) Species with two or more cytotypes (*S. gourlayi*, *S. oplocense*) are counted for every cytotype.

Table 4.2 Numbers of wild and cultivated potato species in each of the taxonomic series, grouped by ploidy level (excluding series *Etuberosa* and *Juglandifolia*)

		Number of species				
		2x	3x	4x	5x	6x
I	*Morelliformia*	1				
II	*Bulbocastana*	2				
III	*Pinnatisecta*	9				
IV	*Polyadenia*	2				
V	*Commersoniana*	1				
VI	*Circaeifolia*	3				
VII	*Lignicaulia*	1				
VIII	*Olmosiana*	1				
IX	*Yungasensa*	7				
X	*Megistacroloba*	8				
XI	*Cuneoalata*	2				
XII	*Conicibaccata*	12		11		2
XIII	*Piurana*	9		1		
XIV	*Ingifolia*	1				
XV	*Maglia*	1				
XVI	*Tuberosa* (wild)	66	2	7		1
XVI	*Tuberosa* (cultivated)	3	2	1	1	
XVII	*Acaulia*		2	1		1
XVIII	*Longipedicellata*		1	6		
XIX	*Demissa*				2	6
		129	7	27	3	10

are rare (or have not yet been found, as in *S. calvescens*). Triploids in *S. bulbocastanum*, *S. cardiophyllum*, *S. commersonii* and *S. microdontum* are very common or very common locally, whilst in others such as *S. jamesii* and *S. venturii* they appear to be rare. They might well be shown to be much more common if the quarantine authorities allowed us to collect and import tuber material for study. Since triploids hardly ever produce true seed they are probably never collected now.

The general picture that emerges is that diploids, tetraploids and hexaploids are sexually fertile and the odd-number polyploids are sterile. The above account refers mainly to wild species, but cultivated ones follow the same pattern, except that no cultivated hexaploids have been found.

There are three cultivated diploids, two of which (*S. stenotomum* and *S. phureja*) are sexually fertile, whilst the third (*S. ajanhuiri*) is less fertile and does not breed true.

The two cultivated triploid species (*S. chaucha* and *S. juzepczukii*) are of hybrid nature and are to a greater or lesser extent sterile (particularly *S. juzepczukii*).

The cultivated tetraploid species, *S. tuberosum*, with its two subspecies, *tuberosum* and *andigena*, is normally fertile except in a number of highly bred clones outside South America.

The one cultivated pentaploid species, *S. curtilobum*, is reasonably fertile in crosses with *S. tuberosum*, but not in attempted selfings.

Meiosis in species and hybrids

Most potato species so far analysed have in general shown very regular meiotic pairing, apart from triploids and pentaploids, where it would not in any case be expected. In fact, since about 1960 cytologists have hardly considered it worthwhile to investigate this subject. Thus, regular meiosis appears in diploid, allotetraploid and allohexaploid species. However, tetraploid domestic potatoes, *S. tuberosum*, function as cytological autotetraploids, even though there is considerable evidence of their having been formed originally as hybrids between two somewhat closely related diploid species.

When crosses are possible, hybrids between pairs of diploids also exhibit regular (or almost regular) bivalent pairing, just as in the parent species themselves (see Magoon *et al.* 1958a, 1958b). When chromosome pairing irregularities are seen in hybrids their frequencies do not seem to differ significantly from those of the species themselves.

Artificial tetraploids of species hybrids made by Howard and Swaminathan (1952) between *S. chacoense* and *S. stenotomum* did not form quadrivalents but tended towards 24 bivalents. On the other hand, in an autotetraploid of the nearly related *S. phureja* there were 3.45 quadrivalents, 16.85 bivalents and 0.50 univalents, typical of an ordinary autotetraploid. They interpreted these results by saying that where homologous chromosomes were absent and replaced by homoeologues from another species in diploid hybrids these homologues and homoeologues paired satisfactorily. In allotetraploids the homologues paired at the expense of the homoeologues. In autotetraploids, where only homologues were present, they tended to form higher associations up to quadrivalents. There thus would appear to be cryptic structural differentiation between the chromosomes of different diploid species, but this is not discernible in simple F_1 hybrids.

Similar work was published by Swaminathan (1953), who showed that multivalent frequencies were lower in amphiploids of crosses between distinct species (*S. phureja* × *S. chacoense*) as compared with autotetraploids. He also showed that there were no significant differences of multivalent frequencies in auto- and allotetraploids if the species involved were closely related (e.g. *S. parodii* and *S. saltense* – now both considered as parts of *S. chacoense*; and *S. yabari* and *S. stenotomum* – the former now considered as part of the latter). This work thus helps to reinforce taxonomic affinities between and within species as postulated from the results of morphological studies.

Crosses between pairs of apparently more distinctly related species have been analysed cytologically by various workers. Thus Matsubayashi (1982) examined hybrids of *S. acaule* (4x) × *S. chacoense* (2x), finding a range of 1–9 trivalents, 3–16 bivalents and 0–11 univalents. He interpreted these results by postulating that one of the genomes of *S. acaule* paired with the *S. chacoense* genome and the other remained as univalents or attached itself to the already paired bivalents. In studies of *S. stoloniferum* (4x) × *S. chacoense* (2x) hybrids, Matsubayashi (1955) obtained F_1 meiotic plates of 1 trivalent + 11 bivalents + 11 univalents. He assumed from this that one of the genomes of *S. stoloniferum* was highly related to that of *S. chacoense* and the other was quite distinct. In another paper, Matsubayashi and Misoo (1977) found little difference between the genomes of *S. jamesii* and *S. × sambucinum* (= *S. pinnatisectum* × *S. cardiophyllum*), the amphiploids behaving like autotetraploids. However, amphiploids of the above species crossed with *S. bulbocastanum* showed a significant reduction in multivalent frequency, compared with their parental autotetraploids. This indicated that the *S. bulbocastanum* genome is distantly related to, though not distinct from, those of the other species. Such results accord well with the taxonomic judgement of separating *S. bulbocastanum* into a separate series (*Bulbocastana*) from *S. jamesii* and *S. × sambucinum* (*Pinnatisecta*).

Before leaving this section mention must be made of Marks' cytological work on species hybrids. Working with series *Demissa*, Marks (1955a) showed that *S. demissum* (2n = 72) could be assigned a genome structure of ABB^1 for the polyhaploid and $AABBB^1B^1$ for the hexaploid. All other hexaploid species studied (*S. brachycarpum*, *S. guerreroense* and *S. hougasii*) showed similar A and B genomes, but differed in the third set: B^2, B^3, etc. He postulated that all these species had been formed as amphiploid hybrids of a common diploid, probably *S. verrucosum*, and various unrelated tetraploid species.

In a second paper, Marks (1958) demonstrated the high degree of possibility that *S. vallis-mexici* (2n = 36) was a natural hybrid of

S. stoloniferum (2n = 48) × *S. verrucosum* (2n = 24). Nevertheless, an artificial hexaploid from this cross does not agree morphologically with any known hexaploid. In a further paper (Marks 1965), the cytological results are seen to agree reasonably well with taxonomic groupings, though exceptions occur. There is general evidence for genomic differentiation amongst polyploids except between *S. guerreroense* and *S. iopetalum* (including *S. brachycarpum*). In the end, one has to admit that the cytological evidence does not always solve problems of species relationships. Nevertheless, Marks considers it likely that *S. oxycarpum* was involved in the formation of the hexaploids *S. iopetalum* (including *S. brachycarpum*) and *S. guerreroense*, whilst *S. stoloniferum* was possibly involved in the formation of *S. demissum* and *S. hougasii*. This hypothesis seems very likely.

Meiotic analysis of series *Conicibaccata* hybrids by L. López (1979; López and Hawkes, in press) showed about 12 bivalents in diploid species crosses, as would be expected. Diploid × tetraploid (both directions) crosses tended toward figures of 12 univalents + 12 bivalents, but with certain numbers of trivalents, indicating that genome differentiation was by no means complete. An exception was seen in *S. flahaultii* × *S. urubambae*, with about 12 bivalents. Tetraploid × tetraploid crosses exhibited a tendency towards 24 bivalents, but some were as low as 15 bivalents and several showed up to 12 univalents. Here again, it is difficult to draw hard and fast conclusions. Tetraploid × hexaploid hybrids (*S. colombianum* (4x) × *S. moscopanum* (6x) and *S. flahaultii* (4x) × *S. moscopanum* (6x)) tended towards 24 bivalents + 12 univalents, but there was much variation around these figures. The tentative conclusions drawn from this work were that all the *Conicibaccata* species possessed the same basic genome which varied to some extent in the different species. However, completely common genomes were found in *S. laxissimum* and *S. santolallae* (x_1) and in *S. urubambae* and *S. violaceimarmoratum* (x_2). Furthermore, the tetraploid species, *S. agrimonifolium*, *S. colombianum*, *S. flahaultii*, *S. longiconicum* and *S. oxycarpum* possessed one genome (x_1) in common, *S. paucijugum* had one genome in common with *S. flahaultii* and another with *S. longiconicum*. Finally, the hexaploid *S. moscopanum* possessed two genomes in common with *S. colombianum*, plus another quite distinct one. It would be interesting to compare these results with data drawn from other disciplines. There is insufficient space to report on all the work published in this field, but the results on the whole conform to the same pattern.

Genome relationships

These have been mentioned in passing, in the previous section. Hawkes (1958) suggested a genome formula of A_1A_1 for series *Tuberosa* and *Commersoniana*, whilst *Acaulia* (4x species) were allotted a formula of $A_2A_2A_3A_3$, observing that the differences between A_1, A_2 and A_3 could not be very great. Thus, although *S. acaule* itself behaves as an allotetraploid, when crossed with a diploid species from series *Tuberosa* and *Commersoniana* the triploid hybrid behaves like an autotriploid. It is assumed that in the absence of homologues the homoeologous chromosomes in the triploid associate randomly, as they would in a true autotriploid.

Matsubayashi (1981) agreed on the whole with these concepts, postulated AA for *Commersoniana* and diploid *Tuberosa*, AAA^aA^a for tetraploid *Acaulia*, A^cA^c for *Cuneoalata*, A^mA^m for *Megistacroloba*, AAA^t for *S. chaucha*, AA^m for *S. ajanhuiri*, AAA^a for *S. juzepczukii*, AAA^tA^t for *S. tuberosum* (both subspecies) and $AAAA^cA^t$ for *S. curtilobum*. The tetraploids in series *Longipedicellata* were characterized as AABB, whilst the triploid *S. vallis-mexici* was given the formula AA^dB (the A^d genome coming from *S. verrucosum*, which was designated A^dA^d). Finally, *S. demissum* was given the formula $A^dA^dC_1C_1C_2C_2$, but the origin of the C genomes is not given in the table. This differs somewhat from Hawkes' (1958) postulate of A_1A_4 (B, C, D) etc. for the several hexaploid species and Marks' (1955a) concept of AABB (B, B^1, B^2, B^3, B^4); the figures in brackets in these two cases represent the third genome which varies in each of the hexaploid species. Only further work could confirm or reject any or all of these three hypotheses.

Crossability and embryo balance number

Crossability between many diploid species is good, indicating that there must be some basic similarity between them, even though, as seen in the last section, more subtle differences are present. Crosses between diploids and tetraploids are also possible. In some of these cases triploid hybrids result, whilst in others the hybrids may be tetraploid, owing to the function of 2n gametes from the diploid parent. Jackson *et al.* (1977, 1978) showed how crosses of *S. tuberosum* subsp. *andigena* (4x) × *S. stenotumum* (2x) could produce 4x, 3x and 2x progeny. The origin of the tetraploids and triploids has just been mentioned. The 2x progeny are dihaploids (spoken of as 'haploids' in many US publications) of *S. tuberosum*. Hougas and Peloquin (1958) were the first to recognize the breeding potential of dihaploid production, though it has been mentioned earlier by Bains and Howard (1950), Dodds (1950) in *S. demissum* and Marks (1955b) in *S. polytrichon*. Thus, dihaploids of *S. tuberosum* can be used to make crosses with diploid wild species, so bringing germplasm from these latter into the cultivated breeding pool (see Hougas and Peloquin 1960 and many other references in the literature).

Returning to the crossability of diploid species, it has long been known that nearly all of them are self-incompatible; some very few diploids are self-compatible, such as *S. polyadenium*, *S. verrucosum*, *S. brevidens*, *S. etuberosum* and *S. morelliforme* (see Hawkes 1958 for references). All tetraploids yet known are self-compatible, apart from *S. tuquerrense* (Marks 1965). All hexaploids are self-compatible also.

Several groups of diploid species are not crossable with the well-known ones, such as *S. chacoense*, *S. microdontum* and *S. bukasovii*. To understand this, Johnson and Hanneman (1978, 1980a, 1980b, 1982) proposed a modification of the hypothesis concerning the normal 2:1 ratio of maternal: paternal genomes in the endosperm itself. They point out that whilst most South American diploids possess an embryo balance number (EBN) of 2, most Mexican and some South American diploids possess an effective EBN of 1. To cross these with the EBN 2 species it is necessary to tetraploidize them, thus bringing the effective number to 2, even though their ploidy will then be 4. Most tetraploid species such as *S. acaule* and *S. colombianum* also possess an EBN of 2, though *S. tuberosum* possesses an EBN of 4. Hexaploid species, such as *S. albicans* and the *Demissa* series hexaploids also possess an EBN of 4.

What all this means in terms of underlying causes is still obscure. However, as we shall see in the next chapter, all the superseries *Stellata* diploids up to and including series VII *Lignicaulia* possess an EBN of 1, followed by an EBN of 2 in the South American *Stellata* diploids of series IX *Yungasensa* and most of the superseries *Rotata* diploids up to and including series XVI *Tuberosa* (though data are not available for series XIV *Ingifolia* and XV *Maglia*).

F$_2$ hybrid analysis

So-called F$_2$ hybrids between diploid species are really F$_1$ sib-matings, since self-incompatibility renders selfing impossible. However, with that in mind we shall continue to refer to F$_2$ families or progenies.

In crosses between distinct species, the F$_2$ families show aberrant plants ranging from seedlings that hardly appear above the soil surface and others that die soon afterwards, through dwarfs and poor unthrifty plants, to those which do not flower, others which flower but do not form fruits, and finally to completely normal ones. Howard and Swaminathan (1952) and Swaminathan (1953) consider that small structural differences between the chromosomes might account for this. I consider it more likely that the adaptive complexes of two distinct species when split up and segregated in the F$_1$ cannot replace each other because the genetic architecture of the two species is too distinct. Thus after segregation many of the progeny will lack the full adaptive and developmental gene complexes of one or the other parent, and 'genetic breakdown' will occur. Some seedlings will possess reasonably good combinations of these complexes and will survive. Others will not and will die. When two species are so similar genetically that chromosome segments from one can replace those from the other, these species could be regarded *either* as parts of the same species *or* as two species that are very closely related. Hawkes (1966) found the latter situation in the Mexican series *Longipedicellata* species, whilst Hawkes and Hjerting (1989, Fig. 1) showed the degree of relationships between certain Bolivian species in various series. Hawkes (1956b) showed that there was no genetic breakdown in crosses between *S. tuberosum* subsp. *tuberosum* and subsp. *andigena* and in unpublished work found that none existed between pairs of *S. stenotomum* clones once considered to be distinct species, such as *S. yabari*, *S. churuspi*, etc. Similar work was undertaken by Hawkes and Hjerting (1969) for pairs of species for Argentina.

The method is therefore useful in pointing out genomic similarities but the results in every case need to be interpreted with care, as for instance where morphological species differences are not backed up by genetic breakdown results.

POTATO EVOLUTION

Species concepts

In most groups of plants studied by experimental taxonomists, the morphological species concept is adopted, then rejected, and finally adopted again even though in a modified form. To distinguish one species from another very similar one it is necessary to find breaks or gaps in the total pattern of diversity. Such gaps indicate a lack of gene flow between two panmictic populations. However, a clear break or gap must mean that there is some underlying mechanism that causes it. An obvious explanation, based on the biological species concept, is that no crossing or gene exchange takes place because of some genetically based sterility mechanism. This sounds fine in theory, but with potatoes very many species will hybridize under experimental conditions and will produce fertile F_1 hybrids, even though in nature they remain distinct. Thus, if the strict biological species definition were applied to potatoes there would be just a few large species, each of which comprised very many blocks of diversity, each looking and remaining very distinct in nature. This, then, would be an illogical and counterproductive solution to the species problem in *Solanum*. A far better concept that most of my colleagues and I have found to be practical and satisfactory is to regard the morphological gaps between species to be due to a variety of causes.

The first of these causes is eco-geographical separation. As we saw in previous chapters, each wild potato species is quite clearly adapted to certain environmental conditions which help to isolate it from others. The second is a difference in the ploidy level. Crosses, for instance, between diploids and tetraploids or between diploids and hexaploids, may take place but the offspring are generally infertile (see Chapter 4). The third mechanism is the difference in embryo balance number (EBN). Thus, among diploids those with an EBN of 1 will not cross with those with an EBN of 2. To take two examples, *S. capsicibaccatum* (EBN = 1) and *S. brevicaule* (EBN = 2) occur together in the same ecological zone in Bolivia but no hybrids are formed. The same situation occurs in Argentina between *S. commersonii* (EBN = 1) and *S. chacoense* (EBN = 2).

Another isolating mechanism is genome difference. Thus, all the hexaploid series *Demissa* species in Mexico will not form fertile F_1s for this reason, even though the EBN number of all of them is 4. This mechanism is not very common in potatoes, however, because of imperfect genome differences between them.

Yet another isolating mechanism is difference of flowering time, as between *S. microdontum* and *S. vernei* in Argentina (Hawkes and Hjerting, 1969). It has to be admitted that this is the only example known to us of such a mechanism in potatoes.

As was mentioned in Chapter 4, species of the same ploidy and EBN often overlap. F_2 hybrids can be made artificially by sib-mating, and where the species possess a distinct 'genetic architecture' many of the F_2 segregants do not possess the total gene complement of either of the parents and are unable to survive. (See also Hawkes and Hjerting 1969, 1989). Such a genetic breakdown might well be considered a barrier to gene exchange. It may indeed be a partial though not complete one, since some plants with the right complement of the adaptive complexes of one or the other parent will be able to survive and set viable seeds. However, these results are based on plants growing under experimental conditions. In the wild they might not be able to do so well.

The potato collector of the twentieth century comes across 'hybrid swarms' resulting from mass natural crosses between pairs of species that possess overlapping distribution areas. This is probably largely due to the influence of man in destroying or modifying the natural plant communities and providing intermediate habitats into which previously isolated species will spread. Examples of this are *S. chacoense* × *S. microdontum* in Argentina; *S. chacoense* × *S. spegazzinii*, also in Argentina; and *S. raphanifolium* × *S. sparsipilum* in the Cuzco valley, southern Peru. In Argentina it was found that hybrid swarms noted and collected some years back had completely disappeared, even though the parents were still present (Hawkes and Hjerting 1969, 459–60). Evidently the hybrids may survive under good weather conditions for a few years, but under drought or other stress may not be able to survive for very long. This would seem to be due to the fact that they possess certain portions of the adaptive gene complexes from the two original parent species but not complete sets from either. This, interestingly, is the reverse of Edgar Anderson's (1952) postulation that hybrids do better than their parent species in 'hybrid habitats' to which neither of the parents is adapted. Presumably different species groups under different conditions may react in different ways.

Are we then to conclude that no gene flow takes place between such potato species that form natural hybrids? Probably not. In Argentina, introgressive hybridization appears to have taken place between *S. chacoense* and *S. microdontum*, not only of morphological but of resistance characters to potato virus Y (Hawkes 1962b). Even so, the vast majority of wild potato species seem to remain very distinct from each other, with very little gene flow taking place between them, or perhaps none at all.

Two final points should be made. Firstly, it is worth noting that some species, such as *S. stoloniferum*, *S. sparsipilum* and *S. chacoense* are highly diverse, rather widespread, and before the first edition of this 'Revision' had been split into a large number of microspecies. As more material was collected, even more microspecies had to be described. Clearly, this was becoming an impossible situation taxonomically. The species were highly variable but because there were no clear-cut morphological boundaries visible between the different forms, the logical solution was to group all the microspecies together in each case under the name of the one that had been first described. Only one fairly clearly defined variant can be identified in each of the species *S. stoloniferum* and *S. sparsipilum*; these have been separated as infraspecific taxa in Chapter 6.

The other point concerns the rather large number of species in series *Conicibaccata* and *Tuberosa* (Peru), each of them generally based on a single or very few collections. Further work is needed with these when more material becomes generally available in order to evaluate them in the way mentioned above.

Origins of *Solanum*, section *Petota*

As we have seen earlier, the tuber-bearing species of this section are very widely distributed in the Americas from the south-western States of the USA to southern Argentina and Chile (see Figs 1.1 to 1.4 and Appendix II).

I have placed in a separate subsection, *Estolonifera*, two series, *Etuberosa* and *Juglandifolia*, which do not bear tubers or stolons. The latter series, *Juglandifolia*, possesses bright yellow flowers and is linked to the tomato genus *Lycopersicon*, probably more closely than to the tuber-bearing members of *Solanum*. In addition, there exists an anomalous yellow-flowered species, *S. pennellii*, with *Lycopersicon* leaves and flowers, but anthers of the *Solanum* type with normal connectives, and not the *Lycopersicon* type which has greatly elongated connectives. Indeed, Correll (1962) places this species, probably rightly, in a separate section, *Neolycopersicum*. All these yellow-flowered species, then, in my view, ought not to be placed with the tuber-bearing *Solanum* species, but until another taxonomist decides as to where they should be transferred I prefer for the present to leave them where they are in their traditional position.

We now come to the other non-tuber-bearing series, *Etuberosa*. This series is found in central to southern Chile and in southern Argentina. Since the species that have been investigated possess an EBN of 1 and can thus be crossed with other species of that number, I am inclined to believe that their relationship to the tuber-bearing species is closer than was first thought possible. According to Hosaka *et al.* (1984) the genome relationship of *S. etuberosum* links up with other EBN 1 species in series *Bulbocastana*, *Pinnatisecta* and *Polyadenia* but at least 22 mutations away (Fig. 5.1). Hosaka's figure, based on results derived from chloroplast genome analyses, also separates the tuber-bearing species and *S. etuberosum* on the

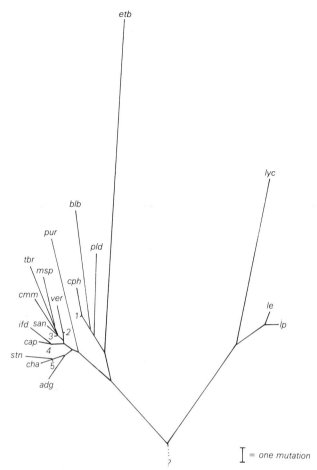

Fig. 5.1 Chloroplast genome relationships (from Hosaka *et al.* (1984), reproduced by kind permission of the authors and the *Japanese Journal of Genetics*.

Key to numbers and symbols:
1.   *S. pinnatisectum* (series *Pinnatisecta*)
2.   *S. stoloniferum* and *S. chacoense* (series *Longipedicellata* and *Yungasensa*)
3.   *S. demissum, S. boliviense* and *S. spegazzinii* (series *Demissa, Megistacroloba* and *Tuberosa*)
4.   *S. leptophyes* and *S. vernei* (series *Tuberosa*)
5.   *S. acaule, S. multidissectum, S. goniocalyx,* and *S. phureja* (series *Acaulia* and *Tuberosa*)

adg = *S. tuberosum* subsp. *andigena* (series *Tuberosa*)
blb   = *S. bulbocastanum* (series *Bulbocastana*)
cap   = *S. capsicibaccatum* (series *Circaeifolia*)
cha   = *S. chaucha* (series *Tuberosa*)
cmm = *S. commersonii* (series *Commersoniana*)
cph   = *S. cardiophyllum* (series *Pinnatisecta*)
etb   = *S. etuberosum* (series *Etuberosa*)
ifd   = *S. infundibuliforme* (series *Cuneoalata*)
le   = *Lycopersicon eculentum*
lp   = *Lycopersicon peruvianum*
lyc   = *S. lycopersicoides* (series *Juglandifolia*)
msp = *S. moscapanum* (series *Conicibaccata*)
pld   = *S. polyadenium* (series *Polyadenia*)
pur   = *S. piurae* (series *Piurana*)
san   = *S. santolallae* (series *Conicibaccata*)
stn   = *S. stenotomum* (series *Tuberosa*)
tbr   = *S. tuberosum* subsp. *tuberosum* (series *Tuberosa*)
ver   = *S. verrucosum* (series *Tuberosa*)

one hand, and *S. lycopersicoides* (series *Juglandifolia*) together with *Lycopersicon* species, on the other.

We can see, also, the close relationships between series *Bulbocastana*, *Pinnatisecta* and *Polyadenia*; and the close relationships of the South American series with *S. demissum* and *S. verrucosum*. The separation of the two subspecies of *S. tuberosum* and the partial isolation of *S. piurae* seem strange, though the rest of the Andean cultivated species are clustered together, as would be expected.

What are the origins of section *Petota*? The most likely source is section *Basarthrum*. Many *Basarthrum* species are easily confused with *Petota* species until the pedicel articulation is studied. This is basal in *Basarthrum* and above the base in *Petota*. It is interesting to note, however, that the pedicel articulation of series *Etuberosa* is very low and almost basal in some species. This may or may not indicate close relationship. Nevertheless, it seems possible that section *Basarthrum* and section *Petota* may have a common ancestor or that *Petota* has been derived from *Basarthrum*.

The evolution of the tuber-bearing wild species

The tuber-bearing species are classified in subsection *Potatoe* which itself is divided into two superseries, *Stellata* and *Rotata*, according to whether the corolla is stellate or rotate. The seemingly more primitive of these is *Stellata*, with its small, star-shaped flowers and EBN of 1.

The account which follows is an attempt to construct a possible scenario for the evolution of the tuber-bearing species. Although a certain amount of inspired guesswork is involved it is based on the results of cytological, serological, EBN, crossability and morphological studies. It thus forms a framework which may need to be modified from time to time when conflicting or additional supporting data become available. I am convinced, however, that the scheme presented here, and based on some 50 years' study of potatoes is basically correct.

Within superseries *Stellata* there is much to be said for regarding *S. morelliforme* (series *Morelliformia*) as the most primitive living representative of the tuber-bearing species, with its very small, deeply stellate corolla, simple leaves and very small berries. Its epiphytic habit is possibly derived. It also possesses the simplest of all immunological spectra against *S. tuberosum*, with one line only, compared with two lines in series *Pinnatisecta* and four lines in series *Tuberosa*, *Demissa*, *Longipedicellata* and *Polyadenia* (Gell *et al.* 1960). The 4-line spectrum of *S. bulbocastanum* in that publication is an error. In fact it should be a 2-line one. These results concur fairly well with those of Hosaka, mentioned above.

All these primitive *Stellata* species in series *Morelliformia*, *Bulbocastana*, *Pinnatisecta* and *Polyadenia* seem to be closely allied; they all possess an EBN of 1 and are confined to Mexico, the south-west USA and Guatemala. This area, or perhaps the central part of it, could well be the centre of origin of wild potato species. Even so, we still need to face the awkward question of their relationship to series *Etuberosa*. Until chloroplast genome analyses are carried out on section *Basarthrum* species it will be difficult to position the primitive *Stellata* vis-à-vis the *Etuberosa* series. If the 'Proto-Petota' originated in South America (a supposition that is by no means certain), they may have moved to Mexico in late Eocene to early Oligocene times, some 37 to 40 million years ago, when a land bridge or island arc between North and South America existed (Hawkes 1988).

A return migration of section *Petota* species, still as primitive *Stellata*, probably took place in the early Pliocene, when the Panamá isthmus was formed, some 3½ millon years ago (see Fig. 5.2). There is good evidence to show that some of these primitive *Stellata* still exist in South America. These are series *Olmosiana*, *Lignicaulia*, *Circaeifolia* and *Commersoniana*, the first three having become stranded in the 'migration race' in northern Peru, southern Peru and Bolivia respectively, whilst *Commersoniana* reached Argentina and the surrounding countries. All of these cross readily with the Mexican *Stellata* species, and have been shown to possess an EBN of 1. They do not cross easily with most of the rest of the South American diploids, which possess an EBN of 2.

The primitive *Stellata* of South America evolved to begin with into what I have termed the 'advanced' *Stellata* (Table 5.1). These are grouped into the series *Yungasensa*, covering parts of Bolivia, Argentina, Paraguay, Uruguay and south-eastern Brazil, with one possible outlier (*S. huanca-bambense*) in northern Peru. It is difficult to decide on the ancestral form of this series, but *S. chacoense* may be close to it. All possess an EBN of 2.

From this advanced *Stellata* stock came the primitive *Rotata*, with substel-late to pentagonal corolla, and the beginnings of corolla pigmentation, mostly absent in the *Stellata* superseries.

One of these primitive *Rotata* is the series *Conicibaccata*. It possesses conical berries and occurs as diploid species in its southern extremity of northern Bolivia and southern Peru. Series *Conicibaccata* is one of those that appear to have carried out a return migration northwards. The diploid species of the south possess a substellate to pentagonal corolla and give rise to tetraploid and even two hexaploid species in the north-western corner of South America. These hexaploids appear to possess limited distributions, but the tetraploids have migrated northwards through Central America (*S. longiconicum*) into Guatemala and Mexico (*S. oxycarpum* and *S. agrimo-nifolium*). By the time that the series *Conicibaccata* reached Central America and Mexico it had developed a completely rotate corolla, and on the present system can then be designated as advanced.

Primitive *Rotata* species in series *Tuberosa* with a substellate to pentago-nal corolla are found in Argentina and Bolivia. There is some evidence for their having branched off from *S. chacoense* in western Argentina (pro-vinces of Mendoza and Córdoba) giving rise to *S. kurtzianum*. In northern Bolivia the corolla lobes broaden out to give the advanced *Rotata* species. All the diploids in both groups possess an EBN of 2, with the exception of two curiously anomalous *Tuberosa* species, *S. chancayense* and *S. mochi-quense*, which have an EBN of 1. Both these are from Peru and occur mostly on the coastal lomas.

Other primitive *Rotata* series with substellate to pentagonal corollas are

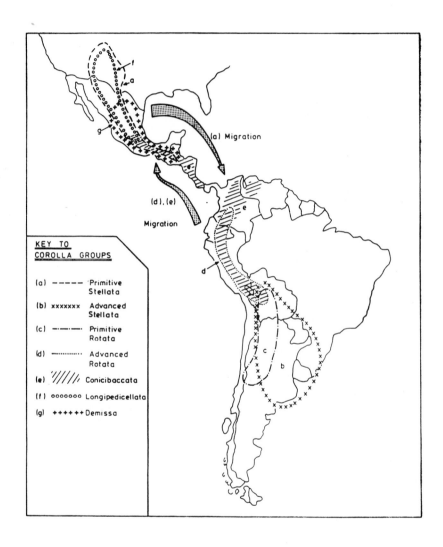

Megistacroloba and *Cuneoalata*. These begin in northern Argentina, progressing through Bolivia northwards into Peru. Series *Maglia* in Argentina and Chile with its pentagonal to sub-rotate corolla might also be classed in the primitive *Rotata* group.

In series *Tuberosa* the advanced stage has begun to appear in northern Bolivia, continuing into Peru, Ecuador, Colombia, Venezuela, and even one species, *S. verrucosum*, in Mexico. Other advanced *Rotata* series are *Piurana* and *Ingifolia*, both in Peru, but *Piurana* also spreads northwards into Colombia.

Particularly interesting are the Mexico/USA tetraploid series *Longipedicellata* and the hexaploid series *Demissa*, both of which can be classed as advanced *Rotata*. These species appear to have arisen through hybridizations between the ancient 'primitive' *Stellata* and more advanced species arriving from South America.

Cytological studies (Matsubayashi 1955) indicate that series *Longipedicellata* possesses the A genome from *S. chacoense* (series *Yungasensa*). Although six tetraploid species of series *Longipedicellata* are known they differ hardly at all in their genetic architecture, since all F_2 families raised by Hawkes (1966) between various species showed no genetic breakdown. So far, no one has been able to synthesize these species experimentally, and the postulated Mexican parent species has not been identified. It is not known either, at about what time this return migration from South America took place, but it was presumably post-Pliocene.

The Mexican hexaploids that have so far been crossed with each other produce sterile F_1 hybrids (Hawkes 1956c). This was explained by Marks (1955) who showed that they possessed two sets of homologous chromosomes, the third set being non-homologous. He suggested that one common set was derived from *S. verrucosum*. The other might have been derived from the South American genome in *S. stoloniferum* or one of the genomes of the tetraploid *Conicibaccata* species in Mexico. The fact that we can at present only make guesses about this indicates that this is a wide-open field for further research.

We have already mentioned that the one tetraploid species in series *Acaulia*, namely *S. acaule* itself, functions as an allotetraploid, with a

---

Fig. 5.2 Suggested evolutionary trends in potato species. Notes: (a) First migration of primitive *Stellata* species southwards from Mexico. Representatives (not shown on map) also found in Peru (series *Olmosiana*, *Lignicaulia*), Bolivia (series *Circaeifolia*), and Argentina, south-eastern Brazil, Paraguay and Uruguay (series *Commersoniana*). (b) Advanced *Stellata* (series *Yungasensa*) (also one species in northern Peru). (c) Primitive *Rotata* (series *Megistacroloba* – should continue further north than shown in map – *Cuneoalata*, and southern parts of *Tuberosa* and *Conicibaccata*). (d) Advanced *Rotata* (series *Piurana*, *Acaulia* and parts of *Tuberosa* and *Conicibaccata*) in central to northern South America. Return migration to Mexico by parts of (d) and (e); formation of (f) series *Longipedicellata* and (g) series *Demissa* by means of hybridization of immigrant species from South America with ones already in existence in Mexico.

Table 5.1   Major corolla groups, taxonomic series and distribution

Superseries (corolla groups)	Taxonomic series	Distribution
Stellata (*primitive*)	*Morelliformia* *Bulbocastana* *Pinnatisecta* *Polyadenia*	South-western USA, Mexico, Central America
	Lignicaulia *Circaeifolia* *Commersoniana* *Olmosiana*	South America
Stellata (advanced)	*Yungasensa*	South America
Rotata (primitive)	*Cuneoalata* *Megistacroloba* *Maglia* Southern forms of *Tuberosa* Southern forms of *Conicibaccata*	Southern to central regions of South America
Rotata (advanced)	*Piurana* *Ingifolia* *Acaulia* Central and northern forms of *Tuberosa* and *Conicibaccata*	Central to northern regions of South America
	Longipedicellata *Demissa* Mexican forms of *Conicibaccata*	South-western USA, Mexico, Central America

genome formula according to Matsubayashi of AAA^aA^a. This points towards some kind of past hybridization between two distinct species, but which ones? We still do not know, though it is possible that one came from series *Megistacroloba* and another from series *Tuberosa*. No one has yet been able to synthesize *S. acaule* from its diploid ancestors or to break it down into dihaploids. This, also, would be a useful field for further research.

The hexaploid species *S. albicans*, in series *Acaulia*, seems clearly on morphological grounds to possess the AAA^aA^a genome from *S. acaule*. It is bushy in habit, has almost white flowers and plentiful long white shaggy pubescence. Perhaps *S. cajamarquense* or some similar species could be a candidate for providing the third genome in *S. albicans*.

We have mentioned earlier in passing (Table 4.1) that certain species possess more than one cytotype. One of these is *S. gourlayi* in Argentina, with diploid and tetraploid cytotypes. Even though the tetraploids may have originated through autotetraploidy, their present status is not clearly understood (Clausen and Okada 1987).

Another species with various cytotypes is *S. oplocence*. The diploid cytotype is rare and has been found only twice. Tetraploid and hexaploid cytotypes are frequent but whether they are auto- or allo-polyploids is unclear.

We know more about the tetraploid Bolivian weed species, *S. sucrense*, which has been shown to be a natural hybrid of *S. oplocense* (4x) × *S. tuberosum* subsp. *andigena* (4x) (Astley 1979, Astley and Hawkes 1979). It possesses much useful genetic diversity inherited from each of its parents (see Hawkes and Hjerting 1989).

The origin of cultivated potatoes

It is possible to speak with more certainty about cultivated potato origins than the wild ones. This is due partly to the greater general interest in cultivated species and also to the fact that they came into existence only 7,000–10,000 years ago.

Vavilov (1951) proposed that the origin of a cultivated plant was to be found in its region of greatest diversity – the 'centres of origin' hypothesis. This was based on the assumption that the longer a crop had existed in an area the greater its genetic diversity. Conversely, by identifying the area of greatest diversity one could assume that the crop had been there for longer than anywhere else and hence had originated there. This hypothesis is based on the assumption that mutation rates and selection pressures for a given crop are everywhere identical, which may not always be so. Nevertheless, Vavilov's hypothesis provides a useful starting point.

Many scientists, myself included, have preferred to pay equal attention to the distribution of wild species and their degree of relationship to cultivated ones. Certainly, with the greater range of techniques now available to us we are able to pinpoint more accurately the wild prototype and centre of origin of a crop than was possible in Vavilov's day.

With cultivated potatoes, the area (rather than the centre) of diversity lies in the central Andes of Peru and Bolivia (Figs 1.1 and 1.2). Somewhere from central Peru to central Bolivia could thus possibly be the point of origin of potato domestication.

It is logical to assume that the most 'primitive' of the diploid species, that is to say, the one most similar to wild ones, might have been the first to be domesticated. This is *S. stenotomum*, which is now grown in the area of Peru and Bolivia mentioned above. In fact the most 'wild-looking' biotypes of this species occur in the general region of the Lake Titicaca basin and especially in northern Bolivia.

How does this accord with the distribution of related wild species? To begin with, we must look at the diploids in series *Tuberosa* occurring in the area mentioned above. The species that most closely conforms to these requirements is *S. leptophyes*, which occurs in northern Bolivia at the same altitudes (3,200–3,950 m) as *S. stenotomum* (3,000–4,000 m) and in the same phytogeographical region.

We have already mentioned (Chapter 2) that early domesticated potatoes were found in central Peru, radiocarbon dated to 7000 BP. This is not exactly in the north Bolivian area but one could easily assume that by 7000 BP the domesticated potato had begun to spread northwards and southwards into other regions, having perhaps originated some one to three millenia earlier.

One of the generally required desiderata for the beginnings of agriculture is a relatively stable population of hunter-gatherers, perhaps settled near river or lake margins where a plentiful food supply was available (Hawkes 1969). The southern margins of Lake Titicaca and the northern margins of Lake Poopó just to the south fulfil these requirements perfectly.

To sum up, then, it would seem that the potato may have been domesticated in what is now the Lake Titicaca to Lake Poopó region of north Bolivia, that it originated from the wild diploid species *S. leptophyes* some 10,000 to 7,000 years ago, and that the first domesticated potato species was *S. stenotomum*.

Potato evolution after domestication

The evolution of potatoes did not by any means end with the formation of *S. stenotomum*. In fact, one might with truth say that this was only the beginning.

As Fig. 5.3 shows, at least four wild potato species were involved in the evolution of cultivated potatos. The first was *S. leptophyes*, as we have already seen. From this was derived the first basic cultivated species, *S. stenotomum*. The other three wild species,*S. sparsipilum*, *S. acaule* and *S. megistacrolobum* played their role *after* the initial domestication step.

The most important event in cultivated potato evolution was the hybridization between *S. stenotomum* and *S. sparsipilum* to form the amphidiploid, *S. tuberosum*. *Solanum sparsipilum* is a weed species with a lower altitude distribution (2,200–3,950 m) on average than that of *S. stenotomum*. However, they overlap in their present-day distribution in the 3,200–3,950 m range, and therefore the opportunity for hybridization may well have been present.

It should at this point be mentioned that some authorities believe that *S. tuberosum* is a straight autotetraploid of *S. stenotomum*, but Cribb and Hawkes (1986) have provided strong evidence in support of the allotetraploid origin of *S. tuberosum*.

The originally formed subspecies of *S. tuberosum* was undoubtedly the Andean subspecies *andigena* (Fig. 1.2). From this was evolved subspecies *tuberosum* in Chile, derived from subspecies *andigena* many millenia ago (see also Chapter 2).

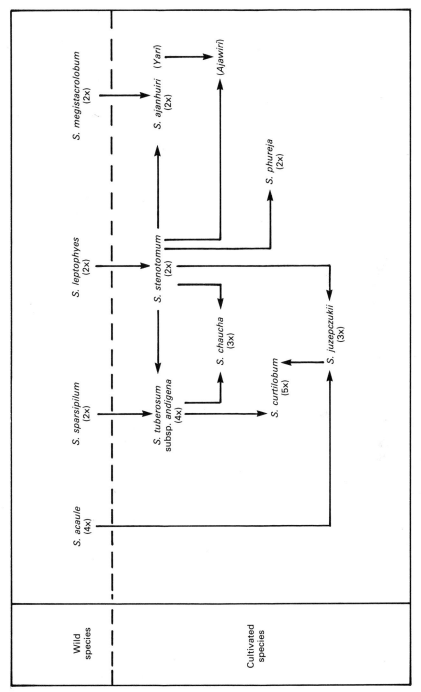

Fig. 5.3 Evolutionary relationships of cultivated potatoes and their ploidy levels.

Then came the incorporation of frost resistance into the cultivated potato. It should be mentioned here, however, that the *time sequence* of these events is not known, apart from the logical fact that *S. chaucha* and *S. curtilobum* must have been formed *after S. tuberosum*.

There were two sequences in the formation of frost-resistant potatoes. The first of these involved natural crosses between *S. stenotomum* and the wild frost-resistant diploid species *S. megistacrolobum* (series *Megistacroloba*) (Huamán *et al.* 1980, 1982, 1983; Johns and Osman 1985; Johns and Keen 1986). The initial stage of this process probably took place on the high Bolivian altiplano near Oruro and gave rise to a group of *S. ajanhuiri* varieties named *Yari*, with very obvious *S. megistacrolobum* features. The second stage involved either a natural F_1 sib-mating or, more likely, backcrosses to *S. ajanhuiri*. These resulted in the *Ajawiri* group of varieties. The latter were evidently more successful than the *Yari* group and spread northwards into the area round Lake Titicaca and thence to Peru, and also southwards to Potosí (see Hawkes and Hjerting 1989, 382–6). Both these groups of *S. ajanhuiri* are highly frost-resistant and were undoubtedly selected by the Aymará Indians who first named them and who praised them in their folk songs (Huamán *et al.* 1980).

Another source of frost resistance in the cultivated potato was the wild tetraploid species *S. acaule*. The cross *S. acaule* × *S. stenotomum* gave rise to highly sterile triploids, named *S. juzepczukii* (Hawkes 1962a; Schmiediche *et al.* 1980, 1982). This is the most frost-resistant of all the cultivated species. It can be grown at altitudes of 3,450–4,500 m, which, together with *Lepidium meyenii* from central Peru, must attain an altitude record for food crops in the New World and probably in the Old World also.

From *S. juzepczukii* a further natural cross, this time with *S. tuberosum* subsp. *andigena*, gave rise to the pentaploid hybrid, *S. curtilobum*. Hawkes (1962a) showed that (as with *S. juzepczukii*) this cross could be re-created artificially, and postulated that a 2n gamete with 36 chromosomes from *S. juzepczukii* had united with a normal 24-chromosome gamete of *S. tuberosum*. Schmiediche *et al.* (1982) were also able to re-create *S. juzepczukii* but could not make the second cross with *S. tuberosum*, even though an alternative method was demonstrated for the creation of *S. curtilobum*, crossing *S. juzepczukii* by *S. stentotomum* (subsp. *goniocalyx*) the latter providing a 2n gamete. It is worth noting that *S. curtilobum* is also frost-resistant and can be cultivated also at the very high altitudes of 3,450–4,400 m.

The other diploid cultigen, *S. phureja*, evolved from *S. stenotomum* by human selection for rapid maturity and lack of tuber dormancy, in order to develop varieties capable of yielding two or even three crops a year in the lower, eastern frost-free Andean valleys. *Solanum phureja* evolved undoubtedly through unconscious selection by the Indian cultivators and it might have been polyphyletic, created several times in different regions by different Indian communities. It is very widely distributed (Fig. 1.1), having spread much further north than *S. stenotomum*. This is probably due to the fact that being adapted to lower valley regions it could bridge the lowland gap in north Peru and southern Ecuador – a feat impossible to the high-altitude adapted *S. stenotomum*. In that way it was able to spread into northern Ecuador, Colombia and Venezuela, in all of which countries it is widely grown and well esteemed.

Finally, a series of triploid hybrid clones exists in Peru and Bolivia, derived from crosses between *S. tuberosum* subsp. *andigena* and *S. stenotomum*. These have been given a species name, *S. chaucha*, for ease of reference. They were investigated and their nature elucidated by M.T. Jackson (Jackson *et al.* 1977, 1978) and are grown at similar altitudes and in the same region as *S. stenotomum* (see also Ochoa 1975).

After the above account of the evolution of wild and cultivated potato species, we can begin to see the main outlines of the process becoming clearer. If this chapter has done anything to point out gaps in our knowledge and areas of possible future research, it will have attained the purpose for which it was intended.

CHAPTER 6

POTATO SYSTEMATICS AND BIODIVERSITY

General

Because of the confusingly large number of species in the genus *Solanum* (some 900 at the last estimate), taxonomists have established various subgenera, of which the subgenus *Potatoe* (G. Don) D'Arcy includes the potatoes and various other groups of species that are assumed to be in some way taxonomically related to them (see p. 64).

Subgenus *Potatoe* has been further subdivided into sections, of which the section *Petota* includes the tuber-bearing species. This section is perhaps better known as *Tuberarium*, a name taken from Dunal (1852) by the German *Solanum* taxonomist Georg Bitter (1912). Unfortunately, this proved to be a synonym of the earlier published *Petota*, which according to the International Code of Botanical Nomenclature has priority in terms of the date of its publication.

Bitter (1912) also divided his section *Tuberarium* into two subsections. Attention was drawn to the fact that the pedicel, or flower stalk, possessed a kind of joint or articulation, which broke off when the flowers withered if they were not fertilized, or when the fruits matured and were ready to be dispersed.

The pedicel articulation seems to be a useful taxonomic character, and Bitter used it to characterize his two subsections. These were *Basarthrum*, in which the pedicel articulation was placed at the base; and *Hyperbasarthrum*, with pedicel articulation above the base. Clearly, of course, there were many other characters which distinguished these two subsections. In the following year (1913) Bitter decided that the two subsections were more distinct than he had at first thought, and he therefore moved *Basarthrum* up in rank to the level of section, where it still remains.

Subsection *Hyperbasarthrum* was also found to be a later synonym for subsection *Potatoe* of G. Don, published in 1838, and therefore taking precedence over *Hyperbasarthrum*. Another subsection, *Estolonifera*, was recently established by Hawkes, in 1989, to accommodate those series which, although very close to the tuber-bearing species in most of their above-ground features, never produce stolons or tubers.

It is unfortunate that so many name changes have recently taken place in the categories lying above the rank of species, but these changes are in fact required to conform with the rules of the International Code of Botanical Nomenclature.

At a lower level of classification (but still above the species level) I have added two superseries, *Stellata* and *Rotata*, to differentiate between species with stellate (or star-shaped) and those with rotate (or wheel-shaped) corollas, respectively (Hawkes 1989). I feel that such groupings help one to understand better the evolutionary relationships between species and series than would otherwise be the case.

Below the rank of superseries come the series themselves, two in subsection *Estolonifera*, nine in superseries *Stellata* and ten in superseries *Rotata*. *Solanum* enthusiasts who are familiar with the classification in the previous editions of this work will see some changes, both in names and sequence. In the present scheme I have tried to group the series into a more meaningful evolutionary sequence (even though this is not really possible to attain satisfactorily in a linear format, of course). I have also tried to group in each series species that seem to be closely related, though, as before, series *Tuberosa* is still not completely satisfactory. Name changes here and there are due partly to the more correct application of the International Rules of Nomenclature and partly to the creation of new series by splitting them off from already existing ones.

Since the above paragraphs may seem a little confusing to the non-taxonomist the new classification is shown below in a condensed form (Table 6.1). More detailed information follows later.

As mentioned already, this sequence of subsections, superseries and series reflects what I believe to be an approximate evolutionary sequence (see Chapter 5). We start with subsection *Estolonifera*, in which the two series *Etuberosa* and *Juglandifolia* do not possess stolons or tubers, but at least seem to bear some sort of relationship to the tuber-bearing species.

We then progress to the true potatoes, grouped in the well-named subsection *Potatoe*. This is divided into two superseries, *Stellata* and *Rotata*, characterized by star-shaped and rotate or wheel-shaped corollas respectively. Nine series are delimited in superseries *Stellata*, most with white or almost white flowers, and all basically diploid.

Superseries *Rotata* includes ten series of which three are basically diploid (*Megistacroloba*, *Cuneoalata* and *Ingifolia*), four are diploid and polyploid (*Conicibaccata*, *Maglia*, *Piurana* and *Tuberosa*), whilst three are completely polyploid (*Acaulia*, *Longipedicellata* and *Demissa*).

It should be noted that many otherwise diploid species give evidence of triploid cytotypes, derived no doubt from the union of normal haploid gametes with 2n gametes. However, these triploid cytotypes could appear to be evolutionary dead ends, since they are highly sterile.

Table 6.1   Classification of potato species and their allies

Genus: *Solanum L.*
  Subgenus: Potatoe (G. Don) A'Arcy
    Section: *Petota* Dumortier
      Subsection: *Estolonifera* Hawkes
        Series I: *Etuberosa* Juzepczuk
        Series II: *Juglandifolia* (Rydb.) Hawkes
      Subsection: *Potatoe* G. Don
        Superseries: *Stellata* Hawkes
        Series I: *Morelliformia* Hawkes
        Series II: *Bulbocastana* (Rydb.) Hawkes
        Series III: *Pinnatisecta* (Rydb.) Hawkes
        Series IV: *Polyadenia* Bukasov *ex* Correll
        Series V: *Commersoniana* Bukasov
        Series VI: *Circaeifolia* Hawkes
        Series VII: *Lignicaulia* Hawkes
        Series VIII: *Olmosiana* Ochoa
        Series IX: *Yungasensa* Correll
        Superseries: *Rotata* Hawkes
        Series X: *Megistacroloba* Cárd et Hawkes
        Series XI: *Cuneoalata* Hawkes
        Series XII: *Conicibaccata* Bitter
        Series XIII: *Piurana* Hawkes
        Series XIV: *Ingifolia* Ochoa
        Series XV: *Maglia* Bitter
        Series XVI: *Tuberosa* (Rydb.) Hawkes
        Series XVII: *Acaulia* Juzepczuk
        Series XVIII: *Longipedicellata* Bukasov
        Series XIX: *Demissa* Bukasov

The detailed taxonomy of section *Petota*

In the treatment of *Solanum* species given in the following pages the species are arranged under their appropriate series as follows:

(i)   Species known from living or herbarium material are listed alphabetically.

(ii)   Species known only from descriptions, but sometimes also from illustrations, are presented in smaller type directly following group (i) in each series and are arranged alphabetically. These are relatively unknown to me and cannot yet be placed with those which I have studied in the living state or as actual herbarium specimens.

(iii)   Species whose identity is doubtful or ambiguous and whose names have been mentioned in the literature with no type specimen cited or even no description (*nomina nuda*). These are listed in Appendix I.

In addition, I have included for easy reference a table (Appendix II) of the better-known species that have been studied in a living state, arranged according to taxonomic series and chromosome number, with a reference to the country or countries to which each species is native.

Species treatments

Each species is named in bold-face type, followed by its author and the journal or book in which the original description was published.

This is followed by a list of synonyms both at the specific and infraspecific level (varieties and forms). I have followed my previous method of distinguishing subspecies as useful taxonomic entities. Where varieties and forms have been described they are mentioned in the text where they seem to be of value taxonomically.

A brief description follows, in which what I believe to be the most easily recognizable characters are noted. (See glossary and figures in Appendix III.)

Following this are notes on the species distribution and its habitat, and altitude where known.

Then comes a phrase headed 'Derivation', which indicates the meaning of the latin names and which may be helpful to those who find them rather daunting.

After this are given the chromosome number(s) (2n) and embryo balance number (EBN) as explained on pp. 48–9.

Finally, information is given on where living material is said to be available, according to the most recent catalogue or inventory that I have. It must be understood that I cannot be held responsible for the material in terms of whether it is still available or whether it is true to type. I have, however, fairly recently revised the living collections in Sturgeon Bay and have checked over most of the Braunschweig material also.

The abbreviations and addresses of the sources of living germplasm material are as follows, the date in the last column indicating when the last inventory was published.

Bal.	Instituto Nacional de Tecnología Agropecuaria (INTA), Estación Experimental Regional, CC 276, 7620 Balcarce, Provincia de Buenos Aires, Argentina	1974
Braun.	Institut für Pflanzenbau und Pflanzenzüchtung, Bundesallee 50, D-3300 Braunschweig, Federal Republic of Germany	1987
CIP	Centro Internacional de la Papa, Apartado 5969, Lima, Peru	1985, but only cultivated materials
CPC	Commonwealth Potato Collection, Scottish Crop Research Institute, Mylnefield, Invergowrie, Dundee DD2 5DA, UK	1969
Gr.Lü.	Institut für Kartoffelforschung Gross Lüsewitz, Deutsche Akademie der	1980

	Landwirtschaftswissenschaften, Gross-Lüsewitz, Postleitzahl 2551, German Democratic Republic	
Stur.	Potato Introduction Station, Sturgeon Bay, Wisconsin 54235, USA	1986
UAC	Universidad Austral de Chile, Casilla 567, Valdivia, Chile	1987
VIR	N.I. Vavilov Institute of Plant Industry, (Attention Professor K. Budin), 44 Herzen Street, Leningrad 190000, USSR	1987

Many other small collections no doubt exist, but I have no inventories of these and cannot therefore list them. My own collection is now with the Commonwealth Potato Collection, but duplicates of most of my accessions can also be found at Braunschweig and Sturgeon Bay.

Key to series and to species

Identification keys are difficult to construct and to use. I included them in the first and second editions and have also done so in this one. Having had no feedback from users I can only conclude that these keys were either satisfactory or that no one had the courage to use them!

When there are very large numbers of species in a series, as in *Conicibaccata* and *Tuberosa*, key construction can become difficult, particularly as potatoes are so phenotypically plastic. However, keying out material should not be too difficult provided that well-grown specimens from the experimental field are examined, with flowers and fruit. Juvenile material or plants from an overheated and overcrowded glasshouse with poor light conditions are very difficult or even impossible to identify. An absence of flowers and fruits also raises problems.

When a specimen has been provisionally identified with the key it should of course be compared with the brief description given in the text. Further information on chromosome number and origin of the accession may also be useful.

Finally, comparison can be made with the excellent plates in Correll's 1962 publication *The Potato and its Wild Relatives*. If material is known to have come from Argentina, Brazil, Paraguay or Uruguay it can be checked by reference to the 1969 publication of Hawkes and Hjerting *The Potatoes of Argentina, Brazil, Paraguay and Uruguay*. Bolivian material can be checked with the 1989 publication by Hawkes and Hjerting *The Potatoes of Bolivia*. Full references to these are given in the bibliography.

It should be noted that no keys are provided for species given in small type, that is to say, those where living or herbarium specimens have not been available for study, or for hybrid species.

KEY TO SERIES WITHIN SECTION *PETOTA*

(1) Plants never developing stolons or tubers
Subsection *Estolonifera* (2)
Plants always developing stolons or tubers at some point in their life cycle Subsection *Potatoe* (3)

(2) Flowers purple or blue, pedicel articulation at or very near the base
Series I *Etuberosa* (p. 69)
Flowers bright yellow: pedicel articulation at some distance above the base Series II *Juglandifolia* (p. 72)

(3) Corolla stellate, its lobes as long or longer than broad, not clearly delimited from acumens Superseries *Stellata* (4)
Corolla rotate, pentagonal or sub-stellate, the lobes broader than long, well delimited from acumens Superseries *Rotata* (14)

(4) Berries ovate-conical, from 1½ to 3 or even 4 times as long as broad
(5)
Berries globular, occasionally ovate or cordate, less than 1½ times as long as broad (8)

(5) Plants covered with abundant glands of an unpleasant odour and dense long spreading hairs Series IV *Polyadenia* (in part) (p. 85)
Plants without glands (6)

(6) Fruits sharp-pointed, flowers white Series VI *Circaeifolia* (p. 89)
Fruits not sharp-pointed, flowers white or purple (7)

(7) Leaflets apically obtuse or rounded; flowers white or white streaked with purple (Argentina, Brazil, Paraguay, Uruguay)
Series V *Commersoniana* (p. 86)
Leaflets apically acute; flowers white (Mexico, USA)
Series III *Pinnatisecta* (in part) (p. 77)

(8) Leaves simple, without lateral leaflets (9)
Leaves with lateral leaflets (10)

(9) Flower very small (to 15 mm diam.); anthers very narrow, somewhat adhering to each other laterally; plant generally epiphytic (Mexico, Guatemala) Series I *Morelliformia* (p. 75)
Flower 2–2.5 cm diam.; anthers broad, not adhering laterally; plant not epiphytic (Mexico, Guatemala)
Series II *Bulbocastana* (p. 75)

(10) Plant covered with glands of an unpleasant odour, and often with some non-glandular hairs (11)
Plant with or without glands; if present of a sweet odour (12)

(11) Plants herbaceous; glandular odour very strong and objectionable (Mexico) Series IV *Polyadenia* (in part) (p. 85)
Plants woody at base; glandular odour fairly strong (Peru)
Series VII *Lignicaulia* (p. 91)

(12) Leaf rachis with an undulating wing; tuber densely and finely pubescent (N. Peru) Series VIII *Olmosiana* (p. 92)
Leaf rachis with normal interjected leaflets or without any, never with an undulating wing; tubers glabrous (13)

(13) Corolla lobes narrow, more than twice as long as broad (Mexico, USA)   Series III *Pinnatisecta* (in part) (p. 77)
Corolla lobes broader, about 1½–2 times as long as broad (Bolivia, Argentina, Paraguay, Uruguay, Brazil)
Series IX *Yungasensa* (p. 92)

(14) Stamens in a loose barrel-shaped column; anthers not clearly delimited from filaments, neither in colour nor shape (Argentina, Chile)   Series XV *Maglia* (p. 127)
Stamens in a conical or cylindrical column; anthers clearly delimited from filaments   (15)

(15) Berries ovate-conical, more than 2 times as long as broad (Bolivia northwards to Mexico)   Series XII *Conicibaccata* (p. 105)
Berries globular to ovoid, less than 2 times as long as broad   (16)

(16) Corolla lobes very short and flat, with small acumens (1.5–2 mm long), giving the flowers a ten-lobed appearance   (17)
Corolla lobes not short and flat, rounded and with acumens longer than 2.5 mm   (18)

(17) Pedicel articulation generally absent, or if present, high up underneath the calyx; plants typically growing as rosettes with very short stem (Peru, southwards to Argentina)
Series XVII *Acaulia* (p. 182)
Pedicel articulation always present, placed above the centre but not just below calyx base; plants with well-developed stems (but often low-growing and bushy in *S. demissum*) (Mexico, Guatemala)
Series XIX *Demissa* (p. 192)

(18) Berries ovoid, with flattened apex; leaves shining, 'varnished', the margin rolled under, especially when dry; leaf and stem glabrous or with inconspicuous hairs (Peru, Ecuador, Colombia)
Series XIII *Piurana* (p. 120)
Berries normally globose; plant without the above combination of characters   (19)

(19) Rachis wings parallel-sided and somewhat lobed (N. Peru)
Series XIV *Ingifolia* (p. 126)
Rachis wings absent or if present smoothly decurrent and diminishing in width from the base of each leaflet   (20)

(20) Corolla pentagonal to substellate; leaf with sessile lobes and broadly decurrent wings; no interjected leaflets present   (21)
Corolla rotate to pentagonal; leaf without broadly decurrent wings; interjected leaflets generally present   (22)

(21) Plants low-growing; terminal lobe much larger than laterals; articulation very high up below calyx base (Argentina, Bolivia, Peru)
Series X *Megistacroloba* (p. 98)
Plants delicate, with pinnatisect leaves and wedge-shaped wings on rachis (Argentina, Chile, Bolivia)   Series XI *Cuneoalata* (p. 103)

(22) Corolla lobes smoothly rounded and acumens large, so giving the corolla a completely circular appearance with acumens standing out sharply from it, or sometimes giving a more pentagonal appearance (Mexico, USA)   Series XVIII *Longipedicellata* (p. 186)

Corolla lobes not formed so as to give circular appearance to the flower (except in certain cultivated forms) (North and South America)   Series XVI *Tuberosa* (p. 128)

Series and species descriptions

Subgenus *POTATOE* (G. Don) D'Arcy
  (Ann. Missouri Bot. Gard. **59**, 276, 1972)
Section *PETOTA* Dumort.
  (Fl. Belg. **39**, 1827)

Subsection *ESTOLONIFERA* Hawkes (Taxon **38**, 490, 1989)

This subsection contains two series of which the species do not bear stolons or tubers. They are, however, related to the true potatoes to some extent, especially series *Etuberosa*, with which hybrids with potato species can be made, although with considerable difficulty.

Series *Juglandifolia* is less related to potatoes and would seem to be a link between them and the tomato genus, *Lycopersicon*.

SERIES I   *ETUBEROSA* JUZ.

(Bull. Acad. Sci., URSS **2**, 301, 1937, *nomen nudum*; *ex* Buk. & Kameraz, Bases of Potato Breeding, 18, 1959)

Herbs with very low, almost basal, pedicel articulation, but without the 'bayonet hairs' typical of section *Basarthrum*. The plants bear no stolons or tubers, though they are sometimes rhizomatous. Corolla rotate, purplish or bluish.
Distribution: central Chile as far south as the island of Chiloé; Nahuel Huapi region of south Argentina; Islands of Juan Fernández.

KEY TO SPECIES

(1) Pedicel articulated completely at the base; calyx, stem and leaf glabrous or glabrescent (Juan Fernández Islands)   **3. *S. fernandezianum***
Pedicel articulated above the base; plant rarely completely glabrous or glabrescent (mainland of Chile and Argentina)   (2)
(2) Calyx with acumen completely absent or not more than 0.5–1 mm long
                (3)
Calyx with well-developed acumen, 1–2 mm long or more   (4)
(3) Plant densely pubescent; pedicel articulation ¼ to ⅓ above the base; anthers minutely puberulous externally (maritime marshes)
                4. *S. palustre*
Plant with short, velvety pubescence or glabrescent; pedicel articulation lower, 2–4 mm above the base; anthers not puberulous
                1. *S. brevidens*

(4) Plant small, less than 20–30 cm tall, subglabrous; interjected leaflets none (very occasionally one)   **5. S. subandinum**
Plant larger, pubescent, with fairly numerous interjected leaflets (always more than three)   **2. S. etuberosum**

1. S. brevidens Phil. (Anal. Univ. Chile, Santiago **43**, 521, 1873)

S. pearcei Phil. (Anal. Univ. Chile, Santiago **91**, 5–6, 1895; non S. pearcei Britton ex Rusby in Mem. Torr. Bot. Cl. **4**, 227, 1895)
S. bridgesii A.DC. (Arch. Sci. Phys. Nat., Ser. 3, **15**, 437, 1886); non S. bridgesii Phil. (Linnaea **33**, 203, 1864–65)
S. tuberosum var. brevidens (Phil.) Reiche (Anal. Univ. Chile, Santiago **124**, 736, 1909)
S. tuberosum var. pearcei (Phil.) Reiche (Fl. Chile **5**, 353, 1910)

A highly polymorphic species, generally with medium dense pubescence (but see below); pedicel articulation 2–4 mm above base; calyx acumens very short (0–0.5 mm); corolla sky blue, paling to white at edges. Berries globose, 1.5–2 cm diam.

S. brevidens var. **glabrescens (Poepp. ex Schlechtd.) Hawkes** comb. nov.

S. palustre Poepp. var. parviflora glabrescens ex Schlechtd. (Hort. Halensis **1**, 5, 1841)
S. palustre var. glabrescens Walp. (Repert. **3**, 39, 1845)
S. caldasii Dun. var. glabrescens (DC Prodr. **13**(1), 37, 1852)
S. etuberosum var. antucense Bitt. (Fedde, Repert **11**, 376, 1912)

Certain forms of S. brevidens which are almost glabrous are listed here. These have been considerably moved around in the older literature. Based on the position of the pedicel articulation and the very short calyx acumens these should for the present be placed with S. brevidens. They come from the Andes of Antuco (prov. Bío-Bío) and should be looked for and collected in the living state to elucidate further their taxonomic status.
General distribution of S. brevidens: south central to south Chile from Bío-Bío to Chiloé and prov. Nahuel Huapi in Argentina.
Note: plant breeders have used material under the name S. caldasii var. glabrescens which really belongs to S. chacoense.
Derivation: Short-toothed, referring to the calyx acumens
2n = 24, EBN = 1
Bal., Braun., CPC, Stur., UAC

2. S. etuberosum Lindl. (Bot. Reg. **20**, t. 1712, 1835)

S. bustillosii Phil. (Linnaea **29**, 24, 1857/8)
S. looseri Juz. (Bull. Acad. Sci. URSS, ser. Biol. **2**, 301–02, 1937)
S. etuberosum var. bustillosii (Phil) Witasek (in Reiche, Fl. Chile **5**, 354, 1910)

S. etuberosum var. *chillanense* Bitt. (Fedde, Repert. **11**, 376–7, 1912)
S. tuberosum var. *polemoniifolium* Hook. f. (Fl. Antarct. **2**, 330, 1846)
S. tuberosum var. *polemoniifolium* (Walp. Repert **6**, 583, 1847)

Distinguished by yellowish-green stems and leaves, with short velvety pubescence and often crisped leaflet margins; pedicel articulation 4–5 mm above the base; calyx with well-marked teeth (1–1.5 mm); corolla rich purple, very showy.
Distribution: north central Chile from prov. Colchagua south to Ñuble and Bío-Bío. Dry mountain forests, from 1,250–2,500 m.
Derivation: Without tubers
2n = 24, EBN = 1
Braun., CPC, Stur., UAC

3. *S. fernandezianum* Phil. (Linnaea **29**, 23–4, 1857–58)

S. brevistylum Wittmack, *nom. nud.* in Berthault (Ann. Sci. Agron. Franç. et Etrang., Ser. 3 **6**(2), 185–6, 1911)
S. tuberosum var. *fernandezianum* (Phil.) Reiche, (Fl. Chile **5**, 353, 1910)

Plant glabrous or glabrescent; pedicel articulation right at the base.
Distribution: Islands of Juan Fernández. Wet forests, from 100–600 m.
Derivation: From the Islands of Juan Fernández
2n = 24, EBN = 1
Braun., Stur., UAC

4. *S. palustre* Poepp. ex Schlechtd. (Hort. Halensis **1**, 5, 1841)

Plant with a very dense white indumentum mostly of glandular hairs; pedicel articulation ¼ to ⅓ above the base; anthers minutely puberulent externally.
Distribution: Chile. Sea marshes near Valparaiso, rare or possibly extinct.
Derivation: From marshes or swampy places

5. *S. subandinum* Meigen (in Engler, Bot. Jahrb. **17**, 271, 293, 1893)

non S. subandinum Phil. (Anal. Univ. Chile, Santiago **91**, 13–14, 1895)
S. kunzei Phil. (Anal. Univ. Chile, Santiago **91**, 6–7, 1895)

Small plants (20–30 cm high or less), subglabrous and rarely with interjected leaflets; calyx acumens fairly well-developed; corolla purple, 1 cm diam. Probably closely related to *S. etuberosum*.
Distribution: Chile. Mountain woods and rocks near Santiago, Valle de San Ramón, Alfalfar and Río Colorado, at 1,700–2,300 m.
Note: chromosome number 2n = 48 (reported in USDA Bulletin 533 **20**, 1958) is probably an error, since this species has not yet been studied in the living state so far as I am aware.
Derivation: From the subandean region

SERIES II *JUGLANDIFOLIA* (RYDB.) HAWKES

(Bull. Imp. Bur. Pl. Breed. Genet., Cambridge, 12, 1944) – as series

Solanum [rankless] *Juglandifolia* Rydberg (Bull. Torr. Bot. Club **51**, 146, 173, 1924)

Plants with herbaceous to woody stems, bright yellow flowers and no stolons or tubers. They are included with the true potatoes because of the position of the pedicel articulation at some distance above the base. They bear obvious resemblances both to section *Neolycopersicon* (*S. pennellii*) and to the genus *Lycopersicon* in their morphology, differing from both in the absence of floral bracts and from *Lycopersicon* in the absence of sterile anther tips. Further research may indicate the removal of series *Juglandifolia* from section *Petota* altogether.

Distribution: mountains of Central America and north-western South America as far south as the coastal ranges of Peru and north Chile.

KEY TO SPECIES

(1)   Leaf irregularly bi-pinnatisect; plant herbaceous or bushy, no more
       than 2.5 m tall   (2)
       Leaf pinnate; plant a perennial woody climber (liane), much more
       than 2.5 m tall   (3)
(2)   Plant glandular-pubescent throughout; stem woody, at least near the
       base   **3. *S. lycopersicoides***
       Plant glabrous, fleshy-leaved, herbaceous   **4. *S. sitiens***
(3)   Leaf rugose, hispid above; interjected leaflets few to absent; berries
       not more than 4.5 cm diam.   **1. *S. juglandifolium***
       Leaf smooth, velvety; interjected leaflets frequent; berries up to 6 cm
       diam.   **2. *S. ochranthum***

1. *S. juglandifolium* Dun. (Synopsis, Montpellier **6**, 1816)

S. lehmannianum Bitt (Fedde, Repert. **10**, 532–3, 1912)
S. juglandifolium var. *lehmannianum* (Bitt.) Bitt. (Fedde, Repert. **11**, 461, 1912)
S. juglandifolium var. *oerstedii* Bitt. (Fedde, Repert. **11**, 461–2, 1912)
S. juglandifolium var. *suprascaberrimum* Bitt. (Fedde, Repert. **11**, 462, 1912)
S. juglandifolium subsp. *cundinamarcae* Bitt. (Fedde, Repert. **12**, 58–9, 1913)

A perennial woody climber (liane); leaf pinnate, 3–4(–5)-jugate, rugose and hispid above; interjected leaflets few or absent; flowers bright yellow, stellate; fruit up to 4.5 cm diam. but generally smaller, globose.

Distribution: Costa Rica, Venezuela, Colombia and Ecuador. High rainfall forests, scrub woodland and hedges at 1,000–3,000 m.

Note: Bitter's one subspecies (*cundinamarcae*) and three varieties (*lehmannianum, oerstedii* and *suprascaberrimum*), based mainly on slight differences of leaf dissection and size, do not merit taxonomic status.
Derivation: Leaf similar to that of *Juglans*, the walnut tree
2n = 24
Stur.

2. *S. ochranthum* **Dun.** (Synopsis, Montpellier **6**, 1816)

S. caldasii Dun. (Synopsis, Montepellier **6**, 1816)
S. ochranthum var. *endopogon* Bitt. (Fedde, Repert. **11**, 464–5, 1912)
S. ochranthum var. *connascens* Bitt. (Fedde, Repert. **11**, 465, 1912)
S. ochranthum var. *septemjugum* Bitt. (Fedde, Repert. **11**, 465, 1912)
S. ochranthum var. *glabrifilamentum* Bitt. (Fedde, Repert. **11**, 466, 1912)
S. ochranthum var. *quinquejugum* Hawkes (Bull. Imp. Bur. Pl. Breed. Genet., Cambridge, 112, 1944)

Habit as for *S. juglandifolium*; leaf pinnate, 4–5(–7)-jugate, smooth and velvety; interjected leaflets very numerous; flowers golden yellow, substellate to pentagonal. Very large berries to 6 cm diam., slightly 3-lobed, resembling a green tomato, though much harder; seeds also tomato-like, large. (Forms known to plant breeders under the name of *S. caldasii* or *S. caldasii* var. *glabrescens* do not belong here, but are classed with *S. chacoense*, q.v.).
Distribution: Colombia, Ecuador and Peru. Humid forests, scrub woodland and hedges at 1,800–3,500 m.
Derivation: ochre-yellow flowers
2n = 24
Braun. (not in inventory), CPC, Stur.

3. *S. lycopersicoides* **Dun.** (in DC Prodr. **13**, I, 38, 1852)

A bush or shrub, to 2.5 m tall. Leaf bi-pinnatisect, very similar to that of the tomato. Flowers bright yellow, rotate. Fruit about 1 cm diam., dark purple.
Distribution: south Peru, dept Tacna. Open ground amongst volcanic rocks, from 2,800–3,150 m.
Derivation: Similar to *Lycopersicon*, the tomato
2n = 24
Stur., UAC

4. *S. sitiens* **Johnston** (Revista Chilena Hist. Nat. **33**, 25, 1929)

S. rickii Corr. (Wrightia **2**, 177–8, 1961)

A herb to 50 cm tall, with bi-pinnatisect leaves and bright yellow corollas, more or less stellate but with broad lobes; fruit globose, to 1 cm diam., the pericarp becoming dry at maturity.

Distribution: north Chile, prov. Antofagasta, at 3,000 m.

Note: this species, better known under the name *S. rickii*, in homage to the distinguished tomato geneticist C.M. Rick, has now unfortunately to be called *S. sitiens* because of the prior publication of that name.

Derivation: Becoming dry, parched, evidently referring to the fruit.

2n = 24

Stur., UAC

Subsection *POTATOE* G. Don (Gen. Syst. **4**, 420, 1838)

This subsection contains the true potatoes, whose tubers are borne on underground stolons, which are true stems, not roots. These stolons are quite long in wild species, often up to several metres. The tubers of wild species are generally quite small, from 1–3 cm long, but can attain a length of 5 cm (or even very occasionally 10 cm – as in *S. vernei*). They are round to oval, borne at the ends of the stolons, or in some species along the length (though near the end), appearing like a pearl necklace. The colours are pale brown to buff, or almost white, sometimes diffused with purple pigmentation, never with any colour patterning.

Cultivated potato species (see series *Tuberosa*) possess short stolons, except when short-day adapted species are grown under long-day conditions. The tubers are much larger than those of wild species and of a wide range of shapes, sizes, colours and colour patterns. Their flesh is generally white or cream to yellow or occasionally tinged or patterned with red or purple anthocyanin. Although the flesh of wild species tends to be watery and of poor flavour, some species such as *S. cardiophyllum* subsp. *ehrenbergii* possess high starch content and good flavour. The tubers of this species are collected and sold in Mexican markets where they command good prices. However, this seems to be a notable exception to the general rule.

Some wild species of *Solanum* in other subgenera also bear tubers, as for example *S. hieronymii* O. Kuntze (= *S. pocote* Hieron.). These appear to be root tubers rather than stem tubers, however.

Superseries STELLATA Hawkes (Taxon, **38**, 490, 1989)

This superseries differs from superseries *Rotata* in the completely stellate corolla which shows no clear distinction between lobes and acumens. The corolla colour is generally white to cream. Exceptions are seen in *S. cardiophyllum* and *S. bulbocastanum* from central Mexico, which show a rather yellowish tinge in the typical subspecies. *S. cardiophyllum* subsp. *ehrenbergii* and one or two other species in series *Pinnatisecta* and *Bulbocastana* exhibit a slight purplish tinge on the corollas, whilst *S. commersonii* subsp. *commersonii* from South America develops strong purple streaks on the outside petal centres. Otherwise, the generally white corolla in this superseries is very well marked.

SERIES I *MORELLIFORMIA* HAWKES

(Scottish Plant Breed. Sta. Ann. Report, 54, 1956)

Small tuber-bearing herbs with a strong resemblance to *S. nigrum*, with predominantly epiphytic habit, simple leaves, very small, white stellate flowers (less than 1.5 cm diam.), long slender anthers which are slightly coherent laterally, and small few-seeded berries. This series, formerly united with *Bulbocastana* Rydb., has been separated on account of the very characteristic flowers. It differs from *Bulbocastana* also in its serological reaction (Gell *et al.* 1960). All indications are that this is closest to the ancestral type of tuber-bearing *Solanums*.
Distribution: Mountain forests of Mexico and Guatemala.

1. *S. morelliforme* Bitt. et Muench (Fedde, Repert. **12**, 154–5, 1913)

A small epiphyte growing on trees and also on moss-covered walls and rocks in dense shade, never on the ground. Distinguished by the simple leaves, small stellate flowers, slender anthers and small, few-seeded berries.
Distribution: central to south Mexico, states of Chiapas, Guerrero, Mexico, Michoacán, Puebla and Veracruz; Guatemala. In wet mountain forests from about 2,000–3,000 m.
Derivation: The name refers to the leaf form, similar to that of black nightshade (*S. nigrum*) or morel
2n = 24
Braun., CPC, Stur., VIR

SERIES II *BULBOCASTANA* (RYDB.) HAWKES

(Bull. Imp. Bur. Pl. Breed. Genet., Cambridge, 15, 1944) – as series

Series *Solanum* [rankless] *Bulbocastana* Rydb. (Bull. Torr. Bot. Club **51**, 146, 172, 1924)
Series *Clara* Graham & Dionne, ex Correll (Texas Res. Found. Contrib. **4**, 243, 1962)

Small tuber-bearing terrestrial herbs with simple leaves, stellate flowers (1.53 cm diam.), short thick anthers and round berries larger than those of series *Morelliformia*.
Distribution: central and southern Mexico; Guatemala.

KEY TO SPECIES

Corolla lobes white to deep cream; leaves more or less cuneate at base, not truncate; base of anther 2-lobed; tubers unpigmented
1. *S. bulbocastanum*

Corolla lobes purple at tip; leaves broadly ovate to cordate, truncate to cordate at base; base of anthers 3–5-lobed; tubers deep rich violet

2. *S. clarum*

1. *S. bulbocastanum* Dun. (in Poir. Encycl. Suppl. **3**, 749. 1813)

S. bulbocastanum var. *latifrons* Bitt. (Fedde, Repert. **11**, 447, 1912)
S. bulbocastanum var. *glabrum* Corr. (US Dept. Agric. Monogr. No. 11, 79, 1952)

Leaf with rounded to cuneate base, generally densely pubescent, varying from ovate to linear-lanceolate according to subspecies. Flowers white to deep cream. Both diploid and (apparently) autotriploid forms are known. General distribution: central to south Mexico; Guatemala. Woods, grassland, rocks and field borders. Often grows under quite dry conditions. Altitude range 1,500–2,300 m.

KEY TO SUBSPECIES

(1) Leaf linear-lanceolate, more than 2.5 times as long as broad
1b. subsp. *dolichophyllum*
Leaf ovate to ovate-lanceolate, less than 2.5 times as long as broad
(2)
(2) Pedicel above articulation and calyx completely glabrous; corolla lobes deeply separated from each other (Guatemala)
1c. subsp. *partitum*
Pedicel above articulation and calyx pubescent (var. *glabrum* not very pubescent); corolla not divided (Mexico)
1a. subsp. *bulbocastanum*

1a. Subspecies *bulbocastanum*

Leaf and stem densely pubescent; leaf ovate in shape, less than 2.5 times as long as broad. Corolla white to cream.
Distribution: central to south Mexico; states of DF, Hidalgo, Jalisco, Mexico, Michoacán, Nayarit, Oaxaca, Puebla, Querétaro, Tlaxcala and Veracruz. Records from Colombia and USA, New Mexico should be treated with reserve, and are probably due to mixed labels.
Note: var. *latifrons* is probably a broad-leaved growth form (?triploid); var. *glabrum* from Oaxaca is intermediate between subsp. *bulbocastanum* and subsp. *partitum*.
Derivation: tuber like a chestnut
2n = 24(36); EBN = 1
Braun., CPC, Gr.Lü., Stur., VIR

1b. Subspecies *dolichophyllum* (Bitt.) Hawkes (Scott. Pl. Breed. Rec., 95, 1963)

S. bulbocastanum var. *dolichophyllum* Bitt. (Fedde, Repert. **11**, 477, 1912)
S. longistylum Corr. (US Dept. Agric. Monogr. No. 11, 87, 1952)

Leaf linear-lanceolate, more than 2.5 times as long as broad, attenuate at base and apex; style varying in length from 6 to 10 mm. Corolla white.
Distribution: central Mexico; states of Guerrero, Jalisco, Mexico, Morelos and Oaxaca.
Derivation: Long leaf
2n = 24; EBN = 1
CPC, Stur.

1c. Subspecies *partitum* (Corr.) Hawkes (Scott. Pl. Breed. Rec., 95, 1963)

S. bulbocastanum var. *partitum* Correll (US Dept. Agric. Monogr. No. 11, 83, 1952)

Leaf ovate to ovate-lanceolate, less than 2.5 times as long as broad; leaf and stem less densely pubescent than in subsp. *bulbocastanum*; pedicel above articulation and calyx complete glabrous; calyx pale yellow-green. Corolla deep cream, the lobes very deeply separated from each other.
Distribution: Guatemala and the State of Chiapas in Mexico.
Derivation: Divided into parts, referring to the corolla
2n = 24; EBN = 1
CPC, Stur.

2. *S. clarum* Corr. (Texas Res. Found. Contrib. **1**, 10–12, 1950)

Leaves typically cordate; corolla lobes purple at tips, becoming white towards the base; base of anther 3–5-lobed. Tubers deep rich violet.
Distribution: Mexico, Chiapas State; Guatemala, depts Huehuetenango, Quezaltenango, Sacatepéquez, Sololá and Totonicapán. High mountain forests, especially under the shade and in leaf litter of *Abies* and *Pinus* trees.
Derivation: Clear, possibly referring to the corolla
2n = 24
Gr.Lü., Stur., VIR

SERIES III *PINNATISECTA* (RYDB.) HAWKES

(Bull. Imp. Bur. Pl. Breed. Genet., Cambridge, 17, 1944) – as series

Solanum [rankless] *Pinnatisecta* Rydberg (Bull. Torr. Bot. Club **51**, 146, 167, 1924)
Series *Trifida* Corr. (Texas Res. Found. Contrib. **1**, 12, 1950)
Series *Cardiophylla* Buk. *ex.* Correll (US Dept. Agric. Monogr. No. 11, 92, 1952).

Herbs with stolons and tubers, imparipinnate to imparipinnatisect leaves and stellate corolla which is white or deep cream coloured, sometimes tinged with purple; berries globular to conical. Further knowledge of the three series cited above has made it impossible to maintain them as distinct entities; even the conical berry which was thought by Correll to be one of the most distinctive features of series *Trifida* is not such a useful diagnostic character as was at first hoped. At least one form of *S. pinnatisectum* and also *S. hintonii* possess conical fruits.

Distribution: south-western United States southwards to central Mexico.

KEY TO SPECIES

(1) Pseudostipular leaves pinnately lobed, or absent, never clasping the stem   (2)

Pseudostipular leaves falcate or semi-lunate, clasping the stem   (3)

(2) Leaves glabrous; leaflets linear-lanceolate, 6–8 paired; corolla lobes only slightly longer than broad   **7. S. pinnatisectum**

Leaves with generally a few hairs; leaflets lanceolate, 2–3(–5)-paired; corolla lobes much longer than broad   **4. S. jamesii**

(3) Berry long oval to conical, apically pointed   (4)

Berry round to short oval, apically obtuse   (5)

(4) Leaflets decurrent on to the rachis, softly densely pubescent
        11. S. trifidum

Leaflets clearly petiolulate, with very sparse pubescence
        3. S. hintonii

(5) Leaflets petiolulate, not or hardly decurrent   (6)

Leaflets sessile to subsessile, decurrent on to rachis   (7)

(6) Leaflets 2–4-jugate; pubescence absent or sparse, not pointing upwards   **2. S. cardiophyllum**

Leaflets 3–5(–7)-jugate; stem hairs short, pointed upwards
        10. S. tarnii

(7) Stem hairs frequent, very minute, 1–3-celled, pointing downward
        (8)

Stem hairs, if present, much longer   (9)

(8) Leaflets (or lobes) lanceolate; leaves rarely exceeding 10 cm long, generally about 6–7 cm long   **1. S. brachistotrichum**

Leaflets (or lobes) linear to linear-lanceolate; leaves more than 10 cm long   **9. S. stenophyllidium**

(9) Long stem hairs pointing downwards; anther base 3-lobed
        6. S. nayaritense

Long stem hairs not pointing downwards; anther base 2-lobed   (10)

(10) Plant essentially glabrous, small and delicate   **8. S. × sambucinum**

Plant not glabrous, robust and erect   **5. S. × michoacanum**

1. S. brachistotrichum (Bitt.) Rydb. (Bull. Torr. Bot. Club **51**, 170, 1924)

S. jamesii Torr. var. *brachistotrichium* Bitt. (Fedde, Repert. **11**, 444, 1912)
S. jamesii Torr. subsp. *septentrionale* Bitt. var. *rupicolum* Bitt. (Fedde, Repert. **12**, 151–2, 1913)
S. brachistotrichum var. *rupicolum* (Bitt.) Corr. (US Dept. Agr. Monogr. No. 11, 105, 1952)

Note: the epithet '*brachistotrichium*' of Bitter was modified by Rydberg (1924) to '*brachistotrichum*'. This spelling was followed by Correll (1952, 1962) and Hawkes (1956, 1963).

Distinguished from other species in this series by the abundant 2–3-celled hairs on leaves and stem pointing *downwards*. Other species, such as *S. stenophyllidium*, may develop some of these hairs but in small numbers only. Leaflets subsessile to petiolulate, always slightly decurrent on to the rachis, 2–3(–4)-jugate. Corolla slightly mauve-tinted towards the acumens, very reflexed. Berries globular, green with white mottling.
Distribution: north-west Mexico in the states of Chihuahua, Durango, Sonora and Zacatecas in dry piñon scrub vegetation at 1,750–2,500 m.

S. brachistotrichum may be closely related to *S. stenophyllidium* but the latter species is insufficiently studied yet for this relationship to be understood fully.
Derivation: very short hairs
$2n = 24$; EBN $= 1$
Braun., CPC, Gr.Lü., Stur., VIR

2. *S. cardiophyllum* Lindl. (J. Hort. Soc. **3**, 70, 1848: non *S. cardiophyllum* Dun in DC Prodr. **13**(I), 89, 1852)

S. cardiophyllum Lindl. var. *oligozygum* Bitt. (Fedde., Repert. **11**, 439, 1912)
S. cardiophyllum Lindl. var. *pliozygum* Bitt. (Fedde, Repert. **11**, 439, 1912)
S. coyoacanum Buk. (*ex*. Rybin, Bull. Appl. Bot. **20**, 700, 1929)

Leaflets ovate-cordate to lanceolate, 2–4-jugate, petiolulate, not decurrent (or only occasionally so); calyx acumens 0.5–1.5 mm long, according to subspecies.

KEY TO SUBSPECIES

(1) Calyx acumens not more than 0.5 mm long; corolla deep cream to buff-coloured **2a. subsp. *cardiophyllum***
Calyx acumens 0.5–1.5 mm long; corolla white to cream, sometimes tinged with mauve towards the tips of the lobes (2)
(2) Leaflets more than 2.5 times as long as broad (very occasionally 2 times as long as broad); calyx acumens 0.5–1 mm long; anthers short, about 5 mm long **2c. subsp. *lanceolatum***
Leaflets less than 2.5 times as long as broad, oblong-lanceolate to lanceolate; calyx acuments 1–1.5 mm long; anthers narrow, often attenuate, to 6–7 mm long **2b. subsp. *ehrenbergii***

2a. Subspecies *cardiophyllum*

Leaflets glabrous, shining, dark green above; calyx acumens not more than 0.5 mm long; corolla deep cream to buff-coloured. Anthers short, 5 mm,

not attenuate above, often tinged with violet inside. Both diploid and (apparently) autotriploid forms are known, the latter being distinguished generally by very much wider (broadly ovate-cordate) leaflets. Most of the material mentioned in the plant-breeding literature as *S. lanciforme* should more correctly be considered as the diploid form of subsp. *cardiophyllum*. Distribution: central Mexico, states of D.F., Hidalgo, México, Michoacán, Morelos, Querétaro and Puebla.
Derivation: leaflet heart-shaped
2n = 24(36); EBN = 1
CPC, Gr.Lü., Stur., VIR

2b. Subspecies *ehrenbergii* Bitt. (Fedde, Repert. **11**, 442–3, 1912)

S. ehrenbergii (Bitt.) Rydb. (Bull. Torr. Bot. Cl. **51**, 169–70, 1924)
S. cardiophyllum var. *ehrenbergii* (Bitt.) Corr. (US Dept. Agric. Monogr. No. 11, 97, 1952)

Differs from the type subspecies by the paler green, non-shining, oblong-lanceolate to lanceolate leaflets and the frequent presence of hairs of varying lengths on leaves and stems. Calyx acumens 1–1.5 mm long; anthers narrow, generally attenuate, 6–7 mm long. Petals often tinged with mauve towards the tips. This subspecies is linked to subsp. *cardiophyllum* in Querétaro State by a series of intermediates. Mostly diploid forms are known, though a triploid (presumably autotriploid) has been recorded in San Luis Potosí State.
Distribution: central to north-west and west Mexico, states of Aguascalientes, Guanajuato, Hidalgo, Jalisco, Michoacán, San Luis Potosí and Zacatecas.
Derivation: named after the German explorer Carl August Ehrenberg, who collected in Mexico between 1831 and 1840
2n = 24; EBN = 1
Braun., CPC, Gr.Lü., Stur., VIR

2c. Subspecies *lanceolatum* (Berth.) Bitt. (Fedde, Repert. **11**, 440–2, 1912)

S. lanceolatum Berth. (Ann. Sci. Agron., ser. 3, **6**, 201–02, 1911; non *S. lanceolatum* Cav. Ic. **3**, 23, t.245, 1794)
S. lanciforme Rydb. (Bull Torr. Bot. Cl. **51**, 169, 1924)
S. cardiophyllum subsp. *lanceolatum* Bitt. var. *endoiodandrum* Bitt. (Fedde, Repert. **11**, 442, 1912)
S. cardiophyllum subsp. *lanceolatum* Bitt. var. *amphixanthandrum* Bitt. (Fedde, Repert., **11**, 442, 1912)

Note: Correll (1962) unites both varieties under var. *endoiodandrum* without recognizing subspecies *lanceolatum*.

This does not differ sufficiently from the diploid forms of subsp. *cardiophyllum* to be ranked as a separate species. Distinguished from subsp.

cardiophyllum by the narrower leaflets (more than 2.5 times as long as broad), the longer peduncle (more than 3.5 cm long) and the 0.5–1.0 mm long calyx acumens. Corolla white or cream-coloured.
Distribution: central to south Mexico, states of Hidalgo, Oaxaca, Puebla and Tlaxcala.
Derivation: leaflet lance-shaped
2n = 24; EBN = 1
CPC

All subspecies occur in dry scrub vegetation in waste places, field borders, old lava fields, and especially as weeds of cultivation. Subsp. *lanceolatum* seems to prefer rocky limestone soils. If this is true it would be the only calcicolous wild potato so far known to exist. The tubers of subsp. *ehrenbergii* are edible. Altitude 1,600–2,550 m.

3. *S. hintonii* Corr. (Wrightia **2**, 139–41, 1961)

A very rare delicate species with 2–3-jugate petiolulate leaflets, and no interjecteds. Rather long peduncle branches give the inflorescence an appearance of a diffuse cymose panicle; calyx acumens 2.5 mm long; corolla lobes narrow lanceolate. Whole plant with sparse pubescence. Fruit conical, green, white-marbled. Perhaps related to *S. trifidum* but differs in the petiolulate leaflets and sparse pubescence.
Distribution: Mexico, México State, near Temascáltepec, by stone walls and among low shrubs under trees. Altitude 1,700–1,850 m.
Derivation: named after its first collector, George B. Hinton, from the USA, who collected in Mexico from 1932–37

4. *S. jamesii* Torr. (Ann. Lyc. N. York **2**, 227, 1828)

S. jamesii var. *heterotrichium* Bitt. (Fedde, Repert. **11**, 444, 1912)
S. jamesii var. *sinclairi* [as *sinclairii*] Bitt. et Correvon in Bitt. (Fedde, Repert. **11**, 444–6, 1912)

(See also *S. tuberosum* var. *boreale* A. Gray (Syn. Fl. **2**(1), 227, 1878); *S. boreale* Bitt. (Fedde, Repert. **11**, 459, 1912))

Plants without typical semilunate pseudostipular leaflets; if present they are pinnatisect and do not clasp the stem. Leaves slightly decurrent, generally pubescent, occasionally glabrous, with (2–)3–4(–5) pairs of leaflets and generally no interjected leaflets. Corolla lobes narrow.
    The white-flowered forms of North American wild potatoes named *S. tuberosum* var. *boreale* A. Gray, very probably belong to *S. jamesii*, but since A. Gray did not designate specimens or give a clear description we cannot be absolutely certain of this. Bitter raised these forms to species rank as *S. boreale*, but the lack of certainty still remains.
    Curious forms with 5-jugate leaves (var. *pentazygum* Hawkes, *ined.*) are

found in Arizona, in the Huachuca mountains, but apparently nowhere else.

Distribution: north-west Mexico, Sonora State; USA, states of Arizona, Colorado, New Mexico, Texas and Utah.

Derivation: named after a US Army surgeon, Dr E. James (1797–1861), and collected by him in 1820

2n = 24(36); EBN = 1

Braun., CPC, Stur., VIR

5. S. × michoacanum (Bitt.) Rydb. (Bull Torr. Bot. Cl. **51**, 171, 1924)

S. jamesii subsp. *nayaritense* Bitt., var. *michoacanum* Bitt. (Fedde, Repert. **12**, 9–10, 1913)

Habit upright with upward pointing leaves; leaf 2–3-jugate with decurrent leaflets and no interjected leaflets, with fairly frequent coarse hairs on both surfaces. Hairs on pedicels and calyx sparse, weak, spreading; corolla white, about 2.5 cm diam. Berries not produced.

Distribution: Mexico, Michoacán State, in general area of Morelia and perhaps elsewhere. Altitude 2,000–2,100 m. In damp grassy fields and amongst rocks.

This is definitely a natural hybrid of *S. bulbocastanum* × *S. pinnatisectum*, both of which parents occur in the same region. It seems to be sterile so far as present information indicates.

Derivation: named after the state in which it is found

2n = 24

Gr.Lü., VIR

6. S. nayaritense (Bitt.) Rydb. (Bull Torr. Bot. Cl. **51**, 170, 1924)

S. jamesii subsp. *nayaritense* Bitt. (Fedde, Repert. **12**, 8–9, 1913)

(The original type of Diguet in Herb. Paris seems to have disappeared. Correll (1962) proposed *Rose 2134* from the same region as Lectotype, but since the type is missing it would be better to call *Rose 2134* NEOTYPE (see Int. Code, 1988, Art. 7.9).)

Distinguished from the other species in series *Pinnatisecta* by the long, weak, spreading hairs over the whole plant, clearly pointing downwards on the stem, peduncles and pedicels – a feature not seen in any other Mexican species. The long hairs also occur on the calyx and tend to point downwards also, though this is not so clear. This is a very robust species. The leaves are 3(–4)-jugate with lanceolate leaflets, with broad wings running down on to the short petiolules and leaf rachis. Interjected leaflets virtually absent. Corolla white, stellate. Anthers long, 8–9 mm, tapering towards the apex and 3-lobed at the base.

Distribution: Mexico, states of Nayarit and Zacatecas, found as a cornfield weed, but probably normally in undisturbed natural vegetation.

Derivation: from the State of Nayarit
2n (unknown, probably 24)
Stur. (not in inventory), VIR

7. S. pinnatisectum Dun. (Dun. Prodr. 13, I, 40, 1852)

S. pinnatisectum var. *heptazygum* Bitt. (Fedde, Repert. **12**, 50–1, 1913)
S. pinnatisectum var. *pentazygum* Bitt. (Fedde, Repert. **12**, 49–50, 1913)

Plant without semilunate pseudostipular leaflets, as in *S. jamesii*. Distinguished from *S. jamesii* by the glabrous leaves, 6–8 leaflet pairs, generally with a few interjected leaflets and large showy corolla with broad triangular lobes. Stigma bifid. Berry round to conical. Bitter's two varieties, *heptazygum* (7 pairs of leaflets) and *pentazygum* (5 pairs of leaflets) cannot be maintained, since all intermediates occur, sometimes even on the same plant.
Distribution: central Mexico, states of Guanajuato, Jalisco, Mexico, Michoacán and Querétaro.
Derivation: leaf is pinnatisect, that is, the division into separate leaflets is incomplete. This feature, new to Dunal, is found in many wild potatoes, especially in series *Megistacroloba*.
2n = 24; EBN = 1
Braun., CPC, Gr.Lü., Stur., VIR

8. S. × sambucinum Rydb. (Bull. Torr. Bot. Cl. **51**, 169, 1924)

A natural hybrid between *S. pinnatisectum* and *S. cardiophyllum* subsp. *ehrenbergii*, which shows segregation to the parental types when grown from seed (Hawkes and Lester 1968). Leaf fairly dark green, with 4–5-paired leaflets which are narrowly lanceolate and both petiolulate and decurrent (thus intermediate between the two parents). Corolla with lobes broader than those of *S. cardiophyllum*, narrower than those of *S. pinnatisectum* (5–6 × 10 mm).
Distribution: central Mexico, states of Querétaro, Guanajuato and Michoacán; a weed of fields and field borders, found in the distribution areas of the two parents, at about 1,800–2,000 m.
Derivation: leaf similar to that of *Sambucus*, the elder tree
2n = 24
Braun. (not in inventory), CPC, Gr.Lü., VIR

9. S. stenophyllidium Bitt. (Fedde, Repert. **12**, 51, 1913)

Leaves lobed, rather than with distinct leaflets. Leaf of type collection, 2–3-jugate, with very narrow 'leaflets', at least 6 times and sometimes more than 10 times as long as broad, linear, sessile or shortly petiolulate and narrowly decurrent along the petiolules and on to the rachis. Interjected leaflets absent. Corolla whitish or tinged with mauve, 2 cm diam.; anthers

7 mm long. Leaves and other green parts provided with numerous minute hairs as in *S. brachistotrichum*.

Under culture the typically 3-jugate leaf lobes are broader, about 5–6 times as long as broad but still very decurrent on the petiolules and rachis. Whole plant (in Mexico and in culture) provided with very frequent, minute 1–3-celled hairs (as in *S. brachistotrichum*), which distinguish it from *S. nayaritense* and *S. tarnii*. The plant is much larger than *S. brachistotrichum* but clearly has some affinities to it. Fruits globular.

Some collections from Aguascalientes State seemed at one time to be related to *S. stenophyllidium* but are seen now to fit best with *S. cardiophyllum* subsp. *ehrenbergii* (Pl. 255527–255530). They were also postulated as natural hybrids but do not segregate when crossed and grown from seed.

Distribution: Mexico, states of Aguascalientes and Jalisco, in dry, hilly rangeland with small *Quercus* and *Mimosa* shrubs and *Opuntias*. Very rare.

Derivation: narrow leaflets

2n = 24

Braun. (?), Gr.Lü. (?), Stur. (?), VIR (?)

10. *S. tarnii* Hawkes et Hjerting (in J.G. Hawkes, J.P. Hjerting and T.R. Tarn, Phytologia **65**(2), 114–16, 1988)

Leaf 3–5(–7)-jugate with 0–3(–7) pairs of interjected leaflets; leaflets narrow lanceolate, the bases rounded (contrast most other species in this series) with 2–5(–8) mm long petiolules. Stem hairs short but appressed or pointed upwards (contrast *S. nayaritense* and *S. brachistotrichum*). Corolla white, 2.5–3.5 cm diam.; anthers 5–8 mm long; style long, 10–13 mm; berries spherical to ovoid with dark green stripes and white spots.

This is a very striking species which surprisingly remained undiscovered until recently.

Distribution: Mexico, states of Hidalgo, Querétaro and Veracruz at altitudes of 2,360–2,650 m. In open vegetation of small shrubs and herbs, amongst rocks with pines or oaks close but very rarely under shade.

Derivation: named in honour of Dr T.R. Tarn, leader of the expedition on which this species was first found

2n = 24

Stur. (not in inventory)

11. *S. trifidum* Corr. (Texas Res. Found. Contrib. **1**, 12–14, 1950)

Leaf 1–3-jugate (thus tri- to septem-fidum!); stem softly, densely pubescent, provided with long hairs and glands; corolla creamy white, with fairly broad lobes. Berries long oval, pointed.

Distribution: western Mexico, states of Michoacán and Jalisco in oak and pine forests, in partial shade (contrast *S. tarnii*), maize fields, roadsides, etc., at altitudes of 2,100–2,400 m.

Derivation: divided into three, referring to the three leaf lobes or leaflets

shown in the type specimen
2n = 24; EBN = 1
Braun. (as *S. michoacanum*), CPC (as *S. michoacanum*), Gr.Lü., Stur.,
VIR

S. nicaraguense Rydb. (see Appendix I, p. 214)

SERIES IV   *POLYADENIA* BUK. ex CORR.

(US Dept. Agric. Monogr., No. 11, 127, 1952)

Tuber-bearing herbs with a very dense indumentum of glandular hairs of
an objectionable odour; most of these glands possess 2-celled stalks – a
feature not known in any other tuber-bearing *Solanum* series. Corolla
white, stellate. Berries ovoid, cordate or conical, somewhat flattened, with
black streaks, especially on the edges.
Distribution: central to southern Mexico on dry stony hillsides or in damp
mountain forests, according to the species.

KEY TO SPECIES

All green parts provided with a very dense covering of many-celled non-
    glandular spreading hairs (as well as the numerous glands), easily visible to
    the naked eye; stem purple-pigmented; berry long-conical **1.** *S. lesteri*
All green parts with very few non-glandular hairs of the type described
    above, and these are not easily visible to the naked eye; stem unpig-
    mented; berry ovate to cordate   **2.** *S. polyadenium*

1. *S. lesteri* **Hawkes et Hjerting** (in Hawkes, Scott. Pl. Breed. Rec., 126,
    1963)

Differs from *S. polyadenium* in the more robust habit, thick purple-
pigmented stem, dense indumentum of long, spreading, multicellular hairs
on all green parts, in addition to the glandular ones, and long-conical,
pointed, 2-grooved and flattened berries. A distinct species, obviously
related to *S. polyadenium*, but occurring under quite different ecological
conditions.
Distribution: endemic to south Mexico (Oaxaca State), in damp mountain
forests at 2,300 m.
Derivation: named after Dr R.N. Lester, a member of the Birmingham
University Potato Collecting Expedition in the USA, Mexico and Central
America, 1958
2n = 24
Braun. (not in inventory), CPC, Stur., VIR

2. *S. polyadenium* Greenm. (Proc. Amer. Acad. Arts & Sci. **39**, 89, 1903)

S. polyadenium subsp. *orizabae* Bitt. (Fedde, Repert. **12**, 7–8, 1913)

Whole plant covered with very frequent, stalked glands; stalks generally 2-celled. Very sparse multicellular non-glandular hairs also present but not easily visible without a lens. Whole plant more slender and less robust than *S. lesteri*. Corolla white, stellate, with fairly broad lobes. Bitter's subsp. *orizabae* does not differ very significantly from the type and in any case a certain amount of variation, chiefly in leaf dissection, exists in natural populations.

Distribution: central Mexico, states of Hidalgo, Jalisco, Michoacán, Oaxaca, Puebla and Veracruz; on dry stony hillsides, by old walls, on old lava and amongst trees and shrubs, from 1,900–2,900 m.

Derivation: with many glands

2n = 24

Braun., CPC, Gr.Lü., Stur., VIR

SERIES V *COMMERSONIANA* BUK.

(in Buk. & Kameraz, Bases of Potato Breeding, 19, 1959)

Tuber-bearing herbs with imparipinnate leaves and stellate corolla with lobes generally less than twice as long as broad. Flowers white or mauve-tinted.

Distribution: South America: Argentina, Paraguay, Uruguay, Brazil. Both species are diploid, though some autotriploid forms occur.

KEY TO SPECIES

Plants erect; leaflets petiolulate, not decurrent; anthers narrow, *c.* 1 mm broad, not clearly delimited from filaments   **1. *S. calvescens***
Plants sometimes erect but generally decumbent or rosetted; leaflets decurrent on to rachis; anthers broad, *c.* 1.5 mm broad, clearly delimited from filaments   **2. *S. commersonii***

1. *S. calvescens* Bitt. (Fedde, Repert. **11**, 436–7, 1912)

Related to *S. commersonii*, and especially to subsp. *malmeanum*, from which it may be distinguished by the larger size, upright growth, curved leaves, more acute lateral leaflets, large flowers, and especially by the curious stamens in which the anthers and filaments are not clearly delimited from each other. Corolla always white, 3–3.5 cm, the lobes as long as broad; anthers very narrow, *c.* 1 mm broad; filaments 2.5 mm long.

Distribution: Brazil, state of Minas Gerais, and perhaps elsewhere; on shady river banks and in cultivated fields, at altitudes of about 1,200 m.

Note: although the anther bases of *S. calvescens* show some similarity to those of *S. maglia* the anther column of *S. maglia* is barrel-shaped and the corolla is rotate.

Derivation: 'becoming bald', presumably because of the short, sparse leaf hairs

$2n = 36$, but probably diploids occur also, though not yet found or studied in a living state. Triploid materials were studied at Birmingham for several years but were sterile and could not be crossed with other species.

2. *S. commersonii* Dun. (Poir. Encyclop. Suppl. **3**, 746, 1813)

S. commersonii Dun. var. *glabriusculum* Hook. f. (p.pte.) (Flora Antarct. **2**, 330, 1846)

S. commersonii Dun. var. *glabratum* Hook. (ibid.)

S. commersonii Dun. var. *pubescens* Sendtn. (*ex* Martius, Flora Brasil. **10**, 12, 1846)

S. tenue Sendtn. (*ex* Martius, Flora Brasil. **10**, 13, 1846)

S. ohrondii Carr. (Rev. Hort. **55**, 496–500, 1883)

S. acroleucum Bitt. (Fedde, Repert. **11**, 435–6, 1912)

S. henryi Buk. & Lechn. (Rev. Argent. Agron. **2**, 182–3, 1935)

S. henryi Buk. et Lechn. f. *pubescens* Lechn. and f. *laticalyx* Lechn. (Rev. Argent. Agron. **2**, 183, 1935)

S. mercedense Buk. (Soviet Plant Industr. Record, No. 4, 12, 1940)

S. sorianum Buk. (Soviet Plant Industr. Record, No. 4, 12, 1940)

S. rionegrinum Lechn. (*nom. nud.*) (Soviet Plant Industr. Record, No. 4, 31–2, 1940)

S. mechonguense Buk. (Rev. Argent. Agron. **7**, 363, 1940)

S. commersonii Dun. f. *mechonguense* (Buk.) Corr. (Wrightia **2**, 173, 1961)

This very well-known species differs from *S. chacoense* in possessing leaflets which are normally obtusely rounded at the apex, sessile or subsessile and generally slightly decurrent; the terminal leaflet is typically much larger than the laterals and the leaf is often sublyrate in shape. Peduncle not or once-branched; branches often very short. Corolla white or often tinted purple on the external surface; berry cordate or conical. Occurs in both diploid and (probably) autotriploid forms, the latter being confined chiefly to the vicinity of Montevideo in Uruguay and prov. Misiones in Argentina.

KEY TO SUBSPECIES

Terminal leaflet much larger than the laterals, which decrease in size rapidly towards the base of the leaf; inflorescence branches generally contracted; corolla generally purple   **2a. subsp. *commersonii***

Terminal leaflet broader but barely longer than laterals, which decrease in size much more slowly towards the base of the leaf; inflorescence branches not markedly contracted; corolla always white

2b. subsp. *malmeanum*

2a. Subspecies *commersonii*

Lateral leaflets decreasing rapidly to base of leaf, often markedly decurrent, normally sessile; peduncle once-forked, the branches somewhat contracted; corolla generally purple externally, the lobes about 1½ times as long as broad or even longer. Most plant breeding and cytological work in the past has utilized this subspecies, often in its triploid forms; certain forms of *S. chacoense*, erroneously identified as *S. commersonii*, have been reported on in studies by various workers. Typical diploid subsp. *commersonii* has sublyrate leaves, elongated and enlarged terminal leaflets and very reduced laterals; the flowers are deep mauve on the outer surface, paler within. The triploid forms are less typical, with wider, less decurrent, often slightly petiolulate leaflets and terminal leaflet not much larger than laterals. They can be distinguished from *S. chacoense* by the *very short* peduncle branches which make the pedicels appear to be arranged in a cymose umbel. The flowers are almost invariably mauve to purple and the berries (when formed) are cordate and pointed.

Distribution: coastal belt of Argentina and Uruguay (estuary of the Río de la Plata), and coastal regions of south Brazil, states of Rio Grande do Sul and Santa Catarina. Grows in a wide variety of habitats, but very frequently in marshy places, fields, river banks, woods and sandy shores (dune slacks), from sea level up to about 400 m.

Derivation: named by Dunal in honour of Philibert Commerson (1727–73) who collected the type specimen (No. 47) in May 1767 at Montevideo. This was probably the first wild potato to be collected on a scientific expedition (see, however, *S. maglia*).

2n = 24, (36); EBN = 1

Bal., Braun., CPC, Gr.Lü., Stur., VIR

2b. Subspecies *malmeanum* (Bitt.) Hawkes et Hjerting (in Hawkes, J.G., Scott. Pl. Breed. Rec., 105, 1963)

S. malmeanum Bitt. (Fedde, Repert. **12**, 447–8, 1913)

S. commersonii var. *pubescens* Chodat (Bull. Herb. Boissier,. Ser. II, **2**, 812, 1902)

S. commersonii var. *pseudostipulatum* Hassl. (Fedde, Repert. **9**, 116, 1911)

S. guaraniticum Hassl. var. *latisectum* Hassl. f. *pilosulum* Hassl. (Fedde, Repert. **9**, 116, 1911)

S. chacoense Bitt. var. *latisectum* Hassl. f. *pilosulum* Hassl. (Ann. Conserv. Jard. Bot. Genève **20**, 186–7, 1917)

S. pseudostipulatum (Hassl.) Buk. (Rev. Argent. Agron. **2**, 180, 1935)

S. millanii Buk. & Lechn. (Rev. Argent. Agron. **2**, 180–2, 1935)

S. commersonii f. *malmeanum* (Bitt.) Corr. (Wrightia **2**, 173, 1961)

Differs from subsp. *commersonii* in the lateral leaflets gradually decreasing to base of leaf, narrowly decurrent and slightly petiolulate; peduncles unbranched or the branches not markedly contracted; corolla always white, the lobes about as long as broad. This subspecies is known in diploid and triploid forms, the latter having been found chiefly in Argentina, prov. Misiones. Like subsp. *commersonii*, it possesses conical berries and is resistant to frost.

Distribution: subsp. *malmeanum* has a more inland distribution and is known in north-east Argentina (chiefly in provs Corrientes and Misiones), Brazil, state of Rio Grande do Sul, north Uruguay and south Paraguay. Inhabits similar places to those in which subsp. *commersonii* is found but seems to prefer shady thickets and woodlands; it has about the same altitude range as subsp. *commersonii*.

Derivation: named after the Swedish collector G.O.A. Malme, who sent to Stockholm a specimen actually collected by Regnell (No. 756), which Bitter used as type.

2n = 24, (36); EBN = 1

Braun., Gr.Lü., Stur., VIR

Forms intermediate between the two subspecies have been found in Argentina, prov. Entre Ríos.

A full discussion of the *S. commersonii* complex is given in Hawkes and Hjerting (1969, 142–80).

SERIES VI *CIRCAEIFOLIA* HAWKES

(Ann. Mag. Nat. Hist., Ser. 12, **7**, 702, 1954)

Tuber-bearing herbs with small leaves, the terminal leaflet enlarged and laterals reduced in size. Corolla white, stellate, less than 1.5 cm diam.; berries narrow-conical, sharp-pointed.

Distribution: north Bolivia; hedges and bushy places at high altitudes.

KEY TO SPECIES

(1) Leaflets linear-lanceolate; terminal as broad as laterals   **3.** *S. soestii*
    Leaflets lanceolate, ovate or cordate; terminal clearly much broader
      than laterals   (2)
(2) Leaflets densely pubescent below, sparsely pubescent above; leaflet
      apex not acuminate   **1.** *S. capsicibaccatum*
    Leaflets entirely glabrous or with sparse to fairly frequent hairs above,
      fewer and shorter below; leaflet apex acuminate **2.** *S. circaeifolium*

1. *S. capsicibaccatum* Cárdenas (Rev. Agric., Cochabamba **2**, 35–6, 1944)

S. capsicibaccatum Cárdenas (in Cárdenas and Hawkes, J. Linn. Soc. (Bot.) **53**, 91–108, 1946)

S. circaeifolium var. *capsicibaccatum* (Cárd.) Ochoa (Phytologia **54**(5), 392, 1983)

Distinguished from *S. circaeifolium* by the softly hairy leaves below, 1–2 pairs of lateral leaflets which are more than half the length of the terminal, rather pubescent inflorescence and grooved stigma.

Distribution: Bolivia, depts Cochabamba, Santa Cruz, La Paz and Potosí; in cloud forest and among bushes and *Polylepis* vegetation at 2,000–4,000 m.
Derivation: berries like those of *Capsicum*, the Chilli pepper
2n = 24; EBN = 1
Braun., CPC, Gr.Lü., Stur., VIR

2. S. circaeifolium Bitt. (Fedde, Repert. **11**, 385–6, 1912)

Leaf glabrescent or sparsely pubescent, simple, or sometimes 1–2(–4)-jugate, the laterals in subsp. *circaeifolium* much less than half the length of the terminal leaflet; stigma simple.

KEY TO SUBSPECIES

Lateral leaflets absent or 1- (very occasionally) 2-jugate; leaf generally
 entirely glabrous   **2a. subsp.** *circaeifolium*
Lateral leaflets (1–)2–3(–4)-jugate; leaf with weak, often fairly frequent,
 hairs chiefly on upper surface   **2b. subsp.** *quimense*

2a. Subspecies *circaeifolium*

This subspecies is rather uncommon, very delicate, and characterized by its ovate acuminate leaf which is generally simple, very rarely with lateral leaflets.
Distribution: Bolivia, dept La Paz, in cloud forest ('ceja') and scrub vegetation from about 2,500–3,600 m.
Derivation: possessing a leaf like that of *Circaea lutetiana*, enchanter's nightshade (Fam. Onagraceae)
2n = 24; EBN = 1
Braun., Gr.Lü., Stur., VIR

2b. Subspecies *quimense* **Hawkes et Hjerting** (Bot. J. Linn. Soc. **86**, 406–8, 1983; ibid. **91**, 445, 1985)

S. circaeifolium f. *lobatum* Correll (Wrightia **2**, 171, 1961)
S. capsicibaccatum var. *latifoliolatum* Ochoa (Phytologia **50**(3), 181–2, 1982)
S. circaeifolium var. *latifoliolatum* Ochoa (Phytologia **54**(5), 392, 1983)
S. capsicibaccatum var. *macrophyllum* Cárdenas, ined.

This subspecies is much more common than subsp. *circaeifolium*. It is distinguished by its (1–)2–3(–4)-jugate leaf, extremely rarely with a pair of interjected leaflets, and with long silky slender hairs when present, on the upper surface, fewer or absent below.
Distribution: Bolivia, depts La Paz, Cochabamba and Santa Cruz, in cloud forest ('ceja') and scrub vegetation from about 2,500–3,600 m.

Derivation: native to the Quime region of dept La Paz, prov. Inguisivi, but found elsewhere, also (see above)

2n = 24; EBN = 1

Braun., Stur.

3. *S. soestii* Hawkes et Hjerting (Bot. J. Linn. Soc. **86**, 406–9, 1983)

A very delicate species some 15–40 cm tall, with narrow lanceolate to linear-lanceolate sessile leaflets. Whole leaf completely glabrous.

Derivation: named in honour of Ir. Loek van Soest, who led the Dutch team in the 1980 expedition to Bolivia

2n = 24 fide Ochoa (Phytologia **57**(5), 315, 1985). I have not examined living material in the experimental stations or seen it in gene banks, though I collected living plants in the field. Unfortunately these did not survive.

SERIES VII *LIGNICAULIA* HAWKES

(Taxon **38**(3), 489–92, 1989)

This is a monotypic series based on the species *S. lignicaule*. It possesses cylindrical rather woody stems, velvety pubescence, white stellate to substellate corolla and globose to ovate fruits.

Lignicaulia may present some affinities with series *Polyadenia*, but such relationships cannot be very close.

For distribution see species.

1. *S. lignicaule* Vargas (Rev. Argent. Agron. **10**, 398, 1943) (Papas Sudperuanas, Univ. Nac. Cuzco, **1**, 89–90, 1949)

S. lignicaule var. *longistylum* Vargas (Papas Sudperuanas, Univ. Nac. Cuzco, **2**, 56, 1956)

S. vargasii Hawkes (Bull. Imp. Bur. Pl. Breed. & Genet., Cambridge, 113, 1944)

Stem cylindrical, strongly woody, with velvety pubescence and strongly scented glandular hairs (also on leaves); leaves with narrow lanceolate to linear-lanceolate acuminate leaflets, 3–4-jugate, with several pairs of small interjected leaflets, yellow-green above whitish below; leaf pubescence softly velvety, denser below. Calyx acumens linear-spathulate. Corolla stellate, creamy white. Anthers 4 mm long; style 8–10 mm long. Fruits globose to ovate. A very distinct species of unknown affinities, endemic to the ruins of the Inca fortress of Pisac.

Distribution: south Peru, dept Cuzco, prov. Calca, on dry bushy slopes and old cultivation terraces at 3,000–3,500 m.

Derivation: woody stem

2n = 24; EBN = 1

Braun., CPC, Gr.Lü., Stur., VIR

SERIES VIII *OLMOSIANA* OCHOA
(An. Cient. Univ. Agr. **3**, 33, 1965)

Tubers pubescent, leaves with broadly winged rachis, the wings being highly irregular in shape and continuing down the petiole almost to its point of insertion. Corolla white, deeply stellate; berry ovoid or pyriform.

This monotypic series stands out sharply from all others by the densely velvety pubescence of the tuber and the extraordinary winging of the leaf rachis and petiole; its deeply stellate flower is unique also for a wild potato in Peru. Possibly related in some way to series *Ingifolia*.

1. *S. olmosense* **Ochoa** (An. Cient. Univ. Agri. **3**(1), 34–7, 1965)

Tubers with densely velvety pubescence. Leaf (1–)2(–3)-jugate with ovate attenuate leaflets and large terminal; the wide and extremely irregular rachis wings extending down the petiole almost to the point of leaf insertion are quite remarkable, but show some similarity to species in series *Ingifolia*. Leaves completely glabrous or with very sparse medium-length hairs. Corolla white to cream, deeply stellate, 2.0–2.5 cm diam.; anthers about 5 mm long; style about 10 mm long. Fruits ovoid to pyriform.
Distribution: north Peru, dept and prov. Lambeyeque, 46 km above Olmos on the road to Chachapoyas. Altitude 1,800 m, amongst bushes in wet ground. Seems to be endemic in this area.
Derivation: from Olmos, though 46 km eastwards of it
2n = 24
No living material is yet available in gene banks apparently

SERIES IX *YUNGASENSA* CORR.
(Potato and Wild Rel., 220, 1962)

Series *Glabrescentia* Buk. (in Buk. et Kameraz, Bases of Potato Breed., 19, 1959 – nom. invalid. without type after 1958)
Series *Tarijensa* Corr. (Potato and Wild Rel., 233, 1962)

Tuber-bearing herbs with imparipinnate leaves and white or creamy yellow stellate corolla with rather broad lobes, generally less than twice as long as broad.
Distribution: South America, Bolivia, Argentina, Paraguay, Uruguay and Brazil. One possible species in Peru.

Formerly grouped in Series *Commersoniana* but separated on a genetical basis and because of the broader lobed white corolla and globular fruits (contrast *S. commersonii*).

All species are diploid, although some autotriploids have been reported.

KEY TO SPECIES

(1) Plant very densely clothed with glistening glandular pubescence (2)
Plant without dense glandular pubescence (3)
(2) Pubescence of short-stalked hairs with 4-celled apical glands (Type A trichome), often also with long non-glandular hairs **4. *S. tarijense***
Pubescence of mixed Type A trichomes and long hairs bearing an apical drop (Type B trichomes), never with simple hairs
6. *S. flavoviridens*
(3) Flower creamy yellow (rarely white); stem wings often 3–5 mm broad
(4)
Flower white; stem wings very narrow (except for some Argentine forms of *S. chacoense*) (5)
(4) Leaf pubescence sparse or entirely absent; occurs in low-altitude, humid tropical zone (Bolivia) **5. *S. yungasense***
Leaf pubescence medium to dense; occurs in medium-altitude, dry forest zone **1. *S. arnezii***
(5) Corolla stellate to substellate (north Peru) **3. *S. huancabambense***
Corolla clearly stellate (Bolivia southwards) **2. *S. chacoense***

1. *S. arnezii* Cárd. (Bol. Soc. Peruana Bot. **5**, 37–41, 1956)

Stem mottled purple, with (1–)2–4 mm broad straight or crinkle-edged wings, leaves generally 4–5-jugate, with medium to dense spreading hairs; corolla creamy yellow (rarely white) very reflexed, deeply stellate; anthers 7–8 mm long; style 8–13 mm long.
Distribution: Bolivia, depts Chuquisaca and Santa Cruz, in partial shade of shrubs and bushes, from 2,000–2,300 m.
Derivation: dedicated by Professor Martín Cárdenas to his pupil, Ing. Victor Arnez, who first collected this species
2n = 24 (?)
Braun.

2. *S. chacoense* Bitt. (Fedde, Repert. **11**, 18, 1912)

S. guaraniticum Hassl. (Fedde, Repert. **9**, 115, 1911); non *S. guaraniticum* A.St. Hilaire, in Mem. Mus. **12**, 321–2, 1825)
S. guaraniticum var. *latisectum* Hassl. p.pte. (Fedde, Repert. **9**, 115, 1911)
S. guaraniticum var. *latisectum* Hassl. f. *glabrescens* Hassl. (Fedde, Repert. **9**, 115–16, 1911)
S. guaraniticum var. *angustisectum* Hassl. (Fedde, Repert. **9**, 115, 1911)
S. bitteri Hassl. (Fedde, Repert. **11**, 190, 1912)
S. subtilius Bitt. (Fedde, Repert. **12**, 6–7, 1913)
S. chacoense var. *latisectum* Hassl. p.pte. (Ann. Conserv. Jard. Bot. Genève **20**, 186, 1917)
S. chacoense var. *latisectum* f. *glabrescens* Hassl. (Ann. Conserv. Jard. Bot. Genève **20**, 186, 1917)
S. chacoense Bitt. var. *angustisectum* Hassl. (Ann. Conserv. Jard. Bot. Genève **20**, 186–7, 1917)

S. gibberulosum Juz. et Buk. (Rev. Argent. Agron. **3**, 225–6, 1936)
S. parodii Juz. et Buk. (Rev. Argent. Agron. **3**, 226, 1936)
S. garciae Juz. et Buk. (Rev. Argent. Agron. **3**, 227–8, 1936)
S. horovitzii Buk. (Rev. Argent. Agron. **4**, 238, 1937)
S. laplaticum Buk. (Rev. Argent. Agron. **4**, 238–9, 1937)
S. boergeri Buk. (Rev. Argent. Agron. **4**, 239, 1937)
S. emmeae Juz. et Buk. (Bull. Acad. Sci. U.R.S.S., ser. Biol. **2**, 321–2, 1937) = *S. dolichostigma* Buk. (*nom. nud.*)
S. knappei Juz. et Buk. (Bull. Acad. Sci., U.R.S.S., ser. Biol. **2**, 322–3, 1937)
S. schickii Juz. et Buk. (Bull. Acad. Sci., U.R.S.S., ser. Biol. **2**, 324–5, 1937)
S. saltense Hawkes (Bull. Imp. Bur. Pl. Breed. & Genet., Cambridge, 113–14, 1944; non *S. saltense* C.V. Morton, in Contrib. U.S. Nat. Herb. **29**, 63, 1944) = *Lycianthes saltensis*
S. horovitzii Buk. var. *multijugum* Hawkes (Bull. Imp. Bur. Pl. Breed. & Genet., Cambridge, 114, 1944)
S. jujuyense Hawkes (Bull. Imp. Bur. Pl. Breed. & Genet., Cambridge, 114, 1944)
S. horovitzii var. *glabristylum* Hawkes *nom. nud.* (ibid. 19, 1944)
S. caipipendense Cárd. (Bol. Soc. Peruana Bot. **5**, 35–6, 1956)
S. cuevoanum Cárd. (Bol. Soc. Peruana Bot. **5**, 36–7, 1956)
S. chacoense subsp. *subtilius* Hawkes (Ann. Rep. Scottish Pl. Breed. Sta., 61, 1956)
S. chacoense f. *gibberulosum* (Juz. et Buk.) Corr. (Wrightia **2**, 172, 1961)
S. chacoense f. *caipipendense* (Cárd.) Corr. (Wrightia **2**, 172, 1961)
S. limense Corr. (Wrightia **2**, 188–9, 1961)

Differs from *S. commersonii* in the petiolulate acute to acuminate leaflets, the terminal leaflet hardly larger than the laterals, the uniformly white corolla and the globular berries. An extremely polymorphic species spreading through south Bolivia, north and central Argentina, Paraguay, Uruguay and south Brazil, generally as a field weed in lowland pastures.

The great range of variation has induced many authors to divide it into a large number of microspecies which cannot now be maintained since they are all apparently fertile with each other and intergrade considerably.

A collection known to plant breeders erroneously as '*S. caldasii*' or '*S. caldasii* var. *glabrescens*' must be included as *S. chacoense*; *S. caldasii* is a synonym of *S. ochranthum* (q.v.), whilst the type material of *S. caldasii* var. *glabrescens* belongs to *S. brevidens*.

KEY TO SUBSPECIES

Lateral leaflets 2–3 times as long as broad   **2a. subsp.** *chacoense*
Lateral leaflets 3.3–4.3 times as long as broad   **2b. subsp.** *muelleri*

2a. Subspecies *chacoense*

Lateral leaflets 2–3 times as long as broad; plains forms are almost glabrous, forming a semi-rosette in the early stages of growth, and also possess very short (not more than 0.75 mm) calyx acumens. Forms of subsp. *chacoense* occurring in the mountain valleys of north-west Argentina and south Bolivia are more pubescent, with shorter petiolules, longer calyx acumens and more developed stem wings. They rarely form the semi-rosette of basal leaves that is seen in *S. chacoense* in the plains. Many of these forms seem to be due to introgression with the species *S. microdontum* and possibly certain other mountain species. It has been thought advisable not to give them separate subspecies rank.
Distribution: Bolivia, Argentina, Paraguay and Uruguay. Waysides, pastures, arable land, scrub and woodland margins, from sea level to 2,350 m.
Derivation: from the Chaco, an area of dry scrub and bush formation occurring in northern Argentina, Paraguay and south-east Bolivia.
2n = 24; EBN = 2
Bal., Braun., CPC, Gr.Lü., Stur., VIR

2b. Subspecies *muelleri* **(Bitt.) Hawkes et Hjerting** (in Hawkes, J.G., Scott. Pl. Breed. Rec., 103, 1963)

S. muelleri Bitt. (Fedde, Repert. **12**, 155–6, 1913)
S. jamesii Torr. var. *grandifrons* Bitt. (Fedde, Repert. **12**, 151–2, 1913)
S. chacoense subsp. *muelleri* f. *densipilosum* Corr. (Wrightia **2**, 173, 1961)

Differs from subsp. *chacoense* by the long narrow leaflets, about 3.3–4.3 times as long as broad, the long petiolules, up to 25 mm on the acroscopic side, the very oblique leaflet bases and rather low pedicel articulation. Plant generally glabrous, very occasionally pubescent (as in Correll's f. *densipilosum*).
Distribution: Argentina (prov. Misiones), south Brazil (states of Rio Grande, Paraná and Santa Catarina). Grasslands, river banks, waysides, fields, forest margins and clearings, at fairly low altitudes (up to 800 m?).
Derivation: Subsp. *muelleri* was named as a species '*S. muelleri*' by Bitter in honour of the collector, 'Frid' Müller, who gave seeds to Professor Hildebrand for sending to the Vienna Botanic Garden for cultivation.

3. *S. huancabambense* Ochoa (Agronomía, Lima, **26**, 109–10, 1959)

Leaflets oblong-elliptic, obtuse, petiolulate; calyx with coarse hairs; corolla white, stellate to substellate, the lobes about 9 mm long with barely distinguishable acumens. This species seems very similar in its stem, leaf, and calyx to *S. chacoense* but it differs in the rather broader corolla lobes; even so, it differs only very slightly from biotypes of *S. chacoense* in Argentina, provs San Luís and Córdoba. Further experimental work is needed on this intriguing species.

Distribution: north Peru, dept Piura, prov. Huancabamba, at 1,800–3,000 m in field borders, roadsides, etc.
Derivation: from Huancambamba
2n = 24; EBN = 2
Braun., Stur., VIR

4. S. tarijense Hawkes (Bull. Imp. Bur. Pl. Breed. & Genet., Cambridge, 114–15, 1944)

Plant with a dense pubescence of simple and short-stalked glandular hairs, pleasantly aromatic; calyx acumens well-marked, linear; corolla white, stellate; berry globular, with white raised spots. Natural hybrids with *S. berthaultii* in Bolivia are quite frequent. In Argentina it may introgress with a purple-flowered species causing a slight purple tinge in the otherwise normally white flowers.
Distribution: Bolivia, depts Chuquisaca, Cochabamba, Potosí and Tarija; Argentina, provs Jujuy and Salta. Scrub and cactus vegetation in dry interandine valleys at altitudes of about 2,000–2,800 m.
    Hybrides with *S. chacoense* are named *S. trigalense* Cárd. (Bol. Soc. Peruana Bot. 5, 41–2, 1956) (see later, No. 8).
    Hybrids with *S. berthaultii* are named *S. zudaniense* Cárd. (ibid. 31–2, 1956) (see later, No. 9).
Derivation: from Tarija
2n = 24; EBN = 2
Bal., Braun., CPC, Gr.Lü., Stur., VIR

5. S. yungasense Hawkes (Ann. Mag. Nat. Hist., Ser. 12, **7**, 697, 1954)

Stem glabrous or sparsely pubescent, with conspicuous straight to crisped wings from 2–3 mm wide. Inflorescence many-flowered; calyx with narrow linear sepal acumens. Corolla stellate 2.5–3.5 cm diam., creamy yellow, with narrow lobes, more than twice as long as broad. Berries globose.
Distribution: north Bolivia, dept La Paz, subtropical forests (Yungas region) at 1,100–1,900 m. (May perhaps also be found in Peru.)
Derivation: from the Yungas subtropical forest region
2n = 24
Braun., Gr.Lü., VIR

6. S. flavoviridens Ochoa (Amer. Potato J. **57**, 387–90, 1980)

I have seen no material of this species, but from the author's description it seems very striking, with yellow-green leaves and stems covered with long and short glandular hairs (trichome Types A and B), white pentagonal to substellate corolla, 3.0–3.5 cm diam., 12 mm long style and globose light green berries.
Distribution: north Bolivia, dept La Paz, in warm humid tropical to subtropical forests at 1,800 m. The author believes it to be a natural hybrid (which I doubt) and considers that it could represent a new potential source for aphid resistant breeding.
Derivation: becoming yellow-green

7. S. × litusinum Ochoa (Phytologia **48**(3), 229–32, 1981)

I have seen no material of this species but the author states that it possesses a large stellate violet-coloured corolla and oval-pyriform berry. The chromosome number is 2n = 24 and he believes that *S. litusinum* should be placed in series *Commersoniana* (*Yungasensa* on the present classification). It seems likely that it might be part of a natural hybrid swarm between *S. tarijense* and *S. berthaultii*. Only experimental plantings and scoring of variability could elucidate this problem.
Distribution: Bolivia, dept Santa Cruz at 2,600 m.
Derivation: from the sea shore, based on the place name 'La Playa', meaning 'beach'.

8. S. × trigalense Cárd. (Bol. Soc. Peruana Bot. **5**, 41–2, 1956)

Plants varying from subglabrous through pubescent to glandular pubescent. Corolla white, stellate, 3.0 cm diam.
Distribution: Bolivia, dept Santa Cruz, at 2,100 m, among bushes.
  This is undoubtedly a natural hybrid between *S. chacoense* and *S. tarijense*. The four plants of Cárdenas's type collection vary greatly in pubescence (see above) and illustrate the segregation of characters from the two parents.
Derivation: from Trigal, where it was collected
2n = 24
VIR

9. S. × zudaniense Cárd. (Bol. Soc. Peruana Bot. **5**, 31–2, 1956)

Plants varying in flower colour from very pale to darker mauve and in shape from stellate to substellate. Leaves with or without long-stalked B-Type trichomes. This is clearly a natural hybrid between *S. tarijense* and *S. berthaultii*.
Distribution: Bolivia, depts Chuquisaca, Cochabamba and Potosí, at about 2,000 m, in fields and on roadsides; also in bushy vegetation with cacti.
Derivation: from Zudáñez, where it was first collected
2n = 24
Braun., Stur.

Superseries ROTATA Hawkes (Taxon **38**, 489–92, 1989)

Differs from superseries *Stellata* in the pentagonal to completely rotate corolla, which always shows a clear distinction between lobes and acumens, even in those rare cases where the corolla is substellate. Corolla varying from white to deep cream, or various shades of mauve and violet.
  Some of the series in superseries *Rotata* can be considered as 'primitive' in that the corolla is pentagonal to substellate. Such series are: X *Megistacroloba*, XI *Cuneoalata*, the southern species of XII *Conicibaccata*, XV *Maglia*, the southern species of XVI *Tuberosa* and two northern species of XVIII *Longipedicellata* (*S. fendleri* and *S. hjertingii*).

The more 'advanced' series in terms of their clearly rotate corolla, are the northern species of XII *Conicibaccata*, XIII *Piurana*, XIV *Ingifolia*, the northern species of XVI *Tuberosa*, XVII *Acaulia*, XVIII *Longipedicellata* (except for two northern species) and XIX *Demissa*.

Note: a key to these series is incorporated into the complete series key on pp. 67–9.

SERIES X *MEGISTACROLOBA* CÁRD. & HAWKES

(J. Linn. Soc. Bot. **53**, 93, 1946)

Rather short-stemmed or decumbent tuber-bearing herbs whose leaves bear a very enlarged terminal leaflet, with the lateral leaflets or leaf lobes much smaller than the terminal or sometimes completely absent. The laterals when present are broadly decurrent on to the rachis at the basiscopic side; peduncle generally very short; pedicel long, with very high articulation; corolla substellate to rotate, purple.

Distribution: north Peru to north-west Argentina, growing in waste places, open mountain pastures, and among rocks and stones, generally at high altitudes.

KEY TO SPECIES

(1) Pubescence on upper stem, peduncles and pedicels very dense, spreading and with short stalked glands (and some long ones?); corolla very large, to 4 cm diam., substellate   **6. S. huanucense**
Pubescence generally less dense, non-glandular; corolla generally smaller, not more than 3–3.5 cm diam., rotate to substellate   (2)

(2) Lateral leaf lobes very minute, placed on the decurrent base of terminal leaflet; corolla rotate (north Peru)   **4. S. hastiforme**
Lateral leaf lobes or leaflets when present not minute, not on decurrent base of terminal leaflet   (3)

(3) Upper pair of leaflets with very broad triangular wings; corolla more or less rotate; plant with upright habit (south Peru)
      5. S. hawkesii
Leaflets not as above; corolla pentagonal to substellate; plant generally rosetted or decumbent   (4)

(4) Leaf very short and broad, with 1(–2) pairs of broad lateral lobes or leaflets and larger broader terminal (north Peru) **3. S. chavinense**
Leaf not of this type, longer and narrower   (5)

(5) Plant more or less erect to decumbent; leaf narrowly lanceolate, simple or occasionally with 1 pair of lateral lobes under culture
      1. S. astleyi
Plant spreading, rosette-like or decumbent, with more or less oval to elliptic or even orbicular lateral and terminal lobes   (6)

(6) Laterals generally absent, but when present shortly petiolulate
      2. S. boliviense
Laterals present in mature plants, never petiolulate   (7)

(7) Leaflets, especially terminal, broad ovate to orbicular, obtuse, narrowly winged, appearing like a radish (*Raphanus*) leaf
8. *S. raphanifolium*
Leaves ovate to ovate-lanceolate, generally broadly winged   (8)
(8) Lateral leaf lobes acuminate, rather narrow   **9. *S. sanctae-rosae***
Lateral leaf lobes obtuse to acute, broad   (9)
(9) Leaf lobes when present with very broad triangular decurrent wings; peduncle 6–8 cm long; calyx acumens decurrent; plant with no odour   **11. *S. toralapanum***
Leaf lobes when present with narrow triangular decurrent wings; peduncle very short, 0–5(–6) cm long; calyx acumens appressed, erect   (10)
(10) Terminal leaflet broadly ovate; inflorescence very robust, with common peduncle 5–6 cm long; corolla rotate   **10. *S. sogarandinum***
Terminal leaflet ovate; inflorescence not robust, with common peduncle short, 0–2 cm long; corolla substellate
7. *S. megistacrolobum*

1. *S. astleyi* Hawkes et Hjerting (Bot. J. Linn. Soc. **90**, 106–8, 1985)

Stem slender, erect; leaf narrow-lanceolate to ovate-lanceolate, generally simple or occasionally with one pair of small lateral lobes under cultivation; interjected leaflets absent. Common peduncle 1.2–2.5 cm long. Corolla pale to medium blue-violet, substellate to pentagonal.
Distribution: Bolivia, dept Potosí, but rather rare; in cultivated fields and waste places from 3,000–3,300 m.
Derivation: named in honour of Dr David Astley who accompanied the author on the 1974 and 1980 expeditions to Bolivia, and who first found this species, together with Dr W. Hondelmann.
2n = 24; EBN = 2
Braun., Stur. (not in inventory)

2. *S. boliviense* Dun. (DC. Prodr. **13**, I. 43, 1852)

Plants rosetted or with weakly erect to decumbent stem. Leaf simple, broadly ovate to elliptic or oblong; lateral leaflets when present much smaller than the terminal, shortly petiolulate. Common peduncle 3–4 cm long. Corolla substellate to rotate, rich blue-purple, about 2 cm diam. Berries globular.
Distribution: central Bolivia, depts Chuquisaca and Potosí, in dry scrub vegetation and cultivated fields, from 2,600–3,750 m.
Derivation: from Bolivia.
2n = 24; EBN = 2
Braun., CPC, Stur., VIR

3. *S. chavinense* Corr. (Wrightia 2, 185–6, 1961)

Plant upright to decumbent, with long, spreading hairs on stems and inflorescence branches. Leaves with enlarged terminals and smaller 1(–2)-

jugate laterals with decurrent bases on to the rachis, rather densely covered below, sparsely above, with medium to long hairs. Common peduncle short, less than 4 cm long; pedicel articulation in the upper third. Corolla broadly substellate to pentagonal, 3–4.5 cm diam. Berries broadly elliptic to globose.

Distribution: Peru, depts Ancash and La Libertad, growing amongst rocks, grass, trees and shrubs, from 3,500–4,200 m.

Derivation: from Chavín, in Ancash dept

Ochoa (Darwiniana **17**, 1972) thinks that *S. chavinense* should be relegated to synonomy under *S. dolichocremastrum*. After a careful study of the type specimens of both those species, I am certain that they are distinct. Material at Sturgeon Bay under the name of *S. dolichocremastrum* should now be named *S. chavinense*, therefore. *S. dolichocremastrum* belongs to series *Tuberosa*.

Stur. (not in inventory)

4. *S. hastiforme* **Corr.** (Wrightia **2**, 187–8, 1961)

Stem upright to decumbent, with coarse spreading hairs. Leaves simple to 1(–2)-jugate, somewhat hastate; terminal ovate-acuminate much larger than laterals; laterals very small, set just below terminal or even on its decurrent wings; leaves densely covered with long shining obliquely pointed hairs, shorter and pointing in various directions below. Inflorescence branches densely pubescent, with coarse hairs; peduncle short, 1–2 cm below fork; pedicel articulation in the upper third, about 5 mm below calyx base. Corolla rotate–pentagonal, rich purple about 3 cm diam.

Distribution: north Peru, dept La Libertad, along a bushy rocky stream, at 3,200 m.

Derivation: with a spear-shaped leaf

2n = 24

VIR

5. *S. hawkesii* **Cárd.** (J. Linn. Soc., Bot. **53**, 95–6, 1946)

Plant large; stem more or less glabrous. Leaf 3–4-jugate, with very broad decurrent triangular wings from the upper pair of lateral leaflets, less so from the other pairs; small interjected leaflets are also present; leaf hairs sparse and short. Peduncle to 6 cm long below fork, subglabrous; pedicels subglabrous with median articulation. Corolla rotate, 3–3.5 cm diam.

Distribution: south Peru, dept Cuzco, Machu Picchu, in humid mountain forests at about 2,000 m.

This species has been collected once only, and unfortunately not in a living state. Further collections, and especially of living material, are necessary to determine its affinities.

Derivation: named in my honour

6. S. huanucense Ochoa (Sol. Tuberif. Silv. Peru, Lima, 190–3, 1962)

Stems long, apparently upright to decumbent. Leaves short, 1–2-jugate, with very large broad terminal leaflets, smaller laterals, quickly diminishing in size below, and no interjected leaflets; laterals sessile, rather decurrent; stem, leaves and inflorescence branches thickly covered with white spreading hairs and short-stalked glands (possibly also some longer ones). Peduncle 2–7 cm long; pedicels articulated in the upper third. Corolla showy, purple, pentagonal to substellate, 4 cm diam.
Distribution: Peru, dept Huánuco, prov. Dos de Mayo, in stony rocky places, at 3,400–3,800 m.
Note: This species has no affinities with *S. dolichocremastrum*. It is not present in any of the living collections according to their inventories.
Derivation: from Huánuco

7. S. megistacrolobum Bitt. (Fedde, Repert. **10**, 536–7, 1912)

S. alticola Bitt. (Fedde, Repert. **12**, 5–6, 1913)
S. alticola var. *xanthotrichum* Hawkes (Bull. Imp. Bur. Pl. Breed. & Genet., Cambridge, 120, 1944)
S. tilcarense Hawkes (Bull. Imp. Bur. Pl. Breed. & Genet., Cambridge, 119–20, 1944)

Rosette-forming or with straggling stem; the terminal leaflet long-ovate to obovate, long-ellipsoid or rhomboid, rounded or obtuse at apex (or with a minute mucron only); entire-leaved rosette forms of this species from north Bolivia were described as *S. alticola*, whilst forms with more rhomboid terminal leaflet from north-west Argentina were named *S. tilcarense*. Most of the differences may be ascribed to variations in habitat.
   The common peduncle in *S. megistacrolobum* is very short, generally 0–2 cm long; pedicels very long, 4–6 cm or more, and articulated 5–10 mm below calyx base. Calyx acumens upright, appressed to corolla. Corolla semi-stellate to pentagonal, 2.5–3.5 cm diam., generally pale blue-lilac. Berries green, globular. The plant possesses a strong characteristic parsley-like (*Petroselinum crispum*) odour when gently rubbed by the fingers – a feature not present in the closely related *S. toralapanum* or any other *Megistacroloba* species.
Distribution: Peru, dept Puno; Bolivia, depts Chuquisaca, La Paz, Oruro, Potosí and Tarija; Argentina, provs Jujuy and Salta. Grows in high mountain grassland and field borders at 3,500–4,450 m.
Derivation: very large terminal lobe (of the leaf)
2n = 24; EBN = 2
Bal., Braun., CPC, Gr.Lü., Stur., VIR

8. S. raphanifolium Cárd. et Hawkes (J. Linn. Soc., Bot. **53**, 94–5, 1946)

Habit spreading, with long decumbent branches. Leaf 2–3(–5)-jugate, with terminal much larger than laterals, broadly ovate to obovate or completely orbicular, obtuse or with a small mucron at apex, basally decurrent on to the rachis as are all the laterals; some few interjected leaflets are also developed; leaf pubescence sparse and short. Peduncle 3–7 cm long; pedicel articulated high up. Corolla violet, substellate to pentagonal, about 2.5 cm diam. Berry globose.

Distribution: south Peru, dept Cuczo, very common in the Cuzco valley system, particularly amongst rocks, grass and shrubs, occasionally in cultivated fields, from 2,800–3,800 m; common on archaeological monuments.

In cultivated fields it forms hybrids with *S. sparsipilum*. Juvenile plants form flat rosettes similar to those of *S. megistacrolobum*, and some workers have assumed *S. raphanifolium* to be a hybrid of *S. megistacrolobum* by *S. canasense* or similar species. Experimental crossings have shown this not to be the case, and that *S. raphanifolium* is a good species in its own right. Note: the original description of Cárdenas and Hawkes in J. Linn. Soc., Bot. **53**, 94–5, 1946, mentions two syntypes. I hereby designate *Cárdenas and Gandarillas 3500* as holotype for *S. raphanifolium* (Herb. Kew).

Derivation: leaf similar to that of *Raphanus*, the radish

2n = 24; EBN = 2

Braun., CPC, Gr.Lü., Stur., VIR

9. S. sanctae-rosae Hawkes (Ann. Mag. Nat. Hist., Ser. 12, **7**, 702–3, 1954)

Distinguished from *S. megistacrolobum* and *S. raphanifolium* by the *acuminate* lateral and terminal leaflets, the small rosette habit, deep blue-purple corolla, with poorly marked acumens and large globose stigma. It possesses the typical *Megistacroloba* habit, rosetted or semi-rosetted plants, decurrent leaflets, rather short peduncle (3–4 cm long), high pedicel articulation (2–3(–6) mm below calyx), and substellate corolla.

Distribution: north-west Argentina, provs Salta, Tucumán, and Catamarca, in high mountain pastures, sandy and rocky places, etc., from 2,500–3,800 m. This is the most southerly of all the series *Megistacroloba* species and is probably most closely allied to *S. megistacrolobum*.

Derivation: from Estancia Santa Rosa, prov. Tucumán, Argentina, referring to the locality of the type specimen

2n = 24; EBN = 2

Bal., Braun., CPC, Gr.Lü., Stur., VIR

10. S. sogarandinum Ochoa (Agronomía, Lima, **19**, 169–72, 1954)

Very closely related to *S. megistacrolobum*; differs chiefly in the very robust inflorescence, the 2–7 cm long peduncle below the fork and 6–7 cm above, which is much longer than in *S. megistacrolobum*, and the rotate corolla. In its leaf it would seem to be no more than a subspecies of *S. megistacrolobum*, but the peduncle length and rotate corolla preclude this decision and indicate that it must be a species in its own right.

Distribution: north Peru, dept La Libertad, in páramos (high Andean grassland), at 3,500 m.

Derivation: from Sogaranda, p·ov. Santiago de Chuco, dept La Libertad
2n = 24; EBN = 2
Braun., Gr.Lü., Stur., VIR

11. *S. toralapanum* Cárd. et Hawkes (J. Linn. Soc., Bot. **53**, 98–9, 1946)

S. decurrentilobum Cárd. et Hawkes (ibid. 97–8)
S. ellipsifolium Cárd. et Hawkes (ibid. 100–1)
S. toralapanum var. *subintegrifolium* Cárd. et Hawkes (ibid. 99–100)
S. ureyi Cárd. (Bol. Soc. Peruana Bot. **5**, 32–3, 1956)

Related fairly closely to *S. megistacrolobum* but differs in the very broadly
triangular decurrent rachis wing, the often very long curved spathulate
terminal lobe (or leaf, when no laterals are present), the lack of a basal
auricle on the acroscopic side of the lateral lobes, the long (6–8 cm)
common peduncle, the spreading to recurved acumens and the lack of the
parsley-like leaf odour.
Distribution: Bolivia, depts Chuquisaca, Cochabamba, La Paz, Oruro and
Tarija; north-west Argentina, prov. Salta. Grows in wetter habitats than *S.
megistacrolobum*, in field margins, rocky and grassy slopes (puna *Stipa*
grassland), etc. from 3,000–4,100 m.
Derivation: from Hacienda Toralapa, dept Cochabamba, where Cárdenas
first found it
2n = 24; EBN = 2
Bal. (as *S. boliviense*), Braun., CPC, Gr.Lü., Stur., VIR

SERIES XI   *CUNEOALATA*   HAWKES

(Bull. Imp. Bur. Plant Breed. & Genet., Cambridge, 118, 1944)

Small straggling tuberiferous herbs with pinnatifid leaf, the rachis with
narrow wedge-shaped decurrent wings between each pair of leaflets.
Corolla purplish, substellate to rotate with well-delimited petal acumens.
Distribution: north Peru to north-west Argentina and north Chile, in dry
cactus deserts and scrub. Possibly drought-resistant.

KEY TO SPECIES

(1) Leaf lobes linear, 7–(9–10)-paired   **3. *S. peloquinianum***
     Leaf lobes lanceolate to narrowly lanceolate, less than 7-paired   (2)
(2) Leaf lobes generally 5–6-paired, falcate (curved) with occasional inter-
     jected leaflets; corolla substellate   **1. *S. anematophilum***
     Leaf lobes generally less than 5-paired, not curved and without inter-
     jected leaflets; corolla pentagonal to rotate **2. *S. Infundibuliforme***

1. S. anematophilum Ochoa (Anal. Cientif. Univ. Agraria, Lima, **11**(4), 391–5, 1964)

A weak decumbent herb, with narrow angled stem. Leaves imparipinnatifid, with (3–)5–6 pairs of lateral lobes, decurrent on to the rachis, the uppermost decurrent wings being quite broad; lobes tending to be falcate and narrowly lanceolate; occasionally 1–2 pairs of interjected lobes can be seen. Corolla substellate, dark purple, 2.5 cm diam. Berries subglobose to ellipsoid.

Distribution: Peru, dept Ancash in shrubby xerophytic woodland with *Trichocereus* and *Opuntia* at 2,700 m.

Derivation: loving the wind

2. S. infundibuliforme Phil. (Anal. Mus. Nac. Chile, 2nd ed. Bot., 65, 1891)

S. infundibuliforme Phil. var. *angustepinnatum* Bitt. (Fedde, Repert. **11**, 388–9, 1912)

S. platypterum Hawkes (Bull. Imp. Bur. Plant Breed. & Genet., Cambridge, 118, 1944)

S. microphyllum Hawkes (Bull. Imp. Bur. Plant Breed. & Genet., Cambridge, 118, 1944; non *S. microphyllum* Dun., Hist. Solan., 187, 1813)

S. glanduliferum Hawkes (Bull. Imp. Bur. Plant Breed. & Genet., Cambridge, 118–19, 1944)

S. pinnatifidum Cárdenas (Rev. Agric., Cochabamba, **2**, 33–4, 1944; non *S. pinnatifidum* Ruiz et Pav., Flora Peruv. **2**, 37, 1798–1802)

S. xerophyllum Hawkes (J. Linn. Soc., Bot. **53**, 108, 1946)

S. infundibuliforme Phil. var. *albiflorum* Ochoa (Phytologia, **46**(4), 223, 1980)

Leaflets or leaf lobes roughly lanceolate, linear-lanceolate to linear. Interjected leaflets entirely absent. Corolla pale mauve to purplish, occasionally white, in shape varying from substellate to completely rotate (circular with well-marked acumens, as in series *Longipedicellata*). A form from the Argentine-Bolivian border previously classed as *S. platypterum* owing to the very wide rachis wings is not sufficiently distinct to be given specific rank; similarly with *S. glanduliferum* which bears some glands on the leaves, and *S. xerophyllum* which possesses narrow linear leaflets, due probably to very poor soil and moisture conditions.

Distribution: Bolivia, depts Chuquisaca, Cochabamba, Potosí and Tarija; north-west Argentina, provs Jujuy and Salta; Chile, provs Antofagasta, Atacama and Tarapacá; dry cactus and scrub deserts at 2,450–4,100 m.

Derivation: funnel-shaped, referring to the shape of the wilted corolla on the type specimen

2n = 24; EBN = 2

Bal., Braun., CPC, Gr.Lü., Stur., VIR

3. *S. peloquinianum* Ochoa (Amer. Potato J. **57**, 33–5, 1980)

Leaves thick, pinnatisect, with 7–(9–10) pairs of leaf lobes and 0–8 interjected leaflets; leaf lobes linear, very long and narrow, slightly falcate, glabrous above, pubescent below; pseudostipules also narrowly falcate. Corolla rotate, rather small (2 cm diam.), purple with dark purple star. Fruit spherical to ovoid, 10–12 mm long.

Distribution: Peru, dept Ancash in xeric habitats mixed with cacti, bromeliads, crassulas etc, at 1,720 m.

Derivation: named in honour of the distinguished American potato geneticist, Stanley J. Peloquin

2n = 24

SERIES XII   *CONICIBACCATA* BITT.

(Fedde, Repert. **11**, 381, 1912)

OXYCARPA Rydb. [grad. ambig.] (Bull. Torr. Bot. Cl. **51**, 146, 172, 1924)

Tuber-bearing herbs with generally well-dissected leaves and acuminate leaflets, rotate to pentagonal or substellate, white to generally purple flowers and ovate-conical to long conical berries.

Distribution: Mexico, southwards to Bolivia; all species grow in humid mountain forests and in other regions of high rainfall.

Conicibaccata is one of the three taxonomic series of wild potatoes to be found both north and south of the Panamá isthmus (the others being *Juglandifolia* and *Tuberosa*). Many of the species are not very well known and are difficult to cultivate. Unfortunately I have not been able to examine more than 23 out of the 40 species now described. With better knowledge it will probably be necessary to reduce some species to synonymy, whilst others might need to be removed to other series.

The polyploid series of species in *Conicibaccata*, with diploid, tetraploid and hexaploid species, is of great theoretical interest and indicates a possibly rather complex evolutionary history, of which we are only just beginning to understand some of the details.

KEY TO SPECIES

(Note: a key to Colombian species is given by Ochoa in Phytologia **49**(5), 486–7, 1981)

(1) Plant with many conspicuous long- and short-stalked glands as well as long non-glandular hairs (Peru)   **5. *S. contumazaense***
    Plant with no conspicuous glandular hairs   (2)
(2) Leaves and inflorescence branches glabrous to subglabrous   (3)
    Leaves and inflorescence branches pubescent   (7)

(3) Leaf with 7(–9) pairs of lateral leaflets and up to 20 pairs of inter-
    jected leaflets (Mexico and Guatemala)   **1. S. agrimonifolium**
    Leaf with 3–5 pairs of lateral leaflets and few interjected leaflets (4)
(4) Leaves completely glabrous   (5)
    Leaves subglabrous, even if only a few sparse hairs present   (6)
(5) Interjected leaflets absent (Central America)   **9. S. longiconicum**
    Interjected leaflets generally present (north Peru)
                                              3. S. chomatophilum
(6) Leaves with narrowly lanceolate, long-acuminate leaflets; berries
    narrow-conical, acute-pointed (Mexico)   **14. S. oxycarpum**
    Leaves with lanceolate acuminate leaflets; berries ovoid-conical,
    blunt pointed (Peru)   **18. S. santolallae**
(7) Leaves very short; leaflets broad-ovate, etc. overlapping each other
    (Colombia)   **6. S. donachui**
    Leaves not of this type   (8)
(8) Corolla with very flat lobes and small acumens, appearing 10-pointed
                                                                        (9)
    Corolla not of this type   (10)
(9) Leaf well dissected, (4–)6(–10)-jugate; articulation more or less
    median (Colombia)   **10. S. moscopanum**
    Leaf poorly dissected, (1–)2(–3)-jugate; articulation very high up,
    just below calyx (Colombia +?)   **7. S. flahaultii**
(10) Leaf poorly dissected, generally with 2(–3) pairs of lateral leaflets
                                                                       (11)
    Leaves better dissected, generally with (3–)4–5(–6) pairs of lateral
    leaflets   (18)
(11) Leaf 2-jugate, the leaflet pairs widely separate, with long petiolules
    and no interjected leaflets (Colombia +?)   **13. S. otites**
    Leaf not with the combination of characaters shown above   (12)
(12) Leaf, inflorescence branches and calyx with dense indumentum of
    shining hairs   (13)
    Leaf, etc. without such features   (15)
(13) Inflorescence very large, up to 100 flowers (south Peru)
                                                 11. S. multiflorum
    Inflorescence smaller, about 5–10-flowers   (14)
(14) Terminal leaflet much larger than laterals (south Peru)
                                                 21. S. villuspetalum
    Terminal leaflet more or less the same size as laterals (south Peru)
                                                 20. S. urubambae
(15) Terminal leaflet only slightly larger than laterals   (16)
    Terminal leaflet much larger than laterals   (17)
(16) Leaf pubescence long and dense, also on the inflorescence branches
    (south Peru)   **17. S. pillahuatense**
    Leaf pubescence not very dense; very sparse and short on inflor-
    escence branches (Central America and Venezuela)
                                                 23. S. woodsonii
(17) Pedicel articulation more or less central (Ecuador +?)
                                                 16. S. paucijugum
    Pedical articulation very low (Colombia)   **12. S. neovalenzuelae**

(18) Leaf very large, to 35 cm long, sparsely pubescent (Peru)
                                                     8. *S. laxissimum*
     Leaf smaller; pubescence well developed   (19)
(19) Leaflets sessile, broadly decurrent, with no interjected leaflets
     (Colombia)   **15. *S. pamplonense***
     Leaflets not decurrent; interjected leaflets generally present   (20)
(20) Stem, leaf and inflorescence branches with long delicate silky hairs
     (Venezuela)   **19. *S. subpanduratum***
     Hairs not of this type   (21)
(21) Stem violet-marbled; leaf fairly densely pubescent (Bolivia)
                                              22. *S. violaceimarmoratum*
     Stem not violet-marbled   (22)
(22) Hairs rather long and dense; calyx conspicuously hairy (south Peru)
                                                     2. *S. buesii*
     Hairs medium-sized, fairly frequent; calyx not conspicuously hairy
     (Venezuela, Colombia and Ecuador)   **4. *S. colombianum***

1. *S. agrimonifolium* Rydberg. (Bull. Torr. Bot. Cl. **51**, 154, 1924)

Leaf large, to 40 cm long or more in well-developed plants, with up to 7(–9) pairs of lanceolate acuminate lateral leaflets and 20 pairs of interjecteds, all subglabrous to sparsely pubescent. Calyx with long linear acumens. Corolla purple, rotate, 2.5 cm diam. or larger. Fruits narrow-conical, apically acute, grooved, 3–4.5 cm long. Plants from Honduras seem to have smaller, less-well dissected leaves than those from further north.
Distribution: south Mexico, Chiapas State (possibly also Oaxaca State); Guatemala, provs Chimaltenango, Huehuetenango, Quezaltenango, San Marcos and Totonicapán; Honduras, dept Morozán. In cloud forest in very humid soils at about 1,600–3,300 m.
Derivation: leaf like that of *Agrimonia*, agrimony
2n = 48; EBN = 2
Braun. (not in inventory), Gr.Lü., Stur., VIR

2. *S. buesii* Vargas (Rev. Argent. Agron. **10**, 396–7, 1943)

Leaf with 3(–5) pairs of lateral and 2–3 pairs of interjected leaflets. Stems, leaves, inflorescence branches and calyx with long coarse hairs, particularly dense on the pedicels and calyx; calyx acumens long (2–3 mm). Corolla abaout 3 cm diam., dark purple. Terminal leaflets not larger than laterals.
   Distinguished from *S. santolallae* by its pubescence and long calyx acumens, as well as the larger, dark purple corolla.
Distribution: south Peru, dept Cuzco, amongst ancient ruins in cloud forest at 3,600 m.
Derivation: named in honour of Ing. Agr. C. Bues from Quillabamba, a local botanical collector

3. *S. chomatophilum* Bitt. (Abhandl. Naturwiss. Ver., Bremen, **25**, 246–8, 1942)

Leaf 3–4-jugate with 0–4 pairs (or sometimes more) of small interjected leaflets; leaflets elliptic or broad lanceolate-elliptic, entirely glabrous. Corolla blue, 4 cm diam. with short lobes; filaments pubescent externally. Distribution: north Peru, depts Amazonas, Ancash, Cajamarca and La Libertad, in woods and grassy places, from 2,000–4,000 m.

On the basis of the leaf, which is not glossy or coriaceous, and the fruit, which is ovoid-conical, I have now transferred this species from series *Piurana* to series *Conicibaccata*. However, certain collections from depts Huánuco, Lima and Piura are still in doubt. A collection from Piura (Ochoa 1795) named by Correll *S. chomatophilum* f. *pilosum* Correll (Wrightia **2**, 180, 1961) should be placed with *S. piurae*. Correll's *S. chomatophilum* f. *angustifolium* (Wrightia **2**, 180, 1961) goes now to *S. colombianum*.

Derivation: liking banks; a ruderal plant
2n = 24; EBN = 2
Braun., CPC, Gr.Lü., Stur., VIR

4. *S. colombianum* Dun. (in DC. Prodr., **13**, I, 33, 1852)

S. dolichocarpum Bitt. (Fedde, Repert. **12**, 4–5, 1913)
S. filamentum Corr. (Wrightia **2**, 174–5, 1961)
S. colombianum var. *trianae* Bitt. (Fedde, Repert. **11**, 382–3, 1912)
S. colombianum var. *trianae* f. *quindiuense* Buk. (Suppl. 47, Bull. Appl. Bot. Genet., Pl. Breed., 225–6, 1930)
S. colombianum, var. *meridionale* Hawkes (Bull. Imp. Bur. Pl. Breed. & Genet., Cambridge, 112–13, 1944)
S. colombianum, var. *zipaquiranum* Hawkes (Bull. Imp. Bur. Pl. Breed. & Genet., Cambridge, 112, 1944)
S. chomatophilum Bitt. f. *angustifoliolum* Corr. (Wrightia **2**, 180, 1961)
S. tundalomense Ochoa (Ann. Cient. Univ. Agr., Lima, **1**(1), 106–9, 1963)

Leaf (3–)4–5-jugate; leaflets elliptic-lanceolate, apically attenuate, with medium-sized, fairly frequent hairs; interjected leaflets present, but laterals vary from 4 pairs in the type to 2 or 3 in '*S. dolichocarpum*' to 5 in var. *zipaquiranum*, f. *quindiuense* and *S. tundalomense*; 4 pairs also occur in Bitter's var. *trianae* and in var. *meridionale*. After studying many collections it seems impossible now to define clearly delimited varieties and forms on the basis of leaf dissection.

Corolla rotate-pentagonal, white to mauve; berries broadly ovate-conical with generally blunt apex, less than 3 cm long. A very polymorphic species.
Distribution: Venezuela, Colombia and Ecuador. Cloud forest at 2,200–3,500 m.
Derivation: from Colombia (but named at a time when Colombia included

what are now Ecuador and Venezuela, from which latter country the type specimen was collected)
2n = 48; EBN = 2
CPC, Gr.Lü., Stur., VIR

5. *S. contumazaense* Ochoa (Ann. Cient. Univ. Agr. **2**(2), 148–51, 1964)

Plant covered thickly with short- and long-stalked glandular hairs and apparently long non-glandular ones also; leaf 3–4(–5)-jugate, with up to 17 interjected leaflets; terminal larger than laterals. Calyx with 7–8 mm acumens. Corolla rotate, creamy white. Berry to 4 cm long × 1.0–1.5 cm broad, acute to subacute.
Distributions: Peru, dept Cajamarca, prov. Contumazá, at 2,840 m (*Ochoa 2485*).
    This species seems to possess the extraordinarily dense glandular pubescence that is already known in *S. berthaultii*, *S. flavoviridens* and *S. neocardenasii* (A and B Type trichomes). It may well be of interest, therefore, to potato breeders in the search for resistance to aphids and other small insects. Ochoa, indeed, compares it with the tomato in its appearance.
Derivation: from Contumazá, where it was first discovered
2n = 24 (fide Ochoa)

6. *S. donachui* (Ochoa) Ochoa (Phytologia **54**(5), 392, 1983)

S. garcia-barrigae var. *donachui* Ochoa (Phytologia **51**(6), 401–2, 1982)

This is a rather curious series *Conicibaccata* species, distinguished from others in north-west South America by its very short, broad leaves, the best developed ones being 8 cm long × 7 cm broad; the leaflets are also rather short and broad, ovate oblong to very broadly ovate, slightly acuminate but apically obtuse, overlapping each other and with no interjected leaflets or very few. The leaves are provided with frequent short hairs. The inflorescence branches are sparsely, shortly hairy and the pedicel articulation low. Corolla said by the author to be white, 15 mm diam., the anthers broad and the style rather short, 6 mm long. The fruit is long-conical.
Distribution: Colombia, dept Magdalena, Sierra Nevade de Santa Marta, Donachui river. Alt. 3,260–3,320 m.
Derivation: from the place where it was collected

7. *S. flahaultii* Bitt. (Fedde, Repert. **12**, 57–8, 1913)

(See also *S. paucijugum* and *S. dolichocremastrum*.)

Stem, inflorescence branches, calyx and leaves covered fairly densely with long, white, thick, spreading hairs, particularly dense on lower leaf surfaces, shorter on pedicels and calyx. Leaf with typically large, ovate terminal leaflet and smaller laterals (1–)2(–3)-jugate, rapidly diminishing in size towards leaf base; leaflet apices somewhat acuminate, but not very acute, often very obtuse. Lateral leaflets ± sessile; generally no interjecteds. Pedicel articulation well above the centre. Calyx acumens short. Corolla violet, about 1.8–2.0(–2.5) cm diam., with very flat lobes and small acumens. Berry blunt ovoid-conical, to about 2 cm long.

Distribution: Colombia, depts Boyacá, Cundinamarca and Santander; also in Venezuela and Ecuador: amongst bushes and in páramo vegetation from 2,700–3,700 m.

This species is very difficult to distinguish from *S. paucijugum*, since both possess fairly long stem and leaf hairs, and a similar leaf shape. However, *S. flahaultii* possesses a very high articulation on the pedicel and very flat corolla lobes (even reminding one to some extent of *S. acaule*). *S. paucijugum* possesses a medium-articulated pedicel and a large corolla with well-defined lobes and large acumens.

Derivation: named in honour of C. Flahault, Professor of Botany at Montpellier University, France

2n = 48

Braun. (not in inventory), Gr.Lü., Stur. (not in inventory), VIR

8. S. laxissimum Bitt. (Beibl. Engl. Bot. Jahrb., No. 119, **54**, 7–8, 1916)

S. rockefelleri Vargas (Papas Sudperuanas, Univ. Nac. Cuzco, **2**, 54–5, 1956)

S. laxissimum Bitt. f. *rockefelleri* (Vargas) Correll, (Wrightia **2**, 175, 1961)

Stem 1.5–2.0 m long; leaves to about 35 × 23 cm with 4–6 very remote pairs of leaflets which are sparsely, shortly hairy, lanceolate, acuminate. Pedicels with rather low articulation, subglabrous. Corolla pentagonal to substellate, blue-violet, 3.0–3.5 cm diam. Berries broadly long conical.

Distribution: Peru, depts Cuzco, Huánuco, Junín and perhaps elsewhere, in mountain rain forests at 2,100–3,100 m.

This species would seem to be closely related to *S. santolallae*, but is much larger in all its parts.

Derivation: having a very loose habit with the parts distinct and away from each other

2n = 24; EBN = 2

Gr.Lü., Stur., VIR

9. S. longiconicum Bitt. (Fedde, Repert. **10**, 534–5, 1912)

S. manoteranthum Bitt. (Fedde, Repert. **11**, 383–4, 1912)

Leaf 3–4-jugate with narrowly lanceolate acuminate shortly petiolulate lateral and terminal leaflets, completely or almost glabrous and completely without interjected leaflets. Inflorescence branches glabrous or with minute hairs and glands; pedicels articulated centrally. Corolla violet, rotate, 1–2 cm diam. with short lobes. Berries narrowly conical, to 4 cm long.

Distribution: Costa Rica, provs Cartago, San José and elsewhere; Panamá, prov. Chiriquí. In humid forests, clearings, roadsides, etc., from 1,600–3,100 m. '*S. manoteranthum*' is a shorter, denser growth form only.
Derivation: possessing long conical berries
2n = 48
Stur.

10. *S. moscopanum* Hawkes (Ann. Mag. Nat. Hist., Ser. 12, **7**, 689–90, 1954)

A spreading bushy species with leaves 10–16 cm long, (3–)4–5-jugate and (4–)6(–10) pairs of interjected leaflets; lateral leaflets ovate-lanceolate to oblong-lanceolate; all leaflets densely covered with medium-lengthened appressed hairs. Pedicels pubescent below, subglabrous above articulation. Corolla pale lilac, to about 2.5 cm diam., with very flat, almost concave lobes, giving it a 10-lobed appearance; anthers finely papillose. Berry ovate-conical, to 27 × 14 mm, not sharp-pointed.
Distribution: Colombia, dept Cauca, in humid pastures and waste places, from 2,900–3,400 m. (Possibly occurs elsewhere.)
This species is interesting in that it was the first hexaploid to be found in South America.
Derivation: from the Páramo of Moscopán, where it was first discovered
2n = 72; EBN = 4
Gr.Lü., Stur., VIR

11. *S. multiflorum* Vargas (Papas Sudperuanas, Univ. Nac. Cuzco, **2**, 55–6, 1956)

A striking plant, to 3 m high, with very large leaves, to 30 cm long × 20 cm broad, but with only (2–)3 pairs of broadly ovate acuminate leaflets and slightly broader terminal, 1 cm long petiolules and dense long glistening hairs pointing diagonally towards the edges of the leaflets. Stems, inflorescence branches and calyx similarly pubescent. Inflorescence immense, at least three times forked, and covering an area when pressed of 20 × 25 cm, with up to 100 flowers; pedicel articulation near the base (about 3 mm above). Calyx acumens linear-spathulate, to about 5 mm long. Corolla pentagonal, with 5–6 mm long acumens, azure blue, 2.5–3.0 cm diam. Berries conical (but only immature ones seen).
Distribution: south Peru, dept Cuzco, prov. Calca, at 2,700 m. In a previous description, in Spanish (Papas Sudperuanas, Univ. Nac. Cuzco, **1**, 93–5), Professor Vargas states that it grows amongst trees, near a stream, and on open slopes, where the dimensions of the plant are not so extreme. It has been found on two other occasions, at Pillahuata (2,300–2,500 m) and at Machu Picchu at 2,100 m.
Derivation: the name refers to the many flowers that this plant develops, on one of the largest inflorescences ever found on the tuber-bearing Solanums.

12. *S. neovalenzuelae* L. López (Caldasia, 14(68–70), 443–6, 1986)

Leaf 2(–3)-jugate; lateral leaflets sessile, slightly decurrent, decreasing in size towards the leaf base; terminal rather larger than laterals; few or no interjected leaflets; leaf with small infrequent hairs, even fewer below. Pedicel articulation very low, just above the base. Corolla somewhat pentagonal, 2.5 cm diam., violet. Berries long conical.

Distribution: Colombia, depts Santander and Bucaramanga, at 3,650 m.

This species may be similar to *S. garcia-barrigae* Ochoa, which unfortunately I have not been able to study.

Derivation: named after Sr E. Valenzuela who described the first wild potato species in Colombia (see *S. papa*, Appendix I)

2n = 48

Stur. (?) not included in inventory

13. *S. otites* Dun. (in DC., Prodr. **13**, 1, 39, 1852)

S. cuatrecasasii Ochoa (Phytologia **49**(5), 485–6, 1981)
S. otites f. *dizygum* Bitt. (Fedde, Repert. **11**, 434, 1912)
S. otites f. *trizygum* Bitt. (Fedde, Repert. **11**, 434, 1912)

Plant very open; leaf 2(–3)-jugate, the leaflet pairs widely separate and with the terminal leaflet much larger; no interjected leaflets present; leaflets broad elliptic lanceolate, acuminate, long-petiolulate, sparsely pilose to glabrescent above. Pedicels articulated in the upper third. Corolla rotate to pentagonal, lilac to white. Berries long-conical, to 2.5 cm diam.

Distribution: Venezuela, Caracas; Colombia, dept Magdalena (and elsewhere?) at 2,600 m in humid mountain forests.

Derivation: 'like an ear', relating to the supposed similarity of the shape of the leaflets

14. *S. oxycarpum* Schiede (in Schlechtd., Hort. Halensis **1**, 5, 1841)

Leaf delicate, 4–5(–6)-jugate, with narrowly lanceolate long-acuminate lateral and terminal leaflets and a general absence of interjected leaflets (if present, one or two only, and extremely minute); leaves glabrous or with sparse very short hairs; lateral leaflets subsessile. Corolla rotate, purple. Berries narrow-conical, sharp-pointed, 3–4 cm long.

Distribution: Mexico, states of Puebla, Oaxaca and Vera Cruz, in humid pine forests and clearings, generally in the eastern Cordillera. This was one of the earliest potatoes to be colleted in Mexico, in 1841.

Derivation: sharply pointed fruit

2n = 48; EBN = 2

Braun., CPC, Gr.Lü., Stur., VIR

15. *S. pamplonese* L. López (Mutisia, Bogotá, **55**, 15, 1983)

Leaves 2–3-jugate, glabrous; leaflets ovate attenuate, basally sessile and broadly decurrent; no interjected leaflets developed; rachis slightly winged. Inflorescence long; peduncle 7.5 cm long below the fork, 13 cm long above; one branch forked twice. Corolla rotate, purple, to 3 cm diam.; style violet. Berries conical, blunt-ended, to about 2 cm long. Distribution: Colombia, dept Norte de Santander, Pamplona. Alt. 3,300 m.

This species could be closely related to *S. otites* but differs in the decurrent leaflets and possibly other features.
Derivation: from the place where it was discovered
2n = 48

16. *S. paucijugum* Bitt. (Fedde, Repert. **11**, 431–2, 1912)

Stem, leaf shape and pubescence very similar to those of *S. flahaultii*. Leaf 2–3-jugate and with some interjected leaflets. Pedicels articulated at about the centre. Corolla lilac to dark purple, rotate-pentagonal, up to 3 cm diam., with rounded lobes and large acumens, about 5 mm long. Berries blunt, ovoid conical.
Distribution: Ecuador, provs Bolívar, Cotopaxi and Tungurahua, at 3,200–4,100 m. Probably spreads into Colombia also. Grows amongst shrubs, rocks, grasses and herbs, in very humid places.

Difficult to distinguish from *S. flahaultii* (see note under that species).
2n = 48
Braun. (this may be *S. flahaultii*), Gr.Lü., VIR

17. *S. pillahuatense* Vargas (Papas Sudperuanas, Univ. Nac. Cuzco, **2**, 53–4, 1956)

Stem sparsely pilose, slender. Leaf (1–)2(–3)-jugate, without interjected leaflets; petiolules about 3 mm long; pubescence of long, dense very coarse hairs, especially on lower surface. Inflorescence branches and calyx very densely covered with long coarse spreading hairs and small glands; pedicel articulation at or slightly below centre. Corolla pentagonal, mauve, 2.5 cm diam. Berries ovoid-conical. Perhaps related to *S. multiflorum*, as shown by the pubescence.
Distribution: south Peru, dept Cuzco, at 2,800–3,650 m, in very humid forest ('ceja').
Derivation: from Pillahuata, the place where this species was first discovered

18. *S. santolallae* Vargas (Rev. Argent. Agron. **10**, 397, 1943)

S. santolallae var. *acutifolium* Vargas (Rev. Argent. Agron. **10**, 397–8, 1943)
S. santolallae f. *velutinum* Corr. (Wrightia **2**, 176, 1961)
S. claviforme Corr. (Wrightia **2**, 174, 1961)

Leaf subglabrous, with very short sparse hairs, (3–)5(–6)-jugate, apically attenuate, basally shortly petiolulate. Inflorescence branches and calyx glabrous. Corolla pale mauve to white, pentagonal, 2–3 cm diam. Berries ovoid-conical, about 2.5 cm long.

Distribution: south and central Peru, depts Cuzco and Huánuco. Growing in cloud forests, thickets and clearings at 2,500–3,600 m.

Var. *acutifolium* does not differ markedly from the type; f. *velutinum* possesses a dense covering of velvety hairs, but otherwise is the same as the type. *S. claviforme* possesses swollen upper pedicels and rather low articulation. It hardly differs enough from *S. santolallae* to be considered a distinct species.

Derivation: dedicated to Ing. Agr. Nicolas Santolalla

2n = 24

Brun. (not in inventory), Gr.Lü., Stur., VIR

19. *S. subpanduratum* Ochoa (Biota, Lima **11**(91), 331–3, 1979)

Leaf 3–4-jugate with 0–5–7 interjected leaflets; terminal slightly larger than laterals, elliptic ovate, subpandurate or obovate; pubescence delicately silky. Stem, inflorescence branches and calyx with long, silky, spreading hairs. Corolla lilac (?), 2 cm diam., rotate. Berries long conical, to 4.5 cm long.

Distribution: Venezuela, Mérida State, 3,400–3,600 m. In shrubby woods with lupins, *Espeletia*, and other composites.

Derivation: somewhat violin-shaped, referring to the terminal leaflet being constricted in the centre, as in a violin. This feature is barely apparent in the isotype specimen examined by me.

2n = 48

Stur., VIR

20. *S. urubambae* Juz (Bull. Acad. Sci. U.R.S.S., **2**, 312–13, 1937)

Leaf to 25 cm long × 21 cm broad, 2(–3)-jugate, with petiolules from 2–17 mm long; laterals to 10.5 × 4.5 cm; no interjected leaflets; leaves with dense short hairs above, very dense below. Stem, peduncle branches and calyx with short, spreading inconspicuous hairs; articulation about median. Corolla dark purple, pentagonal-rotate, 2–3 cm diam. Berries apparently conical.

Distribution: south Peru, dept Cuzco, prov. Urubamba, amongst stones at 2,200–2,700 m.

Correll places this as a possible synonym of *S. multiflorum* and of *S. violaceimarmoratum*, but the denser longer stem and inflorescence pubescence seems to distinguish them well enough. A collection from dept Apurímac (*Vargas 9140*) also fits well with this species.

Derivation: from Urubamba province

2n = 24

CPC, VIR

21. *S. villuspetalum* Vargas (Papas Sudperuanas, Univ. Nac. Cuzco, **2**, 54, 1956)

Stem, inflorescence branches and calyx covered extremely densely with long coarse hairs. Leaf (0–)1–2(–3)-jugate, with terminals longer and

broader than laterals. Lower leaves simple to 1-jugate; no interjected leaflets present. All leaves covered with very shining dense silky yellowish hairs. Pedicel articulation very low. Corolla purple, pentagonal, 3 cm diam., including the 5–6 mm long acumens, densely villose externally. Berries narrowly conical.
Distribution: south Peru, dept Cuzco, prov. Urubamba, on archaeological terraces at 2,500 m.
  This species comes within the group which includes *S. urubambae* and *S. multiflorum*.
Derivation: with soft straight hairs on the petals
$2n = 24$ (according to Ochoa)

22. S. violaceimarmoratum Bitt. (Fedde, Repert. **11**, 389–90), 1912)

S. violaceimarmoratum var. *papillosum* Hawkes (Bull. Imp. Bur. Pl. Breed. & Genet., Cambridge, 113, 1944)

Stem violet-marbled; leaf (2–)3–4(–5)-jugate; laterals ovate-lanceolate, acuminate; terminal leaflet much broader than laterals; interjected leaflets (0–)1–3(–6)-paired, small; leaf pubescence of frequent, shining, diagonally pointing hairs. Inflorescence large, spreading; branches glabrous to pubescent. Calyx generally glabrous. Corolla purple, 1.5–2.5 cm diam., rotate-pentagonal with 5 mm long acumens. Berries ovate-conical to 3 cm long.
Distribution: north Bolivia, depts Cochabamba and La Paz in mountain rain forest ('ceja') from 3,000–3,600 m.
  A natural hybrid of *S. violaceimarmoratum* × *S. microdontum* has been described by Ochoa (Phytologia **46**, 224, 1980) and named *S. microdontum* Bitt. var. *montepuncoense* Ochoa. It was found in dept Cochabamba near Montepunco. (See Hawkes and Hjerting 1989, 183–4.)
Derivation: violet-marbled, referring to the pigment patterning on the stem
$2n = 24$; EBN = 2
Braun., CPC, Gr.Lü., Stur., VIR

23. S. woodsonii Corr. (Wrightia **2**, 137–9, 1961)

Leaflets 2–3-jugate, elliptic to broadly oval and rather blunt, provided with dense short hairs. Corolla rotate-pentagonal, 2.5–3.0 cm diam.; anthers with a medium lobe at the base, as well as the two lateral ones.
Distribution: Costa Rica, Panamá and Venezuela, at 3,250–4,000 m on high páramos (mountain meadows).
Derivation: named after one of the collectors of this species, R.E. Woodson

24. S. ayacuchense Ochoa (Agronomía, Lima, **26**, 312–13, 1959)

Lateral leaflets 3–5-jugate, with very long petiolules (10–20 mm) and pedicels articulated only one-third above the base; corolla rotate; berries long conical, 2.0–2.5 cm long.

Distribution: central Peru, dept Ayacucho, in cloud forests at 3,000 m.

The living collections noted below for Braunschweig and Sturgeon Bay have not been studied sufficiently for me to be certain of their taxonomic position.

Derivation: from Ayacucho in south-central Peru

Braun. (?), Stur. (?) (not in inventory)

25. *S. bombycinum* Ochoa (Amer. Potato J. **60**(11), 849–52, 1983)

(See also Hawkes and Hjerting: Potatoes of Bolivia, 176–77, 1989.)

Leaf 1–2(–3)-jugate, without interjected leaflets; lateral leaflets broadly ovate, acuminate; leaves covered with dense pale straw-coloured to yellowish brown velvety pubescence, as are the inflorescence branches and calyx. Corolla rotate, purple. Ovary conical.

Distribution: north Bolivia, dept La Paz, in humid tropical vegetation at 2,000 m.

I have not seen material of this species, but from its description it would seem to be related closely to the south Peruvian group of species, *S. villuspetalum*, *S. multiflorum* and *S. urubambae*.

Derivation: presumably from the similarity of the hairs to species in the family Bombacaceae, or *Bombax*, the Indian cotton tree

2n = 48

26. *S. burkartii* Ochoa (Biota, Lima **11**(87), 97–8, 1977)

Leaf 4–5-jugate, with many interjected leaflets; lateral leaflets narrow lanceolate, acuminate or subacuminate, with rather short dense pubescence. Inflorescence branches also densely pubescent; pedicel articulated in the upper third. Corolla dark purple, sub-pentagonal. Berries long-conical.

Distribution: north Peru, dept. Amazonas in shrubby woods, at 3,000 m in very humid places.

Derivation: named in honour of the late Professor Arturo Burkart, the distinguished Argentinian botanist

27. *S. cacetanum* Ochoa (Phytologia **46**(7), 495–6, 1980)

Leaf 4–5-jugate, deep green; leaflets narrow elliptic-lanceolate, sessile to subsessile; petiolule 3–4 mm long; with 2–6 interjected leaflets; pubescence short and sparse. Corolla rotate, white, to 1.5 cm diam. Berries conical with acute apex.

Distribution: Colombia, dept Caquetá, in woodland habitats at 2,700 m.

This species, from its description, may be closely allied to *S. colombianum* (material not seen by me).

Derivation: from the name of the Colombian department where it was found

28. *S. calacalinum* Ochoa (Darwinana **23**(1), 227–31, 1981; shows 2 photos)

Leaves glabrous 3–4(–5)-jugate with rarely 1–2 interjected leaflets, long petiolulate, to 2 cm. Corolla showy, rotate, to 4 cm diam., purple. Berry long-conical with obtuse apex, to 2.5 cm long × 2.0 cm broad.

Distribution: Ecuador, prov. Pichincha, mount La Sirena, north-east of Calacalí, at 3,000 m. Found amongst grasses, protected by *Opuntia cylindrica*, *Urtica* sp. along with *Verbena* and other non-tuber-bearing Solanums.

From the description and photographs this species could be closely related to *S.*

colombianum, but it is distinguished apparently by the total lack of pubescence and the long petiolules (material was not seen by me).
Derivation: from the place name Calacalí, where it was collected

29. *S. garcia-barrigae* Ochoa (Biota, Lima, **11**(90), 221–3, 1978)

Plants small, somewhat rosetted at base, covered with dense conspicuous hairs. Leaves 2–3-jugate, without interjected leaflets; terminal leaflet much larger than laerals. Peduncles very short, densely pubescent. Corolla purple, pentagonal. Fruit long-conical, apically acute.
Distribution: Colombia, dept Norte de Santander, Cerro Oroque, at 3,900 m (specimen not seen by me).
Note: a specimen in Hb. Bogotá labelled as *S. garcia-barrigae* is not the type of this species, but of *S. neovalenzuelae* (*López et al. 810011*).
Derivation: named in honour of the distinguished Colombian botanist, Professor Hernando García-Barriga

30. *S. irosinum* Ochoa (American Potato J. **58**(3), 131–3, 1981)

Leaves 4(–5)-jugate, with 2–7 pairs of interjected leaflets, all shortly and densely pubescent; lateral leaflets elliptic-lanceolate, 1–3(–5) mm petiolulate. Pedicel articulation near calyx. Corolla rotate, pale violet to dark lilac, 2.5–3.0 cm diam. Berries ovoid to conical-ovoid, to 2.2 cm long.
Distribution: Peru, dept Cajamarca, Mount Iros, at 3,200 m in a cold foggy region of grasses and bushes.
   No picture of this species was published by the author, and I have not been able to see herbarium or other specimens. It may belong to series *Tuberosa* - see p.151
Derivation: from the name of the mountain where it was collected
2n = 24

31. *S. jaenense* Ochoa (Agronomia, Lima, **27**, 371–2, 1960)

A delicate slender plant with 2–3-jugate, acuminate leaflets, white rotate corolla and acute conical fruits to 10 mm long.
Distribution: endemic to north Peru, dept Cajamarca, at 2,700 m; habitat unknown.
   Correll (1962, 546) considered this species to be a slender form of *S. chomatophilum*, but since he had not seen the type and I saw it once but had no opportunity of studying it further, it would be necessary for the author, Dr C. Ochoa, to comment further on this species.
Derivation: from the name of the province in which it was collected
2n = 24

32. *S. limbaniense* Ochoa (Bol. Soc. Peruana Bot. **7**(1,2), 15–19, 1974)

Tubers white or pink. Leaf dark green above, paler below, glabrescent, 1–2-jugate with no interjected leaflets; main leaflets ovate-cordate, terminal larger than laterals. Inflorescence glabrous. Calyx lobes short, with minute acumen. Corolla rotate, 2.5–3.0 cm diam., pale violet to lilac. Berry conical, 2.0 cm long.
Distribution: south Peru, dept Puno at 3,520 m in the high puna vegetation with *Stipa ichu* grass, *Cajophora* and *Oxalis* species.
   This species is considered by Ochoa to have played an important part in the

evolution of the cultivated potato and to be the ancestor of *S. phureja*, because of its lack of tuber dormancy. However, this would seem to the present writer to be very doubtful, especially since the calyx acumens are quite different from those of *S. phureja* as well as the lack of pubescence. (I have seen no material of *S. limbaniense*.)
Derivation: from the place name Phara-limbani, where it was collected
2n = 24
VIR

33. *S. nemorosum* Ochoa (Amer. Potato J. **60**(6), 389–92, 1983)

Leaf dark green above, paler below, rugose and sparsely pilose, 4–5-jugate with 10–15(–24) interjected leaflets. Inflorescence branches and calyx slightly pilose. Corolla rotate, white with very light lavender shading. Berries long conical, to 2.0 cm long.
Distribution: Peru, dept Cajamarca, prov. San Ignacio, at 2,800 m. In humid forests of shrubs and small trees.
    This is a very interesting species because of the fact that it is a hexaploid – possibly the first in Peru apart from *S. albicans* from the same department. In its general habit it resembles *S. colombianum* but is surely too far south to be related to it.
Derivation: from woods and forests
2n = 72

34. *S. neovargasii* Ochoa (Sol. tuber. silv. Peru, Lima, 53–7, 1962)

Leaflets 2–3-jugate; corolla purple, rotate; stamen filaments sparsely pubescent; berry ellipsoid or conical ellipsoid, to 2 cm long.
Distribution: central Peru, dept Junín, prov. Tarma, at 2,800 m amongst shrubby mountain forests ('ceja').
    From the shape and size of the leaf and other characters this species would seem very probably to be a synonym of *S. laxissimum*, which also occurs in dept Junín. I have seen no living or herbarium material, however.
Derivation: named after the well-known and distinguished Peruvian botanist, Professor C. Vargas, of Cuzco

35. *S. neovavilovii* Ochoa (Amer. Potato J. **60**(11), 919–23, 1983)

Leaves 3–4-jugate, with 0–3 interjected leaflets, densely pilose above. Pedicels articulated above the centre, very densely pilose. Corolla rotate, 2.5–2.8 cm diam., sky blue. Ovary ovate-conical.
Distribution: Bolivia, dept La Paz, at 3,000 m on large moss-covered rocks in cloud forest ('ceja').
    From its morphology and habitat this species is almost certainly a synonym of *S. violaceimarmoratum*, though the plant is much smaller than typical specimens of that species, no doubt due to its habitat. (See Hawkes and Hjerting 1989, 177–84.) (I have seen no specimens.)
Derivation: dedicated to the memory of the great Russian scientist, Academician N.I. Vavilov
2n = 24

36. *S. nubicola* Ochoa (Ann. Cient. Univ. Agr. **8**(3–4), 143–6, 1970)

Leaf 2–3-jugate with a few small interjected leaflets; corolla pale violet, rotate, 2.5–3.0 cm diam.; very short lilac to violet filaments. Berries long-conical, 1.5–2.0 cm diam.

Distribution: Peru, dept Huánuco, at 3,610 m, in small patches of woodland amongst *Buddleia*, *Monnina*, *Fuchsia*, *Stipa*, *Poa*, *Lobelia* etc., in cold, cloudy or densely foggy regions.

This species, of which I have seen no material, is of particular interest in that it is a tetraploid, whilst all other Peruvian species in this series are diploid, or hexaploid (*S. nemorosum*).

Derivation: cloud dweller

2n = 48

37. *S. orocense* Ochoa (Phytologia **46**(7), 496, 1980)

Leaf dark green, 3–4-jugate, with 1–3 pairs of interjected leaflets; with dense very short hairs, velvety on upper surface. Pedicels articulated in the upper third. Corolla rotate, white. Fruit conical, 1.2–1.5 cm long.

Distribution: Colombia, dept Norte de Santander, Cerro Oroque, 3,700–3,900 m. (No habitat given.) (No flowering material seen by me but material in Herb. Bogotá seems close to *S. colombianum*.)

Derivation: from Mount Oroque

38. *S. salasianum* Ochoa (Amer. Potato J. **66**(4), 235–8, 1989)

Stem sparsely short-pilose below, more densely above. Leaf 3–4-jugate; laterals elliptic-lanceolate, acuminate, with 3–7 mm long petiolules; interjected leaflets 2–3-jugate, minute, sessile; leaf more densely short-pilose above, only on veins below. Peduncle 3–4 cm long, densely pilose, as are the pedicels and calyx; hairs very short, pale yellow or whitish; pedicels articulated near base or higher. Calyx 5.5 mm long. Corolla very rotate, 3.0 cm diam., very pale purple, with short broad acumens. Stigma barely thicker than style apex. Berry long conical. (Material not seen by me.)

Distribution: Peru, dept Huánuco, prov. Pachitea, at 2,800–3,000 m, in moist mountain forests.

This species would seem to be rather similar to *S. santolallae* except that it is much more pubescent.

Derivation: named by the author in honour of his assistant, Ing. Agr. Alberto Salas

2n = 24

39. *S. sucubunense* Ochoa (Phytologia **46**(7), 496–7, 1980)

Leaf 2–3-jugate, with 2–4 interjected leaflets; lower laterals smaller than upper ones; lower leaves nearly simple; all leaves are sparsely pubescent, though more densely below. Inflorescence branches and calyx sparsely pubescent; pedicels articulated in the upper third. Corolla rotate, violet, 3 cm diam. Ovary long conical. Fruit not seen.

Distribution: Colombia, dept Cauca, Valle de las Papas, near Valencia, at 2,190 m, near river Sucubún. (Not seen by me.)

Derivation: from the name of the river Sucubún, where this species was found

40. S. trinitense Ochoa (An. Cient. Univ. Agr. 2(3), 245–7, 1964)

Leaf 5–7-jugate with numerous interjected leaflets – to about 12 pairs including some semi-basiscopics; main leaflets lanceolate, marginally crenulate, with few hairs on upper, rather more on lower leaf surfaces; petiolules to 20 mm or more. Pedicels articulated very high up, only 2–3 mm below calyx base. Corolla rotate, white with very short lobes and acumens. Fruit conico-ovoid, with acute to sub-acute apex, 2 cm long.

Distribution: Peru, dept Cajamarca, prov. Contumazá, Trinidad district, at 3,450 m.

This is a very striking species as seen in the photograph reproduced with the published description. Ochoa places it in series *Tuberosa* but the fruit surely indicates that it should be transferred to series *Conicibaccata*. I have seen no material.

Derivation: named from the district of Trinidad where it was found

SERIES XIII *PIURANA* HAWKES

(Ann. Mag. Nat. Hist., Ser. 12, **7**, 693, 1954)

Tuber-bearing herbs with shining ('varnished') glabrous or glabrescent leaves which become leathery and with revolute margin when dry. Corolla large, rotate, showy, blue-purple, white and purple or completely white. Berries ovate, with flattened apex.

Distribution: Colombia, Ecuador, north and central Peru, in a wide range of habitats.

Since the last edition of this Revision was published in 1963, the taxonomic boundaries of this series and the species within it have become clearer, and several species have been removed to series *Conicibaccata* or to series *Tuberosa*. However, there still seems to be some possible inter-grading with series *Tuberosa* in southern Peru, whilst further research may perhaps reveal the presence of synonymity between certain species.

KEY TO SPECIES

(1) Corolla completely white   (2)
    Corolla with at least some pigment   (3)
(2) Terminal leaflet very large, orbicular to broadly ovate (central Peru)
                            6. S. hypacrarthrum
    Terminal leaflet somewhat larger than laterals, lanceolate (central Peru)   **3. S. cantense**
(3) Corolla white with pigment on centre of each petal externally or acumen only   (4)
    Corolla completely purple, violet, etc.   (6)
(4) Corolla with central petal streak of deep lilac pigment on external surface (south Ecuador)   **2. S. albornozii**
    Corolla with external pigment restricted to acumen or one-third below   (5)
(5) Corolla pigment restricted to acumen externally; leaf 3–4-jugate (north Peru)   **12. S. yamobambense**

Corolla pigment at acumen and slightly below; leaf 1–2(–3)-jugate
(north Peru) **8. S. paucissectum**
(6) Terminal leaflet very large compared with laterals (south Ecuador)
4. S. chilliasense
Terminal leaflet only slightly larger than laterals (7)
(7) Leaves 4–6(–10)-jugate with 1–10 pairs of interjected leaflets (8)
Leaves less well-dissected (9)
(8) Leaves 4-jugate, lower surface deep blue-purple; calyx trilabiate
(Ecuador) **5. S. cyanophyllum**
Leaves 4–6(–10)-jugate; lower surface green; calyx not trilabiate
(Colombia, Ecuador) **11. S. tuquerrense**
(9) Leaves 1–2-jugate with no interjected leaflets (10)
Leaves with more pairs of lateral leaflets (11)
(10) Lateral leaflets with long tongue-like acumen (central Peru)
1. S. acroglossum
Lateral leaflets not very acuminate (south Ecuador) **10. S. solisii**
(11) Leaflets sessile, decurrent (north Peru) **7. S. jalcae**
Leaflets petiolulate (north Peru) **9. S. piurae**

1. S. acroglossum Juz. (Bull. Acad. Sci. U.R.S.S. **3**, 313–14, 1937)

Leaf simple to 1-jugate. Lateral leaflets 1(–2)-jugate, sessile, decurrent,
with long tongue-like acumens, obtuse at apex; interjected leaflets absent;
upper leaf surface shining, bright green, paler below; whole leaf more or
less glabrous. Peduncles, pedicels and calyx glabrous. Corolla rotate, 3 cm
diam., dark blue-violet. Fruit unknown.
Distribution: central Peru, depts Junín and Huánuco, at 2,700–3,000 m,
growing among bushes.
Derivation: 'terminal tongue', referring to the long tongue-like acumens
2n = 24 (fide Ochoa)
Gr.Lü. (*Ochoa 11297*), Stur. (*Ochoa 11297*), VIR

2. S. albornozii Corr. (Wrightia **2**, 178–9, 1961)

S. chomatophilum f. *angustifoliolum* Corr. (Wrightia **2**, 180, 1961)

Lateral leaflets petiolulate; upper leaf surface dark green and glabrous
above, rather shining, paler below; margins slightly rolled under. Inflorescence branches and calyx glabrous. Corolla white with a lilac streak on the
back of each petal, rotate, 2.5–3.0 cm diam. Fruit ovoid.
Distribution: south Ecuador, provs Azuay and Loja, at about 3,100 m,
amongst bushes and clearings.
The plant named by Correll *S. chomatophilum* f. *angustifoliolum* fits
better with *S. albornozii* in my opinion, though there are fewer interjected
leaflets.
Derivation: named in honour of the Ecuadorean botanist, Dr G. Albornoz
2n = 24
Stur.

3. *S. cantense* Ochoa (Agronomía, Lima, **26**, 217–18, 1959)

Leaf 2–3-jugate, with no, or very few, interjected leaflets; terminal larger than laterals; laterals sessile to very shortly petiolulate, slightly decurrent, glabrous, shining and darker above, paler below; leaf margins slightly curled under. Inflorescence branches and calyx more or less glabrous. Corolla white, rotate, 2.5–3.0 cm diam. Berry ovate.
Distribution: central Peru, dept Lima, near Canta, at 2,800 m, in shrubby and herbaceous vegetation.
Derivation: from Canta, where it was first discovered
2n = 24 (according to Ochoa)

4. *S. chilliasense* Ochoa (Lorentzia, No. 4, 9–11, 1981)

Leaves deep green, glabrous or glabrescent, shining (varnished) above, pale green glabrescent, opaque below; leaf 2(–3)-jugate, the terminal very large and laterals diminishing rapidly towards leaf base; up to 2 pairs of minute interjected leaflets. Inflorescence branches and calyx glabrous. Corolla rotate, 1.8–2.5 cm diam., lilac with white acumens. Berries ovoid, 1.5–2.0 cm long × 1.2–1.6 cm diam.
Distribution: south Ecuador, prov. El Oro, Cordillera de Chilla, at 3,450 m, amongst shrubs and trees in a humid, foggy, cold habitat.
Derivation: from Chilla
2n = 24 (according to Ochoa)

5. *S. cyanophyllum* Correll (Wrightia **2**, 180–1, 1961)

Leaves 4-jugate, with up to 5 or 6 pairs of sessile interjected leaflets; lateral leaflets petiolulate, lanceolate, long-acuminate to attenuate; upper leaf surface shining, light green, with scattered short hairs; lower surface dark blue, finely pubescent. Inflorescence branches finely puberulent. Calyx deeply trilabiate to below the middle and with two pairs of lobes partially united. Corolla rotate, white mottled with lavender. Fruit unknown.
Distribution: Ecuador, prov. Bolívar, in cleared forest, at about 2,300 m.
  The absence of berries makes it uncertain as to which series this species should belong. In its leaf form it seems similar to *S. colombianum* of series *Conicibaccata*, but Correll places it in series *Piurana* because of the shining leaves. I agree with Correll and defer to his judgement here.
Derivation: blue-leaved, referring to the lower leaf surface

6. *S. hypacrarthrum* Bitt. (Fedde, Repert. **11**, 367–8, 1912)

S. tuberosum var. *puberulum* Hook. f. (Fl. Antarct **2**, 330, 1847)

Leaf 0–2(–3)-jugate, the terminal very large and suborbicular compared with the minute laterals; interjected leaflets absent or with one minute pair; upper leaf surface shining, darker than the lower, glabrous, or with a few delicate hairs which are hardly visible; terminal leaflet apically cuspi-

date. Inflorescence branches and calyx glabrous; pedicels articulated just below calyx. Corolla white, rotate, about 3 cm diam. Berry subglobose, 2 cm diam.
Distribution: central Peru, dept Lima, prov. Canta, at 1,800–2,800 (–3,400) m in western Andean valleys, amongst grasses and bushes.
Derivation: articulation under the apex (of the pedicel)
2n = 24
Stur., VIR

7. *S. jalcae* Ochoa (Agronomía, Lima, **19**, 167–9, 1954)

Leaf 2–3-jugate, thick and leathery, with subsessile decurrent leaflets and winged rachis; terminal larger than laterals; interjected leaflets absent; upper leaf surface glabrous, dark green, glabrous and violet below. Inflorescence branches and calyx glabrous; pedicels articulated in upper third. Calyx dark purple. Corolla rotate, 3.0–3.5 cm diam., medium purple, with short lobes and very small acumens. Berries subglobose.
Distribution: north Peru, dept La Libertad, at 3,100–3,500 m, in páramos and high alpine grasslands. Frost-resistant according to Ochoa.
Note: Correll's var. *pubescens* (Wrightia **2**, 181, 1961) seems to belong to *S. jalcae*, but differs in that it develops up to 4 pairs of minute interjected leaflets, and some pubescence on the leaf.
Distribution: Peru, depts Ancash and Cajamarca, at similar altitudes to the type.
Derivation: from the 'jalcas', a Peruvian word meaning wet windswept moorlands at very high altitudes
VIR

8. *S. paucissectum* Ochoa (Agronomía, Lima, **27**, 365–6, 1960)

Terminal leaflet much larger than the 1–2(–3)-jugate laterals; interjected leaflets absent; leaf completely glabrous, except for minute hairs on the veins, shining above. Inflorescence branches and calyx glabrous; pedicel articulated in the upper third. Corolla white, with lilac streaks at acumen and slightly below, 2.5–3.0 cm diam., rotate. Berries ovoid, to 2 cm long.
Distribution: north Peru, dept Piura, near Huancabamba, at 2,900–3,200 m, in dwarf woodland and amongst grasses.
Derivation: poorly dissected (leaf)
2n = 24; EBN = 2
Braun., Stur., VIR

9. *S. piurae* Bitt. (Beibl. Bot. Jahrb, No. 119, **54**, 5–6, 1916)

S. chomatophilum Corr., f. *pilosum* Corr. (Wrightia **2**, 180, 1961)

Leaves 2–3(–4)-jugate, petiolulate, with 1–4 pairs of interjected leaflets; leaves subglabrous, leathery, shining above, but with a few sparse rough hairs above and below, as well as on the leaflet margins; margins slightly rolled under when dry. Inflorescence branches and calyx glabrous to minutely hairy; pedicels articulated in upper third. Corolla rotate, 2–4 cm diam., purple. Berries ovate to cordate.

Distribution: north Peru, dept Piura, at 2,000–2,900 m, amongst grass and bushes, in humid moorland.

Derivation: from Piura department, Peru

2n = 24

Braun. (not in inventory), Gr.Lü., Stur., VIR

10. S. solisii Hawkes (Bull. Imp. Bur. Pl. Breed. & Genet., Cambridge, 125–6, 1944)

Leaves rosetted towards stem base, 1–2-jugate, with no interjected leaflets; upper surface shining and dark green, paler below, subglabrous on both sides, leathery, and with edges slightly curled under. Inflorescence branches and calyx glabrous. Pedicels articulated in upper third. Corolla rotate, with very short lobes, to 3.5 cm diam., purple. Berries round to oval, about 1 cm long.

Distribution: south Ecuador, provs Azuay and Cañar, at 3,400–3,600 m, in damp grassy and bushy places.

Derivation: named in honour of Dr M. Acosta Solís, Professor of Botany at Quito University, Ecuador

VIR

11. S. tuquerrense Hawkes (Ann. Mag. Nat. Hist., Ser. 12, **7**, 693–7, 1954)

Leaf 4–6(–10)-jugate with 1–10-jugate interjected leaflets; leaf shining, olive green above, paler below, leathery and with the margins slightly curled under, glabrous or with some long, spreading hairs. Pedicels articulated in upper half, slightly pubescent. Corolla showy, blue-purple, very rotate, 2–3.5 cm diam. Berries oval, up to 2.8 cm long × 2.3 cm broad.

Distribution: Colombia, dept Nariño; Ecuador, provs Carchi and Pichincha, at 2,600–3,300 m, amongst shrubs and rough grassland.

Unique amongst tetraploids in being self-incompatible.

Derivation: from Túquerres, in Nariño dept, where it was first collected

2n = 48; EBN = 2

Gr.Lü., Stur., VIR

12. S. yamobambense Ochoa (Agronomía, Lima, **27**, 367–8, 1960) (Correll gives it as a synonym of S. piurae)

Leaves 3–4-jugate, slightly decurrent, with up to 3–4 pairs of interjected leaflets; laterals narrowly lanceolate, acuminate; leaf glabrous or sparsely pilose, darker green above than below. Inflorescence branches and calyx almost glabrous; pedicel articulation in upper third. Corolla rotate, with short lobes and small acumens, 2.5–3.0 cm diam., white but with lilac

pigment on external surface of acumens. Berries ovoid, 1.2 cm long (or more?).
Distribution: north Peru, dept La Libertad, Yamobamba, at 3,160 m, in densely bushy areas, with *Rubus*, *Calceolaria* and *Briza* species.
Derivation: name taken from Yamobamba, where it was first discovered

13. *S. ariduphilum* Ochoa (Bol. Soc. Argent. Bot. **14**(4), 380–4, 1972)

Terminal leaflet much larger than the 1–3-jugate laterals; leaf leathery, 'varnished'. Corolla rotate, dark violet, 3–4 cm diam. Berries 1.5–2.0 cm long, slightly long-conical, ovoid or globular.
Distribution: Peru, dept Huánuco, at 3,340 m, on stony slopes in a semi-arid valley amongst columnar cacti, bromeliads, *Agave* and *Cortaderia* species, etc. (Material not seen by me.)
Derivation: drought-loving

14. *S. blanco-galdosii* Ochoa (An. Cient. Univ. Agr., Lima, **11**(3–4), 157–60, 1973)

Leaf 4–5-jugate, with sub-varnished, rather leathery leaves, glabrous above; first pair decurrent, narrow lanceolate, sometimes falcate; interjected leaflets frequent, varying in size. Corolla rotate, small, dark purple. Berries oval to globose, 1.5–2.0 cm long.
Distribution: Peru, dept Cajamarca, at 2,700 m, in a subxerophytic region with poor vegetation of *Opuntia*, *Fourcroya*, etc.
    Ochoa placed this species in series *Cuneoalata*, but although I have seen no type material, the description indicates that it would fit better into series *Piurana* because of the leaf quality and the large numbers of petiolulate interjected leaflets. I have, however, examined living material of *Ochoa S-68* (not the type) at Sturgeon Bay which confirms my opinion that this species should be placed in series *Piurana*.
Derivation: named in honour of a former student, Ing. Oscar Blanco Galdos, now teaching at the University of Cuzco
2n = 24
Braun. (not in inventory), Stur., VIR

15. *S. pascoense* Ochoa (Agronomía, Lima, **26**, 112–13, 1959)

Leaves 3–4-jugate, with 2–6 small interjected leaflets; laterals petiolulate; all leaflets glabrous, deep green and shining above, paler below with scattered short hairs. Pedicels articulated in upper third. Corolla rotate, blue, 3.0–4.5(–5) cm diam., with short lobes. Berries not described.
Distribution: Peru, dept Pasco, at 3,500–3,600 m. No habitat noted.
    Although the author states that *S. pascoense* belongs to series *Tuberosa*, the leaf, which is dark green and shining above but paler below, strongly indicates series *Piurana*. No type material seen.
Derivation: from the department and province of Pasco, where this species was first collected
2n = 24; EBN = 2
Stur.

SERIES XIV *INGIFOLIA* OCHOA

(Sol. Tuberif. Silv. Peru, Lima, 68, 1962, as 'Ingaefolia'; *ex* Correll, in Texas. Res. Found. Contrib. **4**, 129, 1962)

Tuber-bearing herbs with erect or decumbent habit, thick, winged stems, leaves with broad-winged rachis, the wing continuing along the petiole right to the leaf base. Corolla rotate; ovary ovoid to orbicular.
Distribution: Andes of northern Peru.
Note: Correll includes in this series *S. suffrutescens*, *S. tuquerrense*, *S. jalcae* and *S. jalcae* var. *pubescens*, none of which possess the characteristic rachis and petiole wing which continues to the base of the leaf. These species are therefore excluded in the present treatment, together with *S. lopez-camarenae* Ochoa, which also lacks the rachis and petiole winging. The correct orthography of the earlier names for series Ingaefolia and *S. ingaeifolium* are Ingifolia and *S. ingifolium* respectively.

It is curious that *S. olmosense* (series *Olmosiana*) possesses similar rachis and petiole winging but has a clearly stellate corolla.

KEY TO SPECIES

Leaflets 1–3-paired; rachis and petiole wing broad, smoothly parallel-sided or only slightly narrowing towards the base of the next leaflet; inter-jected leaflets absent   **1. *S. ingifolium***
Leaflets 4–5-paired; rachis and petiole wing rather narrow, interrupted by lobes representing interjected leaflets   **2. *S. raquialatum***

1. *S. ingifolium* Ochoa (Agronomía, Lima, **26**, 319–22, 1959)

A very curious and distinct species with leaves similar to those of the leguminous genus *Inga*. Stem with broad wings; leaves to 43 cm long; lateral leaflets acuminate, decurrent; rachis with broad wings which swell out from the point of insertion of each leaflet pair and sometimes become slightly narrowed towards the next pair below, continuing down the petiole to the leaf base; no interjected leaflets. Inflorescence highly branched, glabrous, as is the calyx. Corolla lilac, rotate, 3.0–3.5 cm diam.
Distribution: endemic to the humid mountain rain forests of north Peru, dept Piura, at altitudes of 2,800–3,000 m.
Derivation: with a leaf similar to that of the leguminous genus *Inga* Braun. (now lost)

2. *S. raquialatum* Ochoa (Agronomía, Lima, **19**, 172–4, 1954)

Differs from *S. ingifolium* in possessing narrow stem wings, shortly petiolu-late lateral leaflets (4–5 pairs instead of 1–3(–4)), interjected leaflets or lobes projecting from the irregularly winged rachis and white rotate corolla.

Distribution: north Peru, dept Piura, rain and mist forests at 1,200–2,300 m.
Derivation: with a winged rachis
2n = 24 (according to Ochoa)

SERIES XV   *MAGLIA* BITT.

(Fedde, Repert. **11**, 360, 1912)

Series *Tuberosa pro parte* Buk. (in Bukasov & Kameraz, Bases Potato Breed., 18, 1959)

Distinguished from all other series by the loose, barrel-shaped anther column and the anthers and filaments not well demarcated from each other, either in colour or form.
Distribution: central Chile and western Argentina.
Bitter (1912) included in this series *S. bijugum* (= *S. microdontum*), *S. microdontum*, *S. megistacrolobum* and *S. hypacrarthrum*; he also created a 'collective species' of *S. maglia* in which he included *S. maglia* itself, *S. weberbaueri*, *S. medians* and *S. hypacrarthrum*. It should be pointed out that collective species are no longer recognized and that the species mentioned above have now been placed in series *Tuberosa*, *Megistacroloba* and *Piurana*. Thus the series *Maglia* as at present defined is monotypic, including only *S. maglia*. Bukasov's definition will be discussed under series *Tuberosa*.

1. *S. maglia* Schlechtd. (Hort. Halensis **1**, 6, 1841)

S. maglia Molina (Walp, Repert. **3**, 1845) *nom. nud.*
S. commersonii Dun. var. *glabriusculum* Hook f. (Fl. Antarct. **2**, 330, 1846) *pro parte*
S. commersonii Dun. var. *glabriusculum* (Walp, Repert. **6**, 583, 1847) *pro parte*
S. collinum Dun. (in DC. Prodr. **13**, I, 36, 1852)
S. maglia var. *collinum* (Dun.) Bitt. (Fedde, Repert. **11**, 364, 1912)
S. maglia var. *witasekianum* Bitt. (Fedde, Repert. **11**, 364–5, 1912)

A large bushy plant with (1–)2–3-paired ovate leaflets, and broader terminal leaflet. Corolla white, pentagonal to rotate. Stamens very characteristic, in a loose, barrel-shaped column; anthers and filaments not well demarcated either in colour or form.
Distribution: central to north Chile, provs Aconcagua, Coquimbo, Ovalle and Valparaiso, generally near the sea coast; Argentina, prov. Mendoza, in dry Andean valleys, at 1,500 m.
Note: G.I. Molina (Saggio Storia Nat. Chili, Bologna, 131, 1782) is sometimes credited with being the first describer of *S. maglia*. This is not correct. He described *S. tuberosum* in latin, but quotes 'Maglia' as an

Indian name for a wild potato, giving no description or reference to specimens collected.
Derivation: from the Indian name (see above) for the wild potato ('Malla' in Spanish transliteration)
2n = (24); 36
Note: all collections but two so far made have proved to be sterile triploids. Of the two diploids one was from Argentina (Quebrada Alvarado), the other from near Valparaiso.
Braun. (from Valparaiso, 2n = 24), Gr.Lü., UAC

SERIES XVI *TUBEROSA* (RYDB.) HAWKES

(Bull. Imp. Bur. Pl. Breed. & Genet., Cambridge, 37, 1944) – as series

Tuberosa [rankless] Rydb. (Bull. Torr. Bot. Club **51**, 146, 147, 1924)
Andigena Buk. (in Bukasov & Kameraz, Bases of Potato Breed., 24, 1959)
Transaequatorialia Buk. (in Bukasov & Kameraz, Bases of Potato Breed., 21, 1959) Name invalid after 1958 without type.
Vaviloviana Buk. (in Bukasov & Kameraz, Bases of Potato Breed., 18, 1959)
Minutifoliola Corr. (Potato and Wild Relat., 216, 1962)
Andreana Hawkes (Bull. Imp. Bur. Pl. Breed. & Genet., Cambridge, 50, 1944) *nom. nud.*

Series *Tuberosa* includes all the cultivated potato species, together with a very wide range of wild and weedy species. With the exception of the Mexican species *S. verrucosum*, *S. leptosepalum* (and USA) and *S. macropilosum*, series *Tuberosa* is confined to the Andes of South America, the adjacent coastal belt in temperate and tropical latitudes, and the precordillera ranges in western Argentina.

It spreads southwards from Venezuela through Colombia, Ecuador, Peru, Bolivia, north-west and west Argentina to Chile as far as about 45° south. The greatest concentration of species is to be found in Peru, with quite a large number in Bolivia and north-west Argentina. Apart from escaped forms of *S. tuberosum*, no wild *Tuberosa* species have yet been found in Chile.

Although most *Tuberosa* species are diploids, a few tetraploids occur; a pentaploid and a hexaploid have been reported, as well as a few autotriploids.

Because of the very large number of species described in this series I have divided them into three geographical groups:

(i)   Mexico, Venezuela, Colombia and Ecuador;
(ii)   Peru;
(iii) Bolivia, Argentina and Chile.

This may seem at first sight very artificial, but in fact the groups are isolated to a large extent by geographical barriers. There is an obvious one between

Mexico and South America, but *S. verrucosum* seems to possess a number of features that link it to the Colombian *S. andreanum*. The second barrier is an area of low mountains between southern Ecuador and northern Peru. No wild *Tuberosa* species seems to occur on both sides of this gap. The third barrier is the highland area of Lake Titicaca. To my knowledge, only two wild species seem to have bridged it, namely, *S. leptophyes*, which only just spreads northward over the frontier into Peru, and *S. sparsipilum*, which as a weed species was probably carried by man unknowingly from north Bolivia into the Cuzco valley system of south Peru, or vice versa.

I have already mentioned that the only wild *Tuberosa* species to be found in Chile and parts of southern Argentina are escaped forms of *S. tuberosum*. To avoid confusion they will be mentioned under both the wild and the cultivated species sections, with appropriate cross-references.

Correll (1962, 44–47, 396–400) was frequently forced to bring distribution data into his keys. I hope that the above suggestions of three geographical groupings will help the reader to understand the species groupings more easily, though in my keys I shall attempt to deal with all the species on the basis of morphological characters only. The keys will not include species of which I have not been fortunate enough to examine actual materials, either dried or living. Neither will they include natural hybrids if previously given scientific names, since the segregation of parental characters makes keying them out almost impossible. The one exception to this rule is the very widespread and relatively uniform *S. sucrense*.

XVI   *Tuberosa* (wild species)

Group (i)   Mexico, Venezuela, Colombia and Ecuador

Only 11 species are so far recognized in this group, of which *S. verrucosum* in Mexico is by far the most common. The other species, apart from the moderately frequent *S. andreanum*, are apparently rare, having been so far encountered as single specimens. Probably further collecting may fill in the gaps and provide evidence for joining several of them together.

KEY TO SPECIES

(1) Berries warty or verrucose, with well-marked, raised white spots
    (Mexico)   **8. *S. verrucosum***
    Berries smooth; if white spots occur they are not raised above the
    surface   (2)
(2) Interjected leaflets completely absent   (3)
    Interjected leaflets present, even if few   (4)
(3) Leaves with frequent coarse hairs on upper surface, 3–5-jugate
    (Ecuador)   **6. *S. regularifolium***
    Leaves with infrequent short hairs on upper surface, 3-jugate
    (Venezuela)   **5. *S. paramoense***

(4) Plant rosetted, with long, coarse, spreading hairs on leaves, stems etc.
   (Colombia)   **3. S. lobbianum**
   Plant without long, coarse, spreading hairs, not rosetted   (5)
(5) Leaves with dense shining pubescence; interjected leaflets very close
   to each other, very frequent (Ecuador)   **4. S. minutifoliolum**
   Plant without the above characters   (6)
(6) Calyx trilabiate, stem rather shrubby (Ecuador)   **7. S. suffrutescens**
   Calyx normal, stem not shrubby   (7)
(7) Leaflets petiolulate, not decurrent (Ecuador)   **2. S. correllii**
   Leaflets sessile, decurrent (Colombia and Ecuador) **1. S. andreanum**

1. *S. andreanum* Baker (J. Linn. Soc. **20**, 498–9, 1884)

S. pichinchense Bitt. et Sodiro (Fedde, Repert. **10**, 533–4, 1912)
S. baezense Ochoa (Phytologia **54**(5), 391–2, 1983)

Leaf (1–)2–3-jugate, with 0–1 pairs of interjected leaflets; all leaflets sessile, decurrent, with medium dense, short hairs on upper surface, much more dense below, ovate to ovate-lanceolate, abruptly acuminate. Corolla very rotate, large, to 3.0 cm diam., with short lobes and small acumens. Berry globose to broadly ovoid, 2 cm long.
Distribution: Colombia, depts Cauca and Nariño; com. Putumayo; Ecuador, provs Imbabura and Pichincha; in high humid mountain valleys amongst trees and bushes at 2,100–2,900 m.
Note: Ochoa (Phytologia **49**, 485, 1981) separates *S. pichinchense* into series *Conicibaccata*, but the globular fruit on the type specimen photograph shows that the species must be placed in series *Tuberosa*. Ochoa's *S. baezense*, originally placed in series *Conicibaccata*, fits best with *S. andreanum*. No fruit is visible on the type specimen.
Derivation: named in honour of the French botanist E.F. André, who made a special point of looking for tuber-bearing *Solanum* species during his travels in the Andes (see Baker 1884).
2n = 24
Braun., Gr.Lü., Stur.

2. *S. correllii* Ochoa (Amer. Potato J. **58**(5), 223–5, 1981)

Leaf 3–4-jugate; leaflets sessile to shortly petiolulate, ovate-lanceolate to lanceolate, with very sparse, long to medium, weak hairs, subglabrous; interjected leaflets 1–3-paired, round, sessile. Inflorescence branches and calyx glabrous. Calyx acumens long linear 3–4 mm. Corolla rotate, 3.0–3.5 cm diam., lilac. Berries ovoid to spherical.
Distribution: Ecuador, prov. Chimborazo, borders of humid forests and scrub, at 2,700 m.
Derivation: dedicated to the distinguished botanist Donovan Correll, author of the 1962 monograph on tuber-bearing *Solanum* species
2n = 24 (according to Ochoa)

3. S. *lobbianum* Bitt. (Fedde, Repert. **12**, 446–7, 1913)

Stem very short; leaf long and narrow, 3–5-jugate, with very few inter-jected leaflets; stem and peduncle with long spreading hairs similar to those of *S. multidissectum* (see Correll, 1962, 423).
Distribution: Colombia (?); exact locality not recorded.

This enigmatic species does not seem to relate to any of the other species in Venezuela, Colombia or Ecuador, being distinguished chiefly by its rosette habit and the very long, coarse spreading hairs on stem, leaf rachis, petiole and inflorescence branches. Although the label states 'Colombia' for its locality, Lobb also collected in Peru, and it is possible for him to have confused his labels and to have collected the type specimen in the area of *S. multidissectum* in southern Peru (manuscript letters at Kew from James Veitch to Sir William Hooker). Another collection by M.T. Dawe on the volcano of Ruíz in Colombia bears some resemblance to Lobb's specimen, but is more probably a pubescent form of *S. colombianum*.
Derivation: named after the collector of the type specimen, William Lobb, who travelled in Argentine, Chile, Brazil, Colombia, Ecuador and Peru, collecting orchids and other ornamental plants for the horticultural firm of James Veitch & Sons.

4. S. *minutifoliolum* Corr. (Wrightia **2**, 191–2, 1961)

Leaf with broad-ovate, long-acuminate terminal leaflet, the laterals 2–3-jugate, smaller than the terminal and diminishing rapidly in size towards leaf base, the lowest pair minute in comparison with the upper two; interjected leaflets about 12-paired, irregularly arranged, very close together and quite small; upper leaf surface with dense, long, shining, yellowish forward-pointing hairs; lower surface with dense, velvety pubesc-ence. Inflorescence branches and calyx with very dense long hairs (and some long-stalked glands?). Corolla purple, substellate. Berries unknown.
Distributions: Ecuador, prov. Tungurahua, in open land or woodland at 1,200–1,500 m.
Derivation: with very small leaflets

5. S. *paramoense* Bitt. (*ex* Pittier, Man. Pl. Usual. Venez., 329, 1926)

Leaf 3-jugate, with no interjected leaflets; lateral leaflets subsessile, ovate, sub-acuminate; third leaflet pair much smaller than others; all leaf surfaces with sparse short hairs. Peduncle long, to 15 cm below fork; pedicels articulated above centre. Calyx with long linear-lanceolate acumens, sub-glabrous, as are inflorescence branches. Corolla to 4.5 cm diam., white (according to Pittier), bright violet (according to label), rotate. No berries seen.
Distribtion: Venezuela, Mérida State, Páramo de la Sal, at 3,300 m.

Bitter determined the specimen from Venezuela but published no de-scription. Without berries it is difficult to be certain as to whether it fits into series *Conicibaccata* or *Tuberosa*. Ochoa (Biota, Lima, **91**, 331, 1979)

states that it belongs to series *Tuberosa*. *S. paramoense* shows some similarities to *S. andreanum* but may not be closely related to it.
Derivation: from the páramo (high humid moorland)
2n = 48 (according to Ochoa)

6. *S. regularifolium* Corr. (Wrightia 2, 194–5, 1961)

Leaves 3–5-jugate with fairly frequent coarse hairs above, short and scattered below: lateral leaflets sessile, very slightly decurrent; interjected leaflets absent. Corolla substellate to pentagonal, pinkish lavender. Probably related to *S. paramoense* and possibly also to *S. correllii*.
Distribution: Ecuador, prov. Chimborazo, on bushy mountain slopes at about 2,150 m.
Derivation: the leaves show regularity in the numbers and positioning of the lateral leaflets

7. *S. suffrutescens* Corr. (Wrightia 2, 183–4, 1961)

Stem stiff, rather woody; lateral leaflets subsessile, slightly decurrent, 4-paired with 0–2 pairs of interjecteds. Calyx trilabiate. Corolla light purple, rotate. Berries globular. Possibly related to *S. andreanum*.
Distribution: Ecuador, prov. Bolívar, roadside, at 2,800 m.
Note: Correll (1962) incorrectly placed this species in series *Ingifolia* Ochoa.
Derivation: becoming somewhat shrubby

8. *S. verrucosum* Schlechtd. (Hort. Halensis **1**, 3, 1841)

S. squamulosum Mart. et Gal. (Bull. Acad. Brux. **12**, 1, 140, 1845)

Distinguished by the upright habit, petiolulate leaflets, terminal larger than laterals, well-defined, rounded corolla lobes whose margins roll inwards, and white verrucose berry. It is very probably an ancestral form of all *Demissa* species, contributing the one genome that they seem to possess in common.
Distribution: Mexico, states of Coahuila, Colima, Distrito Federal, Hidalgo, Jalisco, México, Michoacán, Nuevo León, Oaxaca, Puebla, Tlaxcala and Veracruz. A common species of pine, fir and oak forests, at 2,400–3,200 m.
Derivation: warty or verrucose, referring to the berry
2n = 24; EBN = 2
Braun., CPC, Gr.Lü., Stur., VIR

9. *S. burtonii* Ochoa (Amer. Potato J. **59**, 263–6, 1982)

Leaves short and broad, 3–4-jugate, dark green and shortly pilose above, paler below; lateral leaflets ovate, slightly acuminate; interjected leaflets orbicular, 2–4-paired; terminal broadly ovate, acuminate; leaflets sessile to shortly petiolulate,

rather cordate at base. Corolla rotate, 1.8–2.0 cm diam.; light purple-lilac outside, with white central petal streaks from centre to tip of acumens. Fruit unknown.
Distribution: Ecuador, prov. Tungurahua, at 3,400 m in cloud forest with *Juglans Cedrela*, *Cecropia*, *Chusquea*, etc.
Note: although no fruits are known Ochoa considers this species to belong to series *Tuberosa*. (Specimens not seen by me.)
Derivation: named in honour of the late Dr W.G. Burton, who researched on potato biochemistry and physiology

10. *S. leptosepalum* Corr. (US Dept. Agric. Monogr., No. 11, 158, 1952)

Apart from the slightly longer calyx acumens and apparently non-verrucose berry, this species would seem to be identical with *S. verrucosum* of which it may possibly represent a geographical subspecies. (No authenticated material seen by me.)
Distribution: north-east Mexico and possibly Texas, USA, in oak-pine forests at 2,000 m.
Derivation: with slender sepals

11. *S. macropilosum* Corr. (Wrightia 2, 189–90, 1961)

This might be an extremely hairy form of *S. verrucosum*, but it differs in the less dissected leaf (1–2-jugate) with large terminals and no interjected leaflets. The corolla is said by Correll to be lavender, broadly rotate-pentagonal, and without the characteristic lobes typical of *S. verrucosum*. The dense, long pubescence on stems and inflorescence branches seems to be very far removed from that of *S. verrucosum* also. For the time being it seems best to follow Correll in retaining *S. macropilosum* as a distinct species.
Distribution: Mexico, Nuevo León State, at 3,300 m, on limestone boulders in open pine woods.
Derivation: with great hairiness
    Living material of this taxon is urgently needed.

XVI   *Tuberosa* (wild species)

Group (ii)   Peru

Over 50 species in series *Tuberosa* are recognized for Peru. This is a very large number and indicates an extraordinary range of variation, even though further study may show that some of the Peruvian species may be synonyms.

    One of the reasons for such an extreme speciation in Peru may be accounted for by the large number of closed valley systems in that country compared to the countries to the north and south. Thus, in Peru, many potato populations probably became isolated after the last glaciation that came to an end some 10,000 years ago. They were thus unable to spread up over the high mountain ridges because of their lack of adaptation to cold conditions. Similarly, they were unable to skirt round the bases or lower shoulders of their valleys because they were not adapted to the dry conditions in the west and the very high rainfall in the east.

    On the other hand, species such as *S. canasense* and *S. bukasovii* that are adapted to high cold climates have been able to extend much further than those restricted to isolated medium altitude valleys.

KEY TO SPECIES

(1) Corolla white, creamy white or yellowish (2)
    Corolla purple, lavender, violet, sky blue, etc. (8)
(2) Corolla creamy white to yellow (dept Lima)   **9. S. chrysoflorum**
    Corolla pure white (3)
(3) Leaf completely simple, very large, from 15–30 cm long (dept Cajamarca)   **13. S. guzmanguense**
    Leaf pinnate, always with some lateral leaflets (4)
(4) Leaflets lanceolate to narrow lanceolate (5)
    Leaflets ovate to nearly rotund (6)
(5) Lateral leaflets 6–9-jugate, with up to 16 pairs of interjected leaflets (dept Huancavelica)   **12. S. gracilifrons**
    Lateral leaflets 4–5-jugate, with 0–7 pairs of interjected leaflets (depts Ancash, La Libertad and Lima)   **16. S. immite**
(6) Whole plant glabrous to subglabrous (dept La Libertad)   **7. S. chancayense**
    Plant with easily seen pubescence (7)
(7) Plant with dense, white, thick pubescence; terminal leaflet broad-ovate to sub-rotund (dept Cajamarca)   **5. S. cajamarquense**
    Plant without dense, white, thick pubescence; upper leaf surface shining, with hairs on veins only; margins dentate-undulate (north Peru)   **20. S. mochiquense**
(8) Whole plant covered rather densely with stalked glands, and sometimes very sparse, thin, white hairs (dept Lima) **33. S. wittmackii**
    Glandular pubescence, if present, confined to pedicels (9)
(9) Lateral leaflet pairs (4–)6–8; interjected leaflet pairs (3–)5–20 (10)
    Lateral leaflet pairs 2–4(–5); interjected leaflet pairs 0–3(–6) (17)
(10) Whole plant glabrous to subglabrous; lateral leaflets very long-acuminate (dept Tacna)   **2. S. acroscopicum**
    Plant with obvious hairs on leaves and other organs; lateral leaflets not long acuminate (11)
(11) Hairs on inflorescence branches almost absent (dept Lima)   **23. S. multiinterruptum**
    Hairs on inflorescence branches very frequent (12)
(12) Hairs on inflorescence branches dense, fairly short and somewhat velvety or subappressed (13)
    Hairs on inflorescence branches dense, long and spreading (15)
(13) Leaflet bases cordate (dept Cuzco)   **10. S. coelestipetalum**
    Leaflet bases rounded or cuneate (14)
(14) Leaflet pubesence long, whitish (dept Ancash)   **23. S. multiinteruptum f. longipilosum**
    Leaflet pubescence shining, yellowish, pointing obliquely towards leaf apex (dept Cuzco)   **6. S. canasense**

(15) Leaf pubescence short, dense (dept Apurímac)   **1. *S. abancayense***
      Leaf pubescence crisped, medium lengthed   (16)
(16) Peduncle very long, up to 15–20 cm (central Peru)   **4. *S. bukasovii***
      Peduncle short, 5–10 cm long (south Peru)   **22. *S. multidissectum***
(17) Whole plant glabrous   (18)
      Some hairs always present   (19)
(18) Flowers lavender, with dark stripe on back of petals; interjected
      leaflets frequent (dept Ancash)   **21. *S. moniliforme***
      Flowers without a central petal stripe; interjected leaflets 0–1 (dept
      Lima)   **14. *S. huarochiriense***
(20) Pedicels with short-stalked glands and non-glandular hairs   (21)
      Pedicels with no glands   (22)
(21) Pedicels with upward pointing hairs and glands; lateral leaflets lan-
      ceolate, long-acuminate (dept Ancash)   **25. *S. orophilum***
      Pedicels with spreading hairs and glands; lateral leaflets ovate-
      lanceolate, barely acuminate (dept Apurímac) **26. *S. pampasense***
(22) Pedicel pubescence dense short and velvety (dept Huánuco)
                                                      3. *S. ambosinum*
      Pedicel pubescence sparse, appressed, not velvety (dept Puno; and
      Bolivia)   **17. *S. leptophyes***
(23) Upper leaf surface shining   (24)
      Upper leaf surface not shining, dull   (25)
(24) Upper leaf surface rough; inflorescence and calyx glabrous; corolla
      pale lilac, almost white (depts Cajamarca and Amazonas)
                                                    8. *S. chiquidenum*
      Upper leaf surface smooth; inflorescence and calyx with sparse to
      frequent hairs (depts Apurímac and Cuzco)   **18. *S. marinasense***
(25) Lateral leaflets markedly decurrent on to the rachis   (26)
      Lateral leaflets not markedly decurrent   (29)
(26) Decurrent wings running down rachis to the next leaflet pair below;
      lateral leaflets narrow lanceolate (dept Arequipa – mountains)
                                                    28. *S. sandemanii*
      Decurrent wings only partly decurrent   (27)
(27) Hairs on leaf surface and margins very thick, short and conspicuous
      (dept Tacna)   **31. *S. tacnaense***
      Hairs on leaf surface not as above   (28)
(28) Inflorescence branches with coarse short hairs (dept Lima)
                                               19. *S. medians* (in part)
      Inflorescence branches with spreading hairs and a few glands (dept
      Arequipa – coast)   **32. *S. weberbaueri***
(29) Flower pale lilac, each petal with a dark purple central streak (dept
      Amazonas)   **15. *S. humectophilum***
      Flower not as above   (30)
(30) Flower pale violet, each petal with white central streak that is purple-
      veined (dept Lima)   **24. *S. neoweberbaueri***
      Flower not as above   (31)
(31) Terminal leaflet broadly rhomboid, larger than the lanceolate laterals
      (depts Ancash and Junín)   **27. *S. rhomboideilanceolatum***

Terminal and laterals not as above   (32)
(32) Plants very small, with a basal rosette and 5–9 cm long peduncle
     (dept Cuzco)   **29. S. sicuanum**
     Plants not as above   (33)
(33) Leaf 3–4-jugate with (2–)3–4 or more interjected leaflets; leaf hairs
     sparse, short and inconspicuous (depts Apurímac and Cuzco – also
     Bolivia)   **30. S. sparsipilum**
     Leaf, etc. not as above   (34)
(34) Leaf (1–)2–3-jugate, with short, dense pubescence on upper surface
     (Peru, locality unknown)   **11. S. dolichocremastrum**
     Leaf (1–)2–3(–4)-jugate, with medium-lengthed, dense, coarse hairs
     on upper surface (dept Lima)   **19. S. medians** (in part)

1. *S. abancayense* Ochoa (An. Cient. Univ. Agri. **1**(2), 134–7, 1963)

Leaf 4(–6)-jugate, with 12-jugate or more interjected leaflets; leaflets with
soft, short, dense hairs above, fewer below, but with longer, spreading
hairs on stem, petiole, rachis, inflorescence branches and calyx. Corolla
light purple, rotate 3.0–3.5(–4) cm diam. Berries spherical to slightly
ellipsoid.
Distribution: Peru, dept Apurímac, prov. Abancay, in rain forest, at
2,900–3,600 m, with *Polylepis*, *Eugenia*, etc.
     According to the author, this species is closely related to *S. multiinter-
ruptum*. However, in my view it seems to be closer to *S. pampasense* and
may be synonymous with it. I have not been able to examine the type
specimen, but have seen collections authenticated by the author.
Derivation: from Abancay
2n = 24; EBN = 2
Braun. (not in inventory), Stur., VIR

2. *S. acroscopicum* Ochoa (Agronomía, Lima, **18**, 130–2, 1953)

Leaves 5-jugate, with 6–8(–15) pairs of interjected leaflets, sometimes also
basiscopic and rarely acroscopic; lateral leaflets narrow lanceolate, long-
acuminate, petiolulate, almost glabrous; interjected leaflets sessile. Pedicel
articulation high up, very near calyx. Corolla rotate, 3.0–4.0 cm diam.,
rich purple, very showy. Berries spherical to slightly ovate. Whole plant
almost completely glabrous.
Distribution: south Peru, dept Tacna, amongst bushes, at 3,450 m, in
damp humid-rich soil.
Derivation: 'pointing towards the apex', referring to some of the interjected leaflets
2n = 24
Gr.Lü., Stur., VIR

3. *S. ambosinum* Ochoa (Biota, Lima, **1**, 6–9, 1954)

Leaf 4–5-jugate, with up to 8 pairs of interjected leaflets; laterals broadly
elliptic-ovate, subsessile to shortly petiolulate, endowed with short rather

frequent hairs on both surfaces. Inflorescence branches and calyx provided with fairly dense, short, velvety pubescence. Calyx acumens linear, 1.5–3.0 mm. Corolla purple, rotate, 3.0–3.5 cm diam., with clearly 'shouldered' lobes. Berries spherical, to 1.5 cm diam.
Distribution: Peru, dept Huánuco, prov. Ambo, at 2,500 m, and probably elsewhere, on shrubby mountain slopes.
   Various authenticated collections are grown at Sturgeon Bay. I have not seen the type specimen.
Derivation: from Ambo province
2n = 24; EBN = 2
Braun. (not in inventory), Stur., VIR

4. *S. bukasovii* Juz. (Bull. Acad. Sci. U.R.S.S. **2**, 303, 1937)

S. abbottianum Juz. (Bull. Acad. Sci. U.R.S.S. **2**, 305–6, 1937)
S. neohawkesii Ochoa (Rev. Argent. Agron. **19**, 231–4, 1952)
S. multidissectum subsp. *neohawkesii* (Ochoa) Hawkes (Scott. Pl. Breed. Sta. Rec., 145, 1963)

Stem with frequent, long, white, crisped, sub-appressed hairs. Leaf 3–4(–6)-jugate, with up to 9 or 10 pairs of interjected leaflets; both surfaces with thick, long, densely arranged hairs. Inflorescence branches similarly pubescent. Peduncle long (3–)15–20 cm, bringing the flowers well up above the low-growing bushy foliage; pedicel articulation very high. Calyx densely, coarsely pubescent. Corolla deep purple, rotate, 3.0–3.5 cm diam. Berries spherical.
Distribution: central Peru, depts of Ancash, Huánuco, Huancavelica, Junín, Lima, Pasco (possibly also Ayacucho) from altitudes of 3,300 to 4,300 m, in puna formation and on roadsides, waste places, walls, rocky and shrubby areas, pastures, etc.
   This well-known species seems to be closely related to the south Peruvian *S. multidissectum*, which may be a subspecies of it.
Derivation: named in honour of the famous Russian taxonomist and potato breeder, Professor S.M. Bukasov
2n = 24; EBN = 2
Braun., CPC, Gr.Lü., Stur., VIR

5. *S. cajamarquense* Ochoa (Agronomía, Lima, **26**, 315–15, 1959)

A very distinctive species, the whole plant possessing a dense, coarse pubescence of long, thick, white hairs. Leaf rough, 3-jugate, the laterals diminishing in size rapidly towards the leaf base and not as large as the broad-ovate to sub-rotund terminal; margins undulate-crenulate and apex slightly acuminate; interjected leaflets few to many, very small. Peduncles, pedicels and calyx also densely long-pubescent. Calyx acumens linear-spathulate. Corolla white, rotate, 2.5–3.0 cm diam. Berries spherical, 1.5 cm diam.
Distribution: Peru, dept and prov. Cajamarca, at 2,570–2,800 m, amongst bushes and in grassy places.

Easily recognized by the white shaggy pubescence and the very large sub-orbicular terminal leaflets.

Derivation: from the place name Cajamarca

Stur. (not in inventory)

6. *S. canasense* Hawkes (Bull. Imp. Bur. Pl. Breed. Genet., Cambridge, 123, 1944)

S. lechnoviczii Hawkes (ibid. 124–5, 1944)
S. punoense Hawkes (ibid. 123, 1944)
S. soukupii Hawkes (ibid. 122–3, 1944)
S. espinarense Vargas (Papas Sudperuanas, Univ. Nac. Cuzco **2**, 60, 1956)
S. canasense var. *alba* Vargas (ibid. 57, 1956)
S. canasense var. *calcense* Vargas (ibid. 58, 1956)
S. canasense var. *intihuatanense* Vargas (ibid. 58, 1956)
S. lechnoviczii var. *latifolium* Vargas (ibid. 61, 1956)
S. amabile Vargas (ibid. 58, 1956)
S. canasense var. *latifolium* (Vargas) Ochoa (Sol. Tuber. Silv. Peru, Lima, 170, 1962)
S. soukupii var. *espinarense* (Vargas) Ochoa (ibid. 278, 1962)

A highly variable species with 4–6(–8)-jugate leaf and 3–11(–20) pairs of interjected leaflets; primary laterals ovate-lanceolate, apically acuminate; all leaflets clothed above with dense, silky, slightly yellowish-white, appressed forward-pointing hairs, below with very short, dense hairs. Inflorescence branches and calyx also with dense, silky, subappressed hairs. Corolla very showy, light blue-purple, (2.5–)3.0–4.5(–5) cm diam., rotate with the lobes 'shouldered' and very small 2–3 mm long acumens. Berries round to oval, 1.5–2.0 cm diam.

Distribution: south Peru, common in depts Cuzco and Puno, possibly also in dept Ayacucho, at 2,900–4,100 m, in rocky gravelly slopes, field borders and roadsides.

Derivation: From prov. and river Canas in dept Cuzco, Peru

2n = 24; EBN = 2

Braun., CPC, Gr.Lü., Stur., VIR

6a. *S. canasense* var. *xerophilum* (Vargas) Hawkes, comb. nov.

S. lechnoviczii Hawkes var. *xerophyllum* Vargas (Papas Sudperuanas, Univ. Nac. Cuzco, **2**, 61–2, 1956)

Differs from type in the leaves almost or completely glabrous above, glabrous below.

Distribution: Peru, dept Cuzco, at 2,800–3,300 m, on dry sandy slopes with cacti.

Derivation: referring to the fact that this variety occurs in dry places. (The name *xerophyllum* ['dry leaf'] is surely a mistake by Professor Vargas for *xerophilum* – 'loving dry places'. I have thus altered it accordingly.)

2n = 24; EBN = 2(?)
Braun., CPC, Stur.
(Type: *Vargas 4088*, Peru, dept Cuzco, prov. Calca, Tunasmoko. Living collections: *Petersen & Hjerting 1527*; *EBS 1865, 1887*; *Hawkes 5107, 5112*; *Ochoa 10876*.)

7. *S. chancayense* Ochoa (Agronomía, Lima, **26**, 316–18, 1959)

Small glabrous to glabrescent plants with 2–3(–4)-jugate lateral leaflets and no interjected leaflets; lateral leaflets smaller than terminals, shortly petiolulate and decurrent down the petiolules on to the rachis. Very young shoots and calyx with a few short hairs that drop off later. Corolla white, rotate with very short lobes and small acumens. Berries not noted.
Distribution: Peru, dept Lima, coastal hills (lomas) of Chancay, Lachay and Quilmana. Also dept La Libertad, Trujillo, on coastal hills, at 150–550 m, slightly more pubescent.
Derivation: from Chancay, north of Lima
2n = 24; EBN = 1
Braun., Gr.Lü., Stur., VIR

8. *S. chiquidenum* Ochoa (Biota, Lima, **1**, 5–7, 1954)

Leaves with 1–2 pairs of lateral leaflets, decreasing in size rapidly towards leaf base; interjected leaflets absent, or 1–3 per leaf; leaves with rough shining hairs on both surfaces; leaflet margins crenulate to minutely denticulate. Terminal leaflet larger than laterals. Inflorescence branches and calyx glabrous; articulation of pedicel very high up, just below calyx. Calyx acumens linear. Corolla pale lilac to white, rotate, 2.5–3.5 cm diam., with shouldered lobes and very small acumens. Berries ovoid. This is a very robust species, growing to 1.5 m tall; tubers produced at frequent intervals along the stolon.
Distribution: north Peru, depts Cajamarca and Amazonas, from 2,500–3,350 m on shady banks and amongst shrubs and small trees.

S. chiquidenum var. *cachicadense* Ochoa (Agronomía, Lima, **26**, 318, 1959). Type *Ochoa 1469*
S. chiquidenum var. *porconense* Ochoa (Agronomía, Lima, **27**(4), 369–70, 1960). Type *Ochoa 2340*

The above varieties are only slightly different from the type; var. *cachicadense* is glabrous and approaches *S. cantense*; var. *porconense* is more densely pubescent than the type and the flower is white with a purple star.
Derivation: from the locality Chiquidén, where this species was first found
2n = 24
Stur. (not in inventory), VIR

9. S. chrysoflorum Ochoa (Hickenia **1**(59), 317–20, 1982)

Leaf 3–4-jugate with 4–6 pairs of interjected leaflets; leaf with minute, rather sparse hairs above, slightly denser below; lateral leaflets sessile to subsessile, the uppermost pair slightly decurrent; apex acute to somewhat acuminate. Pedicel articulation in the upper third, to 3 mm below calyx. Corolla rotate, yellow to creamy white, 3.0–3.5 cm diam. Ovary globose; fruit unknown.

Distribution: Peru, dept Lima, prov. Canta, at 3,400 m in humid shrubby thickets.

Even though berries were unknown the author placed *S. chrysoflorum* in series *Tuberosa*. It is unique in subsection *Potatoe* by virtue of its yellow to creamy white flowers.

Derivation: golden-flowered

2n = 24

10. S. coelestipetalum Vargas (Papas Sudperuanas, Univ. Nac. Cuzco, **2**, 59, 1956)

S. ochoae Vargas (ibid. 62–63, 1956)

Leaf 3–4(–5)-jugate, with 3–6(–12) pairs of interjected leaflets; upper surface silky-pubescent, lower surface densely velvety pubescent. Leaflets broad-ovate, very slightly acuminate; inflorescence branches densely pubescent; pedicel articulation in upper third. Calyx acumens long-linear. Corolla sky blue to violet, rotate-pentagonal, 3.0 cm diam. Fruit not described.

Distribution: Peru, dept Cuzco, at 2,400–3,600 m, in shrubby thickets.

This species may bear some affinity to *S. canasense*.

Derivation: with sky-blue petals

2n = 24

Braun., CPC, Stur. (not in inventory), VIR

11. S. dolichocremastrum Bitt. (Fedde, Repert. **12**, 3–4, 1913)

Stem glabrous or with a few appressed hairs above. Leaves (1–)2–3-jugate, leaflets sessile, not or barely decurrent; laterals narrow-lanceolate, obtuse; terminals broadly rhomboid, slightly acuminate, all with dense, short hairs above, sparser below; interjected leaflets absent. Corolla rotate, colour unknown, about 3.0 cm diam. (see figure in Correll, 327, 1962). Fruit unknown.

Distribution: Peru, exact locality unknown. Type and only known collection is *Dombey*(s.n.) in Herb Paris, probably from central Peru.

This enigmatic species may be related to or form a part of *S. medians* Bitt.

Derivation: Long hanging(?). No feature of the plant, as described by Bitter or as seen in the type specimen would seem to justify the use of this name.

12. *S. gracilifrons* **Bitt.** (Beibl. Bot. Jahrb., No. 119, **54**, 6–7, 1916)

Leaf (4–)6–9-jugate, with up to 16 pairs of interjected leaflets; laterals generally petiolulate, very narrowly lanceolate to almost linear. All leaflets glabrous or with very minute hairs seen only through a strong lens. Stem, inflorescence branches and calyx glabrous, or with hairs as leaf. Corolla white, rotate, about 2.5 cm diam. or larger. Berries globular, about 1 cm diam.
Distribution: Peru, dept Huancavelica in the valley of the Mantaro river at 1,900–2,000 m, amongst *Opuntias* and *Lantanas*, and thus in a very warm, dry environment.
Derivation: graceful leaves
2n = 24

13. *S. guzmanguense* **Whalen & Sagást.** (in Whalen, M.D., Sagastegui, A. and Knapp, Sandra. Brittonia **38**(1), 9–12, 1986)

A robust glabrous species up to 1.5 m high, with winged stems and large, simple, ovate leaves, 15–30 cm long, glabrous. Corolla showy, rotate, white, 4–6 cm diam., with 6–9 mm anthers and 10–13 mm style; berries globose 10–15 mm diam.
Distribution: Peru, dept Cajamarca, Contumazá in seasonally humid ravines with shrubs, grasses, etc. at 1,700–2,200 m.
   This very curious species is said by the authors not to be closely related to other species but perhaps nearest to '*S. simplicifolium*' (= *S. microdontum*).
Derivation: from the word Guzmango, the locality where it was collected

14. *S. huarochiriense* **Ochoa** (Sol. tuber. silv. Peru, Lima, 215–17, 1962)

Leaves 3–4-jugate with no interjected leaflets; laterals elliptic obtuse, subsessile; leaf entirely glabrous, as also are the inflorescence branches and calyx. Corolla rotate, blue, 3.0 cm diam. with well-marked lobes and 4 mm long acumens. Berries unknown.
Distribution: central Peru, dept Lima, Huarochirí, at 3,750 m (habitat unknown).
Derivation: from Huarochirí
2n = 24

15. *S. humectophilum* **Ochoa** (Darwiniana **15**(3–4), 550–3, 1969)

Leaves densely pubescent above (1–)2–3-jugate, 0–2-jugate interjected leaflets; terminal larger than laterals which decrease in size rapidly towards leaf base. Corolla with long narrow acumens, rotate, pale lilac with deep purple star. Fruits pear-shaped to long ovoid.
Distribution: Peru, dept Amazonas, prov. Leimebamba, at 2,875 m, in very humid mountain forest, together with *Chusqea*, *Escallonia*, *Fuchsia*, *Calceolaria*, etc.

Although Ochoa places this species in series *Tuberosa* his description of the fruits indicates that it could belong to series *Conicibaccata*; nevertheless, the photograph given with the description shows almost globular berries. I therefore place it where the author wishes it to be, in series *Tuberosa*.

Derivation: loving damp places
Braun. (not in inventory), VIR

16. *S. immite* Dun. (in DC. Prodr. **13**, I, 32, 1852)

S. tuberosum L. var. *multijugum* Hook. f. (Fl. Antarct. **2**, 330, 1846)
S. mathewsii Bitt. (Fedde, Repert. **12**, 53–4, 1913)
S. immite Dun. var. *vernale* Corr. (Wrightia **2**, 181, 1961)

Leaf (3–)4–5-jugate, with 0–7 pairs of minute interjected leaflets; laterals lanceolate to narrow-lanceolate, long-acuminate, glabrous, with 3–15 mm long petiolules. Inflorescence branches and calyx glabrous. Corolla showy, rotate, white, 1.5–3.0 cm diam. Fruit globose, to 1 cm diam.

Distribution: Peru, depts Ancash, La Libertad and Lima, on coastal hills (lomas) from 200–250 m (var. *vernale* Corr.) and in the mountains from 2,400–2,500 m, on rocky hillsides, bushy places and even as a weed of cultivated fields.

Some very minute hairs are sometimes seen on *S. immite*. Correll's var. *vernale* does not differ from the type sufficiently to warrant varietal status. It merely flowers in the spring because of the difference of season between coast and mountain.

Derivation: Rough, harsh, not soft. This is curious, since the plant is soft and almost hairless, quite the reverse of its name!
2n = 24
Braun. (not in inventory), Stur., VIR

17. *S. leptophyes* Bitt. (Fedde, Repert. **12**, 448–9, 1913)

For description see pp. 163–4. This species is almost entirely confined to Bolivia, only just crossing the northern border into south Peru (Hawkes and Hjerting 1989, 303).

Distribution: south Peru, dept Puno, prov. Chucuito, at 3,800 m, on roadsides.

Derivation: slender growth
2n = 24
No Peruvian material available.

18. *S. marinasense* Vargas (Papas Sudperuanus, Univ. Nac. Cuzco, **2**, 53, 1956)

S. marinasense var. *dentifolium* Vargas (ibid. 56, 1956)
S. cuzcoense Ochoa (Agronomía **26**, 219, 1959)
S. pampasense f. *glabrescens* Corr. (Wrightia **2**, 183, 1961)

Leaf (1–)2–3-jugate with 0–2 interjected leaflets; leaflets lanceolate, marginally smooth or denticulate, subglabrous and shining above but with small hairs near and on the margins, below densely felted with short hairs. Inflorescence branches and calyx with sparse to frequent appressed hairs. Corolla showy, rotate, azure blue (to lavender?), 2.5–3.5 cm diam. Berries oval, to 3 × 2 cm.

Distribution: south Peru, dept Cuzco at 3,000–3,500 m; dept Apurímac at 2,200–2,700 m. On rocky slopes amongst shrubs, in hedges and along field borders.

The other taxa grouped here as synonyms do not vary enough to warrant distinction.

Derivation: dedicated to Professor Vargas' pupil, Felipe Marín

2n = 24; EBN = 2

Braun., Gr.Lü., Stur., VIR

19. *S. medians* Bitt. (Fedde, Repert. **11**, 366–7, 1912)

S. medians var. *majorifrons* Bitt. (Fedde, Repert. **12**, 149–50, 1913)
S. medians var. *majorifrons* subvar. *protohypoleucum* Bitt. (Fedde, Repert. **12**, 150–1, 1913)
S. medians var. *autumnale* Corr. (Wrightia **2**, 190–91, 1961)
S. medians var. *angustifoliolum* Ochoa (Sol. Tuber. Silv. Peru, Lima, 242–6, 1962)

A highly variable species, with leaf varying from (1–)2–3(–4)-jugate, the leaflets broad ovate-elliptic, subsessile and often decurrent; interjected leaflets 0–2(–4)-jugate; pubescence of medium-lengthed, fairly dense, coarse hairs above, sparser below; terminal leaflet generally longer and much broader than laterals. Inflorescence branches and calyx with coarse, short hairs; pedicel articulation fairly high. Corolla rotate, rich violet-purple, from 2.0–3.5 cm diam. Berries globular.

Distribution: central Peru, dept Lima, in mountains from 1,800–3,400 m and on coastal hills (lomas) from 200–250 m, growing on rocky hillsides amongst herbs and bushes, roadsides, etc.

The described varieties merely pick out some aspects of the total diversity of this species. Var. *autumnale* refers to the coastal plants which grow and flower at a different season from the mountain plants.

Derivation: 'intermediate', so named by Bitter who considered it to represent the transition from *S. weberbaueri* to *S. hypacrarthrum*.

2n = 24; EBN = 2

Braun., Gr.Lü., Stur., VIR

20. *S. mochiquense* Ochoa (Agronomía, Lima, **26**, 111–12, 1959)

S. earl-smithii Corr. (Wrightia **2**, 135–7, 1961)

Leaflets 3–4(–5)-paired, sessile to shortly petiolulate; 3–12 or more pairs of interjected leaflets; upper leaf surface deep green, shining, with short hairs on veins only, densely felted pubescent below; margins undulate and irregularly crenulate-denticulate. Inflorescence branches and calyx glabrous to minutely pilose. Corolla rotate, white, showy, 2.5–3.0 cm diam., with short acumens. Berries globose.

Distribution: north Peru, depts Cajamarca, La Libertad and Piura, at 1,650–1,700 m in the mountains and 250–500 m on coastal hills (lomas) on rocky hillsides.

Derivation: named after the Moche (Mochica) archaeological cultures of Trujillo and elsewhere

2n = 24; EBN = 1

Braun., Gr.Lü., Stur., VIR

21. *S. moniliforme* Corr. (Wrightia 2, 182–3, 1961)

Whole plant glabrous. Tubers arranged in the form of a necklace. Leaf 3–4-jugate with 0–2 pairs of minute interjecteds; leaflets sessile, elliptic and somewhat decurrent, apically obtuse. Calyx glabrous, dark purple. Corolla lavender with a dark central petal streak, pentagonal, to 5 cm diam. Fruit unknown.

Distribution: Peru, depts Ancash and Lima, at 3,750–3,900 m, amongst boulders on moist mountain slopes.

The affinities of this species are unknown; Correll thought it might be related to *S. chomatophilum* and *S. jalcae*, but the present writer is doubtful about this, considering it more likely to be related to *S. mochiquense*.

Derivation: in the form of a string of beads or a necklace, referring to the tubers

22. *S. multidissectum* Hawkes (Bull. Imp. Bur. Pl. Breed, Genet., Cambridge, 124, 1944)

S. fragariifructum Hawkes (ibid. 129, 1944)
S. lobbianum Bitt. f. *multidissectum* (Hawkes) Corr. (Wrightia 2, 189, 1961)

Habit rosetted or decumbent. Leaf 6–8-jugate, with 10–20 pairs of interjected leaflets, including acroscopics and basiscopics; petiolules 2–12 mm long. Leaf with frequent thick crisped hairs above and below. Stem, petiole, petiolule, rachis, inflorescence branches and calyx with very frequent, long, thick, spreading hairs, very typical of this species. Corolla blue-purple, pentagonal, 2.0–2.5 cm diam. Berries ovate-cordate.

Distribution: Peru, depts Apurímac, Cuzco and Puno (possibly also Ayacucho and Huancavelica) at 3,100–4,175 m, on grass steppe, roadside, moist banks, walls, etc. and amongst rocks and shrubs.

There is still some doubt concerning the taxonomic status of *S. lobbianum*, *S. bukasovii* and *S. multidissectum*, which may finally prove to be a single far-ranging and variable species. The corolla of *S. multidissectum* is smaller and more pentagonal than those of *S. bukasovii* and *S. canasense*

(with which latter species it has also been confused). The coarse curved hairs of *S. multidissectum* also distinguish it from *S. canasense*, which has a very large corolla with strikingly 'shouldered' lobes.
Derivation: much dissected (leaf)
2n = 24; EBN = 2
Braun., CPC, Gr.Lü., Stur., VIR

23. S. multiinterruptum Bitt. (Fedde, Repert. **12**, 56–7, 1913)

Leaf 4–5(–6)-jugate with 5–15 pairs of interjected leaflets; all leaflets sessile to shortly petiolulate; laterals elliptic-oblong, twice as long as broad; leaf with sparse, short, acute hairs above, shorter below. Peduncle very long, about 16 cm; pedicels to 5.5 cm long, articulated very high up, close to calyx base. Inflorescence branches and calyx sparsely, shortly pilose, almost glabrous. Calyx acumens long, linear, to 4 mm. Corolla dark blue to violet, large, 3.5–4.5 cm diam., clearly rotate. Berries globose to oval, to 1.5 cm diam.

Forma *longipilosum* Corr. (Wrightia **2**, 192, 1961)
Differs from the type by the long, spreading hairs on all green parts, particularly conspicuous on inflorescence branches and calyx. Leaflets rather narrower than the type, ovate-lanceolate to lanceolate. (Dept Ancash.)

(Var. *machaytambinum* Ochoa (Agronomía, Lima, **27**, 244–5, 1960). Since the type specimen of this variety possesses long-conical berries, further research would probably place it in series *Conicibaccata*.)

Distribution: Peru, dept Lima (type form) and Ancash (forma *longipilosum*), at 3,300–4,000 m, on bushy and grassy slopes, amongst boulders, etc. Ochoa's var. *machaytambinum* is from dept La Libertad (*Ochoa 2164*).
Derivation: much interrupted, referring to the many interjected leaflets
2n = 24; EBN = 2
Braun., Gr.Lü., Stur., VIR

24. S. neoweberbaueri Wittm. (in Engler, Bot. Jahrb. **50**, Suppl., 540–8, 1914)

S. medians Bitt. f. *neoweberbaueri* (Wittm.) Corr. (Wrightia **2**, 191 1961)

Leaf 2–3-jugate, with 0–1(–2)-jugate interjected leaflets; terminal leaflet generally larger than the ovate-oblong acuminate laterals which are sessile to subsessile, the distal pair often decurrent; all leaflets very sparsely, shortly pubescent above and below, marginally denticulate and slightly crenulate. Inflorescence branches minutely pilose above, glabrescent below. Calyx with spreading hairs and linear-spathulate 4 mm long acumens. Corolla rotate, 3 cm diam., pale violet, with a white violet-veined streak in the middle of each lobe. Fruit not seen.

Distribution: central Peru, dept Lima, on coastal hills (lomas) near Lima at about 250 m; also near Matucana at 2,200 m on rocky slopes.

Although *S. neoweberbaueri* seems close to *S. medians*, its sparse pubescence and pale flower colour distinguish it from that species.

Derivation: a new (or second) species named in honour of the distinguished German botanist, A. Weberbauer

2n = 36 (according to Ochoa)

25. *S. orophilum* **Corr.** (Wrightia **2**, 192–3, 1961)

Stem violet-marbled, with broad straight wings. Leaf 4–5-jugate, with 3–6 pairs of interjected leaflets; lateral leaflets lanceolate, long-acuminate, shortly petiolulate, covered with dense, long, curved, silky pubescence above, shorter and very densely felted below. Pedicels articulated above the centre, covered very densely with upward-pointing hairs and short-stalked glands, as is also the calyx, which has linear acumens. Corolla rotate, pentagonal, 2.5–4.0 cm diam., lavender-purple. Berries globular, about 1.5 cm diam.

Distribution: north Peru, dept Ancash, above Chavín, at 3,500 m on rocky shrubby slope.

Ochoa equates this species with *S. ambosinum*, but the leaflets of *S. orophilum* are narrower, much more acuminate and more densely pubescent, as are the pedicels also.

Derivation: mountain-loving

Stur. (not in inventory)

26. *S. pampasense* **Hawkes** (Bull. Imp. Bur. Pl. Breed. Genet., Cambridge, 125, 1944)

S. longimucronatum Vargas (Papas Sudperuanas, Univ. Nac. Cuzco., **2**, 60–1, 1956)

S. marinasense f. *longimucronatum* (Vargas) Corr. (Wrightia **2**, 181–2, 1961)

Leaf 4–5-jugate, with 3–6-jugate interjected leaflets; lateral leaflets ovate-lanceolate, 2–10(–20) mm petiolulate, margins crenulate, both surfaces densely, shortly pubescent. Peduncle sparsely pubescent; pedicels densely covered with long, spreading hairs and short-stalked glands. Calyx acumens linear, 2.0–5.5 mm long, pubescence as for pedicels. Corolla rotate, 3.0–3.5 cm diam., very pale blue, with rounded lobes, very showy. Anthers long and narrow. Berries globose, to 2 cm diam.

Distribution: Peru, depts Apurímac, Ayacucho and Cuzco, in dry, subtropical interandine valleys at 2,000–2,900 m.

Derivation: from the Río Pampas valley in dept Apurímac

2n = 24; EBN = 2

Braun., Gr.Lü., Stur., VIR

27. *S. rhomboideilanceolatum* Ochoa (Rev. Argent. Agron. **19**, 234–7, 1952)

S. rhomboideilanceolatum var. *ancophilum* Corr. (Wrightia **2**, 195, 1961)
S. ancophilum (Corr.) Ochoa (Phytologia **54**(5), 392, 1983)

Lateral leaflets petiolulate, with long, conspicuous hairs. Terminal leaflet rhomboid, larger than the 1–4-jugate laterals; interjected leaflets few. Corolla rich purple, showy, 3.0–4.5 cm diam., rotate, with well-developed lobes. Anthers 8 mm long. Fruiting calyx with 4 mm long acumens. Berries ovoid.
Distribution: central Peru, depts Ancash and Junín, at 2,600–3,900 m, amongst bushes.
Var. *ancophilum* Corr. differs from the type chiefly in the broad decurrency of the upper laterals on to the rachis. In this it links on to *S. chavinense* but differs in that the decurrency does not follow down the rachis. Further study of living plants of all three taxa is needed.
Derivation: rhomboid-lanceolate leaflets
2n = 24
Braun. (not in inventory)

28. *S. sandemanii* Hawkes (Ann. Mag. Nat. Hist., Ser. 12, **7**, 709–10, 1954)

Leaf imparipinnatisect, 2–3-jugate, with no interjected leaflets (or 1 pair exceptionally); lateral leaf lobes or leaflets decurrent right down the rachis to the next leaflet pair (compare *S. infundibuliforme*); surface with frequent, short, thick hairs, margin more or less entire. Pedicels with dense, spreading hairs and short-stalked glands. Calyx lobes often subspathulate, very pubescent. Corolla showy, bright violet, rotate, 3.0–3.5 cm diam. Berries not described.
Distribution: south Peru, dept Arequipa at 2,600–3,100 m, in sandy soil amongst bushes.
This species is very closely similar to *S. tacnaense* and *S. weberbaueri*. Only studies of all three species collected from their type localities and grown under identical experimental conditions will solve the problem of their possible synonymity. The similarity between *S. sandemanii* and *S. infundibuliforme* when growing under very dry conditions may not indicate a very close relationship.
Derivation: named in honour of the British plant collector, Christopher Sandeman
2n = 24; EBN = 2
All these collections are derived from *Ross 726* = (EBS 1867): Braun., CPC, Gr.Lü., Stur. (as *S. weberbaueri*), VIR

29. *S. sicuanum* Hawkes. nom. nov.

S. pumilum Hawkes (Bull. Imp. Bur. Pl. Breed. Genet., Cambridge, 124, 1944, non *S. pumilum* Dun., in D.C. Prodr. **13**, I, 287, 1852; non *S.* *pumilum* Rojas, in Cat. Hist. Nat. Corrient. **75**, 1897)

A dwarf plant with basal rosette and very long peduncle (5–9 cm). Leaves 2–3-jugate, with 0(–1) pair of interjected leaflets; laterals sessile, very slightly decurrent, provided with rather frequent, thick, appressed hairs; inflorescence branches and calyx with sparse thick hairs; pedicel articulation high. Corolla pentagonal-rotate, dark purple, 2.0–2.5 cm diam. Fruit not seen.
Distribution: south Peru, dept Cuzco, Sicuani, at 3,700–3,800 m, among herbs and mosses.
  Living material of this species might help to reveal its affinities.
Derivation: from Sicuani, where it was collected (*Vargas 9839*)

30. *S. sparsipilum* (Bitt.) Juz. et Buk. (*ex* Vavilov, Theor. Bases Pl. Breed. **3**, 11, 1937)

S. tuberosum L. subsp. *sparsipilum* Bitt. (Fedde, Repert. **12**, 152–3, 1913)

For full list of synonyms, subspecies, description, distribution and other data, refer to this species in (iii) – Bolivia and Argentina (pp. 168–70).
Distribution in Peru: depts Apurímac and Cuzco, at 2,800–3,800 m in fields, walls, field borders, etc.
Derivation: with sparse hairs
2n = 24; EBN = 2
Braun., CPC, Stur., VIR

31. *S. tacnaense* Ochoa (Agronomía **18**(74), 19, 21, 22 [= 133, 135, 136], 1953)

Leaf 4-jugate, with 1–2 pairs of interjected leaflets; laterals sessile to shortly petiolulate, the upper pair shortly decurrent; all leaflets marginally clearly denticulate, each tooth and whole upper surface covered with frequent, short, very thick, conspicuous hairs; lower surface with shorter, thinner hairs. Peduncle to 22 cm long; pedicels to 5 cm long, articulated 5 mm below calyx; both peduncle and pedicels very sparsely pubescent, but calyx densely so, with long spathulate acumens. Corolla deep blue, rotate, 3.0–4.0 cm diam., with flat lobes. Stigma globular, very large. Fruit not seen.
Distribution: south Peru, dept Tacna at 3,000–3,200 m, amongst spiny bushes in a dry region.
  Differs from *S. sandemanii* and *S. weberbaueri* in the very thick, short leaf hairs and denticulate leaf margin; also in the subglabrous very long peduncle. Some slight relationship with *S. oplocense*.
Derivation: from Tacna

32. *S. weberbaueri* Bitt. (Fedde, Repert. **11**, 365–6, 1912)

S. weberbaueri Bitt. var. *poscoanum* Cárd. et Hawkes (J. Linn. Soc. Bot. **53**, 101–2, 1946)

S. weberbaueri Bitt. var. *decurrentialatum* Ochoa (Agronomía, Lima **26**, 219–20, 1959)

Leaf 3(–4)-jugate, with 0(–2) pairs of interjected leaflets; laterals shortly petiolulate to sessile, abruptly decurrent, the terminal much larger; upper surface with sparse, short, inconspicuous hairs, also on margins. Peduncle very short, 3.5–4.0 cm long; pedicels densely covered with spreading hairs and glands. Calyx with dense, coarse hairs and spathulate acumens. Corolla rotate, violet, 3.5–3.8 cm. Fruit not seen.
Distribution: south Peru, dept Arequipa, coastal hills (lomas) at about 500–600 m, among stones and herbaceous vegetation.
Differs from *S. sandemanii* chiefly in the short leaflet decurrency and larger leaflets; from *S. tacnaense* it differs in the fewer, less conspicuous leaf hairs and marginal teeth, and in the much shorter peduncle.
Derivation: named after the distinguished German botanist, A. Weber-bauer
2n = 24
Braun., Gr.Lü., Stur. (all = *S. sandemanii?*), VIR

33. *S. wittmackii* Bitt. (Fedde, Repert. **12**, 546, 1913)

S. tuberosum L. var. *macranthum* Hook f. (F. Antarct. **2**, 330, 1847)
S. wittmackii var. *glauciviride* Bitt. (Fedde, Repert. **12**, 56, 1913)
S. vavilovii Juz. et Buk. (Bull. Acad. Sci. U.R.S.S. **2**, 302–3, 1937)

Leaf 6–7-jugate with about 6–12 pairs of interjected leaflets; leaflets lanceolate-acuminate, petiolulate; all leaves, stems, inflorescence branches and calyx with a very dense covering of stalked glands, as well as some sparse, long, weak, glandless hairs. Calyx acumens linear or spathulate. Corolla rotate, pale lilac, up to 4.5 cm diam. Berries not noted.
Material from different collections differs considerably in the amount of glandular pubescence. In a variety described by Bitter (var. *glauciviride*) it is less dense, whilst in the material of Vavilov (*S. vavilovii*) it is very dense.
Distribution: central Peru, dept Lima. Desert coastal hills (lomas), at 200–350 m, vegetating only during the season of sea mists (garruas) during the months of July to September.
Derivation: named after the distinguished German potao taxonomist, L. Wittmack
2n = 24

34. *S. amayanum* Ochoa (Amer. Potato J. **66**, 1–4, 1989)

Plant with dense, silvery white hairs on all parts. Leaf 3–4(–5)-jugate, with 5–7(–9) pairs of interjected leaflets; terminal larger than laterals. Peduncle 12–15 cm long.

Corolla rotate to rotate-pentagonal, 3.5–4.0 cm diam., purple to dark purple. Berry globose 1.5–2.0 cm diam. (No material seen.)
Distribution: Peru, dept Huancavelica, at 3,000 m on steep hillside.
Derivation: dedicated to Sr Jesús Amaya Castillo, Professor Ochoa's assistant
2n = 24

35. S. antacochense Ochoa (Amer. Potato J. **58**(3), 127–9, 1981)

Leaves dark green, pubescent, 5–6-jugate, with 6–9 pairs of interjected leaflets; leaflets elliptic-lanceolate; all leaflets, petioles and rachis densely canescent. Corolla showy, rotate, to 4.5 cm diam., light purple. Fruit ovoid to conical-ovoid to 20 mm long.
Distribution: Peru, dept Junín, at 3,480 m, in cold *Stipa* grassland with shrubs. (No material seen.)
Derivation: named after the place where it was found, Antacocha
2n = 24

36. S. augustii Ochoa (Bol. Soc. Peruana Bot. **7**(1 & 2), 12–15, 1974)

Leaves 4–5-jugate, with narrow elliptic lanceolate leaflets and many interjected leaflets; lateral leaflets sessile to subsessile and rather varnished, sparsely pilose above. Corolla rotate to subpentagonal, pale azure blue, 3.0–3.5 cm diam. Berries globose, 1.0–1.5 cm diam.
Distribution: Peru, dept Ancash at 3,000–3,200 m. Habitat not noted. (I have seen no material.)
Derivation: dedicated to the distinguished German botanist Augustus Weberbauer, who worked for most of his life on the taxonomy and phytogeography of Peruvian plants.
2n = 24

37. S. aymaraesense Ochoa (Phytologia **64**(1), 36–7, 1987)

Leaves 4–5-jugate (not mentioned in description), ovate, apically obtuse, with 2–5 pairs of interjected leaflets, all provided with minute hairs. Corolla rotate pentagonal, 2.5–2.8 cm diam., pale violet, but darker between star and acumen. Berry globose, 1.0–1.5 cm diam.
Distribution: Peru, dept Apurímac, at 2,500 m in a deep valley, amongst stones and between *Eupatorium*, *Bidens*, *Monnina*, *Calceolaria* etc. (I have seen no specimens, only an illustration.)
Derivation: from the province of Aymaraes, where it was discovered
2n = 24

38. S. bill-hookeri Ochoa (Amer. Potato J. **65**(12), 737–40, 1988)

Stem with long, spreading hairs. Leaf 3–4(–5)-jugate, with terminals larger than the sessile to shortly petiolulate laterals; interjected leaflets 2–4-jugate; leaf with medium dense, long, weak hairs above, much denser below. Peduncles, pedicels and calyx with dense, weak, spreading hairs and some short ones; stalked glands are seen on the pedicels. Corolla sky-blue, showy, 2.5–4.0 cm diam. Berry not seen.
Distribution: Peru, dept Huancavelica at 2,900 m in dry rocky places with *Opuntia* and other drought indicators.

I have not seen the type specimen and the above description is based on an isotype from Herb. US, which differs in some features from the type description, even though they possess the same collection number. I consider this species to be very closely related to *S. pampasense*, which has been recorded in the adjacent department of Ayacucho.

Derivation: dedicated (somewhat informally!) to the well-known American phyto-pathologist, Dr William Hooker

$2n = 24$

39. *S. hapalosum* Ochoa (Bol. Soc. Argent. Bot. **22**(1–4), 297–9, 1983)

Graceful delicate habit. Leaf 5-jugate, with 6–12-jugate interjected leaflets, with very short white hairs, sparsely above, denser below; leaflets elliptic with obtuse to acute apex. Corolla rotate or pentagonal, purple, 2.8–3.0 cm diam. Fruit globose or slightly oval.

Distribution: central Peru, dept Lima, at 3,340 m. (I have seen no material or illustration.)

Derivation: soft, tender, delicate

$2n = 24$

40. *S. incahuasinum* Ochoa (Kurtziana, Córdoba **12–13**, 183–5, 1979)

Leaf pale green, 2–3-jugate, generally without interjected leaflets. (Pubescence not noted.) Laterals narrow elliptic-lanceolate, with entire or slightly undulate margins. Flowers numerous. Corolla white, rotate, large, 5.5 cm diam. Fruits oval to oval-pyriform.

Distribution: Peru, dept Lambayeque, at 2,875 m, in shrubby thickets with ferns, *Calceolarias*, *Salvias*, etc. in damp places by streams.

Ochoa considers that this species may have affinities to *S. mochiquense* and *S. chancayense*. (I have seen no material or illustration.)

Derivation: name taken from Incahuasi, the place where it was discovered

$2n = 24$

41. *S. incasicum* Ochoa (Phytologia **48**(3), 229, 1981)

Leaves densely pilose, 4-jugate, with numerous interjected leaflets; laterals narrowly elliptic-lanceolate; surface with silvery white hairs, margin sinuate-crenate. Corolla lilac, rotate, to 4.5 cm diam. Fruit rotund.

Distribution: south Peru, dept Cuzco, at 3,900 m, in a very cloudy cold region near beautiful archaeological ruins, among shrubs and relic woodlands. (I have seen no material.)

$2n = 24$

42. *S. irosinum* Ochoa (Amer. Potato J. **58**(3), 31–3, 1981)

Leaf 4(–5)-jugate, with 5–15 or more interjected leaflets; leaf shortly, densely pubescent; leaflets elliptic-lanceolate, 1–3 mm petiolulate. Pedicel articulation near calyx base (5–6 mm). Corolla rotate, 2.5–3.0 cm diam., pale violet to dark lilac. Berries ovoid to conico-ovoid.

Distribution: near Peru, dept Cajamarca, Mount Iros, at 3,200 m in copses and open grassland with *Stipa*, in a cold foggy climate and humid soil. (I have seen no material or illustration and this species may belong to series *Conicibaccata* – see p. 117)

Derivation: from Mount Iros

2n = 24

43. *S. longiusculus* Ochoa (Phytologia **63**(5), 329–30, 1987)

Leaf 5-jugate, with 5–7-jugate interjected leaflets; rachis with simple hairs and glands; leaf surfaces densely pilose. Peduncle long (10 cm), many flowered, puberulent; pedicels articulated high up. Corolla rotate-pentagonal, 3.0 cm diam., blue-violet. Berries oval, 1.5 cm long.

Distribution: Peru, dept Apurímac, at 3,400–3,500 m, in cold places, puna and subpuna, amongst rocks and shrubs.

Derivation: moderately long, presumably referring to the peduncle

From the description and illustration this species would seem to be very close to, if not identical with, *S. pampasense*. Since I have seen no material I cannot be certain, however.

2n = 24

44. *S. lopez-camarenae* Ochoa (An. Cient. Univ. Agr., Lima, **12**(1), 12–16, 1974)

Leaf 4–5-jugate, with 3–8-jugate minute interjected leaflets; laterals narrow-lanceolate, strongly acuminate; whole leaf glabrous or glabrescent. Pedicels articulated near calyx. Corolla rotate, purple, 2.5–2.8(–3.8) cm diam. Fruits rotund.

Distribution: north Peru, dept Cajamarca, at 2,700 m in damp shrubby places with *Hypericum, Fuchsia, Miconia,* etc.

Ochoa placed this species in series *Ingifolia*, but since the rachis is not winged in the photograph and drawings exhibited, I prefer to place it for the time being in series *Tuberosa*.

Derivation: dedicated to the Peruvian potato agronomist Pedro López Camarena

45. *S. parvicorollatum* Lechn. (Trudy po Prickl. Bot. Genet. Selek. **105**, 12–13, 1980)

Leaf said to be similar to that of *S. andigenum* [*S. tuberosum* subsp. *andigena*] var. *ccusi*, but with smaller leaflets. Calyx black, slightly bilabiate. Corolla small, blue-violet, 2.6 cm diam., rotate-pentagonal.

Distribution: central Peru, Huancayo, at 2,600 m on the Villarica to Tarma road. Said to be ruderal.

Derivation: with a small corolla

This may very likely be an escape or 'volunteer' ('ground keeper') of a cultivated species, but since I have seen no specimen or illustration I cannot be certain which would be involved – probably subsp. *andigena*, but no chromosome count is given.

VIR

46. *S. quillonanum** Ochoa ined.

S. tenellum Ochoa (Phytologia **63**(6), 455–6, 1987; non *S. tenellum* Bitt., Fedde, Repert. **11**, 219, 1912 – sect. Morella)

Plant small, 20–30 cm tall. Leaf delicate, pale green, 4–5-jugate, with 3–6 pairs of interjected leaflets; lateral leaflets lanceolate to narrow-elliptic, more or less

---

*For some reason Ochoa has now changed this name to *S. chillonanum* Ochoa (Phytologia, **67** (3), 235, 1989).

sessile, above shortly hairy, below only on veins. Peduncle 8 cm long; pedicels with dense short hairs. Corolla white, rotate-pentagonal, 2.5 cm diam. Berry globose. Distribution: Peru, dept Apurímac, near Quillo, at 4,000 m on the high cold puna. Derivation: 'a dwarf Solanum from Quillo', according to the author

This species is said by Ochoa to be rather simlar to *S. gracilifrons* but the two species grow in such distinct habitats that the similarity is perhaps not indicative of true relationship. (No specimen seen.)

47. *S. sarasarae* Ochoa (Phytologia **64**(4), 245–6, 1988)

Leaf (5–)6-jugate, with some 12–15 pairs of interjected leaflets, sparsely pilose. Pedicels articulated high up, 4 mm below calyx base. Corolla rotate or rotate-pentagonal, 2.0–2.5 cm diam., pale blue-violet. Fruit globose, pale green, 1.0–1.4 cm diam.
Distribution: Peru, dept Ayacucho, Sara-sara, at 3,000 m in the *Polylepis*, *Lobivia* zone of the pre-puna.

Ochoa observes that in leaf dissection this species resembles *S. bukasovii*, but differs from it in the delicate pubescence, small corolla and other features. (No specimen seen.)
Derivation: from the place where it was collected
2n = 24

48. *S. sawyeri* Ochoa (Amer. Potato J. **58**(12), 649–52, 1981)

Leaves short, wide, 3–4-jugate, with 1–3-jugate interjected leaflets; leaves of fine texture, delicate, soft, thinly pilose to glabrescent; leaflets broad-ovate, subsessile. Peduncle 2 cm or more long, shortly, sparsely pubescent, as are pedicel and calyx. Corolla rotate, purple, 3.0–3.5 cm diam. Berries orbicular or slightly ovate. (No specimen seen.)
Distribution: south Peru, dept Cuzco, in the humid subtropics at 2,300 m in forests.
Derivation: dedicated in honour of Dr R.L. Sawyer, founder and director of the International Potato Center in Peru
2n = 24

49. *S. scabrifolium* Ochoa (Darwiniana **17**, 427–9, 1972)

Leaves coriacious, 4–5-jugate, with 0–2 pairs of interjected leaflets; margins slightly curled; leaf scabrous above. Corolla rotate, dark violet. Berry round to ovoid.
Distribution: Peru, dept Huánuco, at 2,940 m. Habitat not noted.

Despite seeming to be somewhat related to series *Piurana* the type specimen photograph does not look much like that series. I have not seen the type collection, only another one at Sturgeon Bay from a different place and under another number (S-60), which does not agree too well with the type description.
Derivation: leaf rough to the touch, due to the presence of small spines (really very short stiff projections)
Stur. (? – see above), VIR

50. *S. tapojense* Ochoa (Phytologia **46**(4), 223, 1980)

Leaf 3–4-jugate, with 2–3 small interjected leaflets; leaflets elliptic-lanceolate, all with short hairs above and below. Corolla rotate, small, 2.5–2.8 cm diam., dark purple. Berries globular to oval, 1.0–1.2 cm diam.

Distribution: south Peru, dept Puno, near the Bolivian border, at 3,850 m in puna vegetation.

According to Hawkes and Hjerting (1989, 305) this species is almost certainly a synonym of *S. leptophyes*, which is common in Bolivia and just enters into Peru in the region mentioned by Ochoa. Unfortunately they were not able to see the type specimen.

Derivation: from Tapoje, the place where Ochoa's specimen was collected

51. S. tarapatanum Ochoa (An. Cient. Univ. Agric., Lima, **15**(1–4), 1, 1977)

Leaf long, narrow, delicate, 6–7-jugate, with 5–10 pairs of interjected leaflets. Primary laterals narrow lanceolate, pale green with sparse long hairs above, more dense below. Pedicel articulation in lower third. Corolla rotate, purple, 2.5–3.0 cm diam. Berry round to ovoid.

Distribution: south Peru, dept Cuzco, at 2,600–2,800 m in dry xerophytic vegetation with *Opuntias* etc. (I have seen no material or illustration.)

Derivation: from the place where it was collected

$2n = 24$

52. S. taulisense Ochoa (Lorentzia, Córdoba, No. 4, 13–15, 1981)

Leaf 3–4–(–5)-jugate, with 2–3(–5) interjected leaflets; laterals elliptic to narrow-elliptic, sessile to subsessile, sparsely pilose above, below on the veins also. Corolla rotate, 3.0–3.5 cm diam., violet. Berries ovoid, pyriform, to 2.5 cm long and 2.0 cm diam.

Distribution: north Peru, dept La Libertad, Jalcas (high moors) of Tauli at 3,700–3,800 m in *Stipa* grassland or relic *Polylepis* woodland.

I have seen no material or illustration. Ochoa thinks it might have affinity with *S. chomatophilum* Bitt. (series *Conicibaccata*).

Derivation: from the place where it was collected

$2n = 24$

53. S. velardei Ochoa (An. Cient. Univ. Agr. **1**(3), 216–20, 1963)

Leaf 2–4-jugate, with 0–2 pairs of interjected leaflets; both leaf surfaces with dense, short slender hairs; terminal leaflet much larger than laterals, to sub-orbiculate, with acute or apiculate apex and truncate to cordate base; laterals much smaller and narrower. Corolla rotate to subpentagonal, blue, 3.0–3.5 cm diam., with 2 mm long acumens. Berries subglobose to ovoid, to 1.5 cm long.

Distribution: south Peru, dept Apurímac at 2,200–2,900 m in temperate, dry valleys. (I have seen no material.)

The leaf of this species reminds one of *S. alandiae* from Bolivia, but this may not be indicative of genetic affinity.

Derivation: dedicated to the late Peruvian botanist, Dr Octavio Velarde Núñez

XVI   *Tuberosa* (wild species)

Group (iii)   Bolivia, Argentina and Chile

Series *Tuberosa* species do not occur in Brazil, Paraguay or Uruguay, their place being taken by species in series *Commersoniana* and *Yungasensa*.

There are very few series *Tuberosa* species in Chile, probably only one in fact. This is *S. tuberosum* which has been found as an escape here and there, and has been given various other species names (see under *S. tuberosum*).

Although the region now under discussion is much larger than Peru, there are only some half the number of species in this southern region compared with Peru. Some 24 species and nine species hybrids are now recognized. The reason for the fewer species here may be partly due to the fewer closed valley systems in Bolivia and Argentina, as compared with Peru. Even so, about 14 species are restricted in their distribution, whilst 10 are widespread.

The species of both Argentina and Bolivia have received monographic treatment (Hawkes and Hjerting 1969, 1989) and have been widely collected also by many scientists. Hence all the species from this region are known to me and most are represented in the living state in genetic resources collections.

Note: descriptions and drawings of most of the Bolivian species are to be found in Hawkes and Hjerting (1989) and most of the Argentinian species in Hawkes and Hjerting (1969).

KEY TO SPECIES, EXCLUDING HYBRIDS

(1) Stems and leaves with dense, long- and short-stalked glands   (2)
    Stems and leaves without glands, or at most with a few short-stalked ones   (3)
(2) Flowers white, rotate; interjected leaflets none or few and very minute (Bolivia)   **18. *S. neocardenasii***
    Flowers pale mauve, substellate to pentagonal; leaves with well-developed, interjected leaflets (Bolivia)   **4. *S. berthaultii***
(3) Flowers white   (4)
    Flowers pale blue, purple, mauve, magenta and white, etc.*   (8)
(4) Plant completely glabrous (or occasionally subglabrous   (5)
    Plant pubescent   (6)
(5) Terminal leaf lobe long-ovate; laterals minute; sepal acumens narrow (Argentina)   **31. *S. venturii***
    Terminal leaf lobe broad-ovate; laterals large, though not as large as terminal; sepals ovate, obtuse, without acumens (Bolivia)   **9. *S. gandarillasii***
(6) Leaf 3–4(–5)-jugate; leaflets narrow ovate-lanceolate; terminal same size as laterals (Argentina)   **14. *S. kurtzianum*** (in part)
    Leaf 0–2(–4)-jugate; leaflets broad ovate; terminal much larger than laterals   (7)
(7) Leaves and other green parts densely pubescent; hairs fairly long; stem wings 1–2 mm or more (Argentina and Bolivia)   **16. *S. microdontum***

---

*Some *S. tuberosum* subsp. *tuberosum* varieties also possess white flowers.

Leaves and other green parts sparsely pubescent; hairs short to very short; stem wings very narrow (0–1 mm) (Argentina and Bolivia)
20. *S. okadae*

(8) Leaves with 1–2(–4) pairs of lateral leaflets, diminishing in size rapidly towards leaf base and generally smaller than terminal leaflets (9)

Leaf with at least 4 pairs of more or less sub-equal lateral leaflets, the uppermost similar in size to terminals (14)

(9) Leaf pubescence sparse; leaf thick, fleshy (Argentina)
13. *S. incamayoense*

Leaf pubescence of frequent to dense hairs; leaf not fleshy (10)

(10) Flower very rotate, deep purple, with rounded shoulders (Bolivia)
12. *S. hoopesii*

Flower not as above, rotate/pentagonal (11)

(11) Flower pale blue-mauve; upper leaflet pair decurrent, sessile to subsessile (Bolivia) **2. *S. alandiae***

Flowers darker purple; upper leaflet pair not decurrent (12)

(12) Pubescence soft, densely velvety on upper surface, especially on young leaves (Bolivia) **3. *S. avilesii***

Pubescence not of that type (13)

(13) Leaflets 2–3(–4)-jugate, apically acuminate, petiolulate; plant robust, upright (Bolivia) **33. *S. virgultorum***

Leaflets 1–2(–3)-jugate, apically obtuse to acute, sessile to subsessile; plant delicate, decumbent (Argentina) **19. *S. neorossii***

(14) Leaf large, well-developed; tubers large, edible (south Argentina; south Chile) **29. *S. tuberosum*** (naturalized)

Leaf not as large, or if so, tubers small, inedible (15)

(15) Stigma very minute, no thicker than style apex (16)

Stigma clearly thicker than style apex, globular to clavate (17)

(16) Plant normally growing in a low rosette; style straight, 6–8 mm long; corolla rotate; lobes flat (Bolivia) **1. *S. achacachense***

Plant robust; style curved, 10–14 mm long; corolla pentagonal to substellate; lobes pointed (Bolivia and Argentina)
21. *S. oplocense*

(17) Pubescence of upper leaf surface short and sparse to very sparse (18)

Pubescence of upper leaf surface medium to long and moderately to very dense (20)

(18) Leaflets apically acuminate, basally cuneate and narrowly decurrent on to petiolules and winged rachis (Bolivia) **11. *S. hondelmannii***

Leaflets apically acute to acuminate, basally rounded to subcordate, not or rarely decurrent (19)

(19) Stem wings crisped; upper leaf surface shining, rugose, non-pigmented; stigma clavate (Bolivia, Peru) **25. *S. sparsipilum***

Stem wings straight; upper leaf surface not shining or rugose, often with pink veins and rachis; stigma large, globose (Bolivia)
28. *S. sucrense*

(20) Corolla white with magenta streaks on outside petal centres (Argentina) **14. *S. kurtzianum*** (in part)

Corolla entirely blue, purple etc., never streaked (21)
(21) Pubescence on underside of leaf densely velvety-tomentose; plant tall, vigorous (Argentina) **32. S. vernei**
Pubescence on underside of leaf not densely velvety tomentose; plants of medium growth (22)
(22) Interjected leaflets very numerous, up to 20–25 pairs per leaf (23)
Interjected leaflets not very numerous, generally 2–5 pairs per leaf (24)
(23) Lateral leaflets generally three times as long as broad, frequently sub-opposite; terminal leaflet the same size or slightly smaller than laterals (Argentina) **26. S. spegazzinii**
Lateral leaflets about twice as long as broad, always opposite; terminal leaflet slightly broader than laterals, even though slightly shorter (Bolivia) **30. S. ugentii**
(24) Upper leaf surface pubescence dense, long, appressed; stem violet-marbled (Bolivia) **7. S. candolleanum**
Upper leaf surface pubescence sub-appressed, dense to sparse; stem not violet-marbled (25)
(25) Upper leaf surface hairs sub-appressed, dense; corolla deep, rich purple (Bolivia) **5. S. brevicaule**
Upper leaf surface with medium dense to rather sparse pubescence; corolla medium purple (26)
(26) Plant of medium vigour; leaflets broader in basal leaves than in those near apex (Bolivia) **15. S. leptophyes**
Plant delicate, spreading; leaflets in all leaves delicate, narrow (Argentina, Bolivia) **10. S. gourlayi**

1. S. achacachense Cárd. (Bol. Soc. Peruana Bot. **5**, 30–1, 1956)

Plant very small, generally to 8 cm. Leaf 2–3-jugate, with 0–1-jugate interjected leaflets (but larger numbers and dimensions under cultivation); all leaflets with scattered, coarse, white, short to medium appressed hairs. Pedicels articulated rather high up. Corolla very rotate, with rather flat lobes, blue-violet, 2.0–2.5 cm diam. Style 6–8 mm long. Stigma very minute. Berries globular.
Distribution: north Bolivia, dept La Paz, at 3,900–4,250 m in high moist puna vegetation amongst short grasses and herbs.
Derivation: from Achacachi, near the place where this species is found
2n = 24
Braun.?

2. S. alandiae Cárd. (Bol. Soc. Peruana Bot. **5**, 11–12, 1956)

S. torrecillasense Cárd. (Bol. Soc. Peruana Bot. **5**, 15–16, 1956)

Leaf 2–3(–4)-jugate, with no interjected leaflets except under cultivation; terminal and upper lateral pair very similar, lower pairs much smaller; upper and lower leaf surfaces densely clothed with short, white hairs.

Corolla rotate-pentagonal, 2.0–3.0 cm diam., pale to medium blue-violet. Berries globular.
Distribution: Bolivia, depts Cochabamba and Santa Cruz, generally at 2,300–3,000 m, in dry regions with cacti and drought-resistant shrubs.
Derivation: named in honour of the well-known Bolivian potato agronomist, Ing. Segundo Alandia
2n = 24
Braun., Stur., VIR

3. *S. avilesii* Hawkes et Hjerting (Bot. J. Linn. Soc. **86**, 410–12, 1983)

S. candelarianum Cárd. *pro parte* (Bol. Soc. Peruana Bot. **5**, 12–13, 1956; non *S. candelarianum* Buk., Bull. Appl. Bot. Genet. Pl. Breed., Suppl. 47, 218–19, 1930)

Leaf (1–)2–3-jugate, with 0–2-jugate interjected leaflets; terminal larger than laterals, which decrease in size rapidly towards leaf base. Pubescence soft, densely velvety. Corolla rotate-pentagonal, deep violet-purple, 2.0–3.0 cm diam. Berries globular.
Distribution: Bolivia, dept Santa Cruz, at 2,700–2,950 m, amongst shrubs and degraded forest in a humid climate.
Derivation: named in honour of Ing. Agr. Israel Avilés from Bolivia, who collected this material with Hjerting and myself on our 1980 expedition
2n = 24
Braun., Stur.

4. *S. berthaultii* Hawkes (Bull. Imp. Bur. Pl. Breed. Genet., Cambridge, 122, 1944)

S. vallegrandense Cárd. (Bol. Soc. Peruana Bot. **5**, 23–4, 1956)
S. vallegrandense var. *pojoense* Cárd. (Bol. Soc. Peruana Bot. **5**, 24–5, 1956)
S. candelarianum Cárd. *pro parte* (ibid. 12–13, 1956; non *S. candelarianum* Buk., Bull. Appl. Bot. Genet. Pl. Breed., Suppl. 47, 218–19, 1930)
S. tarijense Hawkes, var. *pojoense* (Cárd.) Corr. (Wrightia **2**, 173–4, 1961)

A very glandular species covered on all green parts with short- and long-stalked glands (trichome Types A and B). Leaf (3–)4–5(–6)-jugate with (0–)5–7(–10)-jugate interjected leaflets, including acroscopics and basiscopics. Corolla pale blue-violet to mauve, pentagonal to substellate, 2.5–3.5 cm diam. Berry globose to sub-ovoid, 1.5–2.5 cm long.
Distribution: Bolivia, depts Chuquisaca, Cochabamba, Potosí and Santa Cruz (but commonest in the first two), at 2,400–2,750 m in rather dry interandine valleys among *Prosopis* scrub and cactus vegetation.
Derivation: named in honour of the distinguished French *Solanum* taxonomist, Pierre Berthault

2n = 24; EBN = 2
Braun., CPC, Gr.Lü., Stur., VIR

5. *S. brevicaule* Bitt. (Fedde, Repert. **11**, 390–1, 1912)

S. liriunianum Cárd. et Hawkes (J. Linn. Soc., Bot. **53**, 106–8, 1946)
S. colominense Cárd. (Bol. Soc. Peruana Bot. **5**, 21–3, 1956)

A low-growing bushy species with (1–)3–4(–6)-jugate leaves and (0–)7(–13) pairs of interjected leaflets; pubescence of very frequent, long, white conspicuous hairs above, shorter below. Corolla deep rich violet-purple, rotate, 2.5–3.0(–4.0) cm diam. Berry globose to slightly oval, 2.0 cm diam.
Distribution: Bolivia, dept Cochabamba, where it is very common, at 3,000–3,850 m, in puna vegetation, *Polylepis* woodland and amongst *Escallonia*, *Berberis*, etc.
'*S. colominense*' was based on poorly developed specimens growing in rocky soil in full sun. '*S. liriunianum*' was described from material in very humid, shaded conditions.
Derivation: so called because of its short stem, but this feature is not diagnostic for *S. brevicaule*
2n = 24; EBN = 2
Braun., CPC, Gr.Lü., Stur., VIR

6. *S.* × *bruecheri* Correll (Wrightia **2**(4), 176–7, 1961)

Said by Correll to show some affinity with several species, but mainly with *S. acaule*, *S. sanctae-rosae* and *S. infundibuliforme*. Type: *Brucher 557(22)*.
   In my view this is undoubtedly a natural hybrid of *S. gourlayi* × *S. infundibuliforme*, occurring in north-west Argentina, prov. Jujuy. I previously thought it to be a hybrid of *S. acaule* × *S. megistacrolobum*. It might occur in Bolivia also but has so far not been found in that country.
Derivation: named in honour of the German geneticist and potato collector Dr Heinz Brücher

7. *S. candolleanum* Berth. (Ann. Sci. Agron., Paris, Ser. 3, **2**, 185, 1911)

S. mandonii A.DC. (Arch. Sci, Phys. Nat. **15**, 438, 1886; non *S. mandonis* Heurck et Muell. Arg. in Heurck, Obs. Bot. **78**, 1870)

Leaf (3–)4–5(–6)-jugate with about 3–6-jugate interjected leaflets; laterals ovate-lanceolate; pubescence of very dense, long, white, appressed hairs above, shorter below. Inflorescence branches with dense, long, rather spreading hairs. Corolla purple, rotate, 2.5–3.5(–4.0) cm diam., with short broad lobes. Berries globular (to oval?).
Distribution: north Bolivia, dept La Paz, from 3,500–4,000 m in high rainfall 'ceja' forest amongst grasses and small shrubs.
Derivation: named by Berthault in honour of the distinguished Swiss

phytogeographer, Alphonse de Candolle
2n = 24
Braun., Stur., VIR

8. *S.* × *doddsii* Corr. (Wrightia **2**, 186–7, 1961)

Leaf 3–5-jugate, glabrescent, with petiolulate laterals and very few interjecteds. Rest of green parts also glabrous. Corolla substellate, light lavender.

This is a hybrid of *S. chacoense* Bitt. × *S. alandiae* Cárd. From a study of living material collected by Hawkes *et al.* in 1971 from the type of locality there is no doubt that this is a hybrid, as shown above, which tends to segregate towards the two parents (see Hawkes and Hjerting 1989 for further details).

Distribution: Bolivia, dept Cochabamba, at 2,600 m. The habitat and the hybrid have now been destroyed.

Derivation: named in honour of the British potato geneticist, Dr K. Dodds

2n = 24; EBN = 2

Stur., VIR

9. *S. gandarillasii* Cárd. (Bol. Soc. Peruana Bot. **5**, 16–20, 1956)

A very distinct species, entirely glabrous, with enlarged terminal and (0–)1–2(–3)-jugate laterals, decreasing in size towards the leaf base; interjected leaflets normally absent. Calyx with curious leafy or bract-like obtuse sepals, with no acumen. Corolla white, pentagonal to rotate (1.5–)2.0–2.5 cm diam. Berries globular to slightly ovoid, 2.0–2.5 cm diam.

Distribution: Bolivia, found very sparingly in depts Chuquisaca, Cochabamba and Santa Cruz, at 1,800–2,500 m in the dry summer-green *Prosopis/Acacia/Jatropha* woodland under bushes and cacti.

Derivation: dedicated to the well-known Bolivian agricultural scientist, Humberto Gandarillas

2n = 24; EBN = 2

Braun., CPC, Gr.Lü., Stur., VIR

10. *S. gourlayi* Hawkes (Bull. Imp. Bur. Pl. Breed. Genet., Cambridge, 120–21, 1944)

Small rosette, semi-rosette or short-stemmed plants with (3–)4–5(–6)-jugate leaf and (2–)4–6(–12) pairs of interjected leaflets; laterals ovate-lanceolate to lanceolate; upper surface with sparse to frequent rather short hairs. Calyx 4–6 mm long. Corolla dark purple, pentagonal, with well-marked acumens, (1.5–)2.0–3.0 cm diam. Berries globular, 1.0–1.5 cm diam.

General distribution: central to southern Bolivia and north-west Argentina. (See below under subspecies.)

This species has been divided into four subspecies.

KEY TO SUBSPECIES

(1) Leaves with slender, medium-lengthed hairs above (Argentina)   (2)
     Leaves with long and silky or very short and thick hairs above   (3)
(2) Terminal leaflet larger than laterals; laterals normally 3-paired;
     petiolules short (Argentina)   **10a. subsp. *gourlayi***
     Terminal leaflet the same size as laterals; laterals normally 4-paired
     (Argentina)   **10b. subsp. *saltense***
(3) Leaves with long, silky hairs above and generally well-marked
     marginal teeth (Argentina and Bolivia)   **10c. subsp. *vidaurrei***
     Leaves with short, thick triangular hairs above; marginal teeth not
     very well-marked (Bolivia)   **10d. subsp. *pachytrichum***

10a. Subspecies *gourlayi*

This tends to be low-growing and semi-rosetted in habit; terminal leaflet
larger than laterals, which are generally 3-paired; leaflets sessile to shortly
(–3 mm) petiolulate.
Distribution: Argentina, prov. Jujuy, at 1,900–3,600 m, in rather dry pre-
puna to puna vegetation amongst grasses, cacti and small shrubs.
   Diploid and tetraploid cytotypes occur.
Derivation: named after the British plant collector, Dr W.B. Gourlay
2n = 24; EBN = 2. 2n = 48; EBN = 4
Bal., Braun., CPC, Gr.Lü., Stur., VIR

10b. Subspecies *saltense* Clausen et Okada (Phytologia **62**(3), 165–7, 1987)

Low-growing, with terminal leaflet the same size as the laterals which are
4-paired; petiolules 2–5 mm long.
Distribution: Argentina, prov. Salta, depts La Poma and Los Andes, at
3,300–3,900 m on rocky hillsides, stream banks and cultivated fields.
Derivation: named after the Argentine province in which this subspecies
occurs
2n = 24; EBN = 2
Bal., Braun., Stur.

10c. subspecies *vidaurrei* (Cárd). Hawkes et Hjerting (Potatoes of Bolivia, 284, 1989)

S. vidaurrei Cárd. (Bol. Soc. Peruana Bot. **5**, 26–30, 1956)

This is a more slender graceful plant with rather narrow leaflets, leaf hairs
long and silky and generally well-marked marginal teeth.
Distribution: Argentina, prov. Salta; Bolivia, depts Chuquisaca and
Tarija, at 2,700–3,450 m, in humid high level grassland and *Polylepis*
woodland.
Derivation: dedicated to the Bolivian botanist, Professor Arturo Vidaurre
2n = 24; EBN = 2
Braun., Stur., VIR

10d. Subspecies *pachytrichum* **(Hawkes) Hawkes et Hjerting** (Potatoes of Bolivia, 284, 1989)

S. pachytrichum Hawkes (Bull. Imp. Bur. Pl. Breed. Genet., Cambridge, 121–2, 1944)

A slender graceful plant with rather narrow leaflets and scattered, very short, thick, few-celled hairs on upper leaf surface. Contrasts with previous three subspecies in the larger number (–12 pairs) of interjected leaflets. Distribution: central Bolivia, depts Chuquisaca and Potosí, at 2,600–2,900 m in drier zones than subsp. *vidaurrei*, and a wide range of natural and man-made habitats.
Derivation: thick-haired, referring to the leaf pubescence
2n = 24
Stur. (*Astley 92*, as *S. leptophyes*), (*Ugent 4909*)

11. *S. hondelmannii* Hawkes et Hjerting (Bot. J. Linn. Soc. **90**, 110–11, 1985)

Leaf 4–5-jugate with 2–3-jugate interjected leaflets; petiolules long, 5–10(–20) mm long; leaflets with very sparse, short, thick hairs, also present on inflorescence branches. Corolla rotate to pentagonal, blue-violet, 1.5–2.5(–3.0) cm diam. Stigma thicker than style apex.
Distribution: Bolivia, depts Chuquisaca and Potosí at 2,600–2,700 m, in dry areas with thorn bushes (*Prosopis*, etc.) and in field borders.
   This species is closely related to *S. oplocense*, differing particularly in the larger numbers of interjected leaflets, longer petiolules, style exserted for only 2–3 mm and larger stigma.
Derivation: named in honour of the distinguished German scientist Professor W. Hondelmann who led the German team on the 1980 Bolivian expedition
2n = 24
Braun., Stur. (not in inventory)

12. *S. hoopesii* Hawkes et Okada (Phytologia **64**(5), 325–27, 1988)

Leaf (2–)3(–4)-jugate, with 0–2(–5)-jugate interjected leaflets; petiolules 3–7(–10) mm long, terminal broader than laterals; upper leaf surface with rather frequent short appressed hairs. Peduncle branches long, from 8 to 21 cm long. Corolla showy, rich purple, rotate, 2.0–3.0 cm diam., with rounded or shouldered lobes. Berries spherical.
Distribution: Bolivia, dept Chuquisaca, prov. Azurduy.
   The tetraploid chromosome number is noteworthy for a species in series *Tuberosa* (see also *S. ugentii*).
Derivation: named in honour of Dr R.W. Hoopes, who worked and collected in Bolivia for many years
2n = 48
Stur. (not in inventory. *Hoopes et al. 160* and *157*)

13. *S. incamayoense* **Okada et Clausen** (Amer. Potato J. **60**(6), 433–9, 1983)

Plants of low habit. Leaf thick, rather fleshy, (2–)3(–4)-jugate; laterals smaller than terminal, decreasing rapidly towards leaf base; interjected leaflets (0–)1(–2)-paired, small, orbicular; leaf sparsely pubescent. Corolla purple-violet or light blue, pentagonal, 2.5–3.0 cm diam. Berry spherical, 1.0 cm diam.
Distribution: north-west Argentina, prov. Salta.

Differs from *S. gourlayi*, to which it bears some resemblance, in the enlarged terminal leaflet, generally broader laterals, glaucous fleshy leaflets and low growth.
Derivation: from the place name Incamayo, where it was first collected
2n = 24
Bal., Braun., Stur., VIR

14. *S. kurtzianum* **Bitt. et Wittm.** (Bot. Jahrb **50**, Suppl., 548–50, 1914)

S. commersonii Dun. var. *pilosiusculum* Hook. f. (Fl. Antarct. **2**, 330, 1846)
S. commersonii Dun. var. *glanduloso-pubescens* Hook. f. (Fl. Antarct. **2**, 330, 1846)
S. velascanum Bitt. et Wittm. (Bot. Jahrb. **50**, Suppl. 551–2, 1914)
S. macolae Buk. (Rev. Argent. Agron. **4**, 239–40, 1937)
S. improvidum Brüch. (Rev. Fac. Cien. Agr., Mendoza, **9**(2), 1114, 1962)

Distinguished by the elliptic-obtuse to oblong leaflets with well-marked marginal hairs set on cushions of tissue and visible without a lens.
Leaf 3–4(–5)-jugate, 0–3(–5)-jugate interjected leaflets. Pubescence of rather short, thick, appressed hairs above, smaller below. Pedicel articulation close to base (1–4 mm above) or to about the centre. Corolla white or white with a rich deep purple central streak on outside of petals, pentagonal to substellate, 1.5–3.0(–3.5) cm diam. Berry globular.
Distribution: Argentina, provs Catamarca, La Rioja, Mendoza and San Juan, at 1,400–2,500 m, in dry areas amongst stones, herbs and bushes in the vegetation zone known as Monte (see Hawkes and Hjerting 1969, 36–7).
Derivation: named in honour of the distinguished German botanist, F. Kurtz, Professor of Botany at Córdoba University, Argentina, from 1884 to 1915.
2n = 24; EBN = 2
Bal., Braun., CPC, Gr.Lü., Stur., VIR

15. *S. leptophyes* **Bitt.** (Fedde, Repert. **12**, 448–9, 1913)

A low-growing slender species with narrow-lanceolate leaflets 3–4 times as long as broad. Leaf (2–)4(–6)-jugate, with (0–)2–5(–8) pairs of interjected leaflets, all with fairly frequent, unequal-lengthed, coarse, appressed hairs.

Corolla violet-purple, rotate-pentagonal, 1.8–2.5(–3.0) cm diam. Berries globular to slightly oval, 2.0 cm diam.
Distribution: Bolivia, depts Chuquisaca, La Paz, Oruro and Potosí; Peru, dept Puno; at 3,200–3,950 m. In puna vegetation, tola heath, *Stipa* grassland, etc. and field borders and roadsides, in medium dry zones.

Under very dry conditions this species develops into a very small plant (as in the type specimen). I think it may well be the ancestor of the cultivated potato, *S. stenotomum*. It is probably the same as Ochoa's *S. tapojense* (see pp. 153–4).
Derivation: slender growth, referring to the very small type specimen, evidently collected from a very dry locality
2n = 24; EBN = 2
Braun., Gr.Lü., Stur., VIR

16. *S. microdontum* Bitt. (Fedde, Repert. **10**, 535–6, 1912; *emend* Hawkes et Hjerting, Phyton, Graz **9**, 144–5, 1960)

S. bijugum Bitt. (Fedde, Repert. **10**, 533, 1912)
S. cevallos-tovari Cárd. (Bol. Soc. Peruana Bot. **5**, 13–15, 1956)
S. higueranum Cárd. (Bol. Soc. Peruana Bot. **5**, 20–21, 1956)

Large plants with winged stems and large, simple to 2(–3)-jugate leaves, the terminal generally much larger than the laterals; interjected leaflets very rare; pubescence coarse, shining, of frequent multicellular, appressed, white to yellowish hairs; leaf margins minutely denticulate, the teeth ending in hairs. Inflorescence branches with appressed upward-pointing hairs. Calyx with unequal-lengthed sepal acumens. Corolla white, substellate to rotate, (1.5–)2.0–3.5(–4.0) cm diam. Berries spherical.
Distribution: very widespread (see subspecies).

KEY TO SUBSPECIES

Stem slender, 1.5–3(–5) mm diam.; wings 0–1(–2.5) mm wide, generally
straight   **16a. subsp. *microdontum***
Stem robust, 3–10(–20) mm diam.; wings 2.5 mm wide, generally undulate
to crisped and marginally crenulate to denticulate
                                                 16b. subsp. *gigantophyllum*

16a. Subspecies *microdontum*

(For synonyms, see above.)

Stem more slender than that of subsp. *gigantophyllum* (see key). Terminal and lateral leaflets more or less the same size, not longer than 8 cm.
Distribution: Bolivia, depts Chuquisaca, Cochabamba, Santa Cruz and Tarija; Argentina, provs Jujuy and Salta; at 1,800–3,100 m, in very humid forests, or shrub and grassland degraded from these forests and particularly associated with *Alnus jorullensis* and *Podocarpus* species.

Derivation: the name refers to the minute teeth on the leaflet margins
2n = 24; EBN = 2
Bal., Braun., Gr.Lü., Stur., VIR

16b. Subspecies *gigantophyllum* (Bitter) Hawkes et Hjerting (Phyton **9**, 144–5, 1960)

S. gigantophyllum Bitt. (Fedde, Repert. **11**, 368–9), 1912)
S. simplicifolium Bitt. (ibid. **11**, 369–70, 1912)
S. simplicifolium subsp. *gigantophyllum* Bitt. (ibid. **12**, 445, 1913)
S. simplicifolium var. *metriophyllum* Bitt. (ibid. **12**, 445, 1913)
S. simplicifolium var. *mollifrons* Bitt. (ibid. **12**, 445–6, 1913)
S. simplicifolium var. *trimerophyllum* Bitt. (ibid. **12**, 446, 1913)
S. simplicifolium var. *variabile* Brücher et Ross (Lilloa **26**, 465–6, 1953)
S. microdontum Bitt. var. *gigantophyllum* (Bitt.) Ochoa (Phytologia **57**(5), 321, 1985)

Stem more robust than that of subsp. *microdontum* (see key). Terminal generally much larger than laterals, at times simple, with no laterals and up to 18(–37) cm long × 9(–16) cm broad.
Distribution: Bolivia, depts Chuquisaca, Cochabamba, La Paz and Tarija; Argentina, provs Catamarca, Jujuy, La Rioja, Salta and Tucumán, at similar altitudes and habitat to subsp. *microdontum*. Subsp. *gigantophyllum* is much more widespread, however, and in the southern parts of its range is found amongst boulders and in rock crevices.
 The rather large number of varieties is indicative of the wide range of phenotypes shown by this species, but they intergrade and are not worthy of true varietal status.
Derivation: with a giant-sized leaf
2n = 24; EBN = 2. 2n = 36 in La Rioja and Catamarca provinces, as well as the usual diploids (Okada 1981)
Bal., Braun., CPC, Gr.Lü., Stur., VIR

***S. microdontum* Bitt. var. *montepuncoense* Ochoa** (Phytologia **46**(4), 244, 1980)
This is a natural hybrid of *S. violaceimarmoratum* × *S. microdontum*. It possesses a violet corolla with white acumens and paler margin. 2n = 24 (see also Hawkes and Hjerting 1989, 183–4).
Distribution: Bolivia, dept Cochabamaba, prov. Carrasco, near Montepunco, hence the name.

17. *S.* × *mollepujroense* Cárd. et Hawkes (J. Linn. Soc. Bot. **53**, 103–4, 1946)

Has affinities with *S. sparsipilum*, but differs in the long, oblong leaflets. The leaf pubescence is of fairly sparse, short, thick hairs. This is almost certainly a hybrid of *S. gourlayi* subsp. *pachytrichum* × *S. sparsipilum*; it is discussed in detail in Hawkes and Hjerting (1989, 294). Two collections from the type locality are analysed.

Distribution: Bolivia, dept Cochabamba, Mollepujro, at 3,600 m.

Derivation: from the name of the locality where it was collected

18. *S. neocardenasii* Hawkes et Hjerting (Bot. J. Linn. Soc. **86**, 411–13, 1983)

All green parts of plant densely covered with short and long glandular hairs (trichome Types A and B). Leaf delicate, narrow (3–)4–5(–6)-jugate; leaflets ovate-cordate, with long petiolules (12–20 mm); interjected leaflets minute, few to none. Pedicel articulation quite high. Corolla rotate, white, 2.0–2.5 cm diam.; anthers pale lemon-yellow. Berries globular.

Distribution: Bolivia, dept Santa Cruz, known only from one locality near Mataral, at 1,400 m under shade of thorn trees amongst spiny ground bromeliads in a dry, very hot locality.

This species, like *S. berthaultii*, is aphid resistant, but bears no close resemblance to *S. berthaultii*.

Derivation: a new (or second) species named in honour of the distinguished Bolivian botanist, Professor M. Cárdenas

2n = 24

Braun., Stur.

19. *S. neorossii* Hawkes et Hjerting (Bot. J. Linn. Soc. **86**, 414–15, 1983)

A low-growing decumbent herb with small (0–)1–3(–4)-jugate leaves and (0–)1–3-jugate interjected pairs; lateral leaflets much smaller than the large, broad-ovate terminal, and diminishing in size rapidly towards the leaf base; leaf pubescence sparse to medium dense, of rather short, appressed hairs. Pedicels articulated quite high up. Corolla rotate, showy, violet purple, 2.5–3.5 cm diam. (to 5.0 cm under cultivation). Style long-exserted (3–4 mm). Berries globular to short oval.

Distribution: Argentina, provs Jujuy and Salta, the latter collections made very near the Bolivian border, at 2,550–3,400 m amongst grasses, shrubs and rocks (Montano phytogeographical district). Probably occurs also in Bolivia.

Derivation: a new species named in honour of the distinguished German potato breeder and collector, Professor Dr Hans Ross

2n = 24

Bal. (as '*S. rossii*', p. 51), Braun., Stur., VIR

20. *S. okadae* Hawkes et Hjerting (Bot. J. Linn. Soc. **86**, 414–17, 1983)

S. venatoris Ochoa (Phytologia **55**(5), 297–8, 1984)

Leaf (0–)1–2(–3)-jugate with 0(–1) pairs of interjecteds; terminal leaflet large (to 7.5 cm long), larger than laterals; leaf shape very similar to that of

S. microdontum; surface with sparse to fairly frequent short hairs. Inflorescence branches and calyx generally with very sparse hairs to more or less glabrous (contrast *S. microdontum*). Calyx acumens long-linear to spathulate. Corolla white, rotate to pentagonal, 2.5–3.5 cm diam. Berries globular, to 2.0 cm diam.

Distribution: Bolivia, depts Cochabamba and La Paz; Argentina, depts Jujuy and Salta; at 2,600–3,200 m generally in high mountain rain forest ('ceja').

Related to *S. microdontum* and *S. venturii*.

Derivation: named in honour of the distinguished Argentinian potato expert, Dr K.A. Okada

2n = 24

Bal. (as *S. venturii*), Braun., Stur., VIR

21. S. oplocense Hawkes (Bull. Imp. Bur. Pl. Breed. Genet., Cambridge, 119, 1944)

Leaf 3–4-jugate with petiolulate but decurrent leaflets and denticulate margin; interjected leaflets generally 0–1-paired; leaf colour typically blue-green, with deep purple to red rachis and primary leaflet veins; pubescence of fairly dense, short, thick hairs. Inflorescence branches and calyx with dense, short, stiff hairs and some glands; pedicel articulation tends to be low. Corolla pentagonal to substellate, blue-violet, (1.7–)2.5–3.0(–3.5) cm diam.; acumens long. Style long, curved, exserted 5–6(–8) mm; stigma minute, not exceeding style thickness.

Closely related to *S. hondelmannii* and *S. sucrense*. The only species yet known with 2x, 4x and 6x cytotypes. The 2x cytotypes are very rare, only found twice and not available in gene banks. The others are common, and nearly all the Argentinian collections are hexaploid.

Distribution: Bolivia, depts Chuquisaca and Potosí; Argentina, prov. Jujuy; at 2,600–3,500 m in dry thorn-bush scrub, hedges, cultivated fields and cactus vegetation.

Derivation: from Oploca in south Bolivia, where this species was first found

2n = 24; EBN unknown. 2n = 48, 72; EBN = 4

Bal., Braun., Gr.Lü., Stur., VIR

22. S. × rechei Hawkes et Hjerting (in Hawkes, Scott. Pl. Breed. Rec., 146, 1963)

Leaf 2–4-jugate; lateral leaflets petiolulate, elliptic-oblong; interjected leaflets generally few; calyx acumens long, linear, 3–5 mm long. Corolla white, rotate-pentagonal or substellate, about 3.0 cm diam.; anthers long-narrow, about 7.0 mm long.

Distribution: Argentina, endemic to prov. La Rioja, in dry valleys in and around Sierra Famatina, at about 1,800–2,000 m.

This is a naturally occurring hybrid of *S. microdontum* subsp. *giganto-phyllum* × *S. kurtzianum*, with probable introgression from S. spegazzinii.

All plants studied so far are triploid (2n = 3x = 36). See also Okada (1981) who states that *S. microdontum* subsp. *gigantophyllum* occurs frequently as triploid cytotypes in the same region.
Derivation: dedicated to the Argentinian botanist, J.O. Reche, who collected materials of this hybrid species and other wild potatoes
2n = 36

23. *S.* × *ruiz-lealii* Brücher (Rev. Fac. Cienc. Agr. **9**(2), 7–11, 1962)

Leaf 4–6-jugate, with 1–3-jugate interjecteds; laterals elliptic, acute, sparsely pilose. Pedicel sparsely pubescent below, articulated in lower third. Corolla white, rotate to subrotate, 2.5–3.0 cm diam. Berries round, 1.0–1.6 cm diam.
Distribution: Argentina, prov. Mendoza (altitude not given), in deep canyons or at the base of *Cortaderia* tussocks.
(I have seen no type material of this species.)
This species is undoubtedly a natural hybrid between *S. chacoense* and *S. kurtzianum* (see Hawkes and Hjerting 1969, 236–7, 239, etc.).
Derivation: named in honour of the Argentinian botanist, Professor A. Ruiz-Leal, from Mendoza province
Chromosome number not given, presumably 2n = 24

24. *S.* × *setulosistylum* Bitt. (Fedde, Repert. **12**, 450–2, 1913)

S. puberulofructum Corr. (Wrightia **2**, 193–4, 1961)

Vegetatively intermediate between *S. chacoense* and *S. spegazzinii*, but with corolla varying from white-stellate to mauve-stellate or pentagonal. Style setae sometimes present. Leaf often highly dissected, 4–7-jugate with 2–13 pairs of narrow-ovate interjected leaflets; all leaflets sparsely and finely pubescent. Corolla to about 3.0 cm diam. Berries subglobose to broadly ovoid. Young fruits sometimes puberulent. This name has been given to hybrid populations derived apparently from natural crosses between *S. chacoense* and *S. spegazzinii*. Since the F_1 hybrids are fertile the variation in these populations is quite extensive.
Distribution: Argentina, provs Catamarca, Salta and Tucumán, at about 1,600–2,100 m in damp to dry places, roadsides, etc.
Derivation: so named because of several bristles or setae on the style
2n = 24
Braun., VIR

25. *S. sparsipilum* (Bitt.) Juz. et Buk. (*ex* Vavilov, Theor. Bases Pl. Breed. **3**, 11, 1937)

S. tuberosum L. subsp. *sparsipilum* Bitt. (Fedde, Repert. **12**, 152–3, 1913)
S. catarthrum Juz. (Bull. Acad. Sci. U.R.S.S. **2**, 308–8, 1937)
S. anomalocalyx Hawkes (Bull. Imp. Bur. Pl. Breed. Genet., Cambridge, 126–7, 1944)
S. brevimucronatum Hawkes (ibid. 127, 1944)
S. lapazense Hawkes (ibid. 127–8, 1944)

S. anomalocalyx var. *llallaguanianum* Cárd. et Hawkes (J. Linn. Soc. Bot.
53, 104–5, 1946)
S. anomalocalyx var. *brachystylum* Cárd. et Hawkes (ibid. **53**, 105, 1946)
S. anomalocalyx var. *murale* Cárd. et Hawkes (ibid. **53**, 106, 1946)
S. calcense var. *urubambae* Vargas (Papas Sudperuanas, Univ. Nac.
Cuzco. **2**, 57, 1956)
S. membranaceum Vargas (ibid. **2**, 62, 1956)
S. sparsipilum var. *llallaguanianum* (Cárd. et Hawkes) Correll (Texas Res.
Found. Contrib. **4**, 465, 1962)
S. ruiz-ceballosii Cárd. (Rev. Agric. Cochabamba **11**, 13–14, 1968)

Leaf (2–)3–4(–5)-jugate with (1–)3–4(–13)-jugate interjected leaflets;
petiolules 3–7(–10) mm long; upper leaf surface with sparse rather short
few-celled hairs. Calyx campanulate or slightly bilabiate; pubescence as for
peduncles and pedicels of sparse to frequent short appressed hairs. Corolla
pale to medium blue-violet, pentagonal to almost rotate (1.5–)2.0–
3.0(–3.5) cm diam. Style 10–11 mm long; stigma much thicker than style
apex. Berries ovate to ovate-cordate, 1.0–2.0 cm long.

KEY TO SUBSPECIES

Leaf 3–4(–5)-jugate; laterals elliptic to elliptic lanceolate, slightly smaller
   than terminal, the bases rounded   **25a. subsp.** *sparsipilum*
Leaf 2–3-jugate; laterals very broad ovate, the first two pairs equal to each
   other and to the terminal leaflet, the bases cordate   **25b. subsp.** *calcense*

25a. Subspecies *sparsipilum*

(Synonyms as for species.)

Differs from subsp. *calcense* in the narrower lateral leaflets and larger
terminals, rounded to cuneate leaflet bases and 2–4 or more pairs of
interjected leaflets.
Distribution: Peru, depts Apurímac and Cuzco; Bolivia, depts Cochabamba, La Paz and Oruro, (and one record each in Chuquisaca and
Potosí), at altitudes of 2,400–3,800 m, in fields, walls, field borders, etc.
Derivation: with sparse hairs
2n = 24; EBN = 2
Braun., CPC, Gr.Lü., Stur., VIR

25b. Subspecies *calcense* **Hawkes nov. comb.**

S. calcense Hawkes (Bull. Imp. Bur. Pl. Breed. Genet., Cambridge,
128–9, 1944)

Differs from subsp. *sparsipilum* in the much broader ovate leaflets with
cordate base and cuspidate apex; uppermost two pairs of lateral leaflets
equal to each other and to the terminal leaflet; third or lowest pair minute;

interjected leaflets 0–1-paired; petiolules 5–10 mm long. Pubescence and flowers more or less similar to the type subspecies.
Distribution: Peru, dept Cuzco, prov. Calca, valley of Río Urubamba, at 2,800–3,000 m, as a weed of fields and field borders, etc.
Derivation: from Calca, where the type specimen was collected
2n = 24; EBN = 2
CPC, Stur.

General: *S. sparsipilum* is a very polymorphic weed species of fields and field borders. Attempts to divide it into different species and forms have not been successful, and the only consistently distinct populations come from the Calca region. These I have placed as a subspecies, *calcense*, based on an original species description.

The similarities to *S. tuberosum* subsp. *andigena* are such that we are led to believe that *S. sparsipilum* was one of its diploid prototypes, the other having been *S. stenotomum* (see Chapter 5).

S. sparsipilum is unique in that it possesses two quite distinct distribution areas. However, this may be due to the tubers of this weed species having been carried by man in sacks of cultivated potatoes from one region to the other. It seems possible that it originated in Bolivia, but this is by no means certain.

26. *S. spegazzinii* Bitt. (Fedde, Repert. **12**, 449–50, 1913)

S. famatinae Bitt. et Wittm. (Bot. Jahrb. **50**, Suppl., 552–3, 1914)
S. sleumeri Corr. (Wrightia **2**, 195–6, 1961)

A widespread and phenotypically highly variable species. Leaf (3–)4–5(–7)-jugate, with (0–)2–7(–18) pairs of interjected leaflets, frequently acroscopically and basiscopically placed, and from 1 mm to 3 cm long; lateral leaflets long-elliptic, narrowing to each end, often decurrent; pubescence of frequent short thick coarse hairs. Corolla medium purple to lilac, substellate to pentagonal. Berries globose to slightly ellipsoid.
Distribution: Argentina, provs Catamarca, La Rioja, Salta, San Juan and Tucumán, at 1,900–3,100 m in dry interandine valleys, under the shade of trees and bushes and in fields and field borders.
Derivation: dedicated to the distinguished Italian mycologist, Carlos Spegazzini (1858–1926), who settled in Argentina and made an extensive herbarium of Argentine plants.
2n = 24; EBN = 2
Bal., Braun., CPC (as *S. leptophyes*), Gr.Lü., Stur., VIR

27. *S.* × *subandigena* Hawkes (Bull. Imp. Bur. Pl. Breed. Genet., Cambridge, 128, 1944)

A weed potato from Bolivia, dept Chuquisaca, near Sucre, at about 2,600 m and possessing some of the characters of *S. tuberosum* subsp. *andigena*, and some of *S. sucrense*. It would seem likely to be a more or less

stabilized hybrid between these two species, so far as can be seen at present (see Hawkes and Hjerting 1989, 357–8). See collections of *Balls 6146* (CPC 161) and *6171* (CPC 174) – probably all living material is now lost. Derivation: almost the same as *S. tuberosum* subsp. *andigena*
2n = 48

28. S. × sucrense Hawkes (Bull. Imp. Bur. Pl. Breed. Genet., Cambridge, 126, 1944)

S. × sucrense var. *brevifolium* Hawkes *nom. nud.* (ibid. 51, 1944)
S. subandigenum Hawkes, var. *camarguense* Cárd. (Bol. Soc. Peruana Bot. **5**, 25–6, 1956)

Leaf (3–)4–5-jugate, with (0–)1–3(–6) pairs of interjected leaflets; lateral leaflets broad ovate to oblong, with (0–)4–6(–15) mm long petiolules; leaf pubescence of sparse to very sparse short appressed hairs; rachis and main veins often pink to purple. Corolla rotate to pentagonal, violet-purple, (1.5–)2.5–3.0(–3.5) cm diam., with long acumens. Stigma large.
Distribution: Bolivia, depts Chuquisaca and Potosí, at 2,600–3,900 m, growing chiefly as a weed of cultivation and amongst cacti and xerophilous shrubs.
  S. sucrense is a widespread somewhat fixed hybrid of *S. oplocense* × *S. tuberosum* subsp. *andigena*. Its nature has been confirmed experimentally by Astley (1979; Astley and Hawkes 1979). Segregation takes place when grown from seed, and backcrosses to the cultivated parent have been found in Bolivia.
Derivation: from the city of Sucre, where this species was first collected
2n = 48; EBN = 4
Braun., CPC, Gr.Lü., Stur., VIR

29. S. tuberosum L. (Sp. Pl., 1, 185, 1753) **subsp. tuberosum**

Escaped and/or Naturalized Materials (for synonyms see pp. 180–81)

1. **Var. vulgare Hook. f.** (Fl. Antarc. **2**, 329–30, 1846)
   This is based on *Darwin 194 bis* from the Chonos Archipelago, Chile.

2. **Var. guaytecarum (Bitt.) Hawkes** (Proc. Linn. Soc. **166**, 130, 1956)
   S. maglia var. *guaytecarum* Bitt. (Fedde, Repert. **12**, 2, 1913)
   This variety is based on *Funck 102c* [or Fonk?], from the Guaitecas Archipelago, Chile.

3. **Var. chubutense (Bitt.) Hawkes** (Proc. Linn. Soc. **166**, 130, 1956)
   S. maglia var. *chubutense* Bitt. (Fedde, Repert. **12**, 452, 1913)
   This variety is based on a collection by *Illin 234* from Chubut, Argentina.

Both these were included by Bitter (Fedde, Repert. **12**, 453, 1913) as *S. maglia* subsp. *meridionale*, but Bitter was mistaken, since they clearly belong to *S. tuberosum*.

4. ***S. molinae* Juz.** (Bull. Acad. Sci., U.R.S.S., Ser. Biol., No. 2, 308–9, 1937) (Collected to Robert Christie.)

5. ***S. leptostigma* Juz.** (ibid. 309–10, 1937) (Collected by Junge.)

These two so-called species were collected in Chile, from the island of Chiloé and grown in Leningrad. They are undoubtedly escapes.

6. ***S. diemii* Brücher** (Darwiniana **13**(1), 108–10, 1964)
From Argentina, prov. Neuquén, Lake Nahuel-Huapi and sent by Sr José Diem. (Type: *Brücher 900*.) Said by Brücher to be triploid, with 2n = 36 chromosomes. Material studied by Hjerting and myself from the same locality was always tetraploid.

7. ***S. sanmartinense* Brücher** (ibid. **13**(1), 111–13, 1964)
From Argentina, prov. Neuquén, San Martín. (Type: *Brücher 1095*.)

I have seen the type specimens of both of these Brücher species. They are undoubtedly naturalized forms of *S. tuberosum*.

8. ***S. oceanicum* Brücher** (Fedde, Repert. **70**, 136–43, 1965)
From Chile, Island of Chiloé, on sea shore and said to be triploid, with 2n = 36 chromosomes. (Type: *Brücher 1196*.) It could perhaps be a chromosome 'sport' of a tetraploid clone, as may well have been the case with *S. diemii*. It would appear to be a naturalized clone, similar to those mentioned above in this respect.

9. ***S. ochoanum* Lechn.** (Trudy po prikl. Bot. Genet. Sel. **62**, 48–9, 1978)
Sent to Lechnovich by Ochoa and collected in Chile, in the Guaitecas Archipelago. (Type *Ochoa s.n. K-11289*.)

10. ***S. zykinii* Lechn.** (ibid. 44–8, 1978)
Sent to Lechnovich by Ochoa and collected in Ancud, Chiloé, Chile. Said to be wild. (Type *Zykin K-11288*.)

These two 'species' described by Lechnovich are also undoubtedly naturalized forms of *S. tuberosum*.

Note: for cultivated forms of *S. tuberosum*, see pp. 180–82.

All these 'species' are undoubtedly infra-specific variants of *S. tuberosum* subsp. *tuberosum*. The use of such names would best be discontinued. Ranks below the level of subspecies can more conveniently be given a non-

Linnean Group classification when thought to be necessary.
2n = 48
VIR

30. *S. ugentii* Hawkes et Okada (Phytologia **64**(5), 327–9, 1988)

Leaf 5–6(–7)-jugate, with very frequent, up to 20 pairs of interjected leaflets, including acroscopics and basiscopics; petiolules 5–15(–25) mm long; pubescence of frequent medium-lengthed hairs, shorter below and on veins only. Peduncles longer above than below fork. Corolla deep rich purple, rotate, 2.5–3.0 cm diam.; stigma large, capitate. Berry spherical.
Distribution: Bolivia, dept Chuquisaca, at about 3,750 m, at the base of cliffs.
This and *S. hoopesii* are noteworthy in series *Tuberosa*, in possessing a tetraploid chromosome number.
Derivation: named in honour of the distinguished American potato taxonomist, Dr Don Ugent
2n = 48
Stur. (not in inventory. *Hoopes et al. 288, 290*)

31. *S. venturii* Hawkes et Hjerting (Phyton **9**, 140–4, 1960)

Leaf with very large terminal and minute 1–3-paired laterals, occasionally simple, with very sparse, closely adpressed, short, 3-celled triangular hairs, visible under a lens only; calyx glabrescent or with a few hairs of same type as leaf hairs. Corolla white, rotate to substellate.
Distribution: endemic to north-west Argentina, provs Tucumán and Catamarca, at 2,000–2,800 m, in high altitude grasslands.
Related to *S. microdontum* but easily distinguished by the very characteristic pubescence. Distinguished from *S. okadae* by the larger terminal and smaller lateral leaflets.
Derivation: named in honour of the Argentine botanist, Santiago Venturi
2n = 24(36); EBN = 2
Gr.Lü., Stur., VIR

32. *S. vernei* Bitt. et Wittm. (Engler, Bot. Jahrb. **50**, Suppl., 550–1, 1914)

A tall robust plant. Leaf (3–)4–5(–7)-jugate, with (0–)2–10(–15) pairs of interjected leaflets; upper leaf surface with short, appresed, fairly frequent hairs, lower with dense, felted/tomentose, whitish-grey pubescence. Calyx dark purple. Corolla large, showy, deep violet purple, pentagonal to substellate, 2.5–4.5 cm diam. Berries more or less globular.

KEY TO SUBSPECIES

Lateral leaflets clearly petiolulate; leaflet apex markedly acuminate; base
    not auriculate   **32a. subsp. *vernei***

Lateral leaflets sessile or very shortly petiolulate; leaflet apex obtuse to acute, base auriculate on basiscopic side   **32b. subsp.** *ballsii*

32a. Subspecies *vernei*

Lateral leaflets petiolulate, basally rounded and apically acuminate; interjected leaflets ovate to cordate and acute. Corolla larger than that of subsp. *ballsii*.

Distribution: Argentina, provs Catamarca and Tucumán, at 2,200–2,800 m in mountain forests, in partial shade of *Polylepis*, *Alnus* and *Sambucus*.

Derivation: dedicated to Professor Claude Verne of Grenoble, who at an early period made living collections of wild potatoes

2n = 24; EBN = 2

Bal., Braun., CPC, Gr.Lü., Stur., VIR

32b. Subspecies *ballsii* (Hawkes) Hawkes et Hjerting (in Hawkes, Scott. Pl. Breed. Rec., 149–50, 1963)

S. ballsii Hawkes (Bull. Imp. Bur. Pl. Breed. Genet., Cambridge, 121, 1944)

Leaflets generally sessile, acute to obtuse apically, auriculate on basiscopic side; interjected leaflets generally shorter than in subsp. *vernei*, obtuse and sessile. Corolla to 3 cm diam.

Distribution: Argentina, provs Jujuy and Salta; not yet seen in Bolivia but might occur there. Altitude 2,700–3,450 m; habitat as for subsp. *vernei*.

Some intermediate forms occur in prov. Salta in a region lying between the distribution areas of the two subspecies.

Derivation: dedicated to the well-known English plant collector, E.K. Balls, who led the 1939 potato collecting expedition to Mexico and South America.

2n = 24; EBN = 2

Bal., Braun., CPC, Gr.Lü., Stur.

33. *S. virgultorum* (Bitt.) Cárd. et Hawkes (J. Linn. Soc. Bot. 53, 103, 1946)

S. boliviense Dun. subsp. *virgultorum* Bitt. (Fedde, Repert. 12, 153–4, 1913)

Leaf (1–)2–3(–4)-jugate, with 0–2(–4) pairs of interjecteds; lateral leaflets with 3–6 mm petiolules, apically abruptly acuminate; terminal leaflet broader than laterals, apically abruptly acuminate; leaf pubescence of dense, fairly short, forward-pointing hairs on upper surface. Peduncles and pedicels with sparse to frequent short hairs. Corolla rotate, violet-purple, 2.5–3.0 cm diam., with rather flat lobes. Berries globose.

Distribution: Bolivia, depts Cochabamba and La Paz, mostly in the latter,

at 2,800–3,000 m or up to 3,900 m, in high altitude rain forest ('ceja') or in areas of bushes and meadows where the forest has been degraded.
Derivation: occurring in thickets and copses
2n = 24
Braun., Gr.Lü., VIR

XVI *Tuberosa* (cultivated species)

These form an interesting group whose mode of origin has now been fairly well elucidated. They occur in a polyploid series with diploids, triploids, tetraploids and pentaploids (see Appendix II).

Bukasov (in Bukasov and Kameraz 1959) classified the Andean species as series *Andigena*, whilst the Chilean materials and certain wild Peruvian coastal species were classified by him in the same publication as series *Tuberosa sensu stricto*. I prefer to keep them as a single series because I believe that they are essentially monophyletic (see Chapter 5).

I have reduced the large number of species described by Bukasov and his colleagues to seven. Dodds (in Correll 1962) suggested a further reduction, by including all the diploid species, one of the triploids (*S. chaucha*), and all the tetraploids under *S. tuberosum*, but distinguishing them as groups and subgroups rather than species. This then reduces the number of cultivated species to three, namely *S. tuberosum*, and the two 'hybrid' species *S. juzepczukii* and *S. curtilobum*. However, since we now know that *S. ajanhuiri*, *S. chaucha* and *S. tuberosum* were also formed by past hybridization, the distinctions made by Dodds cannot be so easily justified. It thus remains for the individual working with this material to choose his own method, and I have given the appropriate cross-references in the account that follows.

Since all cultivated potatoes except *S. stenotomum* and possibly *S. phureja* are of a hybrid nature, I have omitted the hybrid sign (×) in species belonging to this group.

KEY TO CULTIVATED SPECIES

(1) Pedicel articulation high, 2–4(–8) mm below calyx base; always in the upper quarter of pedicel; leaves stiff, not arched at tip   (2)
    Pedicel articulation lower, not higher than two-thirds of pedicel length; leaves often slightly arched at tip   (4)

(2) Corolla roughly pentagonal; upper lateral leaflet pair broadly decurrent on to rachis; leaves softly hairy   **1. S. ajanhuiri**
    Corolla rotate, with very short lobes; upper laterals not (or only barely) decurent on to rachis; leaves not softly hairy   (3)

(3) Pedicel articulation rather indistinct; corolla blue, not more than 2.5 cm diam.; common peduncle short, 0.5–2.0(–4.0) cm long
                                            4. S. juzepczukii
    Pedicel articulation distinct; corolla purple. 3.0–3.5 cm diam.; common peduncle 5–10 cm long or more   **3. S. curtilobum**

(4) Calyx lobes short, with short acumens, generally regularly arranged; main leaflets about twice as long as broad   **7. *S. tuberosum***
Calyx lobes long-ovate, generally arranged irregularly (in 2 + 3 or 2 + 2 + 1 groups); if regular, then leaflets much more than twice as long as broad   (5)
(5) Corolla lobes 2–3 times as broad as long, generally broader than corolla radius; leaves somewhat glossy   **2. *S. chaucha***
Corolla lobes less than or only just as broad as long   (6)
(6) Leaf sparsely pubescent, shining in the living state; tubers yielding in 3–4 months under 12-hour days and with no dormancy period   **5. *S. phureja***
Leaf more densely pubescent, not shining in the living state; tubers yielding in six months (or longer) under 12-hour days and with definite dormancy period   **6. *S. stenotomum***

1. *S. ajanhuiri* Juz. et Buk. (Proc. U.S.S.R. Congr. Genet. **3**, 605, 1929)

(Dodds: Part of Group Stenotomum)

This species is similar in many respects to *S. stenotomum*. It differs, however, in the small regular calyx, smaller blue pentagonal flower, very high pedicel articulation, and stiff leaves. Leaf with 5–6(–7) pairs of lateral leaflets and numerous interjected leaflets. There are two groups, Ajawiri and Yari, the latter with much more broadly decurrent leaflets than the former. (See Hawkes and Hjerting (1989) for a more detailed discussion.) Distribution: Peru, dept Puno; Bolivia, depts La Paz, Oruro and Potosí. Grown at very high altitudes, about 3,800–4,100 m. Frost-resistant.
Derivation: from the Aymará Indian name Ajawiri
     This is a hybrid of *S. stenotomum* × *S. megistacrolobum* (see Chapter 5).
2n = 24
Braun. ?, CIP, CPC, Gr.Lü., VIR

2. *S. chaucha* Juz. et Buk. (Proc. U.S.S.R. Congr. Genet. **3**, 609, 1929)

(Dodds: Group Chaucha)

S. mamilliferum Juz. et Buk. (Proc. U.S.S.R. Congr. Genet. **3**, 609, 1929)
S. tenuifilamentum Juz. et Buk. (ibid. **3**, 603, 1929)
S. coeruleiflorum Hawkes (Bull. Imp. Bur. Pl. Breed. Genet., Cambridge, 131, 1944)
S. chaucha f. *roseum* Hawkes (ibid. 131, 1944)
S. chaucha f. *purpureum* Hawkes (ibid. 131, 1944)

I have grouped under this name all those triploid forms that have been derived from natural crosses between *S. tuberosum* subsp. *andigena* and *S. stenotomum*. It is possible that subsp. *andigena* × *S. phureja* crosses may also have taken place. Some of these, which are most distinct and more widely cultivated, were formerly classed by Juzepczuk and Bukasov (1929) and by myself (1944) as separate species. Many more collections of triploid cultivated potatoes have been made, each of which differs in certain points from the micro-species already described. This is only to be expected when we consider that triploid hybrids could have been formed many times by the crossing of different clones of the three very polymorphic species *S. stenotomum*, *S. phureja* and *S. tuberosum* subsp. *andigena*. If these hybrids are to be named at all, they should be considered merely as nothomorphic forms of one species. I have therefore retained the name *S. chaucha*, since it was the first to be applied to these triploid forms by Juzepczuk and Bukasov. The best way of distinguishing *S. chaucha* from other cultivated species is by the corolla lobes which are in general about three times as broad as long when spread out flat.

Distribution: central Peru to central Bolivia at high altitudes.

Derivation: from the Quechua Indian word indicating a potato which matures in a short time

2n = 36

CIP, Gr.Lü., VIR

3. *S. curtilobum* Juz. et Buk. (Proc. U.S.S.R. Congr. Genet. **3**, 609, 1929)

Distinguished by semi-rosette habit, straight stiff leaves, very high pedicel articulation and large purple *circular* corolla 30–35 mm diam. with very short lobes and acumens. Derived from natural crosses between *S. juzepczukii* and *S. tuberosum* subsp. *andigena* (see Hawkes 1962a). Numerous variations in tuber colour and form are known.

Distribution: central Peru to central Bolivia at very high altitudes. Frost-resistant.

Derivation: short-lobed, referring to the lobes of the corolla

2n = 60

Braun., CIP, Gr.Lü., VIR

4. *S. juzepczukii* Buk. (Proc. U.S.S.R. Congr. Genet. **3**, 603–4, 1929)

S. juzepczukii var. *parco* Hawkes (Bull. Imp. Bur. Pl. Breed. Genet., Cambridge, 131, 1944)

Distinguished by the semi-rosette habit, long, straight leaves, short peduncle (2–4 cm long), pedicels with very high but indistinct articulation, and small blue corolla (to 2.5 cm diam.) with very short lobes and small acumens.

A natural triploid hybrid between *S. acaule* and *S. stenotomum* (see Hawkes 1962a) which has almost certainly been formed more than once, with different varieties of *S. stenotumum* involved in each case.

Distribution: central Peru, southwards to north Bolivia at very high altitudes. Frost-resistant.

Note: Ochoa (Phytologia **65**(2), 106–7, 1988) describes two varieties and five forms of *S. juzepczukii*.

Derivation: named in honour of the distinguished Russian taxonomist and potato collector, S.W. Juzepczuk

2n = 36

CIP, VIR

5. *S. phureja* Juz. et Buk. (Proc. U.S.S.R. Congr. Genet. **3**, 604–5, 1929)

(Dodds: Group Phureja and subgroup Amarilla)

S. rybinii Juz. et Buk. (Proc. U.S.S.R. Congr. Genet. **3**, 606, 1929)
S. boyacense Juz. et Buk. (Proc. U.S.S.R. Congr. Genet. **3**, 609, 1929)
S. caniarense Juz. et Buk. (in Vavilov, Theor. Bases Pl. Breed. **3**, 17, 1937; *nom. nud.*)
S. kesselbrenneri Juz. et Buk. (in Vavilov, Theor. Bases Pl. Breed. **3**, 18, 1937; *nom. nud.*)
S. cardenasii Hawkes (Bull. Imp. Bur. Pl. Breed. Genet., Cambridge, 129–30, 1944)
S. ascasabii Hawkes (Bull. Imp. Bur. Pl. Breed. Genet., Cambridge, 130, 1944)
S. phureja var. *pujeri* Hawkes (Bull. Imp. Bur. Pl. Breed. Genet., Cambridge, 130, 1944)
S. rybinii var. *popayanum* Hawkes (Bull. Imp. Bur. Pl. Breed. Genet., Cambridge, 130–1, 1944)
S. rybinii var. *pastoënse* Hawkes (Bull. Imp. Bur. Pl. Breed. Genet., Cambridge, 131, 1944)

Distinguished by the sparsely pubescent leaf, which is shining in the living state, and rather irregular calyx with lanceolate lobes. Tubers yield in 3–4 months under short-day conditions and possess no dormancy period. This very widespread and highly variable species was formerly separated into a number of smaller units. These have been found to hybridize without lack of vigour or fertility in the F_2 generation under experimental conditions and hence cannot be considered as distinct. The absence of tuber dormancy indicates that *S. phureja* has become specially adapted to regions that are free from long periods of drought or frost.

Distribution: Venezuela, Colombia, Ecuador, Peru and north Bolivia. Wet mountain slopes mostly in the eastern Andes, at lower altitudes than the other cultivated species.

Note: Ochoa (Phytologia **65**(2), 103–4, 1988) describes five varieties and four forms of *S. phureja*.

Derivation: from an Aymará Indian word applied to early-maturing potatoes

2n = 24; EBN = 2

Braun., CIP, CPC, Gr.Lü., Stur., VIR

5a. Subspecies *hygrothermicum* (Ochoa) Hawkes comb. nov.

S. hygrothermicum Ochoa (Econ. Bot. **38**(1), 128–33, 1984)

This is clearly a cultivated potato. From a study of its description and isotope specimen it would seem to agree closely with *S. phureja*. However, since *S. phureja* is diploid and *S. hygrothermicum* is said to be tetraploid, there is clearly some discrepancy. Even so, the leaf pubescence and the irregular calyx clearly indicate *S. phureja*. For the time being, perhaps subspecies rank would be appropriate.

Distribution: Peru, dept San Martín, near river Cumbasa, at 600 m altitude.

Derivation: 'wet and hot', referring no doubt to the climatic conditions where it was found

2n = 48

5b. Subspecies *estradae* (López) Hawkes comb. nov.

S. estradae López (Mutisia, Bogotá, **55**, 5–10, 1983)

This material possesses 4(–5)-jugate leaves with 0–4-jugate interjected leaflets and broad-ovate main leaflets; pubescence of sparse long hairs above, confined to veins below. The author of the description mentions the presence of short-stalked glands.

Although this taxon resembles *S. tuberosum* subsp. *tuberosum* superficially, it does not conform cytoplasmically with that species according to Grun (pers. comm.). The calyx is regular and the corolla 3.5–4.0 cm diam. It crosses with difficulty with diploid cultivated species and easily with tetraploids. Thus the author believes it to be an autotetraploid of *S. phureja*, but a natural cross of *S. phureja* × *S. tuberosum* subsp. *tuberosum* should not be ruled out. For the time being I am placing it as a second subspecies of *S. phureja*.

Distribution: Colombia, dept Quindio at 1,850 m (*López 4702*).

Derivation: named in honour of the distinguished Colombian potato geneticist, Dr Nelson Estrada

2n = 48

6. *S. stenotomum* Juz. et Buk. (Proc. U.S.S.R. Congr. Genet. **3**, 604, 1929)

(Dodds: Group Stenotomum)

S. churuspi Hawkes (Bull. Imp. Bur. Pl. Breed. Genet., 129, 1944)
S. yabari Hawkes (Bull. Imp. Bur. Pl. Breed. Genet., 129, 1944; *pro parte*)

Distinguished from *S. phureja* by the more densely pubescent leaf which is not shining in the living state, tubers produced in 5–6 months or longer and with definite dormancy period. Calyx generally irregular with lanceolate lobes as in *S. phureja*. A very variable species which is possibly ancestral to all the other cultivated potatoes. These have been produced from it either by hybridization (*S. chaucha*, *S. curtilobum*, *S. juzepczukii*, *S. ajanhuiri*), by auto- or allopolyploidy (*S. tuberosum*), or by evolutionary divergence at the same level of ploidy (*S. phureja*). Forms with pinkish-lilac corollas from south Peru which were formerly placed with *S. yabari* and *S. churuspi* (the latter with very short corolla lobes) have now been united with *S. stenotomum*.

Note: Ochoa (Phytologia **65**(2), 104–6, 1988) describes six varieties and 14 forms of *S. stenotomum*.

Subspecies *stenotomum*: includes forms with smaller flowers and unribbed calyx base; leaflets generally 2½ times as long as broad, or even narrower. Calyx very small, regular or irregular in south Peru and north Bolivia, larger in forms from further north.

Distribution: central Peru to central Bolivia at high altitudes.

Derivation: narrowly cut, possibly referring to the narrow leaflets or perhaps to the narrow-lanceolate calyx lobes

2n = 24; EBN = 2

Braun., CIP, CPC, Gr.Lü., Stur., VIR

6a. Subspecies *goniocalyx* (Juz. et Buk.) Hawkes (Scott, Pl. Breed. Rec., 157, 1963)

(Dodds: Subgroup Goniocalyx)

S. goniocalyx Juz. et Buk. (Proc. U.S.S.R. Congr. Genet. **3**, 605–6, 1929)
S. yabari Hawkes (Bull. Imp. Bur. Pl. Breed. Genet., Cambridge, 129, 1944; *pro parte*)

A northern subspecies of *S. stenotomum*, with large white or pink flowers and angled calyx base. Tubers with bright yellow flesh.

Distribution: central to north Peru, at high altitudes.

This subspecies intergrades into subsp. *stenotomum* (forms shown as hybrids in the CIP inventory), and possibly ought not to be maintained. The typical forms from central Peru are easily distinguishable from southern Peruvian and Bolivian ones, but too many intermediates occur for taxonomic comfort.

Derivation: angled calyx

2n = 24; EBN = 2

Braun., CIP, CPC, Gr.Lü., Stur., VIR

7. *S. tuberosum* L. (Sp. Pl. **1**, 185, 1753)

S. esculentum Neck. (Delic. Gallo-Belg. **1**, 119, 1768)
S. sinense Blanco (Fl. Filip, ed. I. 137, 1837)
S. tuberosum L. var. *vulgare* Hook. f. (Fl. Antarct. **2**, 329–30, 1846)
S. tuberosum var. *chiloense* A.DC. (Arch. Sci. Phys. Nat. **15**, 437, 1886)
S. tuberosum var. *cultum* A.DC. (Arch. Sci. Phys. Nat. **15**, 437, 1886)

S. tuberosum var. *sabini* A.DC. *pro parte* (Arch. Sci. Phys. Nat. **15**, 437, 1886)

S. chiloense (A.DC.) Berth. (Ann. Sci. Agron., Paris, **28**, 179, 1911)

S. cultum (A.DC.) Berth. (Ann. Sci. Agron., Paris, **28**, 179, 1911)

S. sabinii (A.DC.) Berth. (Ann. Sci. Agron., Paris, **28**, 179, 1911; *pro parte*)

S. maglia Schlechtd. subsp. *meridionale* Bitt. (Fedde, Repert. **12**, 453, 1913)

S. maglia Schlechtd. var. *guaytecarum* Bitt. (Fedde, Repert. **12**, 2, 1913)

S. maglia var. *chubutense* Bitt. (Fedde Repert. **12**, 452, 1913)

S. molinae Juz. (Bull. Acad. Sci. U.R.S.S. **2**, 309–9, 1937)

S. leptostigma Juz. (Bull. Acad. Sci. U.R.S.S. **2**, 309–10, 1937)

S. tuberosum var. *guaytecarum* (Bitt.) Hawkes (Proc. Linn. Soc., Lond., **166**, 130, 1956)

S. tuberosum var. *chubutense* (Bitt.) Hawkes (Proc. Linn. Soc., Lond., **166**, 130, 1956)

S. diemii Brücher (Darwiniana **13**(1), 108–10, 1964)

S. sanmartinense Brücher (ibid. **13**(1), 111–13, 1964)

S. oceanicum Brücher (Fedde, Repert. **70**, 136–43, 1965)

S. ochoanum Lechn. (Trudy po prikl. Bot. Genet. Sel. **62**, 48–9, 1978)

S. zykinii Lechn. (ibid. 44–8, 1978)

Distinguished from the other species of cultivated potatoes by the pedicel articulation placed in the middle third, short calyx lobes arranged regularly, leaves often slightly arched, leaflets always ovate to ovate-lanceolate, about twice as long as broad, never narrow lanceolate as in some forms of *S. stenotomum* and *S. phureja*. Corolla lobes about half as long as broad. Tubers with well-marked dormancy period.

Two subspecies are now recognized (Hawkes 1956a, and b).

KEY TO SUBSPECIES

Stems few; foliage set at broad angle to stem, arched; lateral leaflets about twice as long as broad; pedicels thickened above **7a. subsp. *tuberosum***

Stems many; foliage set at narrow angle to stem, not arched; lateral leaflets generally more than twice as long as broad; pedicels not thickened above **7b. subsp. *andigena***

7a. Subspecies *tuberosum*

(Dodds: Group Tuberosum)

Distinguished from subsp. *andigena* by the less dissected leaves with wider leaflets, generally arched and set at wider angle to stem. Pedicel thickened above. Corolla often white or pale coloured. Tubers formed under long days or under short days in the tropics at lower altitudes only (500–2,000 m). This subspecies was derived from subsp. *andigena* probably on two separate occasions; first in Chile, where subsp. *andigena* was carried by Indian tribes migrating southwards from the Bolivian Andes; secondly subsp. *andigena* was brought to Europe after the Spanish conquest where under similar climatic and daylength conditions to those of Chile the typical subspecies *tuberosum* was formed again, partly as a result of artificial selection. The evidence for this is set out at length by Salaman (1937, 1949), Hawkes (1956b), and Salaman and Hawkes (1949).

Distribution: originally only from the coastal regions of south central Chile (island of Chiloé and adjacent mainland). Still widely grown in those regions at low altitudes, but now world-wide.

Derivation: tuberous, bearing tubers

2n = 48; EBN = 4

Braun., CIP, CPC, Gr.Lü., Stur. UAC, VIR

7b. Subspecies *andigena* Hawkes (Proc. Linn. Soc. Bot. **166**, 130, 1956)

(Dodds: Group Andigena)

S. andigenum Juz. et Buk. (Proc. U.S.S.R. Congr. Genet. **3**, 609–10, 1929)

S. herrerae Juz. (Bull. Acad. Sci. U.R.S.S. **2**, 310–11, 1937) (*pro parte*)

S. apurimacense Vargas (Papas Sudperuanas, Univ. Nac. Cuzco. **2**, 58–9, 1956)

This subspecies may be distinguished by the narrower, more numerous leaflets, which are generally petiolulate, the leaves set at an acute angle to the stem and generally more dissected; pedicel not thickened at apex; tubers formed at high altitudes only (over 2,000 m) under short-day conditions. (They are, of course, formed under experimental conditions in Europe at low altitudes, but not in the tropics where the temperatures are very high.) This is undoubtedly the ancestral subspecies of *S. tuberosum*, formed either partly or wholly from *S. stenotomum* in the Andes of Peru and Bolivia.

Distribution: Andes of Venezuela, Colombia, Ecuador, Peru, Bolivia, north-west Argentina; also sparingly in Guatemala and Mexico.

Note: Ochoa (Phytologia **65**(2), 108–13, 1988) describes 12 varieties and 28 forms of *S. tuberosum* subsp. *andigena*.

Derivation: born or produced in the Andes

2n = 48; EBN = 4

Bal., Braun., CIP, CPC, Gr.Lü., Stur., VIR

adg × tbr – CIP; tbr × adg – CIP

SERIES XVII   *ACAULIA* JUZ

(Bull. Acad. Sci. U.R.S.S., Ser. Biol. **2**, 316, 1937, *nom. nud.*; *ex* Buk. et Kameraz, Bases of Potato Breeding, 21, 1959)

Low, rosette-forming herbs (occasionally forming long stems), bearing stolons and tubers; leaves with typically obtuse leaflets auricled at the base on the acroscopic side; peduncle very short or absent; pedicel articulation absent or shown only by a ring-of pigment, very rarely well-marked and if so, only a few millimetres below calyx. Corolla small, rotate, and with very short lobes.

Distribution: Peru, Bolivia and north-west Argentina at very high altitudes in alpine meadows, field borders, roadsides, etc.

KEY TO SPECIES

Peduncle unforked; pedicel articulation generally not present, but if so, very high up, 2–3 mm below calyx; style not exserted **1. S. acaule**
Peduncle forked; pedicel articulation lower, 5–7 mm below calyx; style exserted 1.5–2.0 mm above anther column **2. S. albicans**

1. S. acaule Bitt. (Fedde, Repert. **11**, 391–3, 1912)

S. acaule var. *subexinterruptum* Bitt. (Fedde, Repert. **11**, 393–4, 1912)
S. acaule var. *caulescens* Bitt. (Fedde, Repert. **12**, 453–4, 1913)
S. depexum Juz. (Bull. Acad. Sci. U.R.S.S. **2**, 318–18, 1937)
S. schreiteri Buk. *nom. nud.* (Soviet Pl. Indust. Record, No. 4, 13, 1940)
S. acaule var. *checcae* Hawkes (Bull. Imp. Bur. Pl. Breed. Genet., Cambridge, 115, 1944)
S. depexum var. *chorruense* Hawkes (Bull. Imp. Bur. Pl. Breed. Genet., Cambridge, 115, 1944)
S. uyunense Cárd. (Bol. Soc. Peruana Bot. **5**, 33–5, 1956)

Characters and distribution as for series. The fairly wide infraspecific variation has caused certain authors to split *S. acaule* into several micro-species. The fertility and range of variability between all forms so far studied makes it advisable, however, to reunite them into the one original species, divided into geographical subspecies, as follows.

KEY TO SUBSPECIES

(1) Plant very flat-rosetted, bearing long spreading hairs on stem, petiole and leaf rachis (central Peru) **1c. subsp.** *punae*
Plant with less flat rosettes; hairs short, crisped and sub-appressed
(2)
(2) Pedicel articulation well-marked; terminal leaflet much larger than the 0–4-paired laterals which diminish rapidly towards leaf base
1b. subsp. *aemulans*
Peduncle articulation not well-marked, generally completely absent. Terminal slightly larger than the (2–)4–5(–7)-paired laterals which do not diminish rapidly in size towards the leaf base
1a. subsp. *acaule*

1a. Subspecies *acaule*

Lateral leaflets not very much shorter than terminal leaflets, not or only slightly decurrent; pedicel articulation generally invisible or marked by a difference of colour; pubescence of fairly short, crisped hairs. The varieties and species noted above all come within the morphological range of subsp. *acaule*. Phenotypes with stems (var. *caulescens*) have developed amongst rocks and high-growing herbs. For details of others see Hawkes and Hjerting (1989).
Distribution: south Peru, depts Ayacucho, Apurímac, Cuzco, Puno; Bolivia; north Argentina, southwards to prov. La Rioja; generally at altitudes of 3,700–4,200 m, but sometimes even to 4,650 m, in alpine meadows, by paths, walls, ditches, arable fields, etc.
Derivation: stemless
2n = 48; EBN = 2
Bal., Braun., CPC, Gr.Lü., Stur., VIR

1b. Subspecies *aemulans* **(Bitt. et Wittm.) Hawkes et Hjerting** (in Hawkes, Scott. Pl. Breed. Rec., 116, 1963)

S. aemulans Bitt. et Wittm. (in Engler's Bot. Jahrb. **50**, Suppl., 553–5, 1914)
S. acaule var. *aemulans* (Bitt. et Wittm.) Corr. (Wrightia **2**, 169–70), 1961)

Differs from subsp. *acaule* in the short leaf with much enlarged terminal and 0–4 pairs of decurrent laterals; pedicel articulation well-marked but not abscissing when mature. Pubescence as for subsp. *acaule*.
Distribution: Argentina, prov. La Rioja, at 2,950–3,500 m, in open stony places and alpine meadows.
Note: specimens from Argentina, prov. Jujuy, previously thought to be subsp. *aemulans* are more likely to be hybrid derivatives of *S. acaule* and *S. megistacrolobum* (Okada and Clausen, Euphytica **31**, 817–35, 1982 – see *S.* × *indunii*).
Derivation: 'similar to', because the original authors thought it very strongly resembled the Mexican species, *S. demissum*
2n = 48; EBN = 2
Bal., Braun., Gr.Lü., Stur., VIR

1c. Subspecies *punae* **(Juz.) Hawkes et Hjerting** (in Hawkes, Scott. Pl. Breed. Rec., 117, 1963)

S. punae Juz. (Bull. Acad. Sci. U.R.S.S., Ser. Biol. **2**, 316–17, 1937)
S. acaule var. *punae* (Juz.) Hawkes (Bull. Imp. Bur. Pl. Breed. Genet., Cambridge, 23, 1944)

Leaf like that of subsp. *acaule*, but stem very short; pubescence of long, weak, spreading hairs; articulation of pedicel never visible except by a change of colour, observable on living plant only.

Distribution: central Peru, depts Ancash, Huancavelica, Huánuco, Junín, Lima and Pasco, at similar altitudes and habitats to those of subsp. *acaule*.
Derivation: from the Puna, high-altitude grass steppe extending from central Peru southwards into north Argentina
2n = 48(60); EBN = 2
Braun., Gr.Lü., Stur., VIR

2. *S. albicans* (Ochoa) Ochoa (Phytologia **54**(5), 392, 1983)

S. acaule var. *albicans* Ochoa (Agronomia, Lima, **27**, 363–4, 1960)
S. acaule subsp. *albicans* (Ochoa) Hawkes (Scott. Pl. Breed. Rec., 117, 1963)

Habit robust, rosetted to semi-rosetted, with short stem. Leaf 3–4-jugate, with 3–5 pairs of interjected leaflets. All green parts with long weak hairs. Peduncle forked; pedicel with clearly marked articulation in upper third but much lower than in *S. acaule*. Corolla rotate, very pale blue to white, 1.5–2.0 cm diam. Style exserted 1.5–2.0 mm. Berries spherical, not separating at articulation.
Distribution: north Peru, depts Ancash, Cajamarca and La Libertad, at 3,500 m, on páramos or alpine meadows.
  Differs from *S. acaule* in the more robust habit, the generally forked peduncle, much lower and clearly marked pedicel articulation, very pale blue to white corolla and the exserted style. This species is possibly an amphiploid hybrid of *S. acaule* subsp. *punae* with a diploid species from some other series. It has been moved up from varietal, through subspecies to species rank.
Derivation: becoming white, referring to the corolla
2n = 72; EBN = 4
Braun., CPC, Gr.Lü., Stur., VIR

3. *S.* × *indunii* Okada et Clausen (Euphytica **31**, 827–9, 1982)

This is a natural hybrid of *S. acaule* × *S. megistacrolobum* which possesses features of both parent species. It is a sterile triploid and can reproduce only by tubers.
Distribution: north-west Argentina, prov. Jujuy, on high punas, from 3,600–4,000 m.
Derivation: named in honour of the late Argentinian potato breeder, César Induni
2n = 36

4. *S.* × *viirsooi* Okada et Clausen (Euphytica **34**, 227, 1985)

This is a natural hybrid of *S. acaule* × *S. infundibuliforme* which possesses features of both parent species. It is a sterile triploid and reproduces only by tubers.
Distribution: north-west Argentina, prov. Jujuy, on high punas, from 3,500–3,800 m.
Derivation: named in honour of the late Argentinian (previously Estonian) potato specialist Eduardo Viirsoo, who was a pioneer of potato germplasm conservation in his adopted homeland
2n = 36

SERIES XVIII   *LONGIPEDICELLATA* BUK

(in Buk. et Kameraz, Bases of Potato Breeding, 27, 1959)

BOREALIA Corr. (Texas Res. Found. Contrib. **4**, 388–90, 1962)

Herbs with long, creeping stolons; leaves with coarse, white hairs, or glabrous. The arched corolla lobes and large acumens give the corolla a circular appearance with acumens standing out sharply from it. Corolla occasionally, however, substellate to pentagonal.

Distribution: central Mexico to south-west United States on dry plateaux and mountain slopes, medium altitudes. Most species are tetraploid.

KEY TO SPECIES

(1) Pedicel very densely clothed with white spreading hairs, even above
the articulation   **5. *S. polytrichon***
Pedicel sparsely hairy to glabrous, especially above the articulation; if
densely pubescent below articulation then hairs adpressed   (2)

(2) Corolla lobes ± broadly triangular and gradually passing into the
acumens   (3)
Corolla almost circular in outline, except for the sharply delimited
acumens   (6)

(3) Corolla small, never more than 1.5 cm diam., white with darker
acumens or dark purple; plants generally not more than 10 cm tall
                                                    4. *S. papita*
Corolla larger, 2–3 cm diam., dark purple; plants generally larger than
10 cm   (4)

(4) Stem, leaves and calyx completely glabrous or with one or two small
hairs only; leaflets generally petiolulate   (5)
Stem, leaves, peduncle, pedicels and calyx clothed with frequent
coarse hairs; leaflets normally sessile to subsessile
                                          1. *S. fendleri* subsp. *fendleri*

(5) Peduncle and pedicels glabrous; corolla pale mauve, substellate
                                                    2. *S. hjertingii*
Peduncle and pedicels puberulent; corolla dark purple, paler above,
rotate to pentagonal   **3. *S. matehualae***

(6) Corolla white to medium purple; terminal leaflet not differing markedly in size from laterals   **6. *S. stoloniferum***
Corolla dark purple; terminal leaflet broadly obovate to rhomboid,
much larger than laterals   (7)

(7) Anthers 5 mm long; plant robust (central Mexico)
                                                7. *S.* × *vallis-mexici*
Anthers 3 mm long; plant small (Arizona)
                                          1. *S. fendleri* subsp. *arizonicum*

1. S. fendleri Asa Gray (Amer. J. Arts. Sci., Ser. 2, **22**, 284–5, 1856; non *S. fendleri* Huerck et Muell. Arg., Obs. Bot., 180, 1870–71)

S. fendleri var. *texense* Corr. (Wrightia **2**, 187, 1961)

Plant with rather short coarse hairs on stem, leaf, inflorescence branches and calyx; lateral leaflets sessile to subsessile, often decurrent; all leaflets with obtuse apex. Corolla pentagonal to rotate (according to subspecies), purple.

KEY TO SUBSPECIES

Corolla pentagonal to substellate **1a. subsp.** *fendleri*
Corolla rotate with very short lobes **1b. subsp.** *arizonicum*

1a. Subsp. *fendleri*

Leaflets sessile to subsessile. Corolla pentagonal to substellate. Some populations of plants are very much smaller than others. Correll's var. *texense* does not seem to differ sufficiently to warrant varietal status.
Distribution: USA, states of Arizona, Colorado, New Mexico and Texas; Mexico, states of Baja California, Chihuahua and Sonora, at 1,600–2,800 m; in dry oak-pine forests but not under dense shade.
Derivation: dedicated to Mr A. Fendler who first found this species in 1847, in northern Arizona, according to Asa Gray
2n = 48; EBN = 2
Braun., CPC, Gr.Lü., Stur., VIR

1b. Subsp. *arizonicum* **Hawkes** (Scott. Pl. Breed. Rec., 123, 1963)

Differs from subspecies *fendleri* by the rotate corolla with rather small acumens and short lobes, and the small, 3 mm long anthers.
Distribution: USA, Arizona State; Mexico, Chihuahua State; in pine forest clearings and roadsides from about 2,000–2,550 m.
Derivation: from the State of Arizona, where it was first discovered
2n = 48; EBN = 2
CPC, Braun., Gr.Lü., Stur.

2. S. hjertingii Hawkes (Scott. Pl. Breed. Rec., 123, 1963)

Differs from *S. fendleri* in the glabrous or glabrescent stems, leaves, peduncles and calyx, in the generally petiolulate narrow leaflets and the glabrous corolla. Vegetatively extremely similar to *S. cardiophyllum* subsp. *ehrenbergii*, but similar in its floral morphology to *S. fendleri*. *S. fendleri* var. *physaloides* Corr. should be included under *S. hjertingii*, though the calyx does not become accrescent in the latter species as with var. *physaloides* (see below).

Distribution: north-east Mexico, states of Coahuila and Nuevo León, in dry piñon scrub (*Pinus cembroides*, *Juniperus monosperma*, etc.), at 1,750–2,500 m in rather similar habitats to *S. jamesii*.
Derivation: named in honour of the distinguished Danish potato taxonomist and collector, J.P. Hjerting
2n = 48; EBN = 2
Braun, CPC, Gr.Lü., Stur., VIR

S. hjertingii var. **physaloides** (**Corr.**) **Hawkes**, comb. nov.
S. fendleri var. *physaloides* Corr. (US Agric. Monogr. No. 11, 157, 1952)

Plant completely glabrous apart from some short appressed hairs on veins, leaf margins and calyx. Fruit enclosed in bladder-like calyx.
Distribution: Mexico, state of Tamaulipas, at 2,700 m, amongst *Agave* and low herbs. (No living material available.)
Derivation: like *Physalis*, because of the swollen calyx which partly encloses the fruit

3. S. matehualae Hjerting et Tarn (in J.G. Hawkes, J.P. Hjerting and T.R. Tarn, Phytologia **65**(2), 116–18, 1988)

Leaf 2–3(–4)-jugate, with 0(–1) pairs of interjected leaflets per leaf; lateral leaflets broad-ovate to ovate-oblong, with cordate base and obtuse apex; petiolules 3–5(–8) mm long; leaves glabrous or with a few short hairs on the veins; peduncle and pedicels with fairly frequent short appressed hairs. Calyx dark purple, only 3–4 mm long, with very sparse, short, appressed hairs. Corolla dark purple below, paler above, rotate pentagonal, 2.0(–2.5) cm diam., with well-marked lobes and 2 mm long acumens. Anthers 4–5 mm long. Style 12–13 mm long, curved above, exserted up to 8 mm above the stamen column. Berries spherical, 1.0–1.5 cm diam.
Distribution: Mexico, state of San Luis Potosí, at 2,740 m along field borders.
Derivation: from Matehuala, the place where it was first found
2n = 48
Stur. (not in inventory)

4. S. papita Rydb. (Bull. Torr. Bot. Cl. **51**, 148–9, 1924)

S. nannodes Corr. (US Dept. Agr. Monogr., No. 11, 161–2, 1952)

Plant very small and delicate (generally less than 10 cm tall); leaf 3–4(–5)-jugate, with up to 4 pairs of minute interjected leaflets; leaf fairly densely, shortly pubescent, as also the stem, peduncle and pedicel below the articulation; pedicel above articulation glabrous (or with a few stalked glands); calyx small, densely pubescent; acumens 1.0–2.5 mm long. Corolla *either* very pale lilac to white *or* very dark purple, to about 1.5 cm diam., rotate. Anthers 4 mm long. Style exserted about 2 mm. Berries globular, often verrucose.

Distribution: Mexico, states of Chihuahua, Durango, Zacatecas (and Sonora – '*S. nannodes*' – 1,500–1,700 m), at altitudes of 2,150–2,800 m in open juniper, oak and pine woodland and scrub and among rocks and herbs, in rich soil.

This is a characteristically very small, delicate species, with small corolla which is either very pale lilac to white or dark purple, with no intergrading. The same phenomenon is seen in *S. polytrichon*. Correll's *S. nannodes* does not appear to differ sufficiently from *S. papita* to warrant species distinction.

A series of collections known as the '*S. papita* complex' was made mostly in Zacatecas State and rarely in Durango State. These seem to be intermediate between *S. papita* and *S. polytrichon* and clearly need further study.

Derivation: from the vernacular word 'papita', meaning small potato

2n = 48; EBN = 2

Braun., CPC, Gr.Lü., Stur., VIR

5. *S. polytrichon* Rydb. (Bull. Torr. Bot. Cl. **51**, 150, 1924)

S. wightianum Rydb. (Bull. Torr. Bot. Cl. **51**, 149, 1924)

Distinguished by the dense, spreading pubescence of thick white hairs on the whole plant, and especially on the pedicel, both below and above the articulation. Corolla generally white, occasionally mauve; articulation high. Some forms possess sparse leaf pubescence, but the spreading pedicel pubescence is a constant feature. A shade form (cultivated in the USA) has been described by Rydberg as *S. wightianum*; this seems to be no more than a phenotypic variant of *S. polytrichon*.

White-flowered forms known to breeders as '*S. boreale*' should probably be classed as *S. polytrichon* and not as *S. boreale* or *S. fendleri*. If the corolla is stellate, however, it is likely that they may belong to *S. jamesii* (series *Pinnatisecta*). Bitter's *S. boreale* (A. Gray) Bitt. was said to include white-flowered forms mentioned by A. Gray when describing *S. fendleri* and which Bitter himself had not seen. The name 'boreale' is thus a *nomen dubium*, since there is no means of knowing what Gray had in mind when mentioning these white-flowered forms.

Distribution: Mexico, states of Chihuahua, Coahuila, Durango, Guanajuato, Nuevo León, San Luis Potosí and Zacatecas, at 1,800–2,500 m in oak forest, amongst *Opuntia* scrub, in waste places and as a field weed.

Derivation: with many hairs

2n = 48; EBN = 2

Braun., CPC, Gr.Lü., Stur., VIR

6. *S. stoloniferum* Schlechtd. et Bché. (Verh. Bef. Gartenb. Preuss. **9**, 317, 1833; Linnaea **8**, 255 1833)

S. longipedicellatum Bitt. (Fedde, Repert. **11**, 457, 1912)

S. longipedicellatum var. *pseudoprophyllum* Bitt. (Fedde, Repert. **11**, 457–8, 1912)

S. ajuscoense Buk. (*ex* Rybin, Bull. Appl. Bot. Genet. & Pl. Breed. **20**, 699–700, 1929)

S. antipoviczii Buk. (*ex* Rybin, Bull. Appl. Bot. Genet. & Pl. Breed. **20**, 700, 1929)

S. neoantipoviczii Buk. (Bull. Appl. Bot. Genet. Pl. Breed., Suppl. 47, 217, 1930)

S. candelarianum Buk. (Bull. Appl. Bot. Genet. Pl. Breed., Suppl. 47, 218, 1930) (without latin diagnosis)

S. antipoviczii var. *neoantipoviczii* Hawkes (Bull. Imp. Bur. Pl. Breed. Genet., Cambridge, 35, 1944)

S. malinchense Hawkes (Bull. Imp. Bur. Pl. Breed. Genet., Cambridge, 117, 1944)

S. longipedicellatum Bitt. var. *longimucronatum* Hawkes (Bull. Imp. Bur. Pl. Breed. Genet., Cambridge, 117, 1944)

S. tlaxcalense Hawkes (Bull. Imp. Bur. Pl. Breed. Genet., Cambridge, 117–8, 1944)

S. orbiculatibaccatum Lechn. (Trudy po Prikl. Bot. Genet. Selek. **105**, 10–11, 1980)

S. coriaceifoliolatum Lechn. (Trudy po Prik. Bot. Genet. Selek. **105**, 11–12, 1980)

(Note: Lechnovicz's specimens or photographs were not seen by me, but the description clearly indicates that these two species are part of the highly variable *S. stoloniferum*.)

The species, *S. stoloniferum*, is extremely variable, but with the very large number of collections now available to us in the living state it is almost impossible (with one exception) to separate clearly defined specific and subspecific variants. Constant features are the circular corolla outline with large acumens, the coarse appressed hairs over all green parts (not spreading as in *S. polytrichon*), the pedicel glabrous or only sparsely hairy above articulation, and the acuminate leaflets.

At one end of the variation scale are to be found plants with long leaves and white flowers ('*S. longipedicellatum*'); these grade imperceptibly into the pale to medium mauve-flowered forms with rather shorter leaves, formerly classified as *S. ajuscoense*, *S. antipoviczii*, *S. malinchense*, *S. neoantipoviczii* and *S. tlaxcalense*. Even the original collections known to Schlechtendal and Bouché varied in plant size and flower colour. Hawkes (Wiss. Z. Univ. Halle, Math-Nat **6**, 849–54, 1957) established a lectotype, based on the tall specimens with white flowers grown in European botanic gardens in the 1820s and 1830s, coming originally from the base of Mount Orizaba (west or south side, probably).
2n = 48

KEY TO SUBSPECIES

Flower white to various shades of rather pale mauve; plant generally
vigorous **6a. subsp.** *stoloniferum*
Flower deep rich purple; plant generally delicate **6b. subsp.** *moreliae*

6a. Subspecies *stoloniferum*

All green parts with coarse appressed hairs. Leaf (3–)4–5-jugate. Pedicels
glabrous above the articulation. Calyx 5–9 mm long. Corolla white to pale
mauve. Berries 1–2 cm diam. Habit vigorous.
Distribution: Mexico, states of Hidalgo, Mexico, Michoacán, Oaxaca,
Puebla, Querétaro, San Luis Potosí, Tlaxcala and DF.
Derivation: stolon-bearing; this was described at a time when the stolon-
iferous feature was not well known
2n = 48; EBN = 2
Braun., CPC, Gr.Lü., Stur., VIR

6b. Subspecies *moreliae* Hawkes, subsp. nov.

All green parts with less coarse hairs than subsp. *stoloniferum*. Leaf
3–4(–5)-jugate with few, 0–2 pairs, of interjected leaflets and frequently
decurrent lateral leaflets. Pedicel generally glabrous above the articulation.
Calyx very small, 5 mm long. Corolla very dark rich purple. Berries
globular, to about 8 mm diam. Habit delicate.
   Subspecies moreliae *a subspecie* stoloniferum *habitu delicatiore, folio
3–4-jugato, foliolis interjectis paucis, foliolis lateralibus saepe decurrent-
ibus, corolla valde atropurpurea, baccis parvis globosis differt.*
Distribution: Mexico, state of Michoacán. Type: *Hawkes 2530* in Herb.
Kew.
Derivation: named after the City of Morelia, around which this subspecies
appears to be common
2n = 48?
Braun. (EBS 2630), Gr.Lü. (EBS 2630), Stur. (various)

7. *S.* × *vallis-mexici* Juz. (Bull. Acad. Sci. U.R.S.S. **2**, 315–16, 1937)

This hybrid 'species' is distinguished from *S. stoloniferum* by the dark
purple corolla, and broadly obovate to rhomboid terminal leaflet which is
larger than the laterals. Formed as a hybrid between *S. stoloniferum* (2n =
48) and *S. verrucosum* (2n = 24).
Distribution: Mexico, states of México and DF. All localities are in the
Valley of Mexico, where the distributions and altitudes of the two parent
species overlap. In woods, fields, waysides, from 2,400–3,000 m.
Derivation: from the Valley of Mexico
2n = 36
VIR

SERIES XIX *DEMISSA* BUK

(in Buk. et Kameraz, Bases of Potato Breed., 27, 1959)

Series *Demissa* is chiefly distinguished by the very short, rather flattened corolla lobes and high pedicel articulation. All species are hexaploid except two pentaploid species hybrids. The species analysed cytologically possess one genome of *S. verrucosum*, but the nature of the other two genomes is uncertain (see Chapter 5), though some hypotheses have been put forward.
Distribution: Mexico and Guatemala.

KEY TO SPECIES

(1) Corolla white or white splashed with purple; berries globular to ellipsoid   **5. S. hougasii**
Corolla purple (various shades), never white; berries globular to conical   (2)
(2) Habit bushy; stem poorly developed or if long, showing several inflorescences from base upwards; leaflet apex obtuse; berries globular to oval   **2. S. demissum**
Habit normally upright; leaflet apex acute to shortly acuminate; berries conical   (3)
(3) Lateral leaflets sessile, clearly decurrent, diminishing in size rapidly towards leaf base; berry verrucose   **7. S. schenckii**
Lateral leaflets generally petiolulate, not or barely decurrent; berry not verrucose   (4)
(4) Leaf well dissected, with 5–7 pairs of lateral leaflets and 8–11 pairs of interjected leaflets   **4. S. guerreroense**
Leaf moderately dissected, with 2–4(–6) pairs of lateral leaflets and up to 4 pairs of interjected leaflets   (5)
(5) Two distal (uppermost) pairs of lateral leaflets identical in size; corolla pale blue-purple with thin white lines   **1. S. brachycarpum**
Two distal leaflet pairs not always of identical size; corolla showy, deep rich purple   **6. S. iopetalum**

1. S. brachycarpum Correll (US Dept. Agr. Monogr., No. 11, 59–61, 1952)

S. demissum Lindl. var. *longibaccatum* Buk. (Bull. Appl. Bot. Genet. Pl. Breed. Suppl. **47**, 219–20, 1930)
S. oxycarpum Schiede var. *brachycarpum* Corr. (Contr. Texas Res. Found. **1**, 8–10, 1950)

This very widespread and rather variable species may be clearly distinguished from other species in this series by the upright stems, rather poorly dissected leaves with petiolulate leaflets (generally 2–4, occasionally to 6 pairs of laterals), and few (0–3) pairs of interjecteds. A characteristic feature is that the two uppermost leaflet pairs are equal in size and shape; the lower leaflets diminish in size rapidly towards the leaf base. This is very clear under cultivation, less so in wild plants. The corolla is large, with short lobes, rather pale blue-purple in colour with thin white lines. Berries short conical.

Distribution: Mexico, states of Colima, Guerrero, Jalisco, México, Michoacán, Oaxaca (Pacific side), Puebla and Veracruz, at 1,700–3,350 m, in pine and *Abies* forests.

Derivation: short-fruit, comparing it to the longer fruits of *S. oxycarpum*, of which it was once thought to be a variety

2n = 72; EBN = 4

Braun., CPC (as *S. iopetalum* H. 1043), Gr.Lü., Stur., VIR

2. *S. demissum* Lindl. (J. Hort. Soc. **3**, 68–70, 1848)

S. utile Klotzsch (Allgem. Gart.-Ztg. **17**, 315, 1849)
S. demissum var. *klotzschii* Bitt. (Fedde, Repert. **11**, 454, 1912; **12**, 454, 1913)
S. alpicum Standl. et Steyerm. (Publ. Field Mus. Nat. Hist. **7**, 232–3, 1947)

Bukasov described the following forms, but without latin diagnoses, in Rybin, Bull. Appl. Bot. Genet. Pl. Breed., 2nd ser, **20**, 698, 1929; Suppl. 47, 221–2, 1929:

S. demissum f. *adpressoacuminatum* Buk.
S. demissum f. *tlaxpehualcoense* Buk.
S. demissum f. *xitlense* Buk.

In the same publication (p. 224) Lechnovicz described *S. demissum* f. *atrocyaneum* Lechn., also without a latin diagnosis.

In addition the following varieties and forms were described by Hawkes, with latin diagnoses, in Bull. Imp. Bur. Pl. Breed. Genet., Cambridge, 115–16, 1944:

S. demissum f. *calycotrichum* Hawkes
S. demissum f. *tolucense* Hawkes
S. demissum var. *orientale* Hawkes
S. demissum var. *mastoidostigma* Hawkes
S. demissum f. *perotanum* Hawkes
S. demissum f. *longifilamentosum* Hawkes
S. demissum var. *megalocalyx* Hawkes

Grows in rosettes or semi-rosettes but sometimes produces a long stem. Leaflets sessile to subsessile with rounded apex. Corolla purple, generally with very short lobes. Berry globular to oval.

Distribution: Mexico, states of Chihuahua, Guerrero, Hidalgo, México, Michoacán, Morelos, Puebla, Tlaxcala, Veracruz and DF; Guatemala, depts Huehuetenango, Sacatepéquez and Totonicapán.

This is an extremely common and widespread species which has been much collected, especially in the Valley of Mexico and on the slopes of the great volcanoes. All the named varieties and forms come within its general variation. It grows from 2,650–3,800 m in pine and *Abies* forests, generally in shade.

Derivation: low, humble – describing its habit

2n = 72; EBN = 4

Braun., CPC, Gr.Lü., Stur., VIR

3. *S.* × *edinense* Berth. (Ann. Sci. Agron., Paris, **2**, 195, 1911)

Includes all forms that have arisen as hybrids between *S. tuberosum* and *S. demissum*. Lateral leaflets petiolulate, 4–6-paired, with up to 9 pairs of interjecteds. Corolla large, with short lobes, much larger than that of *S. demissum*.

KEY TO SUBSPECIES

Plant low-growing, with short spreading stems and pale flowers

3a. subsp. *edinense*

Plant tall, vigorous, with stems up to about 50 cm long and large dark flowers   **3b. subsp.** *salamanii*

3a. Subspecies *edinense*

Formed as a natural hybrid in the Edinburgh Botanic Gardens and elsewhere, between *S. demissum* and *S. tuberosum* subsp. *tuberosum*.

Distribution: This subspecies has no natural distribution. It has been cultivated in botanic gardens and potato breeding stations for its resistance to *Phytophthora infestans*.

Derivation: from the Edinburgh Botanic Gardens, where Berthault first obtained materials for his description

2n = 60

Apparently not now in cultivation

3b. Subspecies *salamanii* (Hawkes) Hawkes (Scott. Pl. Breed. Rec., 119, 1963)

S. salamanii Hawkes (Bull. Imp. Bur. Pl. Breed. Genet., Cambridge, 116, 1944)

Formed as a natural hybrid in Mexico from *S. demissum* and *S. tuberosum* subsp. *andigena*; leaf much more dissected than in the typical subspecies.

Distribution: Mexico, states of México, Michoacán, Puebla, Tlaxcala, Veracruz and DF, at altitudes of 2,600–3,500 m. Growing as a weed of potato fields where *S. demissum* has invaded or occurs in the immediate vicinity.

Derivation: named in honour of the distinguished potato breeder and historian, Dr Redcliffe N. Salaman

$2n = 60$

Apparently not now available in gene banks

4. S. guerreroense Corr. (US Dept. Agric. Monogr., No. 11, 65–7, 1952)

Distinguished from *S. demissum* by the conical fruits and from *S. brachycarpum* by the well-dissected leaves. Leaf well dissected, with 5–7 pairs of primary leaflets and 8–11 pairs of interjected leaflets. Corolla large, to 3 cm diam., with very short lobes, pale mauve to lavender, with thin white lines on upper surface (as in *S. brachycarpum*). Berries conical, acute, to 3 cm long.

Distribution: Mexico, states of Guerrero and Jalisco, at 2,800–3,000 m altitude, in pine-oak forest.

Derivation: from the State of Guerrero

$2n = 72$; EBN = 4

Braun., Gr.Lü., Stur., VIR

5. S. hougasii Corr. (Madroño **14**, 236, 1958)

S. verrucosum var. *spectabilis* Corr. (US Dept. Agric. Monogr., No. 11, 228, 1952)

S. spectabile (Corr.) Hawkes (Ann. Mag. Nat. Hist., Ser. 12, **7**, 701–2, 1954; non *S. spectabile* Steudel, Nomencl. Bot., ed. 2, pt. 2, 606, 1841)

Habit rather coarse and bushy. Leaves 3–4-jugate, with sessile to petiolulate lateral leaflets, and 1–6-paired interjected leaflets. Stems, leaves and inflorescence branches sparsely and minutely pubescent. Corolla rotate, white or with purple central petal streaks or blotches on the outer surface. Berries globular to ellipsoid.

Differs from *S. demissum* and *S. guerreroense* in its tall upright habit, white corolla (often tinged purple in the centre or along petal centres), longer corolla lobes, and petiolulate leaflets. From *S. brachycarpum* and *S. guerreroense* it differs in the corolla form and colour, and in the round berries. Bears some similarities to *S. stoloniferum* in series *Longipedicellata*.

Distribution: Mexico, states of Jalisco and Michoacán, from 1,600–2,950 m (said by Correll to ascend to 4,000 m but this seems doubtful) in pine-*Abies* forests. Rare.

Derivation: named in honour of the distinguished potato geneticist, Dr R.W. Hougas, who founded the Potato Introduction Station at Sturgeon Bay, Wisconsin

$2n = 72$; EBN = 4

CPC, Gr.Lü., Stur., VIR

6. S. iopetalum (Bitt.) Hawkes (Bull. Imp. Bur. Pl. Breed. Genet., Cambridge, 30, 1944)

S. verrucosum Schlechtd. var. *iopetalum* Bitt. (Fedde, Repert. **11**, 455–7, 1912)

Leaf 4–6-jugate, with 0–2(–4) pairs of interjected leaflets. Lateral leaflets decreasing gradually towards leaf base (contrast *S. brachycarpum*) and slightly decurrent. Inflorescence large, several-branched. Calyx often trilabiate or irregular. Corolla rotate, with flat short lobes, 2.5–3.0 cm diam., showy, deep rich purple. Style exserted 4 mm above anther column. Berries conical.
Distribution: Mexico, States of Hidalgo, Puebla and Veracruz, at altitudes of 1,900–2,360 m, on east-facing escarpment slopes in pine-oak forest.
Note: the habit and leaf of this species are similar to those of *S. brachycarpum* but the flower is very distinct.
Derivation: with violet-coloured petals
2n = 72; EBN = 4
Braun., CPC, Gr.Lü., Stur., VIR

7. S. schenckii Bitt. (Fedde, Repert. **11**, 448, 1912)

S. confusum Corr. (US Dept. Agric. Monogr., No. 11, 63, 1952; non *S. confusum* Morton, Contr. U.S. Nat Herb. **29**, 70, 1944)
S. nelsonii Corr. (Madroño **14**, 236, 1958; non *S. nelsonii* Dun. in D.C. Prodr. **13**, I, 123, 1852)
S. reconditum Corr. (Wrightia **2**, 175, 1961)

Although the type specimen of this species in Berlin was destroyed during the second world war, a drawing was left by Bitter in Herb Göttingen and the species was re-found by Raul Flores Crespo in 1964 in the type locality, near Esperanza, Veracruz State (Agricultura Técnica, Mexico, **2**(8), 374–5, 1968). This compares very closely with the type description and is certainly the authentic species. Unfortunately Flores Crespo did not designate a neotype in this publication. Accordingly, I designate as **neotype** of *S. schenckii*: *Hjerting and Gómez 290*, in Herb. Kew, from Mexico, Puebla State, Esperanza, at 2,470 m; thus, so far as can be seen, this also represents a topotype.
Leaf 2–3(–4)-jugate, the terminal larger than the laterals which diminish rapidly towards the leaf base; lateral leaflets sessile, generally with a long decurrent wing on the rachis; interjected leaflets generally absent but very occasionally one or two minute leaflets are formed. Corolla rotate, to pentagonal, 2.5–3.0 cm diam., dark purple outside, much paler inside. Berry conical, white-verrucose.
Distribution: Mexico, states of Oaxaca, Puebla, Querétaro and Veracruz, from 2,600–3,000 m in pine forests and amongst bushes.

Derivation: named in honour of the original collector, Heinrich Schenck.
2n = 72 (not 2n = 48, as noted by Flores Crespo)
Gr.Lü., Stur.

8. *S.* × *semidemissum* Juz. (Bull. Acad. Sci. U.R.S.S. **3**, 314–15, 1937)

Differs from *S. demissum* in the upright habit and petiolulate leaflets, and
from *S.* × *edinse* in the large terminals and poor leaf dissection (2–4-leaflet
pairs). Is of undoubted hybrid origin produced probably from a *S. demissum* × *S. verrucosum* cross, with the participation of an unreduced *S.
verrucosum* gamete. Rarely forms berries.
Distribution: Mexico, states of México, Morelos and DF in and around the
Valley of Mexico, often on the slopes of the great volcanoes, from
2,500–3,500 m. Grows as a field weed or along hedges and waysides,
sometimes in pine forests.
Derivation: 'half *S. demissum*', that is to say, showing many but not all the
characters of *S. demissum*.
2n = 60
Gr.Lü., VIR

CHAPTER 7

GENETIC RESOURCES OF
THE POTATO

The need for resistance genes

Like all crop plants the potato is susceptible to pests and diseases. This is partly due to the fact that modern agriculture is dependent on the cultivation of standard clones on large areas of land. Thus, if a pest or disease can successfully attack one plant it will be able to run through and decimate the entire crop in a field, a village or even a complete district or country. Under traditional agriculture, on the other hand, where mixtures of different clones or genotypes are grown, a pest or disease does not find it so easy to spread rapidly, because of the genetic diversity of the crop concerned. Even so, whole groups of cultivars or even land races may lack completely any useful genes which could protect the crop from insect or fungal attack. Many crops have been lost because they do not possess resistance to a pathogen newly arrived in a region where there has been no opportunity previously to build up or select for resistance genes.

A well-known but tragic example of this is the rapid loss of the potato crop in Ireland in 1845–1847, when the late blight fungus (*Phytophthora infestans*) destroyed the entire crop, thus causing famine and untold misery.

In the last two decades we have come to rely on chemical methods of pest and disease control. However, these are expensive and out of the financial reach of many poor farmers in the developing world. Plant breeders are thus trying more and more to introduce genetic resistance to pests and diseases into many crops. This has the additional advantage of reducing potential or actual damage to the environment.

Resistance to pests and diseases or ability to withstand environmental extremes of cold, heat or drought was not always available in advanced breeding stocks or highly bred varieties in the first half of the twentieth century. In the last 30 or 40 years, however, breeders have recognized the need for the introduction of a greater range of crop genetic diversity from parts of the world where it still exists. Breeders, collectors and taxonomists have also increasingly made use of resistance and adaptation characters derived from related wild species. Indeed, this had already begun in the late 1920s and early 1930s through the pioneer work of the Russian geneticist, N.I. Vavilov. Nowadays, the use of primitive land races and wild species, which together are classed as the most important elements of genetic resources, is almost taken for granted. Yet, with the potato, because of the vast and barely unutilized diversity of wild species, there is still much to evaluate and introduce into standard cultivars from these and from the wealth of primitive Andean cultivated forms, by a process of resistance breeding, as it is generally called.

Early attempts at resistance breeding

It seems likely that the potato may have been the first crop plant in which resistance breeding was attempted, and this was due particularly to the late blight disaster in Ireland and the continuing threat of outbreaks thereafter.

In the second half of the nineteenth century attempts were made to find late blight resistance in wild or native potatoes brought to the USA and Europe for investigation. Unfortunately, this work did not result in much success until Salaman in 1908 showed that resistance was present in two species, *S. edinense* and *S. demissum* (Salaman 1911). The former was later shown to be a hybrid of *S. demissum* × *S. tuberosum*, and it thus became clear that the blight resistance in both cases came from the same Mexican wild species, *S. demissum*. Seeds of *S. edinense* were also sent from the USA to Germany in 1908 and were used to create the so-called W-races (Ross 1986). These were used to breed the first cultivar with *S. demissum* genes, Sandnudel, in 1934 (Ross 1986). Other researchers, such as Findlay, Wilson and Knappe, were all attempting to introduce blight resistance from *S. demissum* into cultivar breeding at about that time (Ross 1979).

This early work, then, was the beginning of attempts to introduce 'new blood', as it was often called, from Latin American species, both wild and cultivated, into Europe and the USA, and thus to improve resistance to disease. However, we should also mention at this stage the efforts of the Reverend Chauncey Goodrich in the USA, who in 1851 obtained a small collection of tubers from South America. These were bought in the market of Panamá and one of them, which he named 'Rough Purple Chile', particularly impressed him. It is now thought highly likely that these potatoes really did come from Chile, despite Salaman's doubts (Salaman 1949). From this Chilean introduction the variety 'Garnet Chile' was derived from selfed seed, and later 'Early Rose', which was involved in the production of most, if not all, the really early-maturing European varieties. For this reason its ability to form tubers under the long summer days of northern latitudes strongly supported the evidence that its grandparent 'Rough Purple Chile' really came from southern Chile where the day-length conditions are very similar.

Genetic resources exploration

In 1925 a fresh stimulus was given to potato breeding by the Russian expeditons to Mexico and South America (Bukasov 1933; Bukasov and Lechnovicz 1935). The basic thinking behind these was that of N.I. Vavilov, who argued that the chances of success in finding and using useful characters of resistance and adaptation in a crop were likely to be greatly improved if a wide range of material was available to breeders – what we now call 'a broad genetic base'.

The results of the Russian expeditions to Mexico and South America were spectacular. In the first place they claimed to have found 15 distinct cultivated species, within a polyploid series ranging from diploid to penta-ploid; and they described many new wild species, some of which showed frost resistance, others high dry matter, and others blight resistance.

The Russians were enthusiastic taxonomic 'splitters', creating many new species where few existed before. In place of their 15 cultivated species we now recognize only seven. Three of these are sexually reproducing, whilst four are obvious hybrids and highly (though not completely) sterile. Nevertheless, the Russian discovery and careful study of potato genetic diversity in South America and Mexico engendered considerable enthusiasm for potato collecting by potato breeders from other countries, who themselves mounted similar expeditions in the 1930s.

Probably the largest of these expeditions was the British Empire (later, Commonwealth) Potato Collecting Expedition in 1939, in which I was fortunate enough to take part, and whose leader was E.K. Balls, a professional plant collector. The expedition was financed by Common-wealth countries, under the auspices of the Imperial (later, Common-wealth) Bureaux. This expedition collected in Argentina, Bolivia, Peru, Ecuador and Colombia, ending just at the outbreak of the Second World War. Over 1,400 samples of potatoes (mostly cultivated) were collected; additional material was sent later by colleagues in the countries that the expedition had passed through, bringing the total up to over 2,000 (Hawkes 1941, 1944). Extra collections of cultivated diploids were added in the 1960s by Dodds, Simmonds and Paxman, and these are mentioned in the Inventory of the Commonwealth Potato Collection (1969). Some of the materials were lost subsequently but much was later turned into true seed and is still available at the Commonwealth Potato Collection in Dundee, Scotland.

After the War, from 1948–1951, I established a potato research pro-gramme in Colombia and my colleagues and I collected germplasm of cultivated materials and some wild species from that country, and also Ecuador and Venezuela. During that period I made my first collecting trip to Mexico and sent the materials back to the Commonwealth Collection. I collected more material from the USA, Mexico and Central America in 1958 on a Birmingham University Expedition, together with J.P. Hjerting and R.N. Lester (Hawkes 1959). This material formed the main basis of my own germplasm collection, duplicates of which were sent to the newly formed Potato Introduction Station at Sturgeon Bay, Wisconsin. By that time the techniques of potato germplasm conservation had much improved and nearly all those collections are still alive.

Mention should be made here of the very fine potato germplasm collection at Sturgeon Bay, Wisconsin, USA, founded by Dr R.W. Hougas in 1950, and now under the direction of Dr John Bamberg. In the last few years the Sturgeon Bay group have organised, with USDA funding, two expeditions to Bolivia, five to Mexico and one to Chile, with the prospect of several others in the future. The materials are constantly being evaluated cooperatively with other institutions for resistances to pests and diseases, and for adaptation to environmental extremes.

At this point I should record the tremendous advances in potato taxonomy and exploration made by Donovan Correll, who collected extensively in Mexico in 1947 and 1948, and in Chile, Argentina, Bolivia, Peru, Ecuador and Colombia in 1958 and 1960. As a result of these efforts he monographed the USA, Mexican and Central American species (Correll 1952), following this with his magnum opus on the whole group throughout the Americas (Correll 1962). His living material is conserved at the Potato Introduction Station, Sturgeon Bay and his latter work is a point of reference for all potato collectors and taxonomists.

Turning now to Argentina, J.P. Hjerting and his Danish colleague, based in Tucumán, had been assembling collections of wild potatoes from that country since 1948. In 1965–66 J.P. Hjerting, K. Rahn (a *Plantago* specialist), and I spent some five months collecting further germplasm material, some of which we hoped to use in solving taxonomic problems that were as yet unclear to us. We were also joined by K.A. Okada, who later became a first-class potato collector in Argentina, his own country, together with Andrea Clausen, making exploration trips year by year for a very long period. Our 1965–66 Argentine expedition was very successful, and our book on the potatoes of Argentina, Brazil, Paraguay and Uruguay appeared in 1969. (I should add here that I also visited southern Brazil and Uruguay in 1958 to broaden our collections of species from those regions also.)

Bolivia was next tackled. I had found several new species there in 1939, amongst which were *S. berthaultii*, *S. oplocense*, *S. sucrense* and *S. tarijense* – all of considerable value to potato breeders. However, much more work was needed, and to this end Hjerting and I, together with P.J. Cribb (England), and Z. Huamán (Peru), spent four months in southern Peru and Bolivia in 1971, forming another large collection of living material. In 1974 I led a Dutch-funded expedition to southern Peru, Bolivia and north-western Argentina, with A. van Harten, J. Landeo and D. Astley; we were joined in Argentina by J.Th. Hermsen and K.A. Okada. The main purpose of this expedition was to find as wide a range of germplasm as possible with resistance to round cyst nematode biotypes. Finally, in 1980 (with a short follow-up in 1981), we attempted to 'finish off' Bolivia with a three-team international expedition, including besides myself, J.P. Hjerting from Denmark, L. van Soest from Holland, W. Hondelmann from Germany, D. Astley from the UK, Z. Huamán and J. Landeo from Peru (CIP), K.A. Okada from Argentina, and various Bolivian agronomists, notably I. Avilés, A. Moreira, C. Claure and C. Alarcón. We had all been helped tremendously in 1939 and 1971 by the well-known Bolivian botanist, M. Cárdenas and also at times by H. Gandarillas and Ana-Maria Krüger. Now that the Bolivian and Argentine phases have been completed one misses very much the friendly and co-operative botanists and agronomists from those countries, who did so much to help us achieve our aims. The results appeared in a monograph published by Hawkes and Hjerting (1989).

I should also mention two subsequent expeditions to Bolivia funded by the US government, and with R. Hoopes, K.A. Okada and I. Avilés taking part in 1986 and 1987.

It was now high time to turn to Peru. My collections in that country started in 1939. Most of our collections were made in the Puno/Cuzco region in the southern part of the country, where we met the well-known Peruvian botanist, C. Vargas and collected material with him. He invited me back to Cuzco in 1964 to give a series of lectures and before this I was fortunate enough to travel with C. Ochoa from central to northern Peru, an area I had never before had the opportunity of visiting. After the Cuzco lectures Vargas and I made many collections of S. lignicaule, S. raphanifolium, S. sparsipilum and S. marinasense in Cuzco department. References to the excellent earlier works of Vargas and of Ochoa can be sought in their publications (Vargas 1936, 1949, 1956; Ochoa 1962). Later works by Ochoa are quoted in Chapter 6.

A complete new phase of potato germplasm collecting was started with the foundation by R.L. Sawyer of the International Potato Center (CIP) in Lima, Peru, in 1972. Even in 1971 when Sawyer was in Peru with the North Carolina Agricultural Mission, he had kindly loaned us a vehicle; and he supported our Bolivian exploration work also in 1974 and particularly in 1980.

Germplasm exploration, especially of cultigens, was accorded highest priority at CIP, and C. Ochoa, particularly, was involved with this from an early stage, as well as Z. Huamán and other CIP scientists. Over 13,000 cultivar accessions were assembled, but when duplicates had been identified over the years the number of distinct genotypes could be reduced to about 5,000. Very many collections of wild material were made also, probably somewhere about 1,500 accessions. Unfortunately, I have not been able to examine these in any detail, but it would be correct to say that Ochoa's exploratory and taxonomic studies in Peru and elsewhere have added immensely to our knowledge of wild potatoes in Latin America, for which he is to be heartily congratulated.

Another important potato germplasm collection was established co-operatively at Braunschweig between the West German and Dutch governments. This possesses the basic collections made by H. Ross and colleagues in Latin America on the German Botanical-Agricultural Expedition to the Andes in 1959. The expedition travelled in Argentina, Bolivia and Peru, and gathered materials of considerable breeding value, particularly wild species.

Many duplicates from my own collections are held at Braunschweig, and of course the samples gathered by the German, Dutch and British teams on the 1980 expedition to Bolivia are also conserved there.

In the early 1980s the US government funded three collecting expeditions to Mexico led by R. Tarn, accompanied by a staff member, Roman Ross, from the Potato Introduction Station (and J.P.. Hjerting on two occasions). Mexican colleagues were also involved in these collecting trips. Despite the many collecting expeditions of D. Correll and my own, mentioned above, these expeditions were able to locate species unknown before in the living state such as *S. nayaritense* and *S. stenophyllidium*, and two new species, *S. tarnii* and *S. matehualae*. Tarn had previously made collections in Mexico in 1967, and living material of these is also stored at Sturgeon Bay.

In 1988 the newly appointed Sturgeon Bay taxonomist, D. Spooner, went to Mexico for a further US-sponsored exploration trip, together with J.P. Hjerting. Amongst other species they were able to obtain living materials of *S. hintonii* – frequently looked for but never found hitherto.

In early 1989 Spooner collected in Chile, in company with the Chilean agronomist, A. Contreras. They made detailed collections of the non-tuber-bearing species *S. brevidens* and *S. etuberosum*, together with *S. maglia*, which at the time of writing are being studied in the laboratory and experimental field in Wisconsin.

Through lack of information I cannot give details of potato collecting expeditions from Japan (Professor M. Matsubayashi) and later ones from the USSR (Academician P.M. Zhukovsky and Dr A.G. Zykin). Samples were collected in Argentina, Chile and elsewhere by these scientists (Zhukovsky 1959; Zykin 1968) and also by the German geneticist, H. Brücher, and some of these are to be found in Braunschweig and Sturgeon Bay. Many smaller collecting trips were also made from time to time, but unfortunately space does not permit their being mentioned.

This long account (which I am afraid may have been rather tedious to the non-specialist) attempts to show the enormous amount of effort that has gone into the exploration and collection of potato germplasm. Besides the collecting of materials of possible use to breeders in the future, the taxonomist is given the opportunity to observe populations in the wild and to assess their phenotypic diversity. If he is lucky he will be able to compare phenotypes of materials from their native habitat with phenotypes based on the same genotypes in the experimental field and glasshouse. Sometimes changes occur, sometimes not. Often, the type specimen in a herbarium proves to be an extremely aberrant or not very typical example of the particular species range. Without the experience of collecting and observing these materials in nature, and then studying the same genotypes again under controlled conditions, it would have been (and frequently was) quite impossible to understand the taxonomic position and range of the species concerned.

I was fortunate in being able to study and collect wild and cultivated materials in most parts of the Americas where they occur. The regrettable gap in my experience is Chile, where apart from a short visit to Santiago in 1966 I have not been able to collect. Similarly, I have no experience of

Paraguay, but that is perhaps not such a deprivation since the two species there, *S. chacoense* and *S. commersonii* subsp. *malmeanum* occur equally well across the border in Argentina.

All these recent collecting expeditions have taken place in collaboration with scientists from the countries concerned. Furthermore, duplicate samples have been left with the national scientists and institutes, thus completely negating the assertions appearing from time to time in the press that the 'rich nations' are robbing the poorer ones of their plant genetic resources patrimony. Nothing could be further from the truth. Samples from the major germplasm collections such as those at CIP, Sturgeon Bay and Braunschweig are always freely available, together with screening results, to all *bona fide* research scientists.

Gene bank genetic resources conservation

Obviously potatoes when collected need to be conserved in gene or seed banks. True (or botanical) seed of potatoes is easy to conserve, even at room temperature without special drying techniques. Naturally it keeps much better when dried to 4–5 per cent humidity and preserved at sub-zero temperatures ($-10°C$ to $-20°C$). Under these conditions it can easily be kept in a viable condition for 20 to 30 years or more. Even at $+5°C$ in sealed glass containers for 15 years, Howard (1969) found germination percentages ranging from 68 to 92. Even after 25 years (Howard 1980) germination was still remarkably high in some lines (82–100 per cent) though others had fallen to zero. Tubers are more difficult to conserve and normally need to be grown out every year. This is labour-intensive and carries the threat of virus or other disease infection, and possible mixing of stocks through human error. Odd-number polyploids or species hybrids cannot be conserved as seed, and need to be preserved as meristem by means of *in vitro* cultures. Because the cultivated potato is grown from clones and is highly heterozygous, propagation by seed will destroy a particular genotype, and in that case yearly field planting or *in vitro* culture are the only ways of preserving it. On the other hand, if all one needs is to conserve gene pools, one might just as well propagate from true seed and not worry about the fact that every seedling will be a very distinct genotype.

However, there is yet another problem with cultivated potatoes. As we have seen earlier, diploid cultivated species (and most wild ones also) are self-incompatible, and thus seeds can only be obtained by crossing two clones. The recommended practice is to take a set of several clones from a particular location, village or market and mass-pollinate them in a group under isolation, preventing access of pollinating insects. This will ensure that the resulting seeds represent the local gene pool, and if useful resistance characters are identified it will be at once easy to identify the gene pool where they originated, and even to go back to the place where they were collected if more material is needed. If this method is not followed it may be difficult to find out where the possibly useful genes originated.

Tetraploids are self-fertile, and those from the Andes (*S. tuberosum* subsp. *andigena*) will produce seed when self-pollinated. Unfortunately, two or three generations of selfing gives rise to inbreeding depression and loss of fertility. Thus, even with tetraploids, it is better to follow the methods described above for diploids.

This discussion has centred up to now mainly on cultivated potatoes. Wild species are basically similar; diploids, with few exceptions, are self-incompatible and tetraploids may also suffer from inbreeding depression, though the hard evidence for this seems not to be available in the literature. In every case where fresh seed is needed it is best to try to raise at least 20 plants, collect and mix the pollen together and brush the pollen mixture on to the styles of all plants. Roughly equal amounts of seeds are to be harvested from each plant and all bulked together. In this way, with potatoes as well as all other outcrossing plant species, inbreeding depression and genetic drift will be avoided. When the new batch of seed is returned to the gene bank care should be taken not to mix it with the older or original seeds of the same collection.

Records should be kept of the collector and collector's number, the accession number, and other 'passport data' concerned with its collection, such as country and place of origin, altitude, date of collection, latitude and longitude coordinates, habitat, plant characters such as flower colour, vernacular name and farming practices if the sample was from a cultivated species. Some of these data might well figure in the published inventories, together with evaluation information.

The publication of inventories or lists of materials available for breeders and research scientists is of the greatest importance. Now that records can be held on computers it will not be very difficult and certainly not so expensive as it was formerly, to publish updated inventories every five years or so (see Chapter 6, pp. 65–6). In this way breeders can be informed of new materials as and when they are received and multiplied up to provide seed for exchange.

Genetic resources evaluation

Evaluation or screening of gene bank materials is an essential part of genetic resources work. Unevaluated materials are useless, since unless they were collected in an area where useful characters are known to exist as a result of previous screening of other materials from that area, no one will be interested in them and the effort of collecting and maintaining them will be wasted.

On the other hand, materials evaluated for resistance to a particular pest or disease and found to have no, or only a very low level of, resistance should not be discarded. Such material might later be found to possess useful resistance to other pests and pathogens, or qualities whose nature is at present not understood. Clearly identified duplicates (as found at CIP) might well be considered for discarding; even so, although CIP's policy is to eliminate most duplicates of a particular clone, it certainly keeps a few growing, and it retains true or botanical seed for long-term storage of each duplicate, no matter how similar to the others it appears to be.

Many gene bank managers or directors consider that after they have grown out material for characterization no more evaluation is really possible. 'Characterization', in gene bank parlance, means the description of morphological and highly heritable agronomic characters. Standard descriptors and descriptor states are published, crop by crop, by the International Board for Plant Genetic Resources (IBPGR), that for culti-vated potatoes having been published more than 10 years ago (Huamán *et al.* 1977). This descriptor list is far too complex for everyday needs, but fulfilled its purpose excellently in the computer-aided identification of duplicates. A simpler list for everyday needs is now needed for cultivated potatoes.

All inventories should include the results of evaluation for resistance and adaptation. Braunschweig, Sturgeon Bay and CIP provide much useful information of this type. CPC (Scotland) gives some brief characterization data, whilst Balcarce, Gross Lüsewitz and Leningrad provide no screening results of any kind. It is very much to be hoped that information of this sort, which I know to be available through my personal contacts, will appear in future editions.

Many gene bank managers and directors rightly state that they have no time or facilities to carry out evaluation for resistance to pests and diseases and tolerance to environmental extremes. I agree wholeheartedly with them on this point; proper gene bank management is a full-time activity. What can be done, however, is to identify scientists in universities, agricultual research stations and other organizations, who would be inter-ested and enthusiastic enough to carry out such tests. In some cases breeders themselves might become involved, but in general they cannot be expected to carry out large-scale evaluation surveys. To my knowledge, the gene bank directors at Sturgeon Bay and at Braunschweig have found co-operative scientists and funding to carry out such work (see, for example van Soest *et al.* 1980, 1983, 1984; van Soest and Hondelmann 1983; Rowe and Sequeira 1970, etc.). Evaluation work at CIP goes along hand in hand with the germplasm bank activities (see CIP Annual Reports quoted in Hawkes and Hjerting 1989). Finally, a vast amount of evaluation and breeding work was carried out by Professor H. Ross at Cologne and this has been excellently summarized and related to other work (Ross 1986). We shall refer to this in more detail later.

Enough has been said here to stress the need for evaluation to be carried out, published in research papers, and finally to be incorporated in gene bank inventories, so that breeders and others may see at a glance the potential value of the materials available for use.

Evaluation results

There is a vast literature on the evaluation for resistance and adaptation of wild potato species and South American indigenous cultivars, needing a book as long as this present one to show it in any detail. I therefore propose to give an outline of this information in tabular form (Table 7.2) whilst beginning with a useful survey by Huamán (1983) on evaluations of the Andean cultivars at the International Potato Center (Table 7.1). Further details will be found in the CIP Inventory (Huamán 1987). It must be noted that only the barest details can be given in Table 7.2, without any information about the type of resistance and the genes identified. Screening results, where they are detailed enough, generally indicate that only certain lines of a particular species show resistance. The percentage of resistance lines varies by species and areas. Thus *S. demissum* exhibits high percentages of resistance of two types (vertical and horizontal) to

Table 7.1 Data on evaluations conducted at CIP, using native Andean cultivars

Traits evaluated	Accessions evaluated	Accessions with some resistance	
	No.	No.	%
FUNGUS DISEASES			
Late blight	964	224	23.24
Pink rot	2,968	3	0.10
Common scab	927	64	6.90
Wart	1,622	66	4.07
Smut	329	2	0.61
Charcoal rot	2,383	46	1.93
BACTERIAL DISEASES			
Soft rot	226	48	21.24
Pseudomonas wilt	28	15	53.57
VIRUS DISEASES			
PVX	627	181	25.97
PVY	601	41	6.82
PLRV	1,112	27	2.43
NEMATODES			
Globodera pallida	5,264	311	5.91
G. rostochiensis	1,252	213	17.01
Meloidogyne incognita acrita	3,938	643	16.33
INSECTS			
Phthorimaea tuber moth	2,871	404	14.07
ENVIRONMENTAL STRESS			
Frost	341	76	24.63
Hail	3,932	1,319	33.55
Total	29,455	3,683	12.50

(Reproduced by kind permission of the author, Dr Z. Huamán (1983) and the International Potato Center (CIP).)

Table 7.2 General summary of evaluation results on resistance to the major potato diseases and pests, and adaptation to environmental extremes. Only more important species included.

I FUNGUS RESISTANCE

1. *Phytophthora infestans* (late blight)
S. demissum, S. bulbocastanum, S. polyadenium, S. pinnatisectum, S. stoloniferum, S. verrucosum, S. tuberosum subsp. *andigena, S. phureja, S. microdontum, S. berthaultii, S. tarijense, S. circaeifolium, S. vernei.*
2. *Synchytrium endobioticum* (wart)
S. tuberosum (both subspecies), also to R_2 and R_3 races in a range of wild species from Bolivia including *S. sparsipilum, S. acaule* (and *S. spegazzinii* from Argentina).
3. *Streptomyces scabies* (common scab)
S. chacoense, S. commersonii, S. yungasense and various cultivated species.

II BACTERIAL RESISTANCE

4. *Pseudomonas solanacearum* (bacterial wilt)
Promising species are, in particular, *S. chacoense* and *S. sparsipilum*. Resistance is also found in *S. phureja, S. stenotomum* and *S. microdontum*.
5. *Erwinia carotovora* (soft rot; blackleg)
Resistance found in some accessions of *S. bulbocastanum, S. chacoense, S. demissum, S. hjertingii, S. leptophyes, S. microdontum, S. megistacrolobum, S. phureja, S. pinnatisectum, S. tuberosum* subsp. *andigena*, etc.

III VIRUS RESISTANCE

6. **Potato virus X**
S. acaule, S. chacoense, S. curtilobum, S. phureja, S. sucrense, S. tarijense, S. sparsipilum, S. tuberosum subsp. *andigena*, and several other species (Hawkes and Hjerting 1989).
7. **Potato virus Y**
S. chacoense, S. stoloniferum, S. phureja, S. demissum, S. tuberosum subsp. *andigena* (Ross 1986, pp. 70–2).
8. **Potato leaf roll virus**
S. brevidens, S. etuberosum, S. acaule, S. raphanifolium.
9. **Spindle tuber viroid**
S. acaule from Peru (good resistance), *S. berthaultii, S. guerreroense.*

IV INSECT RESISTANCE

10. *Leptinotarsa decemlineata* (Colorado beetle)
S. chacoense, S. demissum, S. commersonii, S. berthaultii, S. tarijense, S. polyadenium.
11. *Myzus persicae, Macrosiphum euphorbiae* (aphids)
S. berthaultii, S. stoloniferum, S. multidissectum, S. medians, S. marinasense, S. lignicaule, S. infundibuliforme, S. chomatophilum, S. bulbocastanum, S. bukasovii.

V NEMATODE RESISTANCE

12. *Globodera rostochiensis, G. pallida* (potato cyst nematode)
S. acaule, S. spegazzinii, S. vernei, S. gourlayi, S. capsicibaccatum, S. boliviense, S. bulbocastanum, S. cardiophyllum, S. oplocense, S. sparsipilum, S. sucrense and several other species from Bolivia and Argentina.

Table 7.2   (*Cont.*)

V NEMATODE RESISTANCE

13. *Meloidogyne incognita* (root-knot nematode)
S. chacoense, S. microdontum, S. phureja, S. sparsipilum, S. tuberosum subsp. *andigena* and *S. curtilobum.*

VI PHYSIOLOGICAL CHARACTERS

14. **Frost**
S. acaule, S. ajanhuiri, S. boliviense, S. brachistotrichum, S. brevicaule, S. brevidens, S. canasense, S. chomatophilum, S. commersonii, S. curtilobum, S. demissum, S. juzepczukii, S. megistacrolobum, S. multidissectum, S. raphanifolium, S. sanctae-rosae, S. toralapanum and *S. vernei.* By far the greatest frost resister is *S. acaule.*
15. **Heat and drought**
S. acaule, S. bulbocastanum, S. chacoense, S. megistacrolobum, S. microdontum, S. papita, S. pinnatisectum and *S. tarijense.*
16. **Lack of tuber blackening**
S. hjertingii.

(Based on Ross 1986, Hawkes and Hjerting 1989, CIP reports, and various inventories.)

Phytophthora infestans. Other species show less. In fact, gene mapping (geographical, not chromosomal) is in its infancy, and could be of great interest in the future. In the table referred to I have in general not included species where fewer than one or two lines show resistance out of many tested.

Another complication is the percentage of resistance alleles in a population. Some populations (or accessions) possess very low percentages of resistance genes; thus the breeder or evaluator is always anxious to discover populations where the resistance allele percentage is very high so that most of his crossed progenies will possess it.

To sum up this section, it is clear that evaluation results point to the presence of useful characters in a wide range of species. In some species the useful characters seem to be widespread and in others sporadic. Different types of resistance are known, and the inheritance of some is certainly much better than others. There are still very large gaps in our knowledge, and when a thorough literature survey is carried out, as for Bolivia recently, one can see what a complex subject this tends to be. Nevertheless, some species are outstandingly promising, as for instance *S. acaule, S. chacoense, S. berthaultii, S. brevidens, S. bulbocastanum, S. demissum, S. microdontum, S. sparsipilum, S. spegazzinii, S. stoloniferum, S. sucrense, S. toralapanum, S. vernei* and *S. verrucosum,* most of which have been much used by breeders.

Use of wild species and indigenous cultivars in breeding

There is a very great difference between the large number of wild species evaluated that show promise and the actual number used in breeding.

H. Ross (1986) concludes that germplasm from only six wild species is frequently incorporated into European cultivars, namely *S. demissum* (late blight and PLRV), *S. acaule* (PVX, PLRV, PSTV, wart, *Globodera* and frost), *S. chacoense* (PVA, PVY, late blight, Colorado beetle, tuber moth), *S. spegazzinii* (*Fusarium*, wart, *Globodera*), *S. stoloniferum* (PVA, PVY) and *S. vernei* (*Globodera*, high starch content). Genes from *S. microdontum*, *S. sparsipilum*, *S. verrucosum*, *S. phureja*, *S. tuberosum* subsp. *andigena*, *S. commersonii* and *S. maglia* have also been used from time to time. It is quite surprising to find (Ross 1986, Table 4) that no less than 97 European cultivars contain genes from one or more of these thirteen species, of which 11 are wild and two are Andean cultivated.

Nevertheless, it comes as rather a shock to be reminded (Chapter 1) that 235 species of wild and cultivated potatoes are recognized but that only 13 have actually contributed genes to potato cultivars. This statement needs qualification, however. I myself have actually seen specimens of 191 species, of which 21 are natural hybrids. The rest are known to me as descriptions or pictures. Even though some of these may be in cultivation at the International Potato Center there is no inventory of wild species published. So, let us for the moment settle on the figure of 191 species which I know through living and dried specimens. How many of these appear in the lists of at least one of the inventories mentioned in Chapter 6? The answer is 128, excluding natural hybrids that have been given species names.

So, 13 wild species out of the 128 known in a living state in gene banks have actually contributed germplasm to European cultivars, that is to say, roughly 10 per cent. However, in all fairness one should mention that probably less than half of these 128 species are well known or have been on offer for over 10 years, which is the minimum time it takes to breed a new variety, whilst if wild species are incorporated it takes even longer. And one can add to this the fact that not all wild species are easy to manipulate. Therefore, taking all this into account and considering that wild species germplasm certainly exists in breeding lines not yet raised to cultivar level, I think that potato breeders are progressing reasonably well. To take as an example a recent survey of Bolivian potatoes (Hawkes and Hjerting 1989), some evaluation work has been carried out on 25 out of the 29 known in a living state, the other four having been known only very recently.

The outlook for evaluation, when material is well distributed through several gene banks, is decidedly promising. It must be said, however, that many breeders are understandably reluctant to use wild species because of the deleterious characters brought over into the hybrids with the useful resistance genes. This means that many generations of backcrossing and selection to the cultivated parent are needed to restore the characters of good flavour, yield and market quality that were diluted by the flow into them of unwanted characters from the wild parent.

This process of putting useful genes from wild species into a cultivated background is known as pre-breeding, parental line breeding or genetic enhancement. It is needed for all crops when crosses from wild species or primitive cultivars are used. It is undoubtedly a very important stage in the process of discovering and transferring useful genetic characters from wild species to the cultivated potato. Yet on the whole not enough pre-breeding has been carried out. One would hope to look forward to the day when, as a continuing process, most useful genes would be transferred from the wild species or the primitive cultivated ones to the good genetic backgrounds of highly selected breeding lines. Up to the present, however, this has been carried out chiefly at CIP and by potato scientists in Germany and Holland such as H. Ross and J. Hermsen, but not universally in all potato breeding countries. If this were done on a major scale potato breeders would not need always to return to the wild species themselves for useful characters, with all the delay caused by this in the production of new varieties. Is it too much to hope that a new kind of breeder, the 'germplasm enhancer' will evolve? Such people are needed for all crops, not just potatoes, but gene bank managers have no time for this work and feel that the breeders should be responsible. On the other hand, breeders have no time for enhancement of the wild germplasm and consider that such activities should be a responsibility of gene bank staff. Somewhere in the future, germplasm enhancement should take its rightful and accepted place in the long process of events lying between the collection of a wild potato in the Andes and the release of new varieties possessing one or more genes derived from it. Let us hope that that time may not be far away.

——————————— APPENDIX I ———————————

Names not included in
the present treatment

In the list which follows I have given names which are unsatisfactory for the following reasons:

(i) *Nomina nuda* Names proposed without any descriptions, or with inadequate descriptions published in a vernacular language, and not in Latin as required by the International Code of Botanical Nomenclature. In each case I have given what I think is the equivalent correct name if I have been able to elucidate this from printed, written or verbal information.

(ii) *Nomina dubia* Names with uncertain application, e.g. where, although a valid description may exist, the application of the name is uncertain and not completely verifiable through lack of type material or imprecision in the description.

(iii) Names given to artificial hybrids; these are unnecessary and should be discontinued.

S. antipochacoense Koopmans, *nom. nud.* (1951). Name given to the artificial amphiploid hybrid of *S. stoloniferum* × *S. chacoense*. (See also *S. artificiale*.)

S. antipophureja Koopmans, *nom. nud.* (1951). Name given to the artificial amphiploid hybrid of *S. stoloniferum* × *S. phureja*.

S. aquinas Bukasov, *nom. nud.* (Zuchter **28**, 65–70, 1958). Name given to Darwin's collections of wild potato from south Chile = *S. tuberosum* subsp. *tuberosum*. (See Hawkes 1956b.)

S. aracc-papa Juzepczuk, *nomen dubium* (Bull. Acad. Sci. U.R.S.S.**2**, 306–7, 1937).

The original collection on which this name was based seems to have been a hybrid population of *S. raphanifolium* × *S. sparsipilum* (or possibly even *S. raphanifolium* × *S. multidissectum*). No type specimen was designated until long after the description was published, and various specimens taken from time to time in the experimental field at Leningrad differ enormously from each other, some being indistinguishable from *S. raphanifolium* and others very close to *S. sparsipilum*. To add to the confusion, even Juzepczuk's original collection seems to have been given two different numbers (1190, 1455). I am convinced that the original collection of this species was a mixed one, and I therefore think that it would be better to class *S. aracc-papa* as a *nomen dubium* and to discontinue its use.

S. arraypitense Firbas et Ross, *nom. nud.* (Z. Pflanzenz **45**, 284, 1961).

S. artificiale Toxopeus, *nom. nud.* (1947). An artificial amphiploid hybrid of *S. chacoense* × *S. stoloniferum* and the reciprocal cross. It is therefore equivalent to *S. antipochacoense* (q.v.).

S. baccale-albescens Zhukovsky, *nom. nud.* (J. Agric. Trop. Bot. Appl. **1**, 257–80, 1954). According to Bukasov (pers. comm.) this name was given in error to a form of *S. phureja*.

S. bonariense Bukasov, *nom. nud.* (Bull. Appl. Bot., Leningrad, Ser. A, **19**, 83–5, 1936). This is a homonym, since the name has already been applied to a non-tuberiferous species. Bukasov later renamed this taxon validly as *S. laplaticum* Buk., placing it under the collective species *S. commersonii* (in the wider sense). I consider that this is incorrect, and in the present treatment I have placed it as a synonym of *S. chacoense* (see p. 94).

S. boreale (A. Gray) Bitt., *nomen dubium* (Fedde, Repert. **11**, 459, 1912). This may refer to *S. jamesii*, to pale flowered forms of *S. fendleri*, or even possibly to *S. polytrichon* (see p. 81).

S. brevistylum Wittm., *nom. nud.* (see Berthault, Ann. Sci. Agron., Paris, **2**, 186, 1911). There seem to be no significant differences between this and *S. fernandezianum* Phil., according to Berthault. Even if there were a valid description, therefore, the name of *S. brevistylum* would probably be a synonym.

S. candelarianum Cárd. (Bol. Soc. Peruana Bot.**5**, 12–13, 1956); non *S. candelarianum* Buk. (see p. 190). This is a homonym, since the name was used by Bukasov in 1930. (See text, p. 158.)

S. catamarcae Bitt., *nom. nud.* This name was proposed by Bitter on the label of a collection of Schickendantz *No. 226* in Herb. Berlin. The collection has been destroyed, even though a photograph exists. The material would seem to have been a hybrid of *S. sanctae-rosae* × *S. venturii*, but there is some element of doubt about it, and the name should be discontinued.

S. cayeuxii Berth., *nomen dubium* (Ann. Sci. Agro., Paris, **2**, 210, 1911). Berthault published a short description in latin, but not sufficient for us to be able to distinguish this species without additional aid. No type specimen has been discovered, and although it seems likely that the material introduced by Cayeux was a Colombian form of the cultivated species *S. phureja*, one cannot be certain of this without type material.

S. chilotanum Hawkes, *nom. nud.* (Bull. Imp. Bur. Pl. Breed. Genet., Cambridge, 79, 1944). A name proposed for the cultivated Chilean forms of *S. tuberosum* subsp. *tuberosum*, but not validated by a latin description.

S. chocclo Buk., *nom. nud.* (in Vavilov, Theor. Bases Plant Breed. 3, 18, 1937). Published with a very short Russian description, and no latin diagnosis. It would seem that the triploid cultivars to which this name was originally applied should be classed under *S.* × *chaucha*.

S. chuga Buk., *nom. nud.* (Lenin. Acad. Agric. Sci., Inst. Pl. Ind., Leningrad, 40, 1933) = *S. cuencanum* Juz. et Buk. (see below).

S. ciezae Buk., *nom. nud.* A name mentioned occasionally in the Russian plant breeding literature, but with no description. It has been applied to a collection (K. 150) made by Schick in Ecuador cr Colombia, of which I have seen a specimen. It undoubtedly belongs to *S. phureja*.

S. compactum Buk., *nom. nud.* = *S. mercedense* Buk. (= *S. commersonii*).

S. cuencanum Juz. et Buk., *nom. nud.* (in Vavilov, Theor. Bases Plant Breed. 3, 18, 1937). This name has not been validated by a latin description. The type material was triploid and might have been a natural hybrid of *S. tuberosum* subsp. *andigena* × *S. phureja*. Since there is considerable doubt about the true nature of *S. cuencanum* it would perhaps be better to discontinue the use of this name.

S. demissorosum Koopmans, *nom. nud.* (1, 51). An amphiploid hybrid of *S. demissum* × *S. tuberosum*, produced artificially. 2n = 120.

S. dolichostigma Buk., *nom. nud.* (in Vavilov, Theor. Bases Plant Breed. **3**, 72, 1937) = *S. emmeae* (according to Zhukovsky, in a written communication). This is a synonym of *S. chacoense*.

S. erlansonii Buk., *nom. nud.* (Bull. Appl. Bot., Leningrad, Ser. A, **19**, 83–5, 1936). A species from Bolivia (not Ecuador, as originally stated), which is probably synonymous with *S. stenotomum*, though it might be identifiable with *S. phureja*; based on Macmillan and Erlanson's collections 440 and 451.

S. fonckii Phil. *ex* Reiche, *nom. nud.* (Fl. Chile **5**, 351, 1910). This is equivalent to *S. tuberosum* subsp. *tuberosum* var. *guaytecarum* (Bitt.) Hawkes. (See p. 171.)

S. gandarae Buk., *nom. nud.* Variously mentioned in the Russian plant breeding literature as *S. antipoviczii* var. *gandarae* or as *S. gandarae* = *S. stoloniferum* Schlechtd.

S. herrerae Juz., *nomen dubium* (Bull. Acad. Sci. U.R.S.S. **2**, 310–11, 1937). Bukasov (verbal comm.) states that the original tubers collected by Juzepczuk grew into a number of rather distinct entities. Certainly some of these were tetraploid escaped forms of *S. tuberosum* subsp. *andigena*. Judging from the two co-lectotypes designated at a much later date by Bukasov, part of the material of *S. herrerae* was quite different, however, and could perhaps be a form of *S. leptophyes*. In view of the doubt and uncertainty about this species it would perhaps be better to discontinue the use of the name *S. herrerae*.

S. juanense Wittm., *nom. nud.* The name was noted on a specimen of Kurtz *No. 9828*, which has since been destroyed, but of which duplicates exist in Herb Córdoba. It is equivalent to *S. kurtzianum* Bitt. et Wittm.

S. kaufmanii Buk., *nom. nud.* (Bull. Acad. Sci. U.R.S.S., Ser. Biol., 715, 1938). Classed by Bukasov in the same subgroup as *S. aracc-papa*. The type specimen, however, is identifiable as *S. canasense* Hawkes.

S. macmillanii Buk., *nom. nud.* (Physis, B. Aires, **18**, 43, 1939). The type specimen of this species can certainly be identified as *S. stenotomum* Juz. et Buk.

S. martinezii Buk., *nom. nud.* (Bull. Appl. Bot. Genet. Plant Breed., Suppl. 58, Plate I. 1933). This was later named *S. antipoviczii* var. *martinezii* Buk., *nom. nud.* It undoubtedly should be classed as *S. stoloniferum*.

S. maydiforme Buk. *ex* Rybin, *nom. nud.* (Bull. Appl. Bot., Leningrad, Ser. 2(2), 46, 1933). A triploid cultivar which could probably be placed under *S.* × *chaucha*.

S. mendozinum Buk., *nom. nud.* (Bull. Appl. Bot. Plant Breed., Ser. A. No. 19. 84, 1936). Was later described by Bukasov under the name of *S. macolae* Buk. (= *S. kurtzianum* Bitt. et Wittm.).

S. nicaraguense Rydb., *nomen dubium* (Bull. Torr. Bot. Cl. **51**, 171–2, 1924). This species was said to have been collected by Flint in Nicaragua, and was classified by Rydberg in series *Pinnatisecta*. From the sublyrate leaf with decurrent laterals and enlarged terminal, and also from the filaments which are fused into a ring below, the type specimen seems to fit very well indeed with *S. commersonii*. Since the latter species comes from South America, it would seem probable that some confusion of collections or labels has taken place. Furthermore, I have searched carefully for this species in Nicaragua, without success, and could not indeed find any habitats in that country which would be suitable for a species of this sort with semi-rosette growth form. In view of the obvious doubts about the validity of *S. nicaraguense*, I consider that it should be classed as a *nomen dubium*.

S. pamiricum Perlova, *nom. nud.* (News Acad. Sci. U.S.S.R., Ser. Biol., No. 4, 81, 1953). A diploid form of the triploid *S. maglia* produced in the Pamir mountains in the Botanic Garden plots. Almost certainly the product of natural hybridization with a diploid wild species growing in adjacent plots.

S. papa Val., *nomen dubium* (Misc. Fondo Quijano Otero, Bogotá, **16**, 1–6, 1809). Although this name has been validly published there seems to be no type specimen. The fruits are rather long (5–7.5 cm), but the description does not differ in other respects from that of *S. colombianum*. Unless a type specimen is found, it will be better to leave this species as a doubtful name, because of the fruit length.

S. paraguariense Dun. (in DC. Prodr. **13**, I, 376, 1852) = *S. renggeri* Schlechtd. (See below.)

S. parviflorum Buk. ined. A name later given to *S. juzepczukii*, and thus invalid.

S. pauciflorum Buk., *nom. nud.* (Bull. Appl. Bot., Leningrad, Ser. A(10), 51–60, 1934) = *S. curtilobum* (type specimen seen).

S. pre-commersonii Kameraz, *nom. nud.* (Soviet Plant Industr. Rec., No. 4, 13, 1940). A diploid form of *S. commersonii* Dun.

S. pseudomaglia Planchon, *nom. nud.* (Ann. Fac. Sci., Marseilles, **18**, 205–24, 1909) = *S. chacoense* Bitt.

S. reddickii Buk., *nom. nud.* (in Vavilov, Theor. Bases Plant Breed. **3**, 51, 73, 1937). Later classed as *S. antipoviczii* var. *reddickii* = *S. stoloniferum*.

S. renggeri Schlechtd., *nomen dubium* (Hort. Hal. **1**, 5, 1841). This species received such a short description that it is quite impossible for us to know which species Schlechtendal had in mind, and it is doubtful whether he himself did more than read through the travel notes of Rengger. No type specimen has been discovered, and from our knowledge of the potatoes of Paraguay, either *S. chacoense* or *S. commersonii* subsp. *malmeanum* may have been seen by Rengger, possibly both.

S. riobambense Juz. et Buk., *nom. nud.* (in Vavilov, Theor. Bases Plant. Breed. **3**, 17, 1937). A triploid cultivar from Ecuador which received a Russian description only. No type material was preserved, and we cannot tell whether it was a hybrid of *S. tuberosum* subsp. *andigena* × *S. phureja*, or a triploid clone of *S. phureja* itself.

S. rionegrinum Lechn., *nom. nud.* (Soviet Plant Industr. Rec., No. 4, 31, 1941). A diploid form of *S. commersonii* subsp. *commersonii* which has received a Russian description only.

S. ruderale Juz., *nom. nud.* (*ex* Rybin, Proc. U.S.S.R. Congr. Genet. **3**, 473, 1929). An unpublished synonym of *S. aracc-papa* Juz., according to Bukasov (verbal comm.).

S. schizostigma Bitt., *nomen dubium* (Fedde, Repert. **11**, 449–50, 1912). The type specimen was in Berlin and has been destroyed. The corolla of this material was white, but this may be due to loss of colour on drying, and I think it likely that *S. schizostigma*, which was said to be almost completely glabrous, may be related to *S. cardiophyllum* or *S. hintonii*. The very bifid stigma, however, renders it distinct from those species, and it will be impossible to identify with any certainty unless an isotype specimen is discovered. Search for isotypes has been unsuccessful.

S. schreiteri Buk., *nom. nud.* (Soviet Plant Industr. Rec., No. 4, 13, 1940). Authenticted material of *S. schreiteri*, kindly supplied by Prof. Bukasov, is synonymous with *S. acaule* subsp. *acaule*.

S. tarmense Buk., *nom. nud.* (in Vavilov, Theor. Bases Plant Breed. **3**, 19, 1937) = *S. andigena* subsp. *tarmense* Buk. according to Zhukovsky (written comm.) = *S. tuberosum* subsp. *andigena* (Juz. et Buk) Hawkes.

S. triferum Schlechtd., *nomen dubium* (Hort. Hal. **1**, 6, 1841). The description was very short and no type specimen exists, since it would seem that Schlechtendal took his description from Pöppig's account of his travels in Peru. Apparently this material refers to cultivated potatoes that yielded in three months in Peru. Ochoa

(1955) mentions it as a very rare cultivar at 500–700 m, but gives no further details. Possibly it represents a form of *S. phureja*, but we cannot be certain as to the plants that Pöppig described, and the name should not be used in future.

S. valenzuelae Pal. (Mem. Mus., Paris, **2**, 340, 1816). A synonym of the *nomen dubium S. papa* Val. (see above).

S. venezuelicum Kameraz, *nom. nud.* (Soviet Plant Industr. Rec., No. 4, 13, 1940). Correll equates this with his newly described species **S. woodsonii**, but I am inclined to think that it is merely a form of *S. colombianum* Dun.

Classification, ploidy level and country of origin of the better- known wild and cultivated potato species and their allies in the genus *Solanum*, section *Petota*

Sub section	Super-series	Series	Species arranged according to chromosome number (x = 12)				
			2x	3x	4x	5x	6x
Estolonifera		I *Etuberosa*	*S. brevidens* (14, 15) *S. etuberosum* (15) *S. fernandezianum* (15)				
		II *Juglandifolia*	*S. juglandifolium* (4, 6, 7, 8) *S. lycopersicoides* (9) *S. ochranthum* (7, 8, 9) *S. sitiens* (15)				
Potatoe	*Stellata*	I *Morelliformia*	*S. morelliforme* (2, 3)				
		II *Bulbocastana*	*S. bulbocastanum* (2, 3) *S. clarum* (2, 3)	*S. bulbocastanum* (2)			

| | | | Species arranged according to chromosome number (x = 12) | | | | |
Sub-section	Super-series	Series	2x	3x	4x	5x	6x
		III *Pinnatisecta*	*S. brachistotrichum* (2) *S. cardiophyllum* (2) *S. jamesii* (1, 2) *S. pinnatisectum* (2) *S. tarnii* (2) *S. trifidum* (2)	*S. cardiophyllum* (2) *S. jamesii* (1)			
		IV *Polyadenia*	*S. lesteri* (2) *S. polyadenium* (2)				
		V *Commersoniana*	*S. commersonii* (11, 12, 13, 14)	*S. calvescens* (12) *S. commersonii* (12, 13, 14)			
		VI *Circaeifolia*	*S. capsicibaccatum* (10) *S. circaeifolium* (10)				
		VII *Lignicaulia*	*S. lignicaule* (9)				
		VIII *Olmosiana*	*S. olmosense* (9)				
		IX *Yungasensa*	*S. chacoense* (10, 11, 12, 13, 14) *S. huancabambense* (9) *S. tarijense* (10, 14) *S. yungasense* (10)				

Potatoe		X *Megistacroloba*	S. *astleyi* (10) S. *boliviense* (10) S. *megistacrolobum* (9, 10, 14) S. *raphanifolium* (9) S. *sanctae-rosae* (14) S. *sogarandinum* (9) S. *toralapanum* (10, 14)	
	Rotata	XI *Cuneoalata*	S. *infundibuliforme* (10, 14, 15)	
		XII *Conicibaccata*	S. *chomatophilum* (9) S. *laxissimum* (9) S. *santolallae* (9) S. *violaceimarmoratum* (10)	S. *agrimonifolium* (2, 3) S. *colombianum* (6, 7, 8) S. *flahaultii* (6, 7, 8) S. *longiconicum* (4, 5) S. *oxycarpum* (2) S. *tuquerrense* (7, 8) S. *moscopanum* (7)
		XIII *Piurana*	S. *albornozii* (8) S. *cantense* (9) S. *hypacrarthrum* (9) S. *paucissectum* (9) S. *piurae* (9)	
		XIV *Ingifolia*	S. *raquialatum* (9)	
		XV *Maglia*	S. *maglia* (14, 15)	S. *maglia* (15)
		XVI *Tuberosa* (i)	S. *andreanum* (7, 8) S. *verrucosum* (2)	
		XVI *Tuberosa* (ii)	S. *acroscopicum* (9) S. *bukasovii* (9) S. *canasense* (9)	

| | | | Species arranged according to chromosome number (x = 12) | | | | |
Sub-section	Super-series	Series	2x	3x	4x	5x	6x
			S. chancayense (9)				
			S. chiquidenum (9)				
			S. coelestipetalum (9)				
			S. immite (9)				
			S. marinasense (9)				
			S. medians (9)				
			S. mochiquense (9)				
			S. multidissectum (9)				
			S. multiinterruptum (9)				
			S. pampasense (9)				
			S. sandemanii (9)				
			S. sparsipilum (9, 10)				
		XVI *Tuberosa* (iii)	*S. alandiae* (10)				
			S. avilesii (10)				
			S. berthaultii (10)				
			S. brevicaule (10)				
			S. candolleanum (10)				
			S. gandarillasii (10)				
			S. gourlayi (10, 14)		*S. gourlayi* (14)		
			S. incamayoense (14)				
			S. kurtzianum (14)				
			S. leptophyes (9, 10)				
			S. microdontum (10, 14)	*S. microdontum* (14)			
			S. neocardenasii (10)				
			S. neorossii (14)				
			S. okadae (10, 14)				
			S. oplocense (10)		*S. oplocense* (10, 14)	*S. oplocense* (10, 14)	
			S. sparsipilum (9, 10)				

Series					
XVI *Tuberosa* cultivated	*S. spegazzini* (14) *S. venturii* (14) *S. vernei* (14) *S. virgultorum* (10) *S. ajanhuiri* (9, 10) *S. phureja* (6, 7, 8, 9, 10) *S. stenotomum* (9, 10)	*S. venturii* (14) *S.* × *chaucha* (9, 10) *S.* × *juzepczukii* (9, 10)	*S. sucrense* (10) *S. tuberosum* (naturalized) (14, 15) *S. tuberosum* (2, 3, 4, 6, 7, 8, 9, 10, 14, 15)	*S.* × *curtilobum* (9, 10)	
XVII *Acaulia*			*S. acaule* (9, 10, 14)	*S. acaule* (9)	*S. albicans* (9)
XVIII *Longipedicellata*		*S.* × *vallis-mexici* (2)	*S. fendleri* (1, 2) *S. hjertingii* (2) *S. papita* (2) *S. polytrichon* (2) *S. stoloniferum* (2)		
XIX *Demissa*				*S.* × *edinense* (2) *S.* × *semi-demissum* (2)	*S. brachycarpum* (2) *S. demissum* (2, 3) *S. guerreroense* (2) *S. hougasii* (2) *S. iopetalum* (2) *S. schenckii* (2)

Key to countries (1) USA. (2) Mexico. (3) Guatemala. (4) Costa Rica. (5) Panamá. (6) Venezuela. (7) Colombia. (8) Ecuador. (9) Peru. (10) Bolivia. (11) Paraguay. (12) Brazil. (13) Uruguay. (14) Argentina. (15) Chile.

Glossary

± more or less

acroscopic (leaflet) a small leaflet set on the petiolule of a lateral leaflet and pointing towards the tip of the leaf (see Fig. 1)

acumen the drawn-out point of certain leaves, leaflets, sepals or petals (see Fig. 2)

acuminate with a long drawn-out apex; tapering to a point

acute sharp-pointed

adaptive complexes the complement of genes that adapt a plant to its environment

allopolyploid a polyploid hybrid between two species in which homologous chromosomes from each pair regularly at meiosis, resulting in good fertility

amphidiploid (or *amphiploid*) a polyploid hybrid between two diploid species, with regular bivalent chromosome pairing at meiosis

anther – see *stamens*

apex the tip of an organ

appressed refers to hairs that are pressed close to the leaf surface

articulation a joint on the pedicel, which breaks off at that point when the berry is ripe or if the flower is not fertilized (see Fig. 2)

attenuate tapering gradually

auricle an ear-like lobe

auriculate with ear-like lobes

autopolyploid a polyploid with more than two sets of homologous

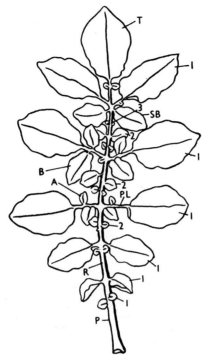

Fig. III.1   Diagram of a potato leaf (adapted from Bukasov, 1933)

T   Terminal leaflet
1   Primary lateral leaflet
2   Secondary lateral leaflet ⎫
3   Tertiary lateral leaflet   ⎬ Interjected
A   Acroscopic leaflet   ⎪ leaflets
B   Basiscopic leaflet   ⎪
SB   Semi-basiscopic leaflet ⎭
P   Petiole
PL   Petiolule
R   Rachis

(Reproduced with the kind permission of Oxford University Press)

chromosomes, and thus with reduced fertility because of irregular chromosome pairing at meiosis

basiscopic (leaflet)   a small leaflet set on the petiolule of a lateral leaflet and pointing towards the base of the leaf (see Fig. 1)

bilabiate   two-lipped, referring to the calyx, with two groups of sepals (2 + 3)

biological species concept   a way of defining a species by means of sterility barriers between it and others apparently closely related to it; see also *morphological species concept*

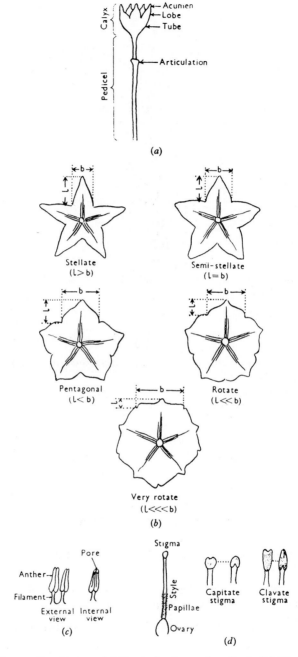

Fig. III.2 Potato floral parts. (a) Typical calyx and pedicel. (b) Various corolla forms. (c) Details of stamen structure. (d) Ovary, style and sigma structure. (Reproduced with the kind permission of Oxford University Press.)

bi-pinnatisect   twice cut pinnately

bivalent   two chromosomes paired together at meiosis

bract   a small leaf-like structure, normally simple, on or near the inflorescence; the sepals of *S. gandarillasii* are bract-like

calcicolous   growing in limestone soil

calyx   the green cup which protects the flower in bud. It is composed of 5 sepals joined toward the base and set on the top of the pedicel. The ends of the sepals bear a point or acumen (see Fig. 2)

canescent   becoming grey or hoary

capitate   more or less globular (see *stigma* and Fig. 2)

ceja forest   high-altitude, high-rainfall cloud forest on the east-facing Andean slopes of Bolivia and Peru (also Colombia?)

centre of diversity   an area where the genetic and specific diversity is very high

chuño   freeze-dried potatoes, the process dating back to very early archaeological horizons and still continued today

CIP   the International Potato Center (Centro Internacional de la Papa), Lima, Peru

clavate   club-shaped (see *stigma* and Fig. 2)

conical (berry)   shaped like a cone, much longer than broad

connective   the tissue in an anther supporting the pollen sacs

cordate   with basally rounded lobes; heart-shaped

coriaceous   leathery

corolla   the brightly coloured part of the potato flower, set into the calyx and composed of 5 petals often fused together for most of the way, free toward the tips and bearing triangular points or acumens; it is generally white or various shades of azure, mauve, lilac, purple or violet but is yellow in series *Juglandifolia*. Its shape varies from stellate to pentagonal and rotate (see Fig. 2)

crenate   with rounded teeth

crenulate   with small rounded teeth

crisped   puckered and crumpled

cuneate   wedge-shaped, generally applied to leaf or leaflet bases

cuspidate   suddenly drawn to a point or cusp

cymose panicle   a very spread-out inflorescence in which each axis ends in a flower and growth continues from one or more side branches *cymose umbel*   a flat-topped cymose inflorescence in which the oldest flowers are in the centre

cytotypes   different chromosome numbers or other cytological phenomena found within a particular species

decumbent   prostrate, with tips rising upwards

denticulate   minutely toothed

dihaploid (= 'haploid' in USA)   a haploid of a tetraploid such as 2x seedling derived from 4x *S. tuberosum*; see also *polyhaploid*

EBN   embryo balance number. Crosses are unlikely to be easy between species with different EBNs. For further explanation see text, pp. 45–6 and 53.

elliptic   in form of an ellipse; broadest at centre

epiphytic   growing on another plant but not parasitizing it

falcate   scythe-shaped; curved laterally

filament   see *stamens*

fruticose   shrubby

genetic architecture   a term used to denote the general genetic structure of a species

genetic breakdown   a term used to indicate the loss of vigour and often the early death of F_2 plants which lack the necessary adaptive complexes of either or both the original parents

genome   a chromosome set

genome formulae   ways of defining different genomes in various species

germplasm   the total amount of genetic diversity within a given group

glabrescent   becoming glabrous as the plant develops

glabrous   without hairs

glaucous   with a blue-green bloom on the leaf

globular, globose (berries)   shaped like a globe or sphere

haploid   a plant with half the number of chromosomes of the normal diploid (see also *dihaploid* and *polyhaploid)*

hastate   spear-shaped, having a large terminal lobe and two very small basal lobes pointing outwards

hispid   with coarse rigid erect hairs, rough to the touch

homoeologous (chromosomes)   chromosomes from two or more different species that although basically similar, will pair only if their homologous partner is not present

homologous (chromosomes)   chromosomes so similar that they will pair regularly at meiosis

hybrid swarms   large populations of plants that are clearly hybrids (F_1s, F_2s, backcrosses, etc.) between two or more parent species

immunological spectrum   a series of precipitin lines produced in a thin agar gel when antigens from one species react with antibodies from this or another species

imparipinnate   pinnate with an unpaired terminal leaflet

imparipinnatisect   leaf not divided completely down to the rachis and with a terminal unpaired lobe

indumentum   hair covering

inflorescence   the part of the plant bearing the flowers. It consists of a *peduncle* below, which is normally once-forked or sometimes twice- (or more) forked. *Pedicels* or flower stalks are borne on the branches

interjected (leaflets)   smaller leaflets set in between pairs of main lateral leaflets (see Fig. 1)

interrupted   refers to the interjected leaflets interrupting the sequence of main lateral leaflets

introgressive hybridization   the limited flow of certain genes from one species to another through hybridization

jalca (vegetation zone)   see *páramo*

jugate (as in unijugate, bijugate, trijugate, etc.)   leaf composed of a single end or terminal leaflet and one, two, three, etc. pairs of lateral leaflets (see Fig. 1). Figures in brackets indicate less common numbers or dimensions

lanceolate   lance-shaped; several times longer than broad, widest below centre

leaf dissection   the way in which a leaf is divided up into various lobes or leaflets

ligneous   woody

ligulate   strap-shaped

linear   long and narrow, with parallel sides

lomas   coastal hills in Peru and northern Chile supporting a seasonal plant growth on the basis of moisture condensing from sea mists

micro-species   species of very small size and range of genetic diversity, which are later generally found to be no more than genetic variants of larger species

morphological species concept   a way of defining a species by looking for clear morphological gaps between it and others apparently closely related to it; see also *biological species concept mucronate*   with an abruptly curved tip or mucro

multivalent   three or more chromosomes linked together at meoisis

oblique   generally referring to the base of a leaflet where the upper and lower sides do not end at the same point

oblong   more or less elliptic but with somewhat parallel sides

obovate   reversed egg-shaped; broadest above centre (contrast *ovate, elliptic*)

obtuse   blunt-pointed

orbicular   circular, round

ovary   this is generally globular to oval, or may be conical, and contains the ovules, which if fertilized will develop into seeds. It is situated at the base of the flower in the calyx cup (see Fig. 2)

ovate   egg-shaped; broadest below centre (contrast *elliptic, obovate*)

ovoid (berry)   egg-shaped, longer than broad but apically rounded

panmictic (population)   populations of plants which through natural hybridization are able to exchange genes with each other

papillose   with very small hairs rounded at the tip

páramo (vegetation zone)   wet, cold moorland vegetation zone at very high altitudes extending from the central to the northern Andes and into Panamá and Costa Rica

pedicels   the flower stalks which grow from the upper branches of the peduncle. The pedicels are jointed or articulate and each bears a flower (or fruit later) at its tip (see Fig. 2)

peduncle   the main flower stalk, often branched once or twice (or more) in its upper part and bearing pedicels near the ends of the branches

pentagonal (corolla)   in which the lobes are rather broader than long, giving the corolla a pentagonal or 5-pointed appearance (see Fig. 2)

pericarp   the outer wall of the fruit

petiole   the stalk of a leaf (see Fig. 1)

petiolulate   with petiolules

petiolule   the stalk of a leaflet (see Fig. 1)

phenotypic   related to the phenotype or plant as it exists – the product of genotype × environment interaction

pilose   hairy

pinnate   a leaf divided into terminal and lateral leaflets (see Fig. 1)

pinnatilobed   with lobed divisions that do not reach the midrib or rachis, characteristic of series *Megistacroloba pinnatisect* or *pinnatifid* a leaf not completely divided into individual leaflets

ploidy a general term indicating the number of sets of chromosomes in a plant, e.g.: diploid = two sets, triploid = three sets, tetrapoid = four sets, pentaploid = five sets, hexaploid = six sets

polyhaploid a plant with half the chromosome number of its polyploid parent, e.g. trihaploid (from *S. demissum*) or dihaploid (from *S. tuberosum*); see also *dihaploid*

polymorphic composed of many different forms

polyploid the condition in which more than two sets of chromosomes are present in the cells of an organism

pre-ceramic (cultures) ancient societies existing before the invention of pottery

Proto-Petota a hypothetical ancestral group that gave rise to the tuber-bearing *Petota* subsection

prototype the ancestral form, as for instance, the wild prototype of the cultivated potato

pseudostipular leaflets leaflets borne on dwarf shoots in the leaf axils appearing to be stipules, though falsely so

puberulent finely hairy

pubescence hairs

puna (vegetation zone) very high-altitude grassland and dwarf shrubland zone in the southern Andes

pyriform pear-shaped

quadrivalent four chromosomes joined together at meiosis

rachis a continuation of the leaf stalk, ending in the terminal leaflet and bearing pairs of lateral leaflets (see Fig. 1)

rachis wing a strip of leaf tissue running down from the base of a leaflet on to the rachis

reflexed bent back

revolute (leaf margin) curled or rolled under

rhizomatous with rhizomes or underground stems

rhomboid more or less diamond-shaped or top-shaped

rosette a cluster of leaves at the base of a plant spreading out on to or near the ground surface

rotate (corolla) rather round in outline, in which the lobe length is about half the breadth or less (see Fig. 2)

rugose   wrinkled, rough

self-compatible (plant)   a plant (or clone) able to form seeds by self-pollination

self-incompatible   a plant (or clone) unable to form seeds by self-pollination

semi-basiscopic (leaflet)   a small leaflet set at the angle between the rachis and petiolule and pointing obliquely towards the base of the leaf (see Fig. 1)

semi-lunate   half-moon-shaped

sessile (leaflet)   not stalked or petiolulate

seta   bristle

shouldered   refers to the corolla lobes which protrude like shoulders on either side of the acumen

sib-mating   brother-sister mating, i.e. pollinating one plant (of an F_1 family) by another to raise an 'F_2' generation

simple (leaf)   not divided up into leaflets

spatulate   formed like a druggist's spatula, thus gradually dilated upwards towards a rounded apex

stamens   the male parts of the flower, composed of filaments below, which are set near the base of the corolla, and anthers above, which contain the pollen (see Fig. 2)

star (of corolla)   the central tongues or strips of the petals, which together take the form of a star

stellate (corolla)   star-shaped, referring to the corolla of a potato flower, in which the petals are slightly or much longer than broad (see Fig. 2)

stem wing   a thin flange of tissue running down from a leaf base and sometimes crinkled or toothed along its edge

stigma   small piece of tissue situated at the top of the style and which, when ripe, is sticky and traps pollen grains; it may be rounded (capitate) or elongated (oval or clavate) and notched above and below (see Fig. 2)

stipules   small bract-like structures developed at the base of the leaf, which are in fact part of it; not seen in section *Petota* (see *pseudostipular leaflets*)

style   a rod-like organ that connects the stigma at its top to the ovary at its base (see Fig. 2)

sub-   somewhat, not completely, almost

subglabrous   almost without hairs

sublyrate somewhat pinnatifid, with the terminal lobe large and rounded, whilst the laterals are very much smaller

subpandurate somewhat violin-shaped

subsessile (leaflet) hardly or only very slightly stalked or petiolulate

substellate or *semi-stellate* (corolla) rather star-shaped, in which the petals are more or less as long as broad (see Fig. 2)

terminal (leaflet) the end leaflet of a compound leaf (see Fig. 1)

tola heath a dry, high-altitude heathland plant community characterized by the tola plant (*Lepidophyllum quadrangulare*)

tomentose with densely matted hairs

trichomes (glandular) glandular hairs of two types: A-type are short-stalked, with a 4-celled glandular tip; B-type are long-stalked with a drop of sticky substance at the tip

trilabiate three-lipped, referring to the calyx, with three groups of sepals (1 + 2 + 2)

trivalent three chromosomes joined together at meiosis

unconscious selection selection by man without a specific end in view or a realization that selection is taking place

undulate wavy

univalent a single chromosome not paired at meiosis

unthrifty (plants) plants that remain small, do not grow well and often die before maturity

varnished with a shiny surface looking as though it had been given a coat of varnish; characteristic of series *Piurana*

verrucose warty

very rotate (corolla) with rather flattened lobes whose length is about a quarter or less than the breadth. Often the ends of adjoining lobes stick out, giving the corolla a 10-pointed appearance (see Fig. 2)

wing see *rachis wing*; *stem wing*

xeric dry

xerophilous liking dry conditions

Series, species and subspecies names, listed taxonomically, with their standard abbreviations[*]

Subsection *ESTOLONIFERA* Hawkes[**]

Series I *ETUBEROSA* Juz	ETU
1. *S. brevidens* Phil.	brd
2. *S. etuberosum* Lindl.	etb
3. *S. fernandezianum* Phil.	frn
4. *S. palustre* Poepp.	pls
5. *S. subandinum* Meigen	sbn
Series II *JUGLANDIFOLIA* (Rydb.) Hawkes	JUG
1. *S. juglandifolium* Dun.	jgl
2. *S. ochranthum* Dun.	ocr
3. *S. lycopersicoides* Dun.	lyc
4. *S. sitiens* Johnston	**sit**

Subsection *POTATOE* G.Don

Series I *MORELLIFORMIA* Hawkes	MOR
1. *S. morelliforme* Bitt. et Muench	mrl
Series II *BULBOCASTANA* (Rydb.) Hawkes	BUL
1. *S. bulbocastanum* Dun.	blb
subsp. *bulbocastanum*	blb
subsp. *dolichophyllum* (Bitt.) Hawkes	**dph**
subsp. *partitum* (Corr.) Hawkes	**ptt**
2. *S. clarum* Corr.	clr
Series III *PINNATISECTA* (Rydb.) Hawkes	PIN
1. *S. brachistotrichum* (Bitt.) Rydb.	bst

*New abbreviations are shown in **bold** face type.
Based on N.W. Simmonds, 1963 (Eur. Potato J. **6, 186–90) and Z. Huamán and R.W. Ross, 1985 (Amer. Potato J. **62**, 629–41).

2. *S. cardiophyllum* Lindl.   cph
   subsp. *cardiophyllum*   cph
   subsp. *ehrenbergii* Bitt.   ehr
   subsp. *lanceolatum* (Berth.) Bitt.   **lcl**
3. *S. hintonii* Corr.   hnt
4. *S. jamesii* Torr.   jam
5. *S.* × *michoacanum* (Bitt.) Rydb.   mch
6. *S. nayaritense* (Bitt.) Rydb.   nyr
7. *S. pinnatisectum* Dun.   pnt
8. *S.* × *sambucinum* Rydb.   smb
9. *S. stenophyllidium* Bitt.   sph
10. *S. tarnii* Hawkes et Hjerting   **trn**
11. *S. trifidum* Corr.   trf

Series IV *POLYADENIA* Buk. ex Correll   POL
1. *S. lesteri* Hawkes et Hjerting   les
2. *S. polyadenium* Greenm.   pld

Series V *COMMERSONIANA* Buk.   COM
1. *S. calvescens* Bitt.   clv
2. *S. commersonii* Dun.   cmm
   subsp. *commersonii*   cmm
   subsp. *malmeanum* (Bitt.) Hawkes et Hjerting mlm

Series VI *CIRCAEIFOLIA* Hawkes   CIR
1. *S. capsicibaccatum* Cárd.   cap
2. *S. circaeifolium* Bitt.   crc
   subsp. *circaeifolium*   crc
   subsp. *quimense* Hawkes et Hjerting   **qum**
3. *S. soestii* Hawkes et Hjerting   sst

Series VII *LIGNICAULIA* Hawkes   **LIG**
1. *S. lignicaule* Vargas   lgl

Series VIII *OLMOSIANA* Ochoa   **OMS**
1. *S. olmosense* Ochoa   olm

Series IX *YUNGASENSA* Corr.   **YNG**
1. *S. arnezii* Cárd.   arz
2. *S. chacoense* Bitt.   chc
   subsp. *chacoense*   chc
   subsp. *muelleri* (Bitt.) Hawkes et Hjerting   mue
3. *S. huancabambense* Ochoa   hcb
4. *S. tarijense* Hawkes   tar
5. *S. yungasense* Hawkes   yun
6. *S. flavoviridens* Ochoa   flv
7. *S.* × *litusinum* Ochoa   lit
8. *S.* × *trigalense* Cárd.   trg
9. *S.* × *zudaniense* Cárd.   zdn

Series X *MEGISTACROLOBA* Cárd. et Hawkes   MEG
1. *S. astleyi* Hawkes et Hjerting   ast
2. *S. boliviense* Dun.   blv
3. *S. chavinense* Corr.   chv
4. *S. hastiforme* Corr.   hsf
5. *S. hawkesii* Cárd.   hwk
6. *S. huanucense* Ochoa   hnu
7. *S. megistacrolobum* Bitt.   mga
8. *S. raphanifolium* Cárd. et Hawkes   rap
9. *S. sanctae-rosae* Hawkes   sct
10. *S. sogarandinum* Ochoa   sgr
11. *S. toralapanum* Cárd. et Hawkes   tor

Series XI *CUNEOALATA* Hawkes   CUN
1. *S. anematophilum* Ochoa   amp
2. *S. infundibuliforme* Phil.   ifd
3. *S. peloquinianum* Ochoa   plq

Series XII *CONICIBACCATA* Bitt.   CON
1. *S. agrimonifolium* Rydb.   agf
2. *S. buesii* Vargas   bue
3. *S. chomatophilum* Bitt.   chm
4. *S. colombianum* Dun.   col
5. *S. contumazaense* Ochoa   ctz
6. *S. donachui* (Ochoa) Ochoa   dnc
7. *S. flahaultii* Bitt.   flh
8. *S. laxissimum* Bitt.   lxs
9. *S. longiconicum* Bitt.   lgc
10. *S. moscopanum* Hawkes   msp
11. *S. multiflorum* Vargas   mfl
12. *S. neovalenzuelae* L. López   **nvz**
13. *S. otites* Dun.   oti
14. *S. oxycarpum* Schiede   oxc
15. *S. pamplonense* L. López   ppl
16. *S. paucijugum* Bitt.   pcj
17. *S. pillahuatense* Vargas   pll
18. *S. santolallae* Vargas   san
19. *S. subpanduratum* Ochoa   sup
20. *S. urubambae* Juz.   uru
21. *S. villuspetalum* Vargas   vsp
22. *S. violaceimarmoratum* Bitt.   vio
23. *S. woodsonii* Corr.   wds
24. *S. ayacuchense* Ochoa   ayc
25. *S. bombycinum* Ochoa   bmb
26. *S. burkartii* Ochoa   brk
27. *S. cacetanum* Ochoa   cct
28. *S. calacalinum* Ochoa   cln
29. *S. garcia-barrigae* Ochoa   gab
30. *S. irosinum* Ochoa   irs

31. *S. jaenense* Ochoa	jnn
32. *S. limbaniense* Ochoa	lmb
33. *S. nemorosum* Ochoa	nmr
34. *S. neovargasii* Ochoa	nvg
35. *S. neovavilovii* Ochoa	nvv
36. *S. nubicola* Ochoa	nub
37. *S. orocense* Ochoa	oro
38. *S. salasianum* Ochoa	**sls**
39. *S. sucubunense* Ochoa	suc
40. *S. trinitense* Ochoa	trt
Series XIII *PIURANA* Hawkes	PIU
1. *S. acroglossum* Juz.	acg
2. *S. albornozii* Corr.	abz
3. *S. cantense* Ochoa	cnt
4. *S. chilliasense* Ochoa	chl
5. *S. cyanophyllum* Corr.	cyn
6. *S. hypacrarthrum* Bitt.	hcr
7. *S. jalcae* Ochoa	jlc
8. *S. paucissectum* Ochoa	pcs
9. *S. piurae* Bitt.	pur
10. *S. solisii* Hawkes	sol
11. *S. tuquerrense* Hawkes	tuq
12. *S. yamobambense* Ochoa	ymb
13. *S. ariduphilum* Ochoa	adp
14. *S. blanco-galdosii* Ochoa	blg
15. *S. pascoense* Ochoa	psc
Series XIV *INGIFOLIA* Ochoa	**ING**
1. *S. ingifolium* Ochoa	igf
2. *S. raquialatum* Ochoa*	raq
Series XV *MAGLIA* Bitt.	**MGL**
1. *S. maglia* Schlechtd.	mag
Series XVI *TUBEROSA* (Rydb.) Hawkes (wild species)	TUB
Group (i) Mexico, Venezuela, Colombia and Ecuador	
1. *S. andreanum* Baker	adr
2. *S. correllii* Ochoa	crl
3. *S. lobbianum* Bitt.	lbb
4. *S. minutifoliolum* Corr.	min
5. *S. paramoense* Bitt.	prm
6. *S. regularifolium* Corr.	rgf
7. *S. suffrutescens* Corr.	sff
8. *S. verrucosum* Schlechtd.	ver
9. *S. burtonii* Ochoa	brt

*Restored to the author's original spelling.

10. *S. leptosepalum* Corr.   lps
11. *S. macropilosum* Corr.   mcp

Group (ii) Peru
1. *S. abancayense* Ochoa   abn
2. *S. acroscopicum* Ochoa   acs
3. *S. ambosinum* Ochoa   amb
4. *S. bukasovii* Juz.   buk
5. *S. cajamarquense** Ochoa   cjm
6. *S. canasense* Hawkes   can
7. *S. chancayense* Ochoa   chn
8. *S. chiquidenum* Ochoa   chq
9. *S. chrysoflorum* Ochoa   crs
10. *S. coelestipetalum* Vargas   cop
11. *S. dolichocremastrum* Bitt.   dcm
12. *S. gracilifrons* Bitt.   grc
13. *S. guzmanguense* Whalen et Sagást.   **gzm**
14. *S. huarochiriense* Ochoa   **hro**
15. *S. humectophilum* Ochoa   hmp
16. *S. immite* Dun.   imt
17. *S. leptophyes* Bitt.   lph
18. *S. marinasense* Vargas   mrn
19. *S. medians* Bitt.   med
20. *S. mochiquense** Ochoa   mcq
21. *S. moniliforme* Corr.   mnf
22. *S. multidissectum* Hawkes   mlt
23. *S. multiinterruptum* Bitt.   mtp
24. *S. neoweberbaueri* Wittm.   nwb
25. *S. orophilum* Corr.   orp
26. *S. pampasense* Hawkes   pam
27. *S. rhomboideilanceolatum* Ochoa   rhl
28. *S. sandemanii* Hawkes   snd
29. *S. sicuanum* Hawkes   **sic**
30. *S. sparsipilum* (Bitt.) Juz. et Buk.   spl
31. *S. tacnaense* Ochoa   tcn
32. *S. weberbaueri* Bitt.   wbr
33. *S. wittmackii* Bitt.   wtm
34. *S. amayanum* Ochoa   **amy**
35. *S. antacochense* Ochoa   atc
36. *S. augustii* Ochoa   agu
37. *S. aymaraesense* Ochoa   **aym**
38. *S. bill-hookeri* Ochoa   **bhk**
39. *S. hapalosum* Ochoa   hpl
40. *S. incahuasinum* Ochoa   inh
41. *S. incasicum* Ochoa   ins
42. *S. irosinum* Ochoa   irs

*Restored to the author's original spelling.

43. *S. longiusculus* Ochoa — **lgs**
44. *S. lopez-camarenae* Ochoa — lpc
45. *S. parvicorollatum* Lechn. — prv
46. *S. quillonanum* Ochoa — **qln**
47. *S. sarasarae* Ochoa — **srs**
48. *S. sawyeri* Ochoa — swy
49. *S. scabrifolium* Ochoa — scb
50. *S. tapojense* Ochoa — tpj
51. *S. tarapatanum* Ochoa — trp
52. *S. taulisense* Ochoa — tau
53. *S. velardei* Ochoa — vlr

Group (iii) Bolivia, Argentina and Chile
1. *S. achacachense* Cárd. — **ach**
2. *S. alandiae* Cárd. — aln
3. *S. avilesii* Hawkes et Hjerting — avl
4. *S. berthaultii* Hawkes — ber
5. *S. brevicaule* Bitt. — brc
6. *S.* × *bruecheri* Corr. — bru
7. *S. candolleanum* Berth. — cnd
8. *S.* × *doddsii* Corr. — dds
9. *S. gandarillasii* Cárd. — gnd
10. *S. gourlayi* Hawkes — grl
    subsp. *gourlayi* — grl
    subsp. *saltense* Clausen et Okada — **sal**
    subsp. *vidaurrei* (Cárd.) Hawkes et Hjerting — vid
    subsp. *pachytrichum* (Hawkes) Hawkes et Hjerting — ptr
11. *S. hondelmannii* Hawkes et Hjerting — hdm
12. *S. hoopesii* Hawkes et Okada — **hps**
13. *S. incamayoense* Okada et Clausen — inm
14. *S. kurtzianum* Bitt. et Wittm. — ktz
15. *S. leptophyes* Bitt. — lph
16. *S. microdontum* Bitt. — mcd
    subsp. *microdontum* — mcd
    subsp. *gigantophyllum* (Bitt.) Hawkes et Hjerting — gig
17. *S.* × *mollepujroense* Cárd. et Hawkes — mlp
18. *S. neocardenasii* Hawkes et Hjerting — ncd
19. *S. neorossii* Hawkes et Hjerting — nrs
20. *S. okadae* Hawkes et Hjerting — oka
21. *S. oplocense* Hawkes — opl
22. *S.* × *rechei* Hawkes et Hjerting — rch
23. *S.* × *ruiz-lealii* Brücher — rzl
24. *S.* × *setulosistylum* Bitt. — stl
25. *S. sparsipilum* (Bitt.) Juz. et Buk. — spl
    subsp. *sparsipilum* — spl
    subsp. *calcense* Hawkes — clc
26. *S. spegazzinii* Bitt. — spg
27. *S.* × *subandigena* Hawkes — sub

28. *S.* × *sucrense* Hawkes   scr
29. *S. tuberosum* L. (escaped forms)   tbr
30. *S. ugentii* Hawkes et Okada   **ugt**
31. *S. venturii* Hawkes et Hjerting   vnt
32. *S. vernei* Bitt. et Wittm.   vrn
    subsp. *vernei*   vrn
    subsp. *ballsii* (Hawkes) Hawkes et Hjerting   bal
33. *S. virgultorum* (Bitt.) Cárd. et Hawkes   vrg

Series XVI *TUBEROSA* (cultivated species)   TUB
1. *S. ajanhuiri* Juz. et Buk.   ajh
2. *S. chaucha* Juz. et Buk.   cha
3. *S. curtilobum* Juz. et Buk.   cur
4. *S. juzepczukii* Buk.   juz
5. *S. phureja* Juz. et Buk.   phu
    subsp. *phureja*   phu
    subsp. *hygrothermicum* (Ochoa) Hawkes   hyg
    subsp. *estradae* (López) Hawkes   est
6. *S. stenotomum* Juz. et Buk.   stn
    subsp. *stenotomum*   stn
    subsp. *goniocalyx* (Juz. et Buk.) Hawkes   gon
7. *S. tuberosum* L.   tbr
    subsp. *tuberosum*   tbr
    subsp. *andigena* Hawkes   adg

Series XVII *ACAULIA* Juz.   ACA
1. *S. acaule* Bitt.   acl
    subsp. *acaule*   acl
    subsp. *aemulans* (Bitt. et Wittm.) Hawkes et Hjerting   aem
    subsp. *punae* (Juz.) Hawkes et Hjerting   pne
2. *S. albicans* (Ochoa) Ochoa   alb
3. *S.* × *indunii* Okada et Clausen   **ind**
4. *S.* × *viirsooi* Okada et Clausen   **vrs**

Series XVIII *LONGIPEDICELLATA* Buk.   LON
1. *S. fendleri* Asa Gray   fen
    subsp. *fendleri*   fen
    subsp. *arizonicum* Hawkes   **azn**
2. *S. hjertingii* Hawkes   hjt
3. *S. matehualae* Hjerting et Tarn   **mat**
4. *S. papita* Rydb.   pta
5. *S. polytrichon* Rydb.   plt
6. *S. stoloniferum* Schlechtd. et Bché.   sto
    subsp. *stoloniferum*   sto
    subsp. *moreliae* Hawkes   **mla**
7. *S.* × *vallis-mexici* Juz.   vll

Series XIX *DEMISSA* Buk.   DEM
1. *S. brachycarpum* Corr.   bcp
2. *S. demissum* Lindl.   dms

3. *S.* × *edinense* Berth.   edn
   subsp. *edinense*   edn
   subsp. *salamanii* (Hawkes) Hawkes   slm
4. *S. guerreroense* Corr.   grr
5. *S. hougasii* Corr.   hou
6. *S. iopetalum* (Bitt.) Hawkes   iop
7. *S. schenckii* Bitt.   snk
8. *S.* × *semidemissum* Juz.   sem

BIBLIOGRAPHY

Acosta, José de (1590) *Historia natural y moral de las Indias.* Seville. English edition translated by E. Grimston, London, 1604. Reprinted by the Hakluyt Society **60**, 1880.

Anderson, E. (1952) *Plants, man and life.* University of California Press, Berkley.

Astley, D. (1979) *Solanum sucrense* Hawkes – a clarification. In Zeven, A.C. and van Harten, A.M. (eds) *Proceedings of the Conference on Broadening the Genetic Base of Crops, Wageningen, 1978,* 223–5. Pudoc, Wageningen.

Astley, D. and **Hawkes, J.G.** (1979) The nature of the Bolivian weed potato species *Solanum sucrense* Hawkes. *Euphytica* **28**, 685–96.

Baines, G.S. and **Howard, H.W.** (1950) Haploid *S. demissum* plants. *Nature, London* **166**, 795.

Baker, J.G. (1884) A review of the tuber-bearing species of *Solanum. Journal of the Linnean Society, Botany* **20**, 489–507.

Bauhin, C. (1596) Phytopinax. Basle.

Bauhin, C. (1598) (In Matthiolus, P.A.). Opera quae extant omnia. Frankfurt-on-Maine.

Bitter, G. (1912) Solana nova vel minus cognita. I. *Fedde Repert.* **10**, 531–32.

Budin, K.Z., Bavyko, N.F. and **Balmasova, M.A.** (1987) Botanical variation of forms in the VIR World Potato Collection. Genetika, Selektsiya i Iskhodnii Material Kartofelya. *Trud. Prikl. Bot. Genet. Selek.,* Leningrad, **115**, 4–7.

Bukasov, S.M. (1933) (The potatoes of South America and their breeding possibilities). *Prilozhenie 58-e K. Trudam po prikladnoi botanike, genetike i selektsii,* Leningrad, 192.

Bukasov, S. M. and **Kameraz, A.Y.** (1959) *Bases of potato breeding.* Gosudarstvennoe Izdatel'sto Sel'skokhozyaistrennoi Literatury, Moscow.

Bukasov, S.M. and **Lechnovicz, V.** (1935) Importancia en la fitotecnia de las papas indigenas de la America del Sur. *Rev. Argent. Agron.* **2**(7), 173–83.

Castellanos, J. de (1886) Elegias de varones ilustres de Indias Part 4. Published by Antonio Paz y Melia under the title 'Historia del Nuevo Reino de Granada, Madrid'. (Manuscript completed on 1 May 1601.)

Christiansen, J. (1967) El Cultivo de la Papa en el Peru. Published privately, pp. 351. Talleres de Artes Gráficas, Lima, Peru.

Cieza de León, Pedro de (1553) La Crónica del Perú. Seville. English translation by Sir Clements R. Markham in Hakluyt Society **33** and **68**, 1864 and 1883, London.

CIP (1973) *Annual report of the International Potato Center* (frontispiece). CIP, Lima, Peru.

Clausen, A.M. and **Okada, K.A.** (1987) The subspecies of *Solanum gourlayi*. *Phytologia* **62**(3), 165–70.

Clusius, C. (1576) Rariorum aliquot stirpium per Hispanias observataram historia. Antwerp.

Clusius, C. (1601) Rariorum Plantarum Historia. Antwerp.

Cobo, B. (1890–93) Historia del Nuevo Mundo. (Written 1650.) Soc. Bibliof. Andal., Seville.

Commonwealth Potato Collection (1969) Inventory of Seed Stocks, 1968. Scottish Plant Breeding Station, Pentlandfield, Roslin, Midlothian, Scotland.

Contreras, A. (1987) Germoplasma chileno de papas (*Solanum* spp.). Anales Simposio Recursos Fitogenéticos, Valdivia, 1984. UACH-IBPGR.

Correll, D.S. (1952) Section Tuberarium of the genus *Solanum* of North America and Central America. USDA Agric. Monograph No. 11, pp. 243.

Correll, D.S. (1962) The potato and its wild relatives. Contributions from the Texas Research Foundation **4**, pp. 606. Texas Research Foundation, Renner, Texas.

Cribb, P.J. (1972) Studies on the origin of *Solanum tuberosum* L., subspecies *andigena* (Juz. et Buk.). Hawkes – the cultivated tetraploid potato of South America. PhD Thesis, University of Birmingham, UK.

Cribb, P.J. and **Hawkes, J.G.** (1986) Experimental evidence for the origin of *Solanum tuberosum*, subsp. *andigena*. In d'Arcy, W.G. (ed.) *Solanaceae: biology and systematics*. Columbia University Press, New York.

D'Arcy, W.G. (1972) Solanaceae studies II: typification of subdivisions of *Solanum*. *Annals of the Missouri Botanical Garden* **59**(2), 202–78.

Dodds, K.S. (1950) Polyhaploids of *Solanum demissum*. *Nature, London* **166**, 795.

Drake, Sir Francis (1628) The World Encompassed. Edited by W.S.W. Vaux. Hakluyt Society **16**, 1854, London.

Dunal, M.F. (1852) Solanaceae, in De Candolle, A. *Prodromus*, **13**, I, 1–385.

Engel, F. (1970a) Exploration of the Chilca Canyon, Peru. *Current Anthropology* **11**(1), 55–8.

Engel, F. (1970b) Recolección y cultivo en los Andes precolombinos. *Anales Científicos UNA* **8**, 122–36.

Engel, F. (1984) *Prehistoric Andean Ecology. Man, Settlement and Environment in the Andes. Chilca.* Humanities Press, Hunter College, City University of New York.

FAO (1985) *Food and Agriculture Organization Production Yearbook for 1985*. FAO, **39**, 331.

Flores Crespo, R. (1968) Colección y estudio de *Solanum schenckii* Bitt. Su confirmación como verdadera especie. *Agric. Técnica, Mexico* **2**(8), 374–5.

Gell, P.G.H., Hawkes, J.G. and **Wright, S.T.C.** (1960) The application of immunological methods to the taxonomy of species within the genus *Solanum. Proceedings of the Royal Society, Series B* **151**, 364–83.

Gerard, J. (1597) The Herball or General Historie of Plants. London. (2nd and 3rd editions in 1633 and 1636 edited and revised by Thomas Johnson).

[Gross-Lüsewitz] Index des Sortimentes knollentragender wilder und kultivierter Kartoffelspecies des Institutes für Kartoffelforschung Gross Lüsewitz. Institut für Kartoffelforschung Gross Lüsewitz, pp. 64.

Hamilton, E. (1934) American treasure and the price revolution in Spain, 1501–1650. *Harvard Economic Studies* **43**, 196.

Hanneman, R.E. and **Bamberg, J.B.** (1986) Inventory of Tuber-Bearing *Solanum* Species. USDA Bulletin, 533, pp. 216.

Hariot, Thomas (1588) A briefe and true report of the new found land of Virginia. London.

Hawkes, J.G. (1941) *Potato Collecting Expeditions in Mexico and South America.* Imperial Bureau of Plant Breeding and Genetics, Cambridge, pp. 30.

Hawkes, J.G. (1944) *Potato Collecting Expeditions in Mexico and South America. II. Systematic Classification of the Collections.* Imperial Bureau of Plant Breeding and Genetics, Cambridge, pp. 140.

Hawkes, J.G. (1956a) A revision of the tuber-bearing Solanums (first edition). *Annual Report Scottish Plant Breeding Station*, 37–109.

Hawkes, J.G. (1956b) Taxonomic studies on the tuber-bearing Solanums. I. *Solanum tuberosum* and the tetraploid species complex. *Proceedings of the Linnean Society, London* **166**, 97–144.

Hawkes, J.G. (1956c) Hybridization studies on four hexaploid *Solanum* species in series *Demissa* Buk. *New Phytol.* **55**, 191–205.

Hawkes, J.G. (1957) On the lectotypes of *Solanum stoloniferum* Schlechtendal et Bouché, *S. oxycarpun* Schiede and *S. verrucosum* Schlechtendal. *Wiss. Zeitschr. Martin-Luther-Univ., Halle-Wittenberg* **6** (1956–7), 3, 849–53.

Hawkes J.G. (1958). Potatoes: taxonomy, cytology and crossability. In Kappert, H. and Rudorf, W. (eds) *Handbuch der Pflanzenzüchtung*, 2nd edn, Ch. 1, vol. 3, 10–43. Paul Parey, Hamburg.

Hawkes, J.G. (1959) The Birmingham University plant collecting expedition to Mexico and Central America. *Univ. Birmingham Gazette* **11**(5), 60–3.

Hawkes, J.G. (1962a) The origin of *Solanum juzepczukii* Buk. and *Solanum curtilobum* Juz. et Buk. *Zeitschrift für Pflanzenzüchtung* **47**, 1–4.

Hawes, J.G. (1962b) Introgression in certain wild potato species. *Euphytica*, Wageningen, **11**, 26–35.

Hawkes, J.G. (1963) A revision of the tuber-bearing *Solanums* (second edition). *Scottish Plant Breeding Station Record*, 76–181.

Hawkes, J.G. (1966) Modern taxonomic work on the *Solanum* species of Mexico and adjacent countries. *American Potato Journal* **43**, 81–103.

Hawkes, J.G. (1967) The History of the Potato. Masters Memorial Lecture, 1966; *J. Roy. Hort. Soc.* **92**, 207–24; 249–62; 288–302; 364–5.

Hawkes, J.G. (1969) The ecological background of plant domestication. In Ucko, P.J. and Dimbleby, G.W. (eds) *The Domestication and Exploitation of Plants and Animals*. Duckworth, London.

Hawkes, J.G. (1988) Evolution of the cultivated potatoes and their wild tuber-bearing relatives. *Die Kulturpflanze* **36**, 189–208.

Hawkes, J.G. (1989) Nomenclatural and taxonomic notes on the infrageneric taxa of the tuber-bearing solanums (Solanaceae). *Taxon* **39**(3), 489–92.

Hawkes, J.G. and **Hjerting, J.P.** (1969) *The Potatoes of Argentina, Brazil, Paraguay and Uruguay. A Biosystematic Study.* Oxford University Press, Oxford, pp. 525.

Hawkes, J.G. and **Hjerting, J.P.** (1989) *The Potatoes of Bolivia. Their Breeding Value and Evolutionary Relationships.* Oxford University Press, Oxford, pp. 472.

Hawkes, J.G. and **Lester, R.N.** (1968) Immunological studies on the tuber-bearing Solanums, III. Variability within *S. bulbocastanum* and its hybrids with species in series *Pinnatisecta*. Annals of Botany **32**, 165–86.

Hoekstra, R. and **Seidewitz, L.** (1987) *Evaluation Data on Tuber-bearing Solanum Species* (second edition). Dutch German Curatorium for Plant Genetic Resources, Braunschweig, pp. 202.

Horton, D.E. (1988) Potatoes: truly a world crop. *SPAN* **30**(3), 116–18.

Horton, D.E. and **Fano, H.** (1985) *Potato Atlas.* International Potato Center (CIP), pp. 135.

Hosaka, K., Ogihara, Y., Matsubayashi, M. and **Tsunewaki, K.** (1984) Phylogenetic relationship between the tuberous *Solanum* species as revealed by restriction endonuclease analysis of chloroplast DNA. *Japanese Journal of Genetics* **59**, 349–69.

Hougas, R.W. and **Peloquin, S.J.** (1958) The potential of potato haploids in breeding and genetic research. *American Potato Journal* **35**, 701–7.

Hougas, R.W. and **Peloquin, S.J.** (1960) Crossability of *Solanum tuberosum haploids with diploid Solanum* species. *European Potato Journal* **3**, 325–30.

Howard, H.W. (1969) The storage of true seeds of potatos. *European Potato Journal* **12**, 278–9.

Howard, H.W. (1980). Storage of true seeds of potatoes for 25 years. *Potato Research* **23**, 241–2.

Howard, H.W. and **Swaminathan, M.S.** (1952) Species differentiation in the section Tuberarium of *Solanum* with particular reference to the use of interspecific hybridization in breeding. *Euphytica* **1**, 20–28.

Huamán, Z. (1983) The breeding potential of native Andean cultivars. *Proc. Internat. Congr.: Research for the Potato in the Year 2000, Tenth Anniversary, 1972–1982.* CIP, Lima, Peru.

Huamán, Z. (1987) *Inventory of Andean Potato Cultivars with Resistance to Some Pests and Diseases and Other Desirable Traits.* CIP, Lima, Peru, pp. 22.

Huamán, Z., Williams, J.T., Salhuana, W. and **Vincent, L.** (1977) *Descriptors for the Cultivated Potato.* IBPGR, Rome, Italy.

Huamán, Z., Hawkes, J.G. and **Rowe, P.R.** (1980) *Solanum ajanhuiri*: an important diploid potato cultivated in the Andean altiplano. *Economic Botany* **34**, 335–43.

Huamán, Z., Hawkes, J.G. and **Rowe, P.R.** (1982) A biosystematic study of the origin of the diploid potato, *Solanum ajanhuiri. Euphytica* **31**, 665–75.

Huamán, Z., Hawkes, J.G. and **Rowe, P.R.** (1983) Chromatographic studies on the origin of the cultivated potato, *Solanum ajanhuiri. American Potato Journal* **60**, 361–7.

Jackson, M.T., Hawkes, J.G. and **Rowe, P.R.** (1977) The nature of *Solanum chaucha*, Juz. et Buk., a triploid cultivated potato of the South American Andes. *Ephytica* **26**, 775–83.

Jackson, M.T., Rowe, P.R. and **Hawkes, J.G.** (1978) Crossability relationships of Andean potato varieties of three ploidy levels. *Euphytica* **27**, 541–55.

Johns, T. and **Keen, S.L.** (1986) Ongoing evolution of the potato on the altiplano of Bolivia. *Economic Botany* **40**(4), 409–24.

Johns, T. and **Osman, S.F.** (1985) Glycoalkaloids of the *Solanum* × *ajanhuiri* domestication complex from western Bolivia [Abstract]. *American Journal of Botany* **72**(6), 914.

Johnston, S.A. and **Hanneman, R.E.** (1978) Endosperm balance factors in some tuber-bearing *Solanum* species. *American Potato Journal* **55**, 380.

Johnston, S.A. and **Hanneman, R.E.** (1980a) Support of the endosperm balance number hypothesis utilizing some tuber-bearing *Solanum* species. *American Potato Journal* **57**(1), 7–14.

Johnston, S.A. and **Hanneman, R.E.** (1980b) The discovery of effective ploidy barriers between diploid *Solanums* [Abstract]. *American Potato Journal* **57**(10), 484–5.

Johnston, S.A. and **Hanneman, R.E.** (1982) Manipulations of endosperm balance number overcome crossing barriers between diploid *Solanum* species. *Science* **217**, 446–8.

Juzepczuk, S.W. and **Bukasov, S.M.** (1929) (A contribution to the question of the origin of the potato). *Proc. U.S.S.R. Congr. Genet. Plant and Animal Breed.* **3**, 592–611.

Koopmans, A. (1951) Cytogenetic studies on *Solanum tuberosum* L. and some of its relatives. *Genetica* **25**, 193–337.

López de Gómara, Francisco (1552) *Historia General de las Indias.* Zaragoza. (Madrid Edition 1922).

López, L. (1979) A biosystematic study of the series *Conicibaccata* of the genus *Solanum.* PhD Thesis, University of Birmingham, UK.

López, L. and **Hawkes, J.G.** (in press) Cytology and genome constitution of the tuber-bearing *Solanum* species in series *Conicibaccata. III International Solanaceae Congress Proceedings.*

Magazzini de Vallombrosa, Father (1623) *Dell'Agricoltura Toscana.* Vallombrosa, Italy.

Magoon, M.L., Cooper, D.C. and **Hougas, R.W.** (1958a) Cytogenetic studies of some diploid *Solanums*, section *Tuberarium. American Journal of Botany* **45**(3), 207–21.

Magoon, M.L., Hougas, R.W. and **Cooper, D.C.** (1958b) Cytogenetic studies of South American diploid *Solanums*, section *Tuberarium. American Potato Journal* **35**, 375–94.

Marks, E. (1955a) Cytogenetic studies in tuberous *Solanum* species. I. Genomic differentiation in the group *Demissa. Journal of Genetics* **53**(2), 262–9.

Marks, E. (1955b) A polyhaploid plant of *Solanum polytrichon* Rydb. *Nature, London* **175**, 469.

Marks, E. (1958) Cytogenetic studies in tuberous *Solanum* species, II. A synthesis of *Solanum × vallis-mexici. New Phytologist* **57**, 300–10.

Marks, E. (1965) Cytogenetic studies in tuberous *Solanum* species. III. Species relationships in some South and Central American species. *New Phytologist* **64**, 293–306.

Martins-Farias, R. (1976) New Archaeological Techniques for the Study of Ancient Root Crops in Peru. PhD Thesis, University of Birmingham, UK.

Matsubayashi, M. (1955) Studies on the species differentiation of the section *Tuberarium* of *Solanum.* III Behaviour of meiotic chromosomes in F_1 hybrid between *S. longipedicellatum* and *S. schickii* in relation to its parent species. *Science Reports of Hyogo University of Agriculture* **2**(1), 25–31.

Matsubayashi, M. (1981) Species differentiation in tuberous *Solanum* and the origin of cultivated potatoes. (In Japanese.) *Recent Advances in Breeding* **22**, 86–106.

Matsubayashi, M. (1982) Species differentiation in *Solanum* Sect. Petota, XI. Genomic relationships between *S. acaule* and certain diploid *Commersoniana* species. *Science Reports of the Faculty of Agriculture, Kobe University* **15**(1), 23–33.

Matsubayashi, M. and **Misoo, S.** (1977) Species differentiation in *Solanum*, Sect. *Tuberarium.* IX. Genomic relationships between three Mexican diploid species. *Japanese Journal of Breeding* **27**(3), 49–58.

Moseley, M. E. (1975) *The Maritime Foundations of Andean Civilization.* California, Cummings.

Ochoa, C. (1950) Papas del sub-grupo Trigonohypsa en el centro del Peru. *Boletin de la Sociedad Peruana de Botánica* **2**(1–4), 5–8.

Ochoa, C. (1955) Species of *Solanum* (Tuberarium) of South America. Present taxonomic status and species use in plant breeding, with special reference to Peru. *Phytopathology* **45**, 247–9.

Ochoa, C. (1962) *Los Solanum Tuberiferos silvestres del Peru (Secc. Tuberarium, sub-secc. Hyperbasarthrum)*. Lima, Peru.

Ochoa, C. (1975?) Las papas cultivadas triploides de *Solanum* × *chaucha* y su distribución geográfica en el Peru. *Anales Científicos* **13**(1–2), 31–44.

Okada, K.A. (1974) *Colección de Solanum tuberíferos de Argentina. Lista de Semillas No. 3, Dicembre, 1974.* Instituto Nacional de Tecnología Agropecuaria, Balcarce, prov. Buenos Aires, Repub. Argentina, pp. 53.

Okada, K.A. (1981) High frequency of triploids of *Solanum microdontum* subsp. *gigantophyllum* on the western mountain ranges of Provinces La Rioja and Catamarca, Argentina. *Bull. Torrey Bot. Club* **108**(3), 331–7.

Okada, K.A. and **Clausen, A.M.** (1982) Natural hybridization between *Solanum acaule* Bitt. and *S. megistacrolobum* Bitt. in the province of Jujuy, Argentina. *Euphytica* **31**, 817–35.

Poma de Ayala, Felipe Guamán (1936) Nueva Corónica y Buen Gobierno. Edited and published by P. Rivet (1936) *Traveaux et Mémoires de l'Institut d'Ethnologie* **23**, Paris.

Quinn, D.B. (ed.) (1955) *The Roanoke Voyages, 1584–1590.* 2 vols. Hakluyt Society **104**, **105**, London.

Rivet, P. (1936) See Poma de Ayala, Felipe Guamán.

Ross, H. (1979) Wild species and primitive cultivars as ancestors of potato varieties. In Zeven, A.C. and van Harten, A.M. *Broadening the Genetic Base of Crops*, 237–45. Pudoc, Wageningen.

Ross, H. (1986) Potato breeding – problems and perspectives. *Supplement 13 to Journal of plant breeding.* (eds W. Horn and G. Röbbelen), pp. 132. Paul Parey, Berlin.

Rowe, P.R. and **Sequeira, L.** (1970) Inheritance of resistance to *Pseudomonas solanacearum* in *Solanum phureja*. *Phytopathology* **60**(10), 1499–1501.

Rybin, V.A. (1930) Karyologische Untersuchungen an einigen wilden und einheimischen kultivierten Kartoffeln Amerikas. *Z. indukt. Abstamm. -und Vererb.-Lehre* **53**, 313–54.

Salaman, R.N. (1911) Studies in potato breeding. In *IVe Conference Internationale de génétique, Paris*, 573–5. Masson, Paris.

Salaman, R.N. (1937) The potato in its early home and its introduction into Europe. *J. Roy. Hort. Soc.* **62**, 61–7; 112–13; 156–62; 253–66.

Salaman, R.N. (1939) Deformities and mutilations of the face as depicted on Chimu pottery of Peru. *Journal of the Royal Anthropology Institute* **69**(1), 109–22.

Salaman, R.N. (1946) The early European potato; its character and place of origin. *Journal of the Linnean Society (Botany)* **53**, 1–27.

Salaman, R.N. (1949) *The History and Social Influence of the Potato* (new edition edited by J.G. Hawkes, 1985). Cambridge University Press.

Salaman, R.N. (1954) The origin of the early European potato. *Journal of the Linnean Society (Botany)* **55**, 185–90.

Salaman, R.N. (1985) See Salaman (1949).

Salaman, R.N. and **Hawkes, J.G.** (1949) The character of the early European potato. *Proceedings of the Linnean Society* **161**, 71–84.

Schmiediche, P.E., Hawkes, J.G. and **Ochoa, C.M.** (1980) Breeding of the cultivated potato species *Solanum juzepczukii* Buk. and *S. curtilobum* Juz. et Buk. I. *Euphytica* **29**, 685–704.

Schmiediche, P.E., Hawkes, J.G. and **Ochoa, C.M.** (1982) The breeding of the cultivated potato species *Solanum juzepczukii* Buk. and *S. curtilobum* Juz. et Buk. II. *Euphytica* **31**, 695–707.

Smith, H.B. (1927) Chromosome counts in the varieties of *Solanum tuberosum* and allied wild species. *Genetics* **12**, 84–92.

Southwell, Sir Robert (1693) Journal Book of the Royal Society of London, 13th December, 1693.

Swaminathan, M.S. (1953) Studies on the inter-relationships between taxonomic series in the section *Tuberarium*, genus *Solanum*. I. *Commersoniana* and *Tuberosa*. *American Potato Journal* **30**(11), 271–81.

Tarn, T.R. and **Hawkes, J.G.** (1986) Cytogenetic studies and the occurrence of triploidy in the wild potato species *S. commersonii* Dun. *Euphytica* **35**, 293–302.

Toxopeus, H.J. (1947) Preliminary account of a new amphiploid: *Solanum artificial*. *Genetica* **124**, 93–6.

Ugent, D., Pozorski, S. and **Pozorski, T.** (1982) Archaeological potato tuber remains from the Casma valley of Peru. *Econ. Bot.* **36**(2), 182–92.

Ugent, D., Dillehay, T. and **Ramirez, C.** (1987) Potato remains from a late Pleistocene settlement in south central Chile. *Econ. Bot.* **4**(1), 17–27.

van Soest, L.J.M. and **Hondelmann, W.** (1983) Taxonomische und Resistenz-Untersuchungen an Kartoffelwildarten und Primitivformen der deutsch-niederlandischen Samelreise in Bolivien 1980. *Landbauforschung Völkenrode* **33**(), 11–23.

van Soest, L.J.M., Hondelmann, W. and **Hawkes, J.G.** (1980) Potato collecting in Bolivia. *Plant Genetic Resources Newsletter* **43**, 32–5.

van Soest, L.J.M., Rumpenhorst, H.J. and **Huijsman, C.A.** (1983) Resistance to potato-cyst nematodes in tuber-bearing *Solanum* species and its geographical distribution. *Euphytica* **32**, 65–74.

van Soest, L.J.M., Schöber, B. and **Tazelaar, M.F.** (1984) Resistance to *Phytophthora infestans* in tuber-bearing species of *Solanum* and its geographical distribution. *Potato Research* **127**, 383–411.

Vargas, C. (1936) *El Solanum tuberosum a través del desenvolvimiento de las actividades humanas.* Imprenta del Museo Nacional, Lima, Peru, pp. 74.

Vargas, C. (1949) *Las Papas Sudperuanas. I.* Univ. Nac. Cuzco, Peru, pp. 144.

Vargas, C. (1956). *Las Papas Sudperuanas. II.* Univ. Nac. Cuzco, Peru, pp. 66.

Vargas, C. (1981) Plant motifs on Inca ceremonial vases from Peru. *Bot. J. Linnean Society* **82**(4), 313–25.

Vavilov, N.I. (1951) The origin, variation, immunity and breeding of cultivated plants. *Chronica Botanica* **13**, 1–366. (Translated from Russian by K. Starr Chester.)

Vilmorin, R. de and **Simonet, M.** (1927) Variations de nombre des chromosomes chez quelques *Solanées*. *C.R. Acad. Sc. Paris* **184**, 164–6.

Wight, W.F. (1916) Origin, introduction and primitive culture of the potato. *Proceedings of the Potato Association of America* **3**, 35–52.

Yen, D.E. (1961/2) The potato in early New Zealand. *The Potato Journal*, Summer 1961/2, 2–5.

Zhukovsky, P.M. (1959) (At the centre of origin of the cultivated plants of Latin America.) *Botanicheskii Zhurnal*, Moskva **44**, 262–72.

Zubeldia, A., López Campos, G. and **Sañudo Palazuelos, A.** (1955) Estudio, descripción y clasificación de un grupo de variedades primitivas de patata cultivadas en las Islas Canarias. *Bol. 33 Inst. Nac. Invest. Agron., Madrid,* 287–325.

Zykin, A. (1968) (A journey to the home of the potato.) (Potato and Vegetables) No. 11, 45–7.

Index

This is an expanded, completely rewritten and updated new edition of Professor Hawkes' definitive botany of the tuber-bearing solanums (potatoes), last revised in 1963. Professor Hawkes is the leading world authority on the history of botany, genetics, and breeding of the potato and this work encapsulates a lifetime's distinguished botanical work. There are descriptions of over 220 species of wild and cultivated potato, which give full details of taxonomy, characteristics and range. Introductory chapters cover the history of the species, their breeding and genetics, cytology and evolution, ecology and geographical distribution and detailed taxonomic descriptions. This is an essential reference work for all scientists concerned with this major food crop, including botanists, geneticists, plant breeders, agriculturalists, biochemists, entomologists and phytopathologists.

Contents